Making Solidarity Work?

The Norwegian Labour Market in Transition

Edited by
Jon Erik Dølvik and Arild H. Steen

SCANDINAVIAN UNIVERSITY PRESS
Oslo - Stockholm - Copenhagen - Oxford - Boston

Scandinavian University Press (Universitetsforlaget AS)
P.O. Box 2959 Tøyen, N-0608 Oslo, Norway
Fax +47 22 57 53 53

Stockholm office
SCUP, Scandinavian University Press
P.O. Box 3255, S-103 65 Stockholm, Sweden

Copenhagen office
Scandinavian University Press AS
P.O. Box 54, DK-1002 København K, Denmark

Oxford office
Scandinavian University Press UK
60 St. Aldates, Oxford OX1 1ST, England

Boston office
Scandinavian University Press North America
875 Massachusetts Ave., Ste. 84, Cambridge MA 02139, USA
Fax +1 617 354 6875

ISBN 82-00-37679-6

Published with a grant from the Research Council of Norway

Design: Astrid Elisabeth Jørgensen
Coverillustration: © NPS/Michael Bennet
Typeset in 9 on 12 point Photina by Formatvisual Limited, UK
Printed on 90 gms Carat offset by Østfold Trykkeri A.s, Norway

Preface

The central issue of this book is the transformation of labour, solidarity and social organisation in a world of growing economic and political interdependence. Focusing on one country, the purpose has been to bring together international researchers to analyse the viability, weaknesses, and strengths of the Norwegian labour market model in a comparative perspective. Rather than searching for clear-cut policy recommendations, our ambition has been to stimulate reflection about recent developments and inspire public debate about viable pathways to full employment.

This book was initiated by the Research Council of Norway (the Programme of Regional and Labour Market Research), which in 1994 asked the Fafo Institute for Applied Social Science to organise an international research team, assigned to undertake a critical examination of possible needs to adjust Norwegian labour market practices, in view of changing international circumstances. The initiative was inspired by a larger Swedish-American project organised by Studieförbundet Näringsliv-Samhälle (SNS) and the American National Bureau of Economic Research (NBER), conducting a thorough appraisal of the Swedish Model (see Richard B.Freeman, B. Swedenborg and R. Topel (eds), NBER-rapporten: *Välfärdsstat i omvandling*, 1995).

Thanks to Fafo-colleague Jon M. Hippe, at the time situated at Harvard University, we were so lucky as to arise the interest of Richard B. Freeman, in charge of the NBER study, to participate in the project. This eased the recruitment of international participants significantly and enabled us to organise a team of distinguished labour market scientists: Professor Gerhard Bosch (IAT/Nortrheine Westphalia); Dr.Phil. Anne Lise Ellingsæter (Institute for Social Research/ISF, Oslo); Professor Richard B. Freeman (NBER/Harvard University); Professor Karl Ove Moene (University of Oslo); Professor Frieder Naschold (Science Center Berlin); Professor Berndt K. Keller (University of Konstanz); Professor Jill Rubery (University of Manchester); and Professor Asbjørn Rødseth (University of Oslo).

The book is the product of a lengthy collective learning process. After an opening conference was held in November 1994, attended by central Norwegian labour market actors and experts, a series of workshops, research visits and interviews have been organised, allowing extensive transnational exchange of hypotheses, views and experiences. Representatives of a large number of Norwegian institutions have generously taken time to share their knowledge, provide material and comment early drafts of our work. These include representatives of central and local trade unions (LO and AF); the employer associations in the private and municipal sectors (NHO and KS); the Ministries of Finance, Administration, and Municipalities and Labour; the Labour Market Administration; individual enterprises; and several research institutions (in particular Statistics Norway, Institute for Social Research, ECON and ARENA). Without their support this book could never have been accomplished. Thus we warmly thank you all and look forward to your participation in critical debate of the outcome, which the authors, of course, are solely responsible for.

At Fafo the work has been organised by a project group consisting of research assistants Alexander W. Cappelen, Mona Bråten and Frode Longva (who have made invaluable efforts to provide practical, administrative and substantial support for the international researchers), Per Kleppe (who has shared his embodied knowledge of Norwegian labour market policies from his time as Minister of Finance and leader of the Norwegian Employment Commission), while Arild H. Steen and Jon Erik Dølvik have been in charge of tying the threads together and editing the contributions. The project has also benefited from numerous conversations, material and comments from colleagues at Fafo.

Finally, we would like to thank the Programme Committee on Regional and Labour Market Research at the Research Council of Norway, headed by Morten Reymert, and Soili Aintila in particular, who have been very supportive and prudently awaited the outcome of the project. We also want to thank the national and international participants of the research team for their enthusiastic collaboration and the interest they have shown for Norwegian pecularities. International research cooperation is troublesome and time-consuming, but the efforts have convinced us that international exchange is invaluable for developing understanding of national distinctions and transnational challenges in the fight against mass unemployment.

Fafo Institute of Applied Social Science,
September 1996

Jon Erik Dølvik and Arild H. Steen

Contents

Chapter 1
Introduction

Jon Erik Dølvik

1. Leaning into the wind

It is widely acknowledged that cross-border market integration, fiercer international competitive pressures, and structural transformations of working life pose profound challenges to national labour market policies in Europe. In comparison, the labour market model in the USA has in recent years produced far more jobs, but also far more inequality and poverty, than that in most European Union (EU) countries (Freeman, 1994: 13). Unemployment has also soared in the Nordic countries, until recently admired as a stronghold of solidaristic full employment policies. Sweden, for decades symbolizing the virtues of the Nordic model, which is distinguished by generous welfare state policies and active labour market measures, has been struggling with soaring budget deficits and harsh economic-political adjustment. In Finland, nearly one-fifth of the workforce is out of a job, and Denmark has coped with persistently high unemployment since the 1970s. Such evidence has led many observers to declare the death of the Nordic model of full employment, suggesting that we are faced with a choice between more inequality or more unemployment, as illustrated by the US example.

Norway, however, with internationally low and falling unemployment, narrow wage differences, a flourishing economy, and remarkable job growth, represents a contrasting case in several respects. Choosing to stay out of the European Union, irrespective of Swedish and Finnish entrance, Norway has positioned itself as a "different country" in the European context. The continuation of ambitious welfare policies, a Keynesian stabilization policy, solidaristic incomes policies, and tight regulation of labour markets have accentuated the divergent features. Norway has, however, conformed to international trends in monetary policy and product market deregulation, widely assumed in the labour movement to halt employment generation and pre-empt the solidaristic welfare state legacy.

Therefore the relative success of Norwegian employment policy, representing a seemingly contradictory blend of market-oriented modernism and social democratic traditionalism, tends to puzzle both advocates of contemporary economic fashion and defenders of orthodox labour policy. While the latter claim the solidaristic legacy of full employment has been eroded by the imperative of market efficiency, the former claim market-efficient job-generation has been fettered by the pervasive solidaristic legacy, tendentially confirming the common perception of each other as antagonists.

This Janus-image might simply indicate that the Norwegian labour market model is in a state of transition from a corporatist paradigm of the past to a market paradigm of tomorrow, smoothed by oil revenues, implying that labour market inequality is likely to escalate in the future. Alternatively it might suggest the hypothesis that Norway is struggling towards a new synthesis beween politics and markets, transcending the dualist conception of an irreconcilable antagonism between equality and efficiency.

This anthology proceeds from a critical view of both (1) the one-sided, micro-oriented, supply-side approach to labour market deregulation of current neo-liberalism, neglecting the important productive impact of human perceptions of distributive justice, fairness, and reciprocity, which distinguish labour market relations from commodity market exchange; and (2) the one-sided, macro-oriented focus on demand-side and distributive features of labour markets represented by welfare state traditionalists, neglecting the problem of inefficient adjustment to the changing needs of production and clients inherent in many well-intended solidaristic arrangements.

As suggested by, among others, Wolfgang Streeck, "diversified quality production presupposes an affirmative polity in which major conditions of competitive performance are, and have to be, collectively created and maintained", representing "an opportunity for a supply-oriented "new deal" between efficiency and equity" (Streeck, 1992: 26). Similarly several of the contributions in this book, from different angles and perspectives, address whether the "hybrid" Norwegian labour market model ingrains contours of a new social compromise, pointing towards a constructive complementarity between solidarity and flexibility, distribution and production, or rather is likely to be torn apart by conflicting internal and external pressures.

Whether Norway has found a new path towards restoring full employment, based on a workable partnership between the state, markets, and societal organizations remains to be seen. But, in view of the entrenched unemployment crisis throughout Europe, we believe the Norwegian example deserves political and scientific attention. How impressive is the actual Norwegian employment record? What could account for the results and what could disturb the fairly bright prospects of today? To what extent can the positive employment trend be attributed to the specific institutional frameworks of Norwegian labour markets and to what extent does it merely reflect Norway's favourable position as a "rentier" oil-state? Given Norway's location on the margins of Europe, how do internationalization and European integration affect Norwegian labour market policies? Does Norway benefit from the advantages of being small and different, which allows greater freedom in labour market policies, or does Norway face even stronger pressures to adapt to external developments than other countries?

These were the kinds of questions we asked a team of distinguished international labour market scientists to address in this study. By throwing a critical, comparative light on central features of the Norwegian labour market approach, the aim is to stimulate debate about its strengths and vulnerabilities and contribute to a better understanding of the critical preconditions for its success or failure. Rather than searching for definite conclusions, we hope the study will stimulate new ways of interpreting current developments and inspire debate about viable paths to full employment.

2. International challenges

In international literature, economic globalization and completion of the European single market have been conceived as major challenges to national employment systems in high-cost European welfare states (Streeck, 1991, 1993; Teague and Grahl, 1992). Increased capital mobility, "regime competition" and "social dumping" have been expected to reinforce restructuring, job competition, and downward pressures on wages, labour, and welfare standards. Intensified cross-border competition is supposed to shift the balance of power in favour of capital, strengthening pressures for labour market flexibility and differentiation of wage determination (Ferner and Hyman, 1992). The emerging regime of fixed exchange rates, possibly leading to a single currency in the EU, has arguably made wage flexibility even more urgent, in order to absorb economic shocks and competitive discrepancies between European countries, in the absence of the devaluation option (Mahnkopf and Altvater, 1995). With a narrowing scope for macroeconomic employment and stabilization policies, the OECD has recommended a restructuring of labour relations, emphasizing decentralization and closer linking of wages to enterprise productivity and international cost levels (OECD, 1994a).

These external transformations have indeed been perceived as a particular challenge to national employment systems such as the Norwegian one with solidaristic wage determination and fairly strict regulation of labour standards.

The shift in Norwegian macroeconomic policy (see Rødseth, chapter 5) and the revitalization of centralized incomes policies since the mid 1980s (see Dølvik et al., chapter 3) were triggered by acute external imbalances and a speculative outflow of capital caused by falling oil prices and previous devaluations. They also reflected, however, a government strategy of adjustment to changing international environments (Mjøset et al., 1995: 67–68). Aspiring at least to become part of the internal market via the European Economic Area (EEA) agreement, the Norwegian social democratic government perceived that major policy revisions would have to be accomplished.

Since the struggle over EC membership in 1972 caused severe cross-cutting cleavages both in society and within the labour movement, Europe had virtually been a non-issue in Norway. The trade agreements with the EC and the European Free Trade Area (EFTA) countries secured customs-free exchange of most manufactured goods, and nearly 80 percent of Norwegian exports went to West European markets. Still, the single market would represent a significant opening of Norwegian domestic markets, and compliance with common rules of competition, product standards, and market regulation implied substantial adjustments of the Norwegian regulatory system. Despite the high export/import ratio, the levels of production costs, prices, and wages as well as welfare and labour standards were considered far above prevailing standards in most EC countries. Income distribution was more egalitarian and the evolution of what has been termed the "negotiative-mixed" Norwegian political economy (Hernes, 1977) had established a far-reaching system of cross-sectoral transfers and regional redistribution. Exposure to open international competition was therefore regarded as a major challenge for large parts of the Norwegian economy (Golombek, 1991).

The reduced latitude for correcting market outcomes by state intervention and the "dual shift" from national to international decision-making, from politics to markets, and possibly also from central to local levels of bargaining (Martin and Ross, 1995) implied that the cornerstones of the Norwegian labour market model could be subject to erosion (Dølvik, 1992,1993). A key issue in the controversy over Norway's relationship with the EC/EU was thus whether or not the single market would lead to a withering of the welfare state (Hagen, 1990) and the political capital that organized labour had vested in the regulatory institutions of the nation-state.

In contrast to such gloomy perspectives, recent developments in Norwegian labour markets may appear surprising. Three years after entry into the single market none of the drastic changes foreseen by the opposition has occurred. Despite the fact that the social democratic government has pursued a policy of "modernization" and committed adjustment to EEA/EU rules, key elements of the solidaristic Norwegian labour market model have seemingly become more entrenched, apparently without impeding economic growth and employment. Nor has the rejection of EU membership had detrimental effects with respect to capital investment and currency stability, as was argued, for instance, by the employers during the EU campaign. On the contrary, according to the World Competitiveness Report, 1996, Norway has climbed the ladder of international competitiveness and attractiveness of investment (Mathiassen, 1996). The time-span is, however, short and the coincidence of international recovery (early 1990s) and soaring oil revenues may have blurred underlying tensions and long-term processes of change. None the less, leaning into international winds has so far apparently been benefitial. The overall issue of whether or not solidaristic labour and welfare policies are compatible with the modern global economic order is analysed by Richard Freeman in chapter 2.

3. Disguised sclerosis, neo-liberalism, or innovative social compromise?

For the sceptical observer the huge oil revenues may tend to render any lesson from the Norwegian case irrelevant for most European countries. According to such a "Manna from heaven" interpretation (Freeman, chapter 2), the seemingly positive development of labour markets in Norway is merely a reflection of a privileged "rentier state" that can afford to continue overly costly and inefficient policies that other states are forced by economic realities to redress. In the view of orthodox economic theory, Norwegian labour market policies may appear dysfunctional. Narrow wage differentials, high minimum income standards, fairly generous unemployment benefits, and densely regulated employment relations, combined with a steadily expanding public sector, potentially crowding out private job creation, fit poorly with conventional OECD wisdom about the path to restore full employment (OECD, 1994). From this perspective, labour market institutions designed to protect the interests of organized "insiders" may lock out low-productive labour and overburden public labour market policies, thereby inhibiting sound employment growth. Norwegian labour markets thus perform relatively well inspite of, rather than because of, their solidaristic institutional frameworks, and they should have done better. Consequently, Norway is deemed to face serious crisis when the price for postponed adjustments has to be paid in the future.

Proponents of a traditionalist labour view share the perception that Norwegian labour markets perform weakly, but for opposite reasons: the government has gone too far in unleashing market forces, delimiting public sector growth, and conducting restrictive economic polices, thereby creating higher unemployment and greater social inequality for the sake of price stability and competitiveness (Brox, 1994).

A more optimist alternative to such dualist interpretations might be that, after unemployment rose as result of economic policy failure in the 1980s, favourable economic circumstances and a careful compromise between market reform and preservation of solidaristic labour market institutions have gradually led to beneficial outcomes. In this view, the persistence of encompassing collective bargaining, low wage dispersion, growing public employment, and a generous welfare system, facilitating female employment, can contribute to labour market integration and reduced unemployment. Even if such policies may not seem overly efficient in terms of providing private or collective goods, they might be quite successful in counteracting "collective evils", *inter alia* by limiting negative hysteresis effects.

Welfare security and broad involvement of women in socioeconomic activity can contribute to a more even distribution of opportunities and burdens across the population, enhancing exit–entry flows and flexibility in labour markets (see Ellingsæter and Rubery, chapter 4). Restraints on short-term external flexibility in the labour market may also promote alternative modes of internal firm adaptation (Blank, 1994: 165–167), contributing positively to the adjustment capacity seen from a long-term societal perspective (see Bosch, chapter 7). According to Sengenberger (1994: 52–55), stable, cooperative labour relations and tightly regulated labour markets can induce industrial restructuring, innovation, and investment in "human capital". Similarly has it been suggested that egalitarian wage bargaining can provide "efficiency of solidarity" effects (Moene and Wallerstein, 1996) and that investment in "collective capital" such as education and a well-equipped public and social infrastructure can enhance economic performance (Crouch, 1995: 76; Streeck, 1992: 22). Consequently, according to such interpretations Norwegian labour markets might perform relatively well because of, rather than in spite of, their institutional frameworks and fragile compromise between market reform and solidaristic traditionalism.

Clearly, the features of continuity and change of the Norwegian labour market model invite diverse interpretations, reflecting the as yet unclear destination of the transformation. The aim of this collection is to contribute to a critical and constructive understanding of the tensions, contradictions, and particular institutional preconditions that shape developments in Norwegian labour markets and tend to puzzle international researchers.

4. Puzzles of interpretation

One puzzle is that Norwegian labour markets in many respects seem to be quite adaptive and flexible, even though the institutional framework displays a range of "rigidities" and "disincentives" that, according to economic orthodoxy, should inhibit adjustment and employment. Despite strong trade unions and high employment, wage growth has been reduced and inflation has been brought down over the past decade, suggesting that the so-called equilibrium rate of unemployment (NAIRU) is among the lowest in Europe. Employment has grown by more than 5 percent over the past three years, the proportion outside the labour force has decreased by 6 percent (16–74 years), and job turnover and labour mobility are similar to the levels found in other OECD countries (Salvanes, 1996: 36). Labour supply seems to be more responsive to fluctuations in demand than it is in most other countries, suggesting that welfare institutions surrounding the labour market do not necessarily distort incentives; they may also provide broader options for social choice, especially among women.

Despite the indications of considerable macro flexibility, there are signs that the functioning of labour markets and work organization at the micro level is insufficient. The development of labour productivity in Norwegian manufacturing was apparently slower than among its trading partners in the period 1988–1994 (Stortingsmelding 2, 1995–96: 52). Despite falling rates, long-term unemployment has prevailed; youth unemployment continues; the number of man-hours worked has slowly caught up; a scarcity of labour and skill mismatches persist in several labour market segments; while a limited proportion of vacancies have been filled by unemployed. After unemployment decreased slowly during the strong recovery in 1993/94, it dropped substantially in 1995/96, but appears to have stabilized at 4.0–4.5 percent, suggesting that structural unemployment has risen (ibid.: 87).

The Norwegian variant of the Nordic model has in many respects been a "light" version of Swedish policies. Whereas international studies claim serious welfare state distortions of labour market incentives in Sweden (Aronsson and Walker, 1995: 136), one reason that similar effects are less evident in Norway might be that small differences create big impacts in terms of behaviour (Card and Freeman, 1994: 217). Whereas the OECD has argued that incentives to work are too weak among certain groups, a study of Statistics Norway suggests that the benefits of paid work compared with various social security programmes are generally significant (Arneberg, 1996).

If apparently tight labour market regulations have not seriously harmed labour market adjustment, one can ask whether alternative sources of flexibility evolve as unintended side-effects, rather than on purpose. The vast numbers of small firms might provide a source of flexibility and, as suggested by Odnes et al. (1990), considerable dynamics can evolve in the "loopholes"; i.e. normative constraints may direct behaviour but social practice often deviates from central regulations in a creative way. Despite their postulated "passion for equality", Norwegians tend to perceive themselves as independent actors reacting quite pragmatically to centrally imposed rules, reflecting a strong anti-centre cultural thrust (Rokkan, 1987: 112). If so, the interaction between macro- and micro-level processes appears critical in detecting sources of rigidity and flexibility in Norwegian labour markets. This issue is discussed by Gerhard Bosch in chapter 7.

Another puzzling feature of Norwegian labour market policies is the mix of conventional policies in some areas and quite radical approaches in other areas, of convergence with and divergence from international trends. Whereas strong emphasis in recent years has been put on sound budgetary policies, controlling inflation, and stabilizing the exchange rate (Norway is over-fullfilling the Maastricht convergence criteria), the most expansionary fiscal policy since World War II was conducted to overcome the recession in the early 1990s (Mjøset et al., 1995: 69). Whereas supply-side liberalization has been conducted, *inter alia*, in the credit system and energy markets, the financial crisis triggered reregulation and takeover of the largest banks by the state in 1990, a revival of "socialism" by default, leading to more extensive state ownership in the economy than ever (ibid.: 69). Owing to limitations on state governance of the economy by traditional means, the governing leader of the Labour Party has argued for more direct modes of state control through joint national ownership structures, including private capital, employees, and the state. If this happens, a supply-side-oriented, re-nationalized mode of state capitalism could paradoxically emerge in response to internationalization.

Job-sharing and reductions in working time as a strategy to combat unemployment have traditionally been rejected by the main social actors, who stick to competitiveness as the overriding policy benchmark. Nevertheless, quite radical reforms, e.g. as regards parental and educational leave, tighter restrictions on temporary employment, and rights to generalize collective agreements to inhibit social dumping by foreign labour have been pursued in recent years. Product market deregulation has gone hand in hand with social and labour market reregulation. In practice, however, a central feature of employment growth during recent decades has been a shortening of working hours and a proliferation of part-time work, suggesting that disguised work-sharing has taken place as an unintended consequence of past institutional reforms. While generous public sector policies have given impetus to employment growth, more restrictive policies are suggested in relation to receivers of social benefits and certain categories of unemployed who are supposed to take part in labour market schemes, according to the so-called "working-line".

The large public sector is another distinctive feature of Norwegian working life, and is often perceived to create rigidities and malfunctioning of labour markets. The rising labour market participation of Norwegian women has predominantly been associated with expansion of the public sector. In contemporary economic wisdom, such expansion is assumed to inhibit growth and disturb the allocation of productive resources, while the welfare-state-dependent dual-income family is suspected of restraining the adjustment of labour supply. Well-paid, subsidized public service jobs are frequently assumed to halt job creation in private, low-productive service sectors, inhibiting female employment opportunities.

The gender order of Norwegian labour markets, engendering tendencies of both reduced inequality and persistent segregation, is analysed by Anne Lise Ellingsæter and Jill Rubery in chapter 4. A central issue is how increased education, gender equality, and dual-income families influence the reconciliation of conflicting expectations in work and family life – between men and women as well as between generations – with respect to renumeration, job opportunities, and social responsibilities. The Norwegian order of relative gender equality is likely to serve as both constraint and opportunity, encouraging new patterns of career and work time, but also renewed tension, legitimacy problems, and a struggle for distribution cutting across gender and class boundaries.

The complexities of labour relations and interest intermediation in the Norwegian public sector are analysed by Berndt Keller in chapter 8, while Frieder Naschold and Robert Arnkil argue in chapter 9 for a critical view of the efficacy and innovative capacity of Norwegian public services, based on, *inter alia*, a comparative study of modernization in state labour market administration.

All in all, Norwegian labour market policies contain few original or surprising single ingredients. The puzzling question is why the coupling of policy ingredients that have not really worked elsewhere seems to function surprisingly well in Norway (even though it could be asked why a country with such economic conditions is not performing better). This question invites three alternative interpretations: (1) favourable demand-side developments have in effect overruled and postponed the negative effects of institutional fetters; (2) the significance of institutionalized labour market regulations is simply overestimated; or (3) the institutional framework is an essential explanatory factor of the improved labour market situation in Norway.

Our assumption is that answers should not be sought in particular measures or a distinct strategic approach. The challenge is rather to understand how and why the specific configuration of institutions and policies tends to produce more favourable outcomes than occur in other countries, probably more by incremental muddling-through policies than by grand design. A central issue therefore is to what degree interaction between various policy components and actors enhances complementarity and coherence, and what kind of mechanism facilitates or impedes such accommodation.

5. A trade-off between equality and flexibility?

The aim of this study has been to analyse how simultaneous changes in the international environment and in domestic conditions exert pressures for adjustment of the Norwegian labour market model. Faced with increased competitive pressures (from outside), restructuring of markets and production (from below), and social change (from within), what are the advantages, vulnerabilities, and critical success factors of the Norwegian approach to restoring full employment?

We were asked by the Research Council of Norway to address the issue of regulation, flexibility, and labour market policies. Despite international literature frequently is reiterating the importance of institutional arrangements in labour markets, political attention is predominantly oriented towards either macroeconomic issues or micro-oriented issues of deregulation and the individual behaviour of firms and employees. During the project the international research team became increasingly concerned with the articulation between macro- and micro-level phenomena, and, hence, with the essential role of institutions in facilitating/inhibiting desirable labour market outcomes. Therefore, when searching for points of change it is important to take account of how labour market processes are embedded in broader patterns of norms, traditions, and ideas, directing actors' behaviour and interaction. Seemingly inadequate practices may serve other, unintended functions than those immediately foreseen. Hence it is frequently reported in the international literature that attempts to import or copy partial labour market reform from outside fail because diverse institutional and cultural prerequisites cause adverse effects (see, for instance, Singh, 1995; Teague, 1994; Streeck, 1992).

In international comparison, one of the most striking features of the Norwegian model is the persistence of an egalitarian wage structure maintained by centralized collective bargaining. As in most Western countries, new expressions of inequality and social exclusion can be found in Norway as well, e.g. among single parents, immigrants, and young unemployed, but among the majority working population, wage differentials have remained stable and even become more compressed over the past decade (OECD, 1995). This "passion for equality" has been perceived internationally as well as by Norwegian capital as a barrier to the adjustment of production and the employment of less productive labour. Evidence of such effects in Norway seems, however, partial and anecdotal, and it might conversely be asked whether the egalitarian legacy might provide comparative advantages, e.g. by containing labour costs among qualified workers and enhancing labour mobility, flexible adjustment, and trust-based cooperation. Most of the international contributions to this book touch on this issue, from different angles and perspectives.

The debate about equality, efficiency, and flexibility has often been conducted at a fairly abstract ideological level. Valid empirical evidence is indeed hard to obtain because similar phenomena tend to serve diverse functions in different national contexts. Before jumping to conclusions, possible unanticipated consequences of the egalitarian legacy – negative as well as positive – therefore ought to be carefully considered. Conceived as a normative order guiding and constraining a multitude of interlinked decisions, the egalitarian legacy cannot easily be modified or redressed on a partial basis. Introduction of increased inequality might well unleash cumulative dynamics and fragmentation of interest intermediation, making a new consensus hard to achieve. It is therefore interesting to note that recent OECD reports appear increasingly concerned with the implications of recommended policies for "social cohesion" and equality (OECD, 1996).

A central concern of this book is thus to encourage reflection about the costs and benefits of the withering but still existing solidaristic order in Norway, and the possible gains and losses of departing from it.

6. Sustainable compromise or crisis management?

A widely held view is that recent developments in Norwegian labour markets have been dependent on cooperation between the state and collective actors with shared perceptions, a reasonable balance of power, and the capacity to aquire legitimacy around agreed policies. Accordingly, the Norwegian case apparently fits well Katzenstein's (1985) thesis that small states with corporatist traditions of governance display a superior flexible capacity to cope with fluctuating international developments. More than in Sweden in recent years, the main labour market parties in Norway have acted together in pragmatic concert with government, in line with the so-called "Solidarity alternative", facilitated by the absence of major political conflict.

This cooperative approach may be founded on precarious conditions; for example, some of the actors in the corporatist triad might pull out, become replaced, or prove unable to sustain internal support. Sceptical observers might well suggest that recent concertation was made possible only by the emergency caused by economic crisis in the mid-1980s; a temporary breakdown in employer strength; and the unusual power of the current union leadership, enabling a tacit peace agreement between capital and labour headquarters, enhanced by their joint interest in EU membership. A decreasing fit between the hegemonic constellation of actors and the changing configuration of social interests might cause uncertainty about the sustainability of the system in its current form. Even if the model appears well entrenched, it cannot be ruled out that fairly minor changes might trigger destabilizing dynamics.

A main concern of Norwegian policy during the last recession (1988–1993) was to ensure wage moderation and a fair distribution of sacrifice through flat pay increases (Kahn, 1996). In the current strong economic recovery, with soaring profits and budget surpluses, these prerequisites may easily be subject to erosion, as illustrated by the conflictual pay round of 1996, which lead to significant real wage increases. Apparently well suited to cope with external pressures, it seems more uncertain whether the Norwegian model is equally capable of handling conflicting pressures from "within". In a context of growing aspirations and diversification of interests, a key question might be whether the Norwegian model has the innovative capacity to reconcile the virtue of distributive justice with the increasingly differentiated demands for productive change, adequate services and meaningful work.

7. Aim, content, and structure

The ambition of this book is not to provide new empirical evidence or policy recipes for Norwegian labour market policy. With some exceptions, the contributions mainly rely on secondary material and interviews with strategic informants. The overriding purpose has been to invite prominent international scholars to take a critical, fresh look at Norwegian labour market developments and re-interpret these experiences in the light of insights from contemporary international research.

Fafo (the Institute for Applied Social Science) has been responsible for organizing interviews with central Norwegian actors and experts and providing background material. Because the international researchers have mainly had the chance to receive "snap-shots" of the system of Norwegian labour market policy, we have encouraged them to convey their personal impressions, thoughts, and even speculation in order to make the most of their role as travelling "devil's advocates".

The risk of such a venture is, of course, that owing to a lack of detailed empirical and background knowledge visiting foreigners may misunderstand certain issues, but we consider this might also be the strength of such an approach. By inviting outsiders, coming like anthropologists to a new tribe, to present their interpretations and participate in dialogue, the insiders may be stimulated to reflect on, and possibly overcome, ethno-centric "blind-spots". The inhabitants of an inherited national model naturally learn to take national distinctions for granted and reify domestic perceptions of reality, which can serve to overlook the strengths, weaknesses, and vulnerabilities of customary national practices. Therefore we are convinced that international exchange, aimed at enhancing comparative perspectives, is fruitful for developing insight, consciousness, and self-reflection about reality, and, it is hoped, contributing positively to change and continuity of national policy.

Accordingly, the international scholars were asked to focus on issues with policy relevance and implications. This does not imply that the study provides specific policy recommendations, but we are convinced their contributions will stimulate new ways of conceptualizing, understanding, and discussing viable pathways to the restoration of full employment.

The book is organized in the following way. In chapter 2, Richard B. Freeman discusses whether or not solidaristic wage and welfare policies are compatible with the restoration of full employment in the modern global economy. In chapter 3, Jon Erik Dølvik, Mona Bråten, Frode Longva, and Arild H. Steen describe the background and institutional frameworks of Norwegian labour market policies, with particular emphasis on the system of labour relations and collective bargaining. In chapter 4, Anne Lise Ellingsæter and Jill Rubery analyse Norwegian labour market developments from a gender perspective. A central issue is how institutional arrangements and tension between labour market participation and family commitments influence the adaptiveness of labour markets and inequalities across gender and class boundaries. In chapter

5, Asbjørn Rødseth analyses to what degree macroeconomic policy changes can account for the growth in Norwegian unemployment in the late 1980s and discusses the potential for returning to full employment by means of macroeconomic strategies. In chapter 6, Karl Ove Moene, Ragnar Nymoen, and Michael Wallerstein present a conceptual discussion of the relation between fixed and flexible manpower regimes of employers and the development of unemployment. In chapter 7, Gerhard Bosch discusses relations between labour market regulations and mechanisms of labour force adaptation in private firms, with an emphasis on functional flexibility as regards working time, work organization, and training. In chapter 8, Berndt Keller analyses the role of the public sector in Norwegian employment policy with a focus on interaction between labour relations and labour market developments. In chapter 9, Frieder Naschold and Robert Arnkil present a comparative study of the effectiveness and modernization of Norwegian labour market placement services and invite a critical view of the innovative capacity and effectiveness of the large public sector in Norway. In chapter 10, Jon Erik Dølvik resumes joint efforts to synthesize the main conclusions and future questions of policy relevance that can be derived from the study.

References

Arneberg, M. W. (1996) Lønner det seg å jobbe? Kompensasjonsgrader i den norske velferdsmodellen. *Økonomiske analyser* 4/96, Statistics Norway, Oslo.

Aronsson, T. and J. R. Walker (1995) Velferdsstatens effekter på arbeidsutbudet. In R. B. Freeman et al. (eds), *Velferdsstat i omvandling. Amerikansk perspektiv på den svenske modellen.* Stockholm: NBER-rapporten, SNS-forlag.

Brox, O. (1994) *Norge mot tusenårsskiftet. Arbeid for alle – eller flere rike og ny fattigdom?* Oslo: Gyldendal.

Crouch, C. (1995) Exit or voice: Two paradigms for European industrial relations after the Keynesian welfare state. *European Journal of Industrial Relations* 1(1).

Dølvik, J. E. (1992) The Nordic trade unions and the dilemmas of European integration. In J. Fagerberg and L. Lundberg (eds), *European Economic Integration: A Nordic Perspective.* Aldershot: Avebury.

Dølvik, J. E. (1993) *Nordic Trade Unions and the Social Dimension of European Integration. Towards Europeanisation or Renationalisation of Trade Union Strategies?* Oslo: FAFO-Paper.

Ferner, A. and R. Hyman (1992) Introduction. In A. Ferner and R. Hyman (eds), *Industrial Relations in the New Europe.* Oxford: Blackwell.

Freeman, R. B. (1994) How labor fares in advanced economies. In R. B. Freeman (ed.), *Working under Different Rules.* New York: Russell Sage Foundation.

Golombek, R. (1991) *Lønnsomheten i norsk industri.* Oslo: SNF-rapport 28/91.

Hagen, K. (1990) *Nasjonalstat, velferdspolitikk og europeisk integrasjon.* Oslo: FAFO-rapport 104.

Hernes, G. (1977) *Forhandlingsøkonomi og blandingsadministrasjon.* Oslo: Scandinavian University Press.

Kahn, L. K. (1996) Against the wind: Bargaining recentralization and wage inequality in Norway 1987–91. Mimeo, Cornell University, Ithaca, NY.

Katzenstein, P. J. (1985) *Small States in World Markets.* Ithaca, NY: Cornell University Press.

Kvinge, T., L. Lindholt, and L. Stle (1996) *Nyskaping i norsk arbeidsliv.* Oslo: FAFO-rapport 191.

Mahnkopf, B. and E. Altvater (1995) Transmission belts of transnational competition? Trade unions and collective bargaining in the context of European integration. *European Journal of Industrial Relations* 1(1).

Martin, A. and G. Ross (1995) Labor and Europe: European institutions and the precarious construction of interest representation. Paper, Harvard Center for European Studies, Boston.

Mathiassen, S. (1996) Norge på vei mot topplass. *Dagens Næringsliv.* 28 May 1996.

Mjøset, L., . Cappelen, J. Fagerberg, and B. S. Tranøy (1995) Norway: Changing the model. Særtrykk 95/1, Oslo, from P. Anderson and P. Camiller, *Mapping the European Left.* London: New Left Review

Moene, K. O. and M. Wallerstein (1996) Economic integration and unemployment in EFTA countries. In B. Eichengreen, J. Frieden, and J. von Hagen (eds.), *Monetary and Fiscal Policy in an Integrated Europe.* Springer Verlag.

Odnes, D., A. Hompland, A. Pape, and T. R. Larsen (1990) *Kampen om framtiden. Frontlinjer 2006.* Oslo: FAFO-rapport 98.

OECD (1994) *Jobs Study. Evidence and Explanations.* Paris.

OECD (1995) *Economic Surveys – Norway.* Paris.

OECD (1996) *The OECD Jobs Strategy. Pushing ahead with the strategy.* Paris.

Rokkan, S. (1987) *Stat, nasjon klasse.* Oslo: Scandinavian University Press.

Salvanes, K. G. (1996) *Job Creation and Job Destruction in Norway 1976–1992.* Oslo: Ministry of Finance.

Sengenberger, W. (1994) Labour standards in the international economy – Challenges and perspectives. In G. Bosch (ed.), *International Integration and the Regulation of Working Conditions.* Gelsenkirchen: SAMF/Institut Arbeit und Technik.

Singh, A. (1995) Institutional requirements for full employment in advanced economies. *International Labour Review* 134(4–5).

Stortingsmelding 2 (1995–96) *Revidert Nasjonalbudsjett.* Oslo: Finansdepartementet.

Streeck, W. (1991) More uncertainties: German unions facing 1992. *Industrial Relations* 30(3).

Streeck, W. (1992) *Social Institutions and Economic Performance. Studies of Industrial Relations in Advanced Capitalist Economies.* London: Sage.

Streeck, W. (1993) The rise and decline of neocorporatism. In L. Ulman et al. (eds), *Labor and an Integrated Europe.* Washington DC: The Brookings Institution.

Teague, P. (1994) Between new Keynesianism and deregulation: Employment policy in the European Union. *Journal of European Public Policy* 1(3).

Teague, P. and J. Grahl (1992) *Industrial Relations and European Integration.* London: Lawrence & Wishart.

Chapter 2

Are Norway's Solidaristic and Welfare State Policies Viable in the Modern Global Economy?

Richard B. Freeman

In the latter half of the 20th century, West European countries developed extensive welfare states and modes of institutional determination of wages that compressed the distribution of earnings and raised the living standards of low-income persons. The Scandinavian countries, including Norway, were among the leaders in creating this social democratic brand of capitalism. In the 1960s, the government share of GDP in Norway averaged around 33 percent; in the 1970s, it averaged around 45 percent; in the 1980s, it increased to around 50 percent.[1] In 1990, Norway was the fifth-highest ranking OECD country in terms of its government share of GDP (OECD, 1996a: appendix table 28). Throughout the 1980s and 1990s, collective bargaining in Norway raised the earnings of low decile workers toward the median (OECD, 1995a: fig. 16) and produced a spread of earnings more compressed than in any country, including Sweden.

From the 1950s through the 1970s, the large welfare state and solidaristic pay policies succeeded in reducing poverty without harming economic performance. Economic growth in Western Europe exceeded that of the United States. Centralized collective bargaining with solidaristic wage-setting cut pay differentials without creating unemployment. Unemployment rates were lower in Western Europe than in the USA.

In the 1980s and 1990s, however, the situation changed. Growth of GDP per capita in Western Europe roughly matched that in the USA, but the European employment record was abysmal. Most countries in Western Europe developed high persistent unemployment and substantial budget deficits that led many analysts and policy-makers to question

---

1 These data are from OECD, *Historical Statistics*, 1960–1990. They are based on GDP figures for Norway calculated before the 1995 European System of Accounts was introduced. Figures based on the new accounting system will show lower levels of government spending to GDP.

the size of the welfare state and the value of associated solidaristic policies. The exemplar welfare state, Sweden, fell into economic depression and was forced to reassess its welfare policies. The Maastricht criterion for a common European currency required that European Union countries lower fiscal deficits, which often meant cutbacks in welfare state benefits. Business groups throughout Europe campaigned for deregulation of the labour market.

Norway stands out among advanced countries as an exception to this trend in policy. During the 1990s Norway developed a "solidarity alternative" policy to strengthen centralized bargaining and maintain egalitarian goals. Rather than seeking to cut welfare state benefits, Norway increased some benefits[2] while strengthening the work orientation of other benefits and tried to target them more on the needy (Kuhnle, 1996). Unlike Sweden, which plummeted in league tables of per capita income, possibly in part because of inefficiencies arising from a large welfare state, Norway rose in those tables. Norway emerged as the exceptional case of an economy succeeding with all the "old" policies and commitment to egalitarianism.

How come? What explains Norwegian exceptionalism? What lessons, if any, can we draw about the long-term viability of welfare state spending and solidaristic wage policies from the Norwegian experience? What are the risks to maintaining the Norwegian model as the country enters the 21st century?

This paper considers four hypotheses for Norway's successful welfare state and solidaristic policies through the 1990s: the Welfare Autarky hypothesis, that the world economy does not force countries into the lowest common denominator social policy but rather leaves considerable scope for national choice; the Solidaristic Welfare State Efficiency hypothesis that narrow income distributions have efficiency benefits that exceed their costs; the Golden Mean hypothesis that there is an optimal level of welfare state/solidaristic wage-setting that Norway managed to find; and the Manna from Heaven hypothesis that Norway's oil revenues gave it the wherewithal to fund welfare state/egalitarian policies with only modest inefficiency costs, via the deadweight losses due to taxation.

The chapter begins by laying out some of the key welfare state and solidaristic wage policies of Norway, and the evidence that Norway is an economic success story compared with most other advanced OECD economies. Then I examine the hypotheses for Norway's success. When

2 Norway made child allowances more generous in the 1990s, extended maternity leave from 18 weeks in 1977 to 52 weeks by 1995; and extended benefits to parents with sick children.

I began the project, I believed that Norway was doing fine because of its oil revenues. But, as you will discover, I have changed my views. That oil enables Norway to do more than many other countries is true, but I now believe that the key to understanding "Norwegian exceptionalism" lies in the political economy forces that led the country to spend those monies judiciously and to balance carefully the costs and benefits of welfare state/solidaristic policies – the golden mean story.

Throughout, I treat the welfare state and solidaristic wage policies as a single economic system. One can imagine substantial welfare state spending independent of solidaristic wage-setting (a huge pension and medical care system might coexist with highly unequal wages), but the large welfare states of Western Europe, particularly of the Nordic countries, combine the two, so this seems the more realistic way to proceed.[3] I also take as given attitudes in Norway toward the distribution of income and the role of the state and institutions in influencing that distribution. Norwegians, like other Western Europeans, support government/union interventions to limit inequality and poverty. The question in these countries is not whether solidaristic/welfare state policies are desirable (which many in the USA doubt) but whether they are viable. If they are, Norwegians seem to want them. Hence, I consider the viability, not the desirability, of these policies.

1. Norwegian solidaristic/welfare state policies

The level and direction of change in Norwegian labour institutions, economic outcomes, and welfare state policies differ from those in most advanced countries.

Unionization and centralized collective bargaining

In the 1970s, union density increased in most European countries while falling in the USA. In the 1980s–1990s unionization fell or stabilized in most advanced countries. Some countries "de-institutionalized" their labour market along various dimensions (the UK, New Zealand, the USA). Others moved from centralized wage-setting to more decentralized

---

3 There are good reasons to expect solidaristic pay-setting and a large welfare state to accompany one another. One reason is that unions are likely to be an important supporter of both, so that strong unions should lead to reduction of pay differentials through collective bargaining and extensive welfare state benefits. Another is that solidaristic pay policies may be more acceptable to workers when taxes are high: if skilled workers do not gain all that much from higher pay because of taxes, they may accept reductions in skill differentials.

Table 2.1 Important features of Norway's labour market

1. *Union density*	
Level, 1993	
Norway	58.1
OECD median	38.1
Change in density, 1970–1993	
Norway	3.2
OECD median	–3.3
2. *Earnings differentials*	
90/10, 1991	1.97
Change, 1980–1991	–0.09
std dev of industry earnings, 26 industries 1980–1990 average (lowest of 17 countries)	0.12
3. *Rate of unemployment, 1995*	
Norway	4.9
including those on programmes	6.7
USA	5.6
EU	11.2
4. *Employment–population ratios, 1995*	
Norway	74.0
USA	73.5
OECD-Eur	60.1
5. *Employment—population ratios, men aged 55–64, 1994*	
Norway	69.1
USA	62.9
Sweden	68.8
Germany	45.0
France	39.1
6. *Labour participation by education, men aged 30–39, 1993*	
Primary school	88
Secondary level I	92
Secondary level II	93
University level	96
7. *Hours worked per person in employment, 1994*[a]	
Norway	1415
USA	1780
8. *Part-time work, 1995*	
Norway, % part time	26.5
USA, % part time	18.6

Sources: line 1 – J. Visser ('Unionization Trends Revisited', mimeo, University of Amsterdam, 1996), with medians calculated as average of countries ranked 9 and 10 from list of 18; line 2 – OECD (1993: table 5.2); industry earnings from STAN Data Set; line 3 – OECD (1995b: table 1.3; table B); adjusted for programmes based on Try (1994), I assume the same rate of involvement of unemployed young people as in the whole population and a ratio of programme participants to unemployed the same in 1995 as in 1993; line 4 – OECD (1996: table A); line 5 – OECD (1996 : table 13); line 6 – Norway Official Statistics (1993: table 16); line 7 – OECD (1996: Table C); line 8 – OECD (1996 : Table E).

[a] OECD (1996b) shows a bigger difference in hours worked owing to its use of different US data. For 1995 it shows Norway 1424 and USA 1952. But the revised US data seem too high since 18 percent of Americans work part time and US employees get about 3 weeks of vacation and holiday pay. In 1985, mean usual hours per week for non-farm wage and salary workers was 38.4, giving a total hours worked of 1882 for those with 3 weeks off.

---

bargaining (Italy abandoned the Scala Mobile; Australia chose more plant-level bargaining; Swedish employers abandoned centralized wage-bargaining). Although collective bargaining coverage remained stable in Western Europe, even in countries such as the Netherlands or Austria where union density fell, union influence on wage-setting and economic policies lessened.

Norway went in a different direction. After a set of industry-level negotiations in 1982 and 1984, Norway re-centralized collective bargaining from 1987. The contrast with Sweden, where the employers' association shut down its centralized bargaining unit in 1990, is stark. Union density rose in Norway in the 1980s/early 1990s (Table 2.1, line 1), widening the gap between unionization in Norway and most other OECD countries. Overall, unions remained as important in the labour market as ever before. Analysts place Norway at or near the top in corporatist or centralized wage-setting arrangements (OECD, 1994: table 5.1).[4]

Solidaristic wage structure

In the 1980s/early 1990s market forces greatly widened the wage structure in the USA and UK and raised inequality in some other OECD countries, albeit more mildly (OECD, 1996b: chapter 3). By contrast, Norway's earnings distribution grew more compressed (Table 2.1, line 2) as collective bargainers negotiated a guaranteed wage for the lowest paid in a branch or enterprise linked to the average wage in manufacturing

---

4 The bargaining system is more accurately described as a two-tier system, beginning with a centrally fixed frame level between LO and NHO, or at industry level followed by plant-level amendments, which can produce significant wage drift (Holden, 1989).

(from 1987, average at branch level). Earnings differences by education, occupation, and industry were narrow, and Norway reduced its male–female differential considerably, so that in 1994 it had the lowest such differential in the advanced world (Bradshaw et al., 1996: 49, table 6.1).

Still, Norway is not an extreme outlier in earnings inequality. Many advanced OECD European countries maintained compressed wage structures through the mid-1990s. Where Norway deviates from other West European countries is that it combined a narrow wage structure with low unemployment and a high rate of employment to population. Prior to the 1990s, Sweden also had low unemployment, high employment, and a narrow wage structure that risked job loss for the least skilled. But Swedish unemployment jumped in the early 1990s when the economy fell into a major depression, leaving Norway as the primary low unemployment/narrow wage distribution economy in Western Europe.

The size of the welfare state

Norway has an extensive welfare state. The share of GDP that passes through state hands is large. With the GDP accounting system used through 1994, government expenditures as a share of GDP were 55 percent (see Table 2.2, line 1) – a high figure but one surpassed by several other OECD countries, including Germany, France, and Italy, all of which had sizeable public sector deficits. As in the other Nordic countries, most government expenditures in Norway are transfers: the public share of consumption was about one-fifth of GDP. Government revenues in 1994 were 57 percent of GDP, a level exceeded only by Sweden, Denmark, and Finland. In 1995 Norway revised its GDP accounts to follow the European System of Accounts that all Eurostat countries are expected to adopt by 1999. This raised GDP per capita by about 10 percent, reducing the estimates of government's share of outlays or receipts (see 1995 in Table 2.2, line 2). The new estimates are not comparable to those for other countries, which have not published statistics using the new accounting system, as of this writing.

What distinguishes Norway from other large welfare states is that substantial public spending does not involve a huge government deficit. In 1995, Norway had a public sector surplus of 3.1 percent of GDP compared with a 5.3 percent deficit in EU countries, and an 8.1 percent deficit in Sweden.[5] Norway has huge net assets in the form of oil that permit sizeable public spending at a given tax burden without a deficit.

5 OECD (1996a: table A-30).

Table 2.2 Government budgets and oil revenues, 1994 and 1995

	1994[a]	1995
1. *Government outlays as % of GDP*		
Norway	55.6	47.4
Sweden	68.8	
OECD	40.8	
2. *Government receipts as % of GDP*		
Norway	55.3	50.5
Sweden	58.4	
Europe-OECD	37.0	
3. *Government oil receipts as % of GDP*		
Norway	5.6	–
4. *Government financial balances as % of GDP*		
Norway	−0.2	3.1
Sweden	−10.4	−8.1
Europe-OECD	−3.8	−3.6
5. *Government net financial assets as % of GDP*		
Norway	14.3	26.3
Sweden	−23.4	−27.8
Europe-OECD	−43.4	−45.7
6. *Petroleum and natural gas production as % of GDP, 1991*		
Norway	13.1	

Sources: line 1 – OECD (1995c, 1996a: table 28); line 2 – OECD (1995c, 1996a: table 29); line 3 – calculated by dividing government receipts from petroleum activities, in OECD (1995a: table 14) by gross domestic product; line 4 – OECD (1995c, 1996a: table 30); line 5 – OECD (1995c, 1996a: table 31); line 6 – OECD (1995c, 1996a: table 35); line 7 – OECD (1993: table C).

[a] The 1994 figures are based on the national income accounts system used in Norway and other countries prior to the revision of national income accounting procedures in the European System of Accounts that all Eurostat countries are expected to adopt by 1999. Norway revised its GDP accounts in 1995 to follow the new system. This raised GDP per capita by about 10 percent, giving estimates of government's share of outlays or receipts that are not comparable to those in countries that have not yet revised their GDP accounts.

In 1995 the general government in Norway had net financial *assets* relative to GDP of 26 percent compared with an OECD average net financial *liability* of 46 percent.

Another way to measure welfare state activity is by the public sector share of employment. In 1993, 30 percent of Norwegian workers were public employees (Norway, 1993: table 2), which puts Norway in third position in the OECD (Sweden and Denmark have higher shares). Between 1973 and 1993 private sector employment grew by 3 percent while public sector employment grew by 94 percent. To some extent the high public share of employment reflects state production of some service activities privately produced in other countries. To some extent it reflects counter-cyclical policies that raise government employment when private sector employment is slack. But even in 1987, when non-government employment peaked at 1.6 million, the government share of employment was 25 percent, compared with 19 percent in 1973 and 14 percent in 1964 (Norway, 1993: table 2). In 1987 the share of employment in personal services was 6.7 percent in Norway compared with 12.5 percent in the USA; hotel and restaurant employment was 2.7 percent of the total compared with 7.0 percent in the USA (Erhvervsministeriet, 1995: 41).

A high government share of resources makes the efficiency of the public sector, which does not face the same market test as private firms, a critical determinant of economic well-being.

Oil revenues

Since 1975 Norway has enjoyed a windfall gain in oil and natural gas. In 1985 the share of GDP from crude petroleum and natural gas production reached a peak of 18 percent. In 1991, petroleum and natural gas was 13 percent of GDP. Although it is hard to imagine that a windfall gain can be bad for an economy, many countries with oil bonanzas have in fact done poorly (Gelb, 1988). Rates of growth of GDP tend to be inversely related to the natural resource proportion of exports (Sachs and Warner, 1995). Countries with natural resource windfalls can incur the "Dutch Disease": rising effective exchange rates that create competitiveness problems for non-natural resource sectors in world markets; and reduced work effort by a suddenly enriched population. These countries can also suffer from rent-seeking, as different groups fight over the disposition of the natural resource windfall. In Nigeria and Venezuela, politicians stole or wasted much of the national dividend from the rise in oil prices. In Norway, the danger was that oil revenues would lead to excessive welfare state spending and/or a breakdown of coordinated wage-setting and labour market controls on inflation as different groups sought their share of the proceeds.

The petroleum sector is critical in Norway's trade and public sector accounts. Merchandise exports of oil make up nearly one-third of Norwegian exports (see line 3 of Table 2.4). These exports allow the country to run a deficit in other goods and services while maintaining a current account balance. Approximately 5 percent of GDP consists of oil production/revenues for the state. Petroleum revenues constitute some 13 percent of government receipts and fund 10–11 percent of government expenditures. These receipts allow Norway to operate a large welfare state without a public sector deficit, though the country could choose to deficit finance an even larger welfare state.

2. National income and employment

The viability of any economic system depends on how well it produces goods and services for its citizens. With a narrow distribution of wages and income, the issue for Norway and other welfare state economies is whether the economy grows at a healthy pace and generates sufficient employment to keep unemployment at modest levels.

Table 2.3 shows GDP per capita in purchasing power parity ("ppp") units for major OECD countries from 1970 to 1993. Over this period Norway rose smartly in the country ranking, closing nearly one-half of the gap with the USA. In 1993, it was the fifth-highest country in per capita income in the OECD. Comparisons of GDP per capita in "ppp" units in any given year are, however, far from perfect, particularly for countries closely bunched together, so that Norway could easily drop a few places in ensuing years: in 1992, it was 11th in "ppp" per capita ranking. In addition, Norwegian GDP per capita and growth are greatly affected by petroleum activity. From 1988 to 1994, GDP excluding North Sea petroleum production, oil platforms, and ships grew 1–2 percent per year less rapidly than total GDP (OECD, 1995a: fig. 1). Absent the petroleum wealth, GDP per capita would be 5–10 percent lower and 1970–1993 growth less impressive. Still, as noted, many countries fail to turn natural resource wealth into economic success. And the exemplar welfare state, Sweden, dropped significantly in per capita income after its 1991 depression and suffered high unemployment in the 1990s.

The Norwegian record in unemployment and employment puts it near the top of OECD countries. In 1995 the unemployment rate was 4.9 percent compared with 5.6 percent in the USA, 7.7 percent in Sweden, and 11.2 percent in the EU (line 3 of Table 2.1). Norway's youth unemployment rate was 9.4 percent whereas the rates for many OECD countries, including the USA, were in double digits (OECD, 1996b: table B).[6] Because persons on labour market programmes in Norway are not

6 Despite country differences in student employment and participation and involvement in employment programmes, Norway's low youth unemployment appears to hold up in more refined data (OECD, 1996b: chapter 5).

Table 2.3 Norway's GDP per capita as a percentage of USA and ranking in comparison with 20 other advanced countries

	1970	1989	1993
United States	1.00	1.00	1.00
Norway	0.54	0.72	0.80
Sweden	0.77	0.77	0.69
Australia	0.70	0.73	0.70
Austria	0.61	0.73	0.79
Belgium	0.64	0.72	0.80
Canada	0.72	0.88	0.79
Denmark	0.71	0.75	0.80
Finland	058	0.76	0.64
France	0.71	0.77	0.77
Germany	0.74	0.82	0.76
Greece	0.29	0.34	0.36
Italy	0.60	0.72	0.73
Japan	0.57	0.77	0.84
Netherlands	0.72	0.71	0.72
New Zealand	0.70	0.63	0.64
Portugal	0.30	0.37	0.49
Spain	0.45	0.52	0.55
Switzerland	1.03	0.95	0.95
UK	0.66	0.73	0.70
Norway's ranking	16	14	5

Sources: GDP per capita, 1970 and 1989 – US Bureau of the Census, *Statistical Abstract 1994*, table 1370; 1993 – US Bureau of the Census, *Statistical Abstract 1995*, table 1374.
Note: Rankings can change sharply from year to year, with business cycle changes and revisions of purchasing power parity deflators. In 1992, Norway was 11th, according to OECD international comparative data in OECD (1995a). I have left Luxembourg out of this table; the *Statistical Abstract* data show that it had higher per capita income than the USA.

included in the unemployment total, however, Norwegian unemployment rates are biased downward relative to those of the USA. Employment–population ratios, which do not vary with how countries count people on labour market programmes or with whether or not the jobless report looking for work (which may depend on benefit programmes), are potentially more informative in cross-country comparisons. In 1995 among 15–64 year olds, the rate of employment in Norway was 74.0 percent, which put the country with the USA, Japan, and Denmark at the top of the OECD rankings. For adults 25–54 years old, the rate was 82.8 percent, compared with 79.7 percent in the USA. Among men aged 55–64, who retire early in many advanced countries, Norway also records a high rate of work participation (line 5 of Table 2.1)

– second only to Japan in the OECD. Equally impressive is the high labour participation of younger men with limited schooling (line 6 of Table 2.1).

But again, comparisons with the USA are biased. On average, Norwegians work 20 percent fewer hours than Americans, so that person-hours of work per adult are less in Norway than in the USA at comparable employment–population rates (line 7 of Table 2.1).[7] One reason for the lower hours worked is that many Norwegians, particularly women, work part time. In 1994, 27 percent of the Norwegian workforce consisted of part-timers, placing Norway second to the Netherlands in part-time work among reporting OECD countries. By comparison, 19 percent of Americans work part time. Among full-time workers in manufacturing, Norwegians take more vacation/holiday weeks than Americans, though fewer than other Europeans. In 1986, LO and NHO bargained for a standard workweek in Norway of 37.5 hours, which is lower than in most other OECD countries. The 37.5 hour standard workweek explains a large proportion of the gap between the annual hours of Americans and Norwegians in manufacturing (Bell and Freeman, 1996: table 5.2). A short bargained workweek does not, however, mean that Norwegians are unable to work long hours when they want. Overtime hours in industry averaged 5–6 per week in 1990–1994. And many Norwegians hold second jobs: 6.3 percent in 1993 (Norway, 1993: table 46) compared with 6.2 percent of Americans in 1991 (US Bureau of the Census, *Statistical Abstract 1993*, table 640). Finally, surveys regarding preferences for hours of work across several countries show that Norwegians fit in about the middle of the distribution of desire for work and work effort.[8] In sum, evidence on income per capita,

7 The gap in hours worked between Norwegians and Americans is much larger in OECD (1996b) because the OECD uses a different hours series for the USA that I find implausible, for the reasons given in the table notes.

8 The 1989 International Survey of Social Science Programmes questioned persons in Norway, the USA, and seven other countries or entities regarding preferences for hours and attitudes toward work. Respondents were asked if they preferred: (1) longer hours and more money; (2) the same number of hours and the same money; (3) fewer hours and less money – 24 percent of Norwegians said they preferred more hours; 69 percent wanted the same hours and pay; and 7 percent wanted fewer hours. These figures place Norway near the middle of the distribution of respondents. Americans had the highest proportion wanting more hours of work (33 percent) and Germans had the lowest proportion wanting more hours of work (13 percent) (see Bell and Freeman, 1996: table 4). Another question asked respondents "How hard do you work?" Forty-five percent of Norwegians said they would "work hard even if it interfered with family life", compared with 62 percent of Americans; 13 percent of Norwegians said that they would work "only as hard as they had to", compared with 8 percent of Americans. In this case also, however, Norwegians were close to the middle of the distribution of respondents by country. Americans were distinct with their devotion to work.

employment and unemployment, and worktime shows that Norway succeeded with a large welfare state and egalitarian wage policies in an epoch when the competitive market seemed to demand inequality or joblessness in advanced countries. Why? What enabled the big welfare state/solidaristic wage policy to remain alive and well in the fjords whereas it had run into such troubles in other European countries, including neighbouring Sweden?

3. Explanations

There are four possible explanations for the Norwegian success.

The first two are "cases against the case against" the viability of a large welfare state. The *Welfare Autarky Hypothesis* rejects the claim that the global economy makes large welfare state/solidaristic wage-setting unviable owing to competition in world markets from low-wage less developed countries (LDCs) or from advanced countries with more market-driven policies. The *Solidaristic Welfare State Efficiency Hypothesis* holds that critics of the large welfare state overstate the efficiency costs of solidaristic/welfare state interventions and ignore important efficiency benefits.

The second set of hypotheses relates specifically to Norway. The *Golden Mean Hypothesis* asserts that there is an optimum level of solidaristic/welfare state intervention that balances the costs of those interventions against the costs of inequality. By intervening more modestly than Sweden and more extensively than the USA, Norway has found the right balance. The *Manna from Heaven Hypothesis* is that Norway's oil wealth permits it to fund greater welfare state interventions than other countries. The economic costs of solidaristic/welfare state interventions are large, but manageable with extra wealth.

Welfare Autarky

The argument that the global economy severely limits, if not eliminates, the ability of individual countries to choose a solidaristic wage structure or a large welfare state is grounded in the factor price equalization proposition. This theory holds that, given certain assumptions, free trade makes worldwide factor endowments rather than domestic labour market conditions the determinant of the relative and real pay of factors of production in trading countries. It suggests that in the emerging global economy countries with high wages and labour standards will face great pressures to reduce unskilled worker wages and to cut taxes/welfare state spending.

The debate over the effects of trade on the earnings distribution in the USA and on unemployment in Europe provides a substantial body of evidence on these claims (see *Journal of Economic Perspectives*, Summer 1995). The emerging consensus from this research is that trade with LDCs has a modest effect in shifting labour demand away from unskilled workers in advanced countries rather than a massive effect. One reason the effect of trade seems to be modest is that imports from LDCs constitute only 2 percent or so of GDP in most countries, and are concentrated in apparel, leather, etc., which employ a limited number of largely female unskilled workers. If LDC trade was the main cause of labour market problems, the growth of manufacturing imports from LDCs should have reduced the pay and employment of low-skill women. In fact, throughout the OECD the wages and employment of women rose relative to those of men. Developments in non-traded goods and services, where the vast bulk of employees are found, dominate the job market for low-skill women workers. In addition, if a trade-induced decline in unskilled-labour-intensive industries was the main cause of falling labour demand for less skilled workers, many of those workers would have sought jobs outside traded goods, raising the unskilled share of employment in non-traded sectors. To the contrary, the proportion of unskilled workers fell in virtually all sectors. Finally, if trade affected wages or employment according to the precepts of the Heckscher–Ohlin trade model, industry prices would have fallen sharply in industries that use many unskilled workers (or, in the short run, in industries subject to LDC import competition). But changes in industry prices are only moderately correlated with the share of unskilled employment. The bottom line is not that the LDC trade has no effect on national labour markets, but that its effect is not sufficiently powerful to threaten national wage structures or policies.

What about Norway? Line 4 of Table 2.4 shows that 15 percent of Norwegian imports are from countries other than the advanced countries. Some of these imports are from the former communist countries. Some are from the newly industrialized East Asian countries. Given that imports are roughly 40 percent of GDP (Table 2.4, line 1), about 6 percent of GDP consists of imports from non-advanced countries; approximately half of these from LDCs. In terms of employment, if we take textiles, wood, and ships and boats as sectors that face substantial LDC low-wage competition, 2.7 percent of the Norwegian workforce was in direct competition with LDC workers – a proportion that nearly halved from 1981 to 1991. Line 7 of Table 2.4 shows that a disproportionate number of the experienced unemployed were previously employed in import-competing activities, but they constitute just 7 percent of the unemployed.

Table 2.4 Norway's international trade record

Trade flows	
1. Imports of goods and services as share of GDP	
(1989–1994 average)	39.6%
2. Exports of goods and services as share of GDP	
(1989–1994 average) total	43.5%
exclusive of oil	36.8%
3. Exports of oil and gas as share of total exports (1991)	31.4%
4. LDC imports' share of all imports (1991)	15.0%
of which: NICS	4.0%
COMECON	3.0%
Other	8.0%
Employment	
5. Employment in import-competing manufacturing	
As share of employment, 1993	7.9%
Change in share, 1973–1993	–6.3%
6. Employment in LDC import-competing sectors	
As share of employment in textiles, wood, shipping, 1991	2.7%
Change in share, 1981–1991	–2.5%
Unemployment	
7. Experienced unemployed in import-competing activities, 1993	
As share of experienced unemployed	13.0%
As share of total unemployed	7.0%
8. Rates of unemployment by group, 1993	
Total	5.1%
Immigrant	10.7%
LDC immigrant	17.8%

Sources: lines 1 & 2 – OECD (1995a), basic statistics of Norway; line 3 – Melchior (1994 : table D-12); line 4 – OECD (1995a: table 1); line 5 – Norway Official Statistics (1993: table 2); line 6 – Norway Official Statistics (1991: table 5.19); line 7 – Norway Official Statistics (1993: table 65); line 8 – Norway Official Statistics (1993: table 78).

Immigration is another important link among countries in the global economy. An immigrant increases the labour supply of his or her skill group, raising the rewards to cooperating inputs but reducing the pay/employment of natives with comparable skills. Immigration into Norway is modest – 3.8 percent of the population were foreign born in 1993, of whom 20 percent were from other Nordic countries. Immigrants are concentrated in Oslo, where the foreign born make up 10 percent of the population (OECD, 1995d: 111). Immigrants have roughly twice the unemployment rate of other residents of Norway. Unemployment is exceptionally high among LDC immigrants (line 8 of Table 2.4). But immigration is too small in Norway to have a major effect on the job market, either by altering the composition of the workforce or by reducing opportunities for natives.

Some analysts worry that as China, India, Indonesia, and the former European communist countries enter the global economy, pressures for factor price equalization will grow. The magnitudes are daunting. There are more workers in Shanghai or Calcutta or Djakarta than in Norway. But pressures from LDCs on the labour markets for unskilled work in advanced countries depend on the number of unskilled workers who produce goods that compete with LDC imports. In a Heckscher–Ohlin model with infinitely elastic product supply schedules, LDC trade has *no* effect on the wages of unskilled workers in advanced countries if *all* of those workers are employed in sectors that do not compete with LDC produced goods. For instance, if no low-skill Norwegians produce, say, children's toys that compete with those made by cheap labour in China, increased imports of such toys are purely a benefit to low-skill Norwegians. The number of Norwegians employed in industries competing with LDC workers is not zero, but it is sufficiently close to zero to dispel fears that increased LDC trade will create enough pressures on pay to make solidaristic policies unviable.[9]

What about trade with advanced countries? To what extent might Norway suffer from solidaristic wage policies or high welfare state taxes that raise costs compared with those in other advanced countries? Labour compensation of production workers in manufacturing is higher in Norway at market exchange rates than in many other advanced countries, including the USA, Sweden, and the EU (Table 2.5). But hourly compensation in manufacturing is mediated by productivity in determining the unit labour costs that affect international competitiveness. And, with the appropriate product mix and quality of goods, Germany and Japan have remained world exporters despite exchange rate appreciations that have given them extremely high hourly compensation costs. The total labour cost of production depends, finally, on the earnings of non-production workers as well as on the earnings of production workers. To the extent that solidaristic wage-setting reduces inequality by cutting the pay of non-production/white-collar workers, those policies may have no net effect on *total* labour costs. Edin and Topel (1996) have shown that "taxing" skilled workers to pay for the less skilled can be consistent with full employment for some time, though it risks reducing the supply of skilled labour in the long run.

9 Several East and Central European countries, however, produce goods more similar to the Norwegian export structure (e.g. metallurgies, chemicals, timber, paper, and energy) and are likely to pose new challenges when they catch up in the future.

Table 2.5 Hourly compensation costs for production workers in manufacturing, Norway vs USA, Sweden, Germany, Japan, EU countries and exchange rates

	Indices of hourly compensation (NW=100)					Change in index of hourly compensation 1975–1994	Change in US$ per currency 1975–1994
	1975	1980	1985	1990	1994		
Norway	100	100	100	100	100	0	–21%
USA	94	85	125	69	82	–13%	0%
Germany	94	107	93	102	131	39%	59%
Sweden	105	109	93	97	90	–14%	–46%
Europe	77	88	78	82	94	22%	–10%
Japan	44	48	61	60	102	131%	186%

Sources: US Department of Labor, *Monthly Labor Review* (October 1985: 6, 8), with exchange rates for Norway from OECD (1996a: table 37) and IMF, *Financial Statistics* (1990).

Panel A of Table 2.6 summarizes data on changes in compensation, unit labour costs, and labour productivity for all employees in the business sector in Norway, the USA, and the EU. From 1983 to 1993 Norway had exceptionally rapid increases in unit labour costs in the business sector, owing to large percentage increases in money wages in the early/mid-1980s' industry-level wage negotiations. Toward the end of the 1980s, unit labour costs increased less rapidly in Norway than in the USA or EU, as wage growth moderated and productivity growth picked up. Panel B of Table 2.6 summarizes OECD data for Norway, the

Table 2.6 Changes in compensation, unit labour costs, and productivity, Norway, the USA, and the European Union, 1983–1995

	1983–1993	1994	1995
A BUSINESS SECTOR			
Norway			
Compensation	6.0	2.9	2.5
Unit labour costs	4.4	–0.8	1.6
Implied productivity	1.6	3.7	0.9
USA			
Compensation	4.2	2.5	2.8
Unit labour costs	3.2	2.0	2.8
Implied productivity	1.0	0.5	0.0
European Union			
Compensation	6.3	3.3	3.3
Unit labour costs	4.0	–0.1	1.2
Implied productivity	2.3	3.4	2.1
B NATIONAL ECONOMY			
Norway			
GDP	2.7	5.7	3.7
Employment	0.3	1.5	2.0
Implied productivity	2.4	4.2	1.7
USA			
GDP	2.9	3.5	2.0
Employment	1.8	2.3	1.6
Implied productivity	1.1	1.2	0.4
European Union			
GDP	2.3	2.8	2.5
Employment	0.4	–0.3	0.6
Implied productivity	1.9	3.1	1.9

Source: OECD (1996b: tables 1.1, 1.2, 1.4).

USA, and the EU on changes in GDP, employment, and productivity in the entire economy. Economy wide, productivity grew more rapidly in Norway than in the USA or EU and employment growth was reasonably healthy in Norway. The two panels show that Norway's economic performance has fluctuated over time relative to the comparison groups, but has not deteriorated owing to the Dutch disease, solidaristic pay-setting, or some other economic malady.

There are ways to maintain international competitiveness even when wage determination raises unit labour costs. One way is through currency devaluation, which acts as a general sales tax to pay for the higher wages of the low skilled. Devaluations have worked fairly well in the medium run in the Nordic countries. But the traditional Nordic model of wage-setting is supposed to prevent labour cost problems and devaluations. Ideally, collective bargainers in the traded sector set wages on the basis of productivity changes in the sector and price changes in foreign competitors. Unit labour costs thus increase at rates that enable exporters to compete with foreign producers at a fixed exchange rate. Workers in other sectors of the economy are supposed to accept similar pay increases.[10]

The declining proportion of workers in manufacturing and increased unionization of workers outside traded goods poses a threat to this mode of wage-setting. If labour market conditions differ between traded goods industries and the protected sector, why should workers in the latter – professionals, white-collar employees, unskilled workers in the service or government sector – allow changes in their pay to depend on what an increasingly small number of metalworkers in the export sector decide? Be it through wage drift or separate union bargaining, groups of workers facing different labour market conditions may seek separate wage settlements. This institutional problem is potentially a great danger to a centralized wage-setting model. The more heterogeneous the workforce, the more trade unions and trade union groupings, the harder is it to maintain the Nordic mode of export-led national pay-setting (Freeman and Gibbons, 1995). Social capital must continually be applied to maintain what amounts to a national wage-setting cartel, just as firms must apply pressures on competitors to maintain industrial cartels.

10 The model is more complicated if collective bargainers seek to reduce the manufacturing–service sector pay differential. Then manufacturing workers have to accept pay increases below those elsewhere in the economy. The differential in pay increases will affect the costs of traded goods (which presumably use non-traded goods and services), which will require either that manufacturing wages increase at less than productivity plus the costs overseas or that the currency devalue.

For a country with oil, the situation is more difficult. Increases in labour costs in manufacturing may have little effect on currency markets dominated by oil sales. The currency may appreciate regardless of what happens in manufacturing. In its 1995 *Economic Survey of Norway*, the OECD (1995a: 62–63) argued that petroleum production crowded out export-oriented and import-competing activities through such a scenario. This sort of crowding out appears, however, limited to the early 1970s when the oil price shock first occurred. From 1975/76 through 1994, increases in relative unit labour costs and the exchange rate did not affect non-oil trade in a significant way. Melchior, who studied trade for Norway from 1976 to 1991, reports that "Norway's trade deficit in non-oil goods decreased in proportion to total trade" (1994 : 8), though trade in goods and services dropped relative to GDP. Exports minus imports of non-oil goods were about 10 percent before 1973 and about 10 percent in 1993 – hardly what one would expect if Norway was suffering from a serious "Dutch disease" problem (Melchior, 1994a: 45, chart 2).

Turning from wage policies to welfare state expenditures, some analysts worry that the payroll taxes that fund certain welfare state benefits create a cost problem for firms that compete in international markets with firms in countries with less welfare state spending and lower payroll taxes. I reject this argument on two grounds. First, analyses of the incidence of payroll taxes suggest that they are largely borne by workers, not by the firm (Ehrenberg, 1994). As long as workers value the unemployment insurance or benefits that payroll taxes fund, these taxes do not add to the cost of labour. Second, in the case of Norway, welfare state benefits are funded largely through income and value added taxes, not through payroll taxes, so that the proportion of compensation due to the supplementary cost of hiring an employee does not differ much from that in the USA.[11] My bottom line is that the Welfare Autarky hypothesis is basically correct. The world economy does not dictate any given wage structure/social spending policy. The problem of adjusting to a more open world economy lies with internal conditions relating to wage-setting institutions, not with trade per se.

---

11 According to the US Department of Labor, in 1994 social insurance expenditures were only 16.9 percent of hourly compensation of production workers in Norway; pay for time worked in Norway was 71.5 percent of hourly compensation. This compares with social insurance expenditures that were 23.1 percent of hourly compensation costs in the USA and 70.5 percent of costs that were for time worked. Countries with large social insurance expenditures were France with 29.2 percent and Italy with 30.6 percent. Countries with low levels of compensation in the form of pay for time worked were Italy, 50.3 percent, Belgium, 52.3 percent, and France, 54.2 percent (US Department of Labor, *Monthly Labor Review*, 1995: 9, table 3).

Solidaristic welfare state efficiency

The solidaristic efficiency hypothesis holds that a large welfare state and solidaristic wage-setting policies increase macroeconomic and microeconomic efficiency more than they create inefficiencies due to deadweight losses from taxes or wage structures that are overly compressed.

Consider first the alleged macroeconomic benefits of coordinated wage-setting. Generalizing from the 1970s' experience of countries with centralized wage-setting, some observers, such as Bruno and Sachs (1985), argued that centralized institutions had superior employment–wage inflation outcomes. Analysts of corporatism attribute this to bargainers' internalizing the externalities of the macro costs that might result from any given settlement. This claim has not fared well in the 1980s and 1990s. Swedish centralized wage-setting did not constrain pay settlements noticeably, so that periodic devaluations were necessary for Swedish goods to remain competitive in world markets. Among centralized bargaining states, Austria and Norway kept employment high, but in the 1980s–1990s other European economies, that save for the UK or Eire rely on some form of "corporatist" wage-setting, had poor employment performances (though good real wage growth) compared with the decentralized USA.

The consensual view at this writing is that centralized and decentralized bargaining have comparable macroeconomic effects and that industry-level bargaining has the least desirable macroeconomic consequences (Calmfors and Driffil, 1988). Industry bargainers do not internalize the inflationary costs of agreements, are less bound by competitive forces than plant-level wage-setters, and are thus prone to make monopolistic wage settlements. Although I contributed to this categorization of 1980s' experience (Freeman, 1988), I doubt that it will prove correct over the long run. The effectiveness of any bargaining regime in dealing with macroeconomic problems depends on whether union, business, and government leaders learn from past experiences and adapt to new circumstances. It is possible that some bargaining regimes facilitate learning and adaptability in all circumstances, but it is equally plausible that some facilitate learning and adaptation under some conditions whereas others do better under other conditions (centralized bargainers may respond better to cyclical demand side shocks; whereas industry bargainers may respond better to supply shocks). We lack the well-grounded knowledge needed to rate the learning/adaptability of alternative bargaining regimes in particular countries. Absent such, I am as suspicious of generalizations about collective bargaining structures that ignore organizational specifics, national leadership, and the fact that unions, employer federations, and governments learn from past experiences, as macroeconomists are of analyses of fiscal and monetary policies that fail to allow for citizens to adjust to the policy initiatives, per the "Lucas critique".

An active labour market programme (ALMP) is the single policy of the large welfare states that the OECD has endorsed. Comparisons of the rates of joblessness in countries with differing expenditures on active labour market programmes in the 1980s showed low unemployment in countries with larger ALMPs, such as Norway and Sweden. This led some analysts to conclude that those programmes succeeded in reducing joblessness (OECD, 1993; Layard, Nickell, and Jackman, 1991). The evidence from the 1990s, however, rejects this claim. Sweden's extensive labour market programmes did little to keep employment high when the economy collapsed in 1991. Between 1990 and 1994, the proportion of the workforce on ALMPs increased from 1.1 to 4.7 percent, while open unemployment remained high. Some macro-analysts argue that the programmes have deleterious macroeconomic effects by removing workers from active job search (Calmfors, 1992). Others claim that excessive belief in the effectiveness of active labour market policies misled Swedish policy-makers into policy errors (Robinson, 1995). Microeconomic analyses of active labour market policies for Sweden find that these programmes have negligible effects on how employees fare in the job market (Forslund and Krueger, 1996).

Table A.13 (in the Appendix) shows that Norway has not invested as much in ALMP programmes relative to GDP as has Sweden. Has the lower spending produced a more effective set of programmes? Extant evaluations suggest that at best Norway's ALMPs have modest positive effects. Evaluating job training, Raaum, Torp, and Goldstein (1995) found no difference in the employment of persons who completed a training programme and those who applied to the programme but had been rejected, but reported greater employment among those who obtained a written occupational qualification as part of the training programme. Summarizing studies of ALMP programmes, Try (1996) concludes that they may have an overall positive effect on individual work skills, but that the effect is hard to detect. The one area in which Norwegian active labour programmes appear to do better than those in Sweden is in their unintended effects on wage settlements. In Norway, the programmes seem to reduce inflationary wage changes (Raaum and Wulfsberg, 1996), not to increase them, as some believe to be the case for Sweden. In general, the economic effects of ALMPs differ noticeably depending on the details of design of the programme, the market for the particular group being aided, and the state of the economy. Training programmes presumably work better in a tight labour market in easing labour shortages than in creating employment in a period of labour surplus.

Reading the evidence on ALMPs generously, I conclude that they can be a modest tool in the economic policy arsenal, but are not a big gun in the fight against unemployment. You don't ALMP your way out of unemployment except by changing the statistics.

Welfare state spending as investments

Some welfare state expenditures, particularly those devoted to education and children's well-being, are investments rather than government consumption. They can have potential beneficial effects on long-run economic growth and efficiency. To the extent that expenditures on child care and schooling raise the competency of young persons in ensuing years, redistributions through child allowances, parental leave, and generous state-funded schooling should be viewed differently than, say, greater pension support of the elderly. Cross-country regressions invariably find that GDP is higher the greater the education of the workforce, and many studies find that government spending on education raises productivity growth (Barro, 1991; see Benabou, 1996, for a summary).

Sinn (1995) has argued that welfare state policies have a more subtle effect on national investment. By providing a high safety net that lowers the cost of business failure, the welfare state could induce individuals to undertake risky investments that in the aggregate will raise growth. But high progressive taxes operate in the opposite direction, and the other regulations associated with welfare state policies may discourage small business formation. Empirically, venture capital and risk-taking are greater in the USA than in most European countries, so I doubt that this is more than a theoretical fine point.

Many analysts of solidaristic pay policy worry that institutionally induced reductions in pay will compress skill differentials excessively and create a long-term problem of human capital formation. If employees lack the motivation to undertake training or to shift to jobs the economy needs, or if the supply of young people to higher education falls short of what it otherwise would be, economic growth might slacken and factor endowments would move closer to those in LDCs. For Sweden, Edin and Holmlund (1995) show that the compression of university differentials reduced the growth of supply of university graduates, while Edin and Topel (1996)suggest a similar supply effect in on-the-job skill acquisition. In the USA, enrolments in specific university fields as well as in the aggregate fluctuate with market conditions (Freeman, 1976). Recognizing that compressed differentials reduce the incentive for human capital formation, Norway modestly subsidizes higher education with loans and scholarships. And in reality Norway is a leader, not a laggard, in enrolment of college age students. In 1991, 29 percent of 22-year-old Norwegians were enrolled in full-time education, compared with 18 percent of Swedes and Americans – a proportion just behind Germany (including apprenticeships) and Finland (OECD, 1994: table 1.18). The share of young Norwegians enrolled in higher education increased through the early 1990s.

Solidaristic pay-setting and efficiency

Many proponents of solidaristic pay-setting, such as Moene and Wallerstein (1995a, b), stress a different aspect of solidaristic pay policy: that it reduces pay differentials among otherwise similar workers. In theory, the competitive labour market should squeeze out differentials based on anything but skill or work conditions that enter employee utility functions. But, in fact, pay varies widely among observably similar workers across firms and sectors in economies that rely extensively on market wage determination, such as the USA or UK. Many, though not all, labour economists read this as showing that the labour market fails to accomplish this goal.[12] Thus there is a market failure that solidaristic wage policies can cure. Imposing a single rate of pay for comparable work raises productivity by driving inefficient firms out of the market (these firms are in business only because they pay low wages) and by shifting labour and capital to more efficient firms.

Hibbs and Locking (1995) have examined the hypothesis that solidaristic pay is efficient in Sweden, using a set of time-series production function models. They estimate the relation between output, standard factor inputs, and the dispersion of pay between industries/plants and the dispersion in pay within industries/plants in Sweden from 1963 to 1993. They find that lower dispersion of pay *between* industries/plants was productivity enhancing, whereas lower dispersion of pay *within* industries/plants due to skill compression was productivity reducing. Findings from a single study based on time-series production functions are hardly definitive. Still, these results suggest that there is substance to both the solidaristic pay–efficiency hypothesis and to fears that compressed skill differentials harm productivity.

12 The alternative interpretation of these differentials is that they reflect either unmeasured skills of workers or unmeasured differences in work conditions that induce compensating differentials.

Golden mean

The welfare state/solidaristic efficiency hypothesis directs attention to the possible efficiency gains from those policies. But, even granting some efficiency gains, nearly everyone, including proponents of a large welfare state, recognizes that solidaristic/welfare state policies can go too far: at some expenditure level, the costs of these policies exceed their benefits. On the other side, a society can have too small a welfare state and too great inequalities. The problem is to find the balance between the costs that welfare state policies incur, on the one side, and the costs of the inequality that they reduce on the other side.

It is easy to state the principle for determining the right balance. Programme by programme, one should compare programme benefits, including consumer/worker surplus produced and efficiency gains, with programme costs, including indirect efficiency costs in the form of deadweight losses due to behavioural responses to the programme and the taxes raised to fund it. Under standard assumptions, costs rise more rapidly than benefits: deadweight losses depend on the square of costs so that, as a welfare state programme grows, its true economic costs increase rapidly. Assuming declining marginal benefits to the programme or, more conservatively, less than parabolic increases in benefits, there is an optimal welfare state expenditure for a given programme, and, with due allowance for externalities of one programme on another, for the total size of the welfare state. The optimal size of the welfare state will depend on the composition of welfare state programmes – it will be larger if a country chooses more productivity-enhancing programmes – and on how individual programmes fit together into a consistent system.

Beyond these broad generalizations, which are simply verbal statements of optimizing conditions from the calculus, there is not much one can say absent detailed analysis of particular programmes and of the linkage among programmes. The efficiency costs of some welfare state/solidaristic policies are fairly easy to establish. Consider for example the 1980s' sick leave policy of Sweden (since reformed), under which the state paid for sick leave at a 90 percent rate of replacement of earnings from the first day someone was sick. This law encouraged employees to take more days off than their actual health justified and gave employers no incentive to monitor or discourage such behaviour. As a result, Swedish workers had more days off sick than workers in many other advanced countries. In the 1990s Swedish policy-makers reduced the replacement rate, required firms to pay sickness benefits for the first two-week sick period, added a waiting day before sick pay could be received, and raised employees' contributions. These policies reduced sickdays considerably. Similarly, deadweight losses of high taxation are identifiable, though difficult to pin down in standard labour supply data for men. The NBER–SNS study of the Swedish welfare state (Freeman, Swedenborg, and Topel, 1996) documented the costs of some welfare state policies but lacked evidence on others. Going beyond Scandinavia, there is evidence from many countries that the longer the duration of unemployment benefits, the greater is the amount of time people wait before finding a job. But there is little evidence on the costs of many other specific European welfare state policies (Blank, 1994).

For a rational assessment of the golden mean, evidence is also needed on the benefits of programmes. One great virtue of the private sector is that society can rely on consumer evaluations to determine the commodities that should be produced. Barring externalities, if a commodity exists, it must have a benefit–cost ratio greater than one. In the public sector, by contrast, the mere fact that a programme exists does not mean that it has substantial benefits to consumers. If a subsidized housing project costs X dollars, and the subsidy is such that people in the project pay 0.3X dollars, they will support the programme even if they value it at 0.5X dollars. By getting the rest of society to pay, they have chosen a public programme whose benefits fall short of its costs.[13] Blank and Freeman (1994) point out the remarkable lacunae of studies documenting the benefits of most welfare state programmes. For instance, we have no detailed analysis of the valuation that workers place on the insurance benefits of unemployment insurance. All too often, advocates of programmes simply assert their virtues.

As for the costs of inequality that welfare state spending might be expected to reduce, the social problems afflicting the USA in the mid-1990s provide some clue to how inequality can be socially expensive. In 1995, the USA had roughly half a million people homeless and a rate of child poverty above the rates in other advanced countries, and was incarcerating in prison over 2.5 percent of its potential male employees. Despite the highest GDP per capita in the OECD (exclusive of Luxembourg), the real (purchasing power parity adjusted) earnings of American workers in the lower third or so of the earnings distribution fell short of those of West European workers in the lower third of their country's earnings distribution (Freeman, 1994).

The work needed to assess welfare state programmes one by one is suf-

---

13 Becker (1974) argues that the smaller the benefit–cost ratio of any government programme – the less efficiently it transfers money from one group to another – the less likely it is to prevail in the political market. But this does not rule out programmes where costs exceed benefits.

ficiently daunting that many analysts take a more aggregative approach to studying the economic effects of the welfare state. They regress growth rates of GDP per capita across countries on levels of welfare state spending, or some other measure of government activity. Atkinson's review of nine studies linking welfare state spending with growth shows an even split in findings: four studies report that welfare state spending reduces growth, four studies report that welfare state spending raises growth, while one study shows no effect (Atkinson, 1995). Benabou's review of studies linking government spending in general with growth shows that most studies find that government consumption reduces growth but that redistributive expenditures and tax rates are unrelated to growth (Benabou, 1996). Slemrod's review of studies linking taxation with growth also concludes that aggregative analyses have yielded inconclusive results. He argues that one reason is that the studies fail to differentiate adequately between the effect of government on the economy and the reverse effect of the economy on government. Differences in years and countries covered and in the specification of the welfare state variable and of the outcome equation seem to matter greatly in this work (Slemrod, 1995). Given the difficulty in finding any relation between growth and welfare state spending, no researcher has dared estimate what the golden mean of such spending might be.

Muddying the waters even more, the welfare state programmes and spending appropriate for one period of time may be inappropriate for another. Solidaristic pay policies may be efficient under some technologies of production but not under others. This implies that the location of the "golden mean" in the welfare state/solidaristic policy-economic outcomes landscape will change over time. Decision-makers in business, labour, and government must thus continually adjust policies to fit changing circumstances. In the Norwegian case, the shock of the oil price drop in 1986 and accompanying unemployment may have been salutatory in focusing attention on the dangers of pushing welfare state spending to the point of committing oil revenues to social goals; and may have alerted decision-makers to the need to reassess policies in changing circumstances.

In sum, it is difficult to determine where the "golden mean" lies at any point in time, and thus to assess the golden mean hypothesis for Norway. Still, with a share of GDP going to government and spent on social security lower than in Sweden, whose welfare state has proven unsustainable,[14] and higher than in the USA, which has its own prob-

14 According to NOSOSCO (1995), the proportion of GDP spent on social security in Norway in 1991 was 31 percent compared with 40 percent in Sweden.

lems, Norway may just have got it right. Or maybe Norway has simply been lucky with its oil bonanza.

Manna[15]

In the early/mid-1990s, sizeable fiscal deficits forced Sweden to cut back some welfare state programmes, such as unemployment insurance benefits and child allowances. If the Invisible Hand dropped a permanent 5 percent extra GDP in the form of government resources on Sweden, would this manna from heaven have prevented its financial problems and allowed the government to avoid painful and hard decisions? The fiscal deficit in Sweden in 1995 was about 8 percent of GDP, compared with an EU average of 5.3 percent. The 5 percent Manna bonus would have moved Sweden from the top of the country table in fiscal problems into the normal problem range. Although a 3 percent deficit exceeds the growth of GDP in Sweden, placing the country under some financial stress, this deficit would perhaps not be enough to induce the country to cut welfare state programmes.

Now consider the opposite scenario: what might happen to Norway if its oil revenues disappeared in the 1990s. In 1995, the immediate effect would be to move the country from fiscal surplus to a rate of deficit/GDP of around 2 percent – below the OECD average – and readily manageable with a growth rate of GDP above 2 percent. But, given generous unemployment benefits and safety net guarantees to citizens, Norway would have been in a "danger zone", much as Sweden was in the late 1980s. The danger for a large welfare state is that an unexpected adverse economic shock can create a major drain on the treasury because the state is committed to maintaining the living standards of citizens in adverse states of the world. One important lesson of the 1980s–early 1990s has been that *large welfare states cannot sustain high unemployment for very long.* With fewer people paying taxes and unemployment benefits close to wages, high rates of joblessness almost guarantee a budget crisis. Some simple numerics make this point. Assume that the state pays the unemployed the going wage and that 5 percent are jobless at the outset. The tax to fund unemployment is 5.3 percent. Now let the unemployment rate double. The necessary tax rises to 11

15 The permanent increase in GDP due to the oil revenues depends on various factors, such as the size of the reserves and the price of oil. According to OECD (1995a: 61, table 14), government receipts as a share of mainland GDP were 8.5 percent in 1985/86, 3.2 percent in 1987–1989, and 7.2 percent in 1990–1992. The Norwegian Longterm Programme 1994–1997 estimated that the permanent income from petroleum reserves was equivalent to 5–7 percent of GDP (OECD, 1995a: 66).

percent. Unless unemployment insurance taxes are doubled, there will be a crisis with unemployment funds. By contrast, a state with less commitment to its unemployed workers, either through lower unemployment benefits or with shorter durations of benefits, would face no such crisis. This mechanical scenario implies that, without its oil revenues, Norway would be risking a Swedish-style welfare state crisis in an economic downturn if it ran an otherwise defensible fiscal deficit. But would Norwegian policy-makers and public take such a risk with their welfare state?

My discussions in both countries suggest that policy-makers have a different attitude toward the risks of welfare state implosion. Even after the Swedish fiscal crisis, Sweden's body politic was reluctant to cut back welfare state benefits. In Norway, by contrast, there is considerable concern about the risks entailed by reliance on oil revenues, and a desire to establish "clear blue water" between the welfare state and potential financial disaster if the economy or the oil sector hit the skids. Norway's plan to establish an oil fund and invest some of the monies overseas rather than to fund higher non-oil budget deficits is a prudent way of saving money for the proverbial rainy day. Perhaps these plans will prove infeasible, with the public demanding more immediate benefits from the oil revenues. But perhaps the experience of Sweden will convince citizens that a cautious policy is in the interest of the welfare state.

In sum, without gainsaying the manna from heaven hypothesis, I find it incomplete. The oil revenues have helped Norway fund a large welfare state, but they could have been spent profligately, and still could be so spent. The key to understanding why these monies have helped the country succeed lies in the political economy decision on how to spend/husband those resources. As the oil revenues gradually decline over time, Norway will have to develop alternative income-earning sources from investments in human capital or physical capital, including investments overseas, that the oil revenues can help fund.

4. Conclusion: maintaining viability

In an epoch when economic forces are decentralizing wage-setting and raising inequality in market-driven job markets, Norway has maintained a centralized collective bargaining system and high welfare benefits and solidaristic wage policies without suffering the unemployment or fiscal deficits that forced Sweden to tighten its welfare state. Going against the wind, Norway rose in league tables of GDP per capita. Whether this is because Norway chose a less expansive welfare state than Sweden, per the golden mean argument, or because of its oil revenues, per the manna from heaven argument, or for reasons having to do with the efficiencies of welfare state/solidaristic policies, Norwegian exceptionalism seems healthy and sound. The modern global economy has reduced the policy tools available for the state to manage the economy (notably in the form of capital or currency controls), but it has not emasculated collective bargainers or the ability of states to tax and spend. I see no *necessary* reason for a country that chooses to maintain egalitarian wage-setting and welfare spending to run aground in the modern economic world. In the case of Norway, its solidaristic/welfare state system has, in fact, some advantages that may give it a competitive edge in the 21st century. If the job structure continues to shift toward service sectors that have historically been female intensive, Norway's use of female workers could ease the transition from a male-dominated economy to one where women play a more significant role in the market. Norway's high social wage – consumption covered by the state – and small wage differentials give it leeway to reduce relatively the marginal costs of unskilled labour in private services, e.g. by differentiated reduction of employer levies on labour, or otherwise subsidize their work if this is needed to maintain high employment.

But I also see risks to solidaristic/welfare state policies. An institutionally driven economy, such as Norway's, places great responsibility on business, labour, and government leadership to learn and adjust to economic changes. Resources have to be spent to control "prisoner's dilemma" temptations for particular groups to move away from the (fuzzy and uncertain) golden mean level of egalitarianism into rent-seeking that is harmful to the economy. Internal conflicts could develop among workers owing to their increasing heterogeneity and interests, which the labour relations system may be unable to contain. Reductions of skill differentials beyond some (fuzzy and uncertain) point risk cutting the rate of growth of the supply of the skilled. A different sort of danger is that the public sector may fail to make the productivity advances that an efficient private sector would make in a similar economic and technological environment. With a large public sector, the drag on the economy of such a failure would be substantial.

In the fiscal sphere, pressures for spending the oil revenues rather than "saving them for a rainy day" for various reasons could push government spending beyond the "golden mean" point. With a rate of unemployment in Norway in the mid-1990s below that in most other advanced countries and an employment–population ratio at a peak level, spending the oil revenues to try to reduce joblessness to 1970s' levels would seem to run against the golden mean principle. A large welfare state needs "clear blue water" between its national finances and what it will spend in an economic crisis because of its commitment to maintain economic well-being even in difficult times. This means running surpluses in good years, to permit large deficits in bad years. Put differently, more than countries less committed to providing a safety net for citizens, a welfare state must maintain a safety net for itself as well. Norway's oil revenues give it the resources to do that, but also give it the resources to go beyond the "golden mean". So, skål. But not too many skåls. And none before driving home.

Acknowledgements

I have benefited from the comments of Per Kleppe, Stein Regaard, Karl-Ove Moene, and the FAFO editors.

References

Alessina, A. and R. Perotti (1994) *The Welfare State and Competitiveness*. NBER Working Paper 4810, July 1994.

Allen, S. and R. Freeman (1996) Quantitative flexibility in the U.S. labour market (with Steven G. Allen). In Edward J. Amadeo and Susan Horton (eds) *Labour Productivity and Flexibility*). London: Macmillan. Also presented at the 65th Annual Conference of the Southern Economic Association, 18–20 November, 1995.

Atkinson, T. (1995) *The Welfare State and Economic Performance*. STICERD Welfare State Working Paper Programme, WSP 109, May 1995.

Barro, R. (1991) Economic growth in a cross-section of countries. *Quarterly Journal of Economics* 106(2): 407–443.

Becker, G. (1974) A theory of social interactions. *Journal of Political Economy* 82 (November/December): 1095–1117.

Bell, L. and R. Freeman (1995) Why do Americans and Germans work different hours? In F. Buttler, W. Franz, R. Schettkat, and D. Soskice, *Institutional Frameworks and Labor Market Performance*. London: Routledge.

Bell, L. and R. Freeman (1996) Working hard. Paper delivered in Toronto, June 1996.

Benabou, R. 1996. Inequality and growth. Forthcoming in *NBER Macroeconomics Annual* 1996.

Bjørklund, A. and R. Freeman (1996) Generating equality and eliminating poverty: The Swedish way. In R. Freeman, B. Swedenborg, and R. Topel, *Reforming the Welfare State: The Swedish Model in Transition*. Chicago: University of Chicago Press and NBER.

Blank, R., ed. (1994) *Social Protection versus Economic Flexibility: Is there a tradeoff?* Chicago: University of Chicago Press and NBER.

Blank, R. and R. Freeman (1994) Evaluating the connection between social protection and economic flexibility. In R. Blank (ed.), *Social Protection versus Economic Flexibility: Is there a tradeoff?* Chicago: University of Chicago Press and NBER.

Bradshaw, J., S. Kennedy, M. Kilkey, S. Hutton, A. Corden, T. Eardley, H. Holmes, and J. Neale (1996) *The Employment of Lone Parents: A comparison of policy in 20 countries*. London: Family Policy Studies Centre.

Bruno, M and J. Sachs (1985) *The Economics of Worldwide Stagflation*. Cambridge, MA: Harvard University Press.

Calmfors, L. (1992) *Lessons from the Macroeconomic Experience of Sweden*. IIES Seminar Paper No. 522.

Calmfors, L. and J. Driffil (1988) Bargaining structure, corporatism, and macroeconomic performance. *Economic Policy* 6: 13–61.

Edin, P.-A. and B. Holmlund (1995) The Swedish wage structure: The rise and fall of solidarity wage policy? In R. Freeman and L. F. Katz (eds), *Differences and Changes in Wage Structures*. Chicago: University of Chicago Press and NBER.

Edin, P.-A. and R. Topel (1996) Wage policy and restructuring: The Swedish labor market since 1990. In R. Freeman, B.Swedenborg, and R. Topel (eds) *Reforming the Welfare State: The Swedish Model in Transition*. Chicago: University of Chicago Press and NBER, forthcoming.

Ehrenberg, R. (1994) *Labor Markets and Integrating National Economies*. Washington DC: The Brookings Institution.

Erhvervsministeriet, (1995 *Efterspørgsels- og beskæftigelsespotentialet i forbrugs-service*. Copenhagen

Forslund, A. and A. Krueger (1996) An evaluation of the Swedish active labor market policy: new and received wisdom. In R. Freeman, B. Swedenborg, and R. Topel (eds) *Reforming the Welfare State: The Swedish Model in Transition*. Chicago: University of Chicago Press and NBER, forthcoming.

Freeman, R. (1976) *The Overeducated American*. New York: Academic Press.

Freeman, R. (1988). Labour market institutions and economic performance. *Economic Policy* 3: 64–80.

Freeman, R., ed. (1994) *Working under Different Rules*. New York: Russell Sage Foundation.

Freeman, R. (1995b) The large welfare state as a system. *AER Proceedings*, May.

Freeman, R. and R. Gibbons (1995) Getting together and breaking apart: The decline of centralised collective bargaining. In R. Freeman, and L. Katz (eds), *Differences and Changes in Wage Structures*.Chicago: University of Chicago Press and NBER.

Freeman, R., B. Swedenborg, and R. Topel (1996). *Reforming the Welfare State: The Swedish Model in Transition*. Chicago: University of Chicago Press and NBER, forthcoming.

Gelb, A. (1988) *Oil Windfalls: Blessing or Curse?* New York: Oxford University Press for the World Bank.

Hibbs, D. and H. Locking (1995) Solidarity wage policies and industrial policy in Sweden. *Nordic Political Economy* 22: 95–108.

Holden, S. (1989) Wage drift and bargaining: Evidence from Norway. *Economica* 56: 419–432.

Kmitch, J., P. Laboy, and S. Van Damme (1995) International comparisons of manufacturing compensation costs. *Monthly Labor Review* October: 3–9.

Kuhnle, S. (1996) European integration and the national welfare state. Mimeo, 21–22 March.

Layard, R., S. Nickell, and R. Jackman (1991) *Unemployment*. Oxford: Oxford University Press

Lindbeck, A. (1993) *The Welfare State: The Selected Essays of Assar Lindbeck*, vols I and II. England: Edward Elgar.

Lindbeck, A. (1995) Welfare state lessons. Austin Robinson Lecture, IEA Congress, Tunis, December.

Melchior, A. (1994a) Export specialisation in small countries: A case for the standard goods hypothesis? Oslo: NUPI, No 184.

Melchior, A. (1994b) Intra-industry trade: A matter of scale or skills? Oslo: NUPI, No 183.

Moene, K. O. and M. Wallerstein 1992. The decline of social democracy. October 1992 (mimeo). Department of Economics, University of Oslo, Working Paper, no. 21.

Moene, K. O. and M. Wallerstein (1995a) Job creation and job destruction with local and centralised wage-setting. May 1995 (mimeo). Presented at Conference in honor of Assar Lindbeck, "Unemployment and wage dispersion: is there a trade-off?" Stockholm. June 16–18, 1995.

Moene, K. O. and M. Wallerstein (1995b) How social democracy worked: Labor-market institutions. No 10, February 1995 (mimeo). Department of Economics, University of Oslo, Working Paper, no. 10.

Norway Official Statistics (1991) *National Accounts.*

Norway Official Statistics (1993) *Labour Market Statistics*

Norway (1993) *Labour Force Statistics.*

NOSOSCO (1995) *Social Security in the Nordic Countries.* Copenhagen: Nordic Social Statistical Committee, 2.

OECD (1992) *Historical Statistics 1960–1990.* Paris.

OECD (1993) *Employment Outlook.* Paris.

OECD (1994) *Employment Outlook.* Paris.

OECD (1995a) *Economic Surveys, Norway.* Paris.

OECD (1995b). *Employment Outlook.* Paris.

OECD (1995c) *Economic Outlook.* Paris, June.

OECD (1995d) *SOPEMI Trends in International Migration.*

OECD (1995e) *Education at a Glance.* Paris.

OECD (1996a) *Economic Outlook.* Paris, June.

OECD (1996b) *Employment Outlook.* Paris.

Perotti, R. (1996) Growth, income distribution, and democracy: What the data say. *Journal of Economic Growth.*

Raaum, O. and H. Torp (1996) Impact of training on earnings. Testing alternative models. EALE Conference, Crete, 19–22 September.

Raaum, O. and F. Wulfsberg (1996) *Unemployment, Labour Market Programmes, and Wages in Norway.* Foundation for Research in Economics and Business Administration, 26 June.

Raaum, O., H. Torp, and H. Goldstein (1995) *Employment Effects of Labour Market Training in Norway.* Department of Economics, University of Oslo.

Robinson, P. (1995) *The Decline of the Swedish Model and the Limits to Active Labour Market Policy.* Centre for Economic Performance, Discussion Paper 259, August.

Rosen, S. (1996) Public employment and the welfare state. In R. Freeman, B.Swedenborg, and R. Topel, *Reforming the Welfare State: The Swedish model in transition.* Chicago: University of Chicago Press and NBER, forthcoming.

Sachs, J. and A. Warner (1995) *Natural Resource Abundance and Economic Growth.* NBER Working Paper 5398, December.

Sinn, H.-W. (1995) *A Theory of the Welfare State.* Centre for Economic Policy Research Discussion Paper 1278, November.

Slemrod, J. (1995) What do cross-country studies teach about government involvement, prosperity, and economic growth? *Brookings Papers on Economic Activity* 2: 373–431.

Statistics Norway (1995) Revised Norwegian national accounts. *Economic Survey* 3/95, 18–28.

Try, S. (1996) *Effekter av den aktive arbeidsmarkedspolitikken.* Kommunal og Arbeidsdepartementet, Arbeidsavdelingen, Arbeidsnotatserie No 1: 106.

Try, S. (1994) Effects and Evaluation of Large Scale Labour Market Programmes. FAFO Seminar, 17 October.

US Bureau of the Census (various years) *Statistical Abstract 1993.*

US Bureau of Labor Statistics (1995) *International Comparisons of Hourly Compensation Costs for Production Workers, 1994.* Report 893, June.

Visser, J. (1996) *Unionization Trends Revisited.* Amsterdam.

Chapter 3

Norwegian Labour Market Institutions and Regulations

Jon Erik Dølvik, Mona Bråten, Frode Longva, and Arild H. Steen

1. Scope and issues

The institutional and regulatory frameworks of Norwegian labour market policy represent a variant of the broader Nordic model.[1] The aim of this chapter is twofold: first, to present an overview of the main developments and features of the regulatory and institutional context of Norwegian labour market policy; second, to discuss the central role of labour relations and collective bargaining in facilitating social compromise conducive to employment generation and equality. Specific attention will be paid to continuity and change in the configuration of organized actors, interests, and powers that have contributed to institutionalize and preserve the solidaristic Norwegian legacy.

The chapter thus departs from two central assumptions: (1) the centralized system of solidaristic bargaining and interest intermediation has represented a crucial and, in the Norwegian context, often underestimated nucleus between macroeconomic and microsociological prerequisites of labour market policy; (2) this institutionalized social compromise is subject to potential erosion from three angles – from "above" owing

1 The concept of a distinct Nordic societal model is contested (see, for instance, Mjøset, 1992), but for pragmatic reasons we interchangeably use the terms 'model', 'system', and 'pattern' of Nordic labour relations, referring to the broad common traits and features of post-war Scandinavian labour market organization, associated with strong and relatively unitary organizations of labour and capital and a centralized system of solidaristic collective bargaining within a framework of political concertation based on active labour market policies, extensive welfare state provision, and Keynesian macroeconomic policies of full employment, often under the auspices of a hegemonic social democratic party (see, for instance Kjellberg, 1992; Goetschy, 1995: 8). It should, however, be noted that, with regard to labour market developments, important distinctions have evolved between the Nordic countries, for example as to unemployment, the role of the state, law vs. collective bargaining, dispute management, the degree of centralization, and union organisational structures (see, e.g. Kjellberg, 1992; Dølvik, 1993; Scheuer, 1992; and Strøby Jensen et al., 1994).

to diminished scope for ensuring full employment by macroeconomic means, reflecting the restraining effects of internationalized capital markets; from "below" owing to increased pressures from market competition both nationally and internationally; and from "within", owing to changes in the social and occupational structure, altering the balance of power and prompting renewed and more differentiated perceptions of interests, (class) identification, justice, and solidarity. Faced with such pressures, the recent revitalization of the solidaristic Norwegian model may appear to be a paradox. A central purpose thus is to raise questions that could stimulate debate about (a) factors that can account for the persistence of the post-war model of social partnership; (b) factors that may undermine this model; and (c) prospects for accommodating pressures for change to the preservation of the egalitarian legacy within a renewed and more encompassing social compromise. An underlying presumption is that if such a reconstructed compromise is not achieved, the existing model is likely to be subject to fragmentation, possibly making full employment even more difficult to achieve.

This chapter gives an overview of the institutional and economic-political frameworks of labour market policy in Norway, then discusses the development of labour market outcomes, regulatory frameworks, the system of education and vocational training, active labour market policy, the development of the Norwegian system of collective bargaining, and prospects for continuity and change.

2. Background and overview

The main features of the Norwegian system of labour market institutions were shaped in the immediate pre- and post-war era, facilitated by broad class compromises and a spirit of national reconciliation under the auspices of a long-lasting Labour Party hegemony (Dølvik and Stokland, 1992). After a turbulent period of class struggle, economic crisis, and unemployment, culminating with depression and large-scale industrial conflict in 1931, a cooperative system of labour relations became institutionalized throughout the 1930s. The Basic Agreement, signed in 1935, laid down the fundamental rules of conduct between the two sides of industry and paved the way for the peaceful evolution of an encompassing, centralized system of collective bargaining. In the same year, a crisis pact between the Labour Party and the Agrarian Party enabled organized labour to enter into government. This cross-cutting coalition between labour, small farmers, and fishermen, between centre and periphery, has been a persistent feature of the political configuration in which Norwegian labour market policies have been embedded (Rokkan,

1987: 138). Accordingly, extensive regional policies aimed at sustaining a scattered pattern of population have remained a central feature of Norwegian employment policies.

The economic-political basis of the Norwegian labour market system was marked by late and limited industrialization. As a small, open economy with an import ratio around 40 percent, exports have predominantly been founded on natural resources such as fisheries, forestry, and utilization of cheap hydro-power for the production of semi-finished metals and chemicals. In addition, shipping has played an important historical role. Weakness of national capital, reflecting an industrial structure of small enterprises, allowed foreign capital to play an important role in the development of manufacturing, often in close cooperation with the state (Mjøset et al., 1995: 56). Today roughly one-third of Norwegian enterprise shares are owned by foreign capital (Kvinge, 1994). From early on the state became an important economic actor as regulator, as owner of key enterprises, often located in the districts, and as manager of an extensive state bank system. Since the petroleum industry took off in the 1970s the state has become the leading accumulator of capital in Norway, today controlling roughly 23 percent of shares on the Oslo stock exchange. The newly deregulated private banking system was brought to the verge of collapse in 1990, but was rescued by a government bail-out, re-installing the state as a leading actor in the finance system. Together with an extensive public system of industrial and regional transfers and the evolution of public infrastructure and the welfare state, such factors have enabled the state to play a powerful governing role in economic and labour market developments.

During the post-war period the governing Labour Party advocated Keynesian stabilization policies, but in practice fiscal policies were kept tight, whereas credit policies and the state banks were used for countercyclical purposes within a regime of low interest rates and a fixed exchange rate (Mjøset et al. 1995: 60). Production and employment grew steadily, inflation was low, and unemployment was negligible.

Wage determination was closely coordinated with economic policies, giving priority to the competitiveness of exposed sectors. Labour relations were marked by a close interplay between negotiations and political governance via legislation and state intervention. Organization rates have been fairly high, union density has stabilized around 56–57 percent, and the peak organizations of private business (NAF/NHO) and blue-collar workers (LO) have commanded strong central authority over a multi-tier negotiating system. From the late 1970s, local wage drift tended to erode central negotiations, but in the late 1980s a vigorous recentralization of bargaining and strict incomes policies were pursued.

Throughout the 1960s and 1970s major welfare state reform, regulation of labour markets, and development of public services were pursued. Universal public pension schemes (Folketrygden) were established, education and healthcare expanded rapidly, and legislation promoting workplace democracy, protection of the working environment, and the world's most generous system of sick pay were established. Working time and retirement age were gradually reduced, though the latter is still among the highest in Europe (67 years).

These developments contributed to an unprecedented employment growth in the 1970s, facilitating the entry of women into the labour market. The public sector has grown continuously and employs more than 30 percent of the labour force. More than 70 percent of women of working age (15–64) are occupationally active, predominantly in the public sector. The participation rate of women is far beyond the level in most continental European countries, although lower than in Sweden and Denmark (see Tables A5 and A3 in the Appendix). The universal social security system, financed by taxation, is assumed to enhance labour market mobility and restrain indirect labour costs, having left less scope for private and occupational welfare schemes than in most West European countries (Hippe and Pedersen, 1996; Hippe, 1996). Nevertheless, roughly half of employees are covered by supplementary occupational pension schemes (ibid.). Demographic factors, causing long-term ageing of society and relative labour force decline and prompting uncertainties about the future financing of the social security system, have raised new debates about pension funds and occupational and private welfare. These concerns have also become a main argument for the pursuit of the so-called "working-line", aimed at increasing labour force participation especially among receivers of social benefits.

Active labour market policies have traditionally played a modest role compared with Sweden, although public investment has been accelerated and labour market schemes have been initiated during times of recession. Unemployment benefits are part of the public social security system and are managed by the Labour Market Administration (Arbeidsdirektoratet), which is responsible for placement services and labour market schemes for training and temporary employment. Since the recent recession, strong emphasis has been laid on active labour market programmes to raise qualifications and prevent marginalization of the long-term unemployed, a policy that has been continued on a reduced scale in the current recovery in order to enhance re-employment and improve the matching of skills in labour markets.

Since the early 1970s, petroleum activities have gained increasing economic significance. Being the major recipient of capital investment and the leading export sector, oil activities now account for more than 30 percent of total exports. Controlled by the state, which granted the state-owned company, Statoil, a key role in developing petroleum industries, the state-capitalist features of the Norwegian political economy have thus been reinforced (Mjøset et al. 1995: 63). Today Norway is the third-largest oil exporter in the world and the state's net cash flow from petroleum's activities represents a significant part of government incomes, roughly 7 percent in 1994, and some 3.5 percent of GDP in the same year (Statistics Norway, 1996: 385). Oil production is still rising and revenues are expected to increase in coming years, while investment in the Norwegian continental shelf is expected to decline.

While fluctuating oil prices are a potentially destabilizing factor in the Norwegian economy, the oil revenues contribute to a cyclical pattern that is not synchronized with Norway's main European trade partners. This may inhibit pursuit of monetary policies locked to the emerging European regime of fixed exchange rates, and the conjunctural discrepancy between domestic sectors and export industries may aggravate the problem of designing macroeconomic policies that suit both. As analysed by Rødseth (Chapter 5) macroeconomic policy in the first half of the 1980s tended to function pro-cyclically. The renaissance of corporatist incomes policies in Norway can plausibly be interpreted as a response to fluctuating external economic conditions and the specific problem of containing cost pressures in an oil economy where domestic sectors represent an ever-growing proportion of employment.

Recent policy developments

Whereas unemployment throughout the post-war period was almost negligible until the mid-1970s and grew slowly in the early 1980s, an unprecedented acceleration of unemployment occurred from 1988. Within a few years the proportion of the labour force out of an ordinary job had risen to more than 8 percent, including 2–3 percent in active labour market schemes, whereas employment and participation rates fell substantially. In addition, the number of people on disability pension rose sharply during the 1980s, but has thereafter stabilized around 8–9 percent of the working age population (Visher and Midtsundstad, 1993: 90).

These developments reflected substantial policy shifts during the 1980s. First, extensive deregulation of credit markets and housing was pursued by a conservative government in the early 1980s, leading to an extraordinary growth in credit-financed private consumption, services, and employment. Wages and inflation soared and competitiveness declined further, in spite of continuous depreciation of the currency. In 1986, prompted by falling oil prices and external imbalances, the "boom" collapsed and a change of policies eventually evolved. The reasons and character of this policy shift are explored by Rødseth in Chapter 5, but the central ingredients were the introduction of a fixed-exchange-rate regime; austerity policies and anti-inflationary measures; further liberalization of credit policies and capital flows, and the use of interest rates to cool the economy; complemented by expansion of active labour market measures and education. The two sides of industry played a key role in securing wage moderation, underpinned by wage laws making excessive pay increases unlawful.

This economic policy turn was succesful in redressing the external imbalances, helped by favourable international conjunctures and rising oil prices, but the consequence was domestic recession and accelerating unemployment. In recent years expansionary policies have been pursued (1990–1993) and the labour market situation has improved, but unemployment is still unacceptably high by Norwegian standards (around 4 percent registered unemployed and 1.5 percent in labour market programmes, Fall 1996).

In short, these changes transformed the central pillars of the orthodox macroeconomic Norwegian model, notably state control over credit policies, in parallel with the revival of other features of this model, notably corporatist incomes policies. According to some observers and the leftist forces of the labour movement, this change of policy regime signalled a paradigmatic farewell to the Norwegian model (Fagerberg et al., 1990: 88; Notermans, 1995), while others have seen it as a mixture of modernization and a partial return to early post-war deeds (Dølvik, 1994). None the less, the turn-around did converge with international trends of liberalizing monetary policies, whereas it diverged as regards incomes policies and subsequently also fiscal policies. A striking feature, however, is that, despite misgivings from labour traditionalists and a supposed withering of labour constituencies, this relatively profound transformation has seemingly bolstered the position of the minority labour government and its close allies in the LO, while their political opponents remain divided. A key question for the future is whether the leading actors of the social compromise, partly imposed "from above" in a context of economic crisis, can continue to muster popular support and legitimacy for this variant of solidaristic policy in a context of economic recovery and growing expectations.

3. Labour market outcomes and processes

The main distinctions of Norwegian labour markets compared with other OECD countries over the past 20 years can be summarized as follows (see also the comparative labour market statistics in the Appendix).

- Significant growth of labour force participation and employment, especially among women. In the 1970s the total labour force grew on average by 2 percent per year, in the 1980s by more than 1 percent, until it fell by 0.6–1.3 percent in 1989–1991 and then stagnated. Since 1993 the labour force on average has increased by more than 1 percent a year, while employment has expanded even more, exceeding 2 percent in 1994–1995 and probably 3 percent in 1996. The Norwegian participation rate of 77.8 per cent is among the highest in the OECD (OECD, 1996a).

- This development has been enhanced by the expansion of public services, where employment more than doubled from 1972 to 1990, implying that the public sector today employs more than 30 percent of the working population (SSB, 1992:20). Private services too have increased considerably, while employment in manufacturing fell by about 20 percent in 1970–1990, to 14.5 percent of employment in 1994 (Kvinge et al., 1992: 18).

- After a drastic fall in private employment in 1987–1993, it has picked up and grown by more than 4.5 percent since, especially in construction and services, but also in manufacturing, while public employment growth has flattened out (Stortingsmelding 2, 1995–96, pp. 36–37).

- Female employment and labour participation rates increased by more than 20 percent in 1970–1990 to 71 percent in 1994, predominantly in the public sector. In the municipal sector more than 70 percent of the workforce are women (SSB, 1992: 22) and nearly 47 percent of female employees work part time. Overall, 26.5 percent of employees worked part time in 1995, exceeded only by the Netherlands and Switzerland (OECD, 1996a).

- Despite the number employed proliferating, total man-hours worked have remained fairly stable in recent decades, reflecting the impact of part-time work and reduced standard working hours. Working time was reduced from 42.5 to 40 hours per week in 1976 and to

37.5 hours in 1986. Among part-timers, roughly half worked fewer than 20 hours a week. Despite considerable overtime work, mainly among men, the average of 1415 work-hours per year in Norway is the lowest in any OECD country (OECD, 1996a).

- In spite of restrictive regulations 14 percent of all employees were employed on temporary contracts in 1996 (Nergaard and Stokke, 1996), with great variation between sectors. The proportion of temporary employed was lower in the private sector and considerably higher in the public sector, especially in the municipalities.

- Unemployment remained below 2 percent in the 1970s, reached 3 percent in 1983, and then fell until it accelerated from 1987 and exceeded 6 percent in 1993, when more than 8 percent of the work-force were out of an ordinary job. Unemployment has been lower among women than among men and among high-skilled than low-skilled, while high unemployment persists among the limited number of immigrant workers (13.9 fall, 1995). Since 1994, registered unemployment has gradually decreased and fallen to below 4 percent (77 000, November 1996). Still, youth unemployment (11.8 percent 1995) and a core of long-term unemployment (over 26 weeks) persist, indicating that skill-mismatches prevail, even though this group has shrunk to below 30 000.

- After nominal wage growth surpassed 10 percent in the early 1980s, it declined from 1987 and has remained stable around 3.5 percent per year on average from 1990 to 1995 (NOU, 1996: 19). Owing to inflation, real wages increased very slowly in the 1980s, but have caught up in recent years, growing by 1.2 per cent in 1993/94, 0.3 percent in 1994/95, and over 2 percent in 1995/96. Contrary to most OECD countries, wage dispersion in Norway has in recent years become more compressed, reflecting solidaristic wage policies marked by flat pay increases, giving priority to the low-paid and women (OECD, 1995: 38; Kahn, 1996: 5, 13).[2]

---

2 The reduction in wage inequality primarily reflects a lifting of the bottom relative to the middle of the wage distribution, while relative wages in the upper part of the ladder have remained fairly stable (Kahn, 1996: 13). Studies of the disposable income of households, however, suggest a modest increase in income dispersion in 1986–1994 measured by the proportion of income earned by the lowest and highest decile of households, while relative incomes for the other groups has been stable (Statistics Norway, 1996b: 13).

As to the widely discussed "jobless-growth" hypothesis, there is no evidence that the overall employment intensity of growth in Norway has declined over recent decades. Clearly capital intensity, productivity, and labour shedding have accelerated in certain industries, but the shifts in the industry structure towards more labour-intensive social services imply increased employment effects of growth. Productivity growth in the Norwegian manufacturing sector decreased from 5 percent in the 1960s, to 3 percent in the 1970s, and to 1.4 in the 1990s, suggesting increased employment effects of growth (OECD, 1995a). Although GDP growth in the 1970s averaged 4.8 percent and man-hours increased by 1.1 percent on average, similar growth rates under the current recovery have had a stronger impact on employment. This Norwegian pattern is in line with a general tendency within the OECD (Glyn, 1995).

The personal burden and societal costs of unemployment, indeed, depend on the duration and in-out-flows of unemployment. Figures from the Directorate of Labour indicate that roughly 300 000 persons in Norway experience a spell of unemployment during any one year (LO, 1995), suggesting that the rotation of jobs and employees is considerable. According to the OECD (1995a), as much as 20 percent of the stock of unemployed left unemployment in any given month in 1994, the highest in the OECD, while the chance of entering unemployment was slightly higher than in most OECD countries (0.7 percent). As to the risk that lasting unemployment causes withdrawal from the labour force and possibly social marginalization, Colbjørnsen and Larsen (1995) concluded that the active labour market programmes had contributed to keeping most of the long-term unemployed within the workforce and had reduced long-term unemployment by 45 000 in 1993 (ibid.: 37). OECD estimates suggest that the active labour market policy may have contributed to reducing the long-term level of unemployment by as much as 2.5 percent (OECD 1994, in Try, 1996: 14).

As to labour and job turnover, evidence reveals quite high Norwegian labour market mobility compared with the levels of most OECD countries (OECD, 1994a; Salvanes, 1996). In the case of manufacturing, Salvanes found a gross job reallocation rate of 16.8 percent (1977–1992) whereas the rate in the USA and Canada was about 20 percent (ibid.: 23). The dominant source of job reallocation is within industries and regions, differs considerably between sectors, and by far exceeds what is necessary to accommodate net changes in job positions (ibid.: 53, 56). Internal migration between regions has remained stable since the mid-1970s and is among the highest in the OECD area – 2.6 percent of the population compared with1.1 in Germany and 2.8 in the USA in 1987 (OECD, 1994a: 66).

During the last recession the labour force declined by 2.5 percent

(15–64 years), and has increased significantly under the current recovery (Colbjørnsen and Larsen, 1995: 22). The responsiveness of labour supply to unemployment shifts in both a short- and long-term perspective is among the highest in the OECD area (ibid.: 23). The population (16–74 years) outside the labour force increased from 45 percent to 49 percent in 1985–1992, and it decreased to 44 percent in 1995 (Stortingsmelding 2, 1995–1996: 37). During the recession the Norwegian system of higher education was expanded considerably, illustrated by a 60 percent increase in available student places. These factors presumably contribute to explaining the relatively low level of unemployment in Norway compared with most other OECD countries (according to Colbjørnsen and Larsen, 1995: 24).

Still, the share of vacant jobs that are filled by unemployed – roughly 30 percent during the strong employment growth in 1994–1995 – suggests that skill mismatches account for a considerable part of current Norwegian unemployment. This concern is reflected in the strong emphasis by the government on qualificational upgrading, through both labour market programmes and educational reform (this is discussed in more detail by Bosch in Chapter 7).

However, fresh evidence does not fit with the expectation of rapidly growing skill requirements. A study of employer recruitment policies in 1993–1995 showed that a substantial part of employment growth occurred in jobs demanding only modest or low qualifications and the supposed relative decline in low-skilled jobs is as yet difficult to trace. Estimates suggest that roughly 15 percent of current positions require no more than primary education. Given the soaring supply of high-skilled labour and the fact that educational upgrading by far exceeds the decline in low-skilled jobs, a plausible scenario is that Norway may actually experience a shortage of low-skilled labour over the next few years and a potential mis-match in terms of over- or mis-qualification (Larsen, 1996a). This scenario gains support from long-term forecasts of labour supply and demand produced by Statistics Norway (Cappelen and Stølen, 1995). However, under the current recovery labour markets have shown a surprising capacity to absorb high-skilled labour, suggesting that the potential for upward substitution associated with generational change in the labour force is considerable. If so, social tension mediated by age and education may arise, reflecting a situation in which leading positions, held by senior employees with modest formal education, are challenged by incoming, highly educated young colleagues (Larsen, 1996b). Considering that ideas for a new large-scale educational reform have been launched by the LO and the government, aimed at providing workers with the right to continuous vocational training over the life-cycle, a rationing of job opportunities between groups of employees with different skills and ages might become a more contested terrain of distributional struggle than the distinction between insiders and outsiders in the labour market in the years to come.

4. Regulatory frameworks of Norwegian labour markets

The individual employment relationship as well as collective labour relations in Norway are extensively regulated by a dual system of framework legislation and legally binding collective agreements. While individual employment rights are predominantly regulated by laws such as the Work Environment Act of 1977, collective labour relations are mainly regulated by collective agreements within legal rules of conduct, management of disputes, etc. This section will present some general findings from international research on the relationship between employment regulation, international competitiveness, and employment patterns, and also a short overview of the Norwegian regulatory system of individual employment rights (collective labour relations are analysed in section 7).

Internationalization, labour regulation, and employment

In contemporary political discourse it is often assumed that internationalization and regime competition imply that states with regulatory regimes marked by high labour standards and tight restrictions on employers' manpower policy will suffer in terms of reduced competitiveness, domestic investment, and employment creation.[3] Empirical evidence to support this thesis is, however, as yet meagre and ambiguous. According to OECD (1994b: 157) there is no correlation between labour standards and aggregate trade performance (although the relationship is different in certain low-cost sectors). A certain correlation can be traced between labour standards and outward investment, although large deviations can be observed from this relationsship in a number of countries (ibid.: 160). As noted by Bosch (1995a), outward investment in countries with stringent labour standards tend to accompany rising exports and reflect competitive companies' desire to be present in export markets, suggesting that the relationship between employment regula-

3 "Labour standards" here broadly refers to regulations that govern working conditions (e.g. dismissals, temporary work, working time, health and safety, and worker representation) (OECD, 1994b: 137).

tions and investment flows is a spurious one. In corollary, OECD (1994b: 161) concludes that "the degree of government intervention in the determination of labour standards appears to have little effect on final outcomes, as evidenced by the lack of association between the index for stringency of regulations on labour standards and per capita GDP and wages".

In the Norwegian case, outward direct investment has been among the highest in the OECD area and has increased over the past decade, while inward direct investment has been more volatile and lower than average within the OECD area (Hødnebø and Stokland, 1994: 11). In (1994–1995 outward direct investment more than doubled, mostly to EU countries, and inward direct investment declined, while in Sweden the opposite tendency occurred (NHO, 1996). Norwegian outward investment has predominantly been market driven (Hammervold and Heum, 1993; Stokland, 1994: 82), whereas inward investment has been restrained by the limited scope of Norwegian markets (Hødnebø and Stokland, 1994: 19). As to Norway's attractiveness for inward direct investment, a recent study by FAFO found that economic-political stability was judged by multinational companies as a positive factor and labour market conditions and the bargaining system were conceived as positive (49 percent) or neutral (36 percent) (ibid.: 130).[4]

The implications of national employment regulations therefore seem to be more important for the form, distribution, and growth of employment opportunities in domestic labour markets, but the direction and strength of such effects are difficult to judge (Emerson, 1988: 777). Efficiency wage theory and implicit contract theory suggest that strict protection can be mutually beneficial to employers and employees, by reducing risk and wages (ibid.: 777), while strict protection against firing may encourage different forms of atypical work, e.g. fixed contracts and part-time and temporary work (ibid.: 776).

OECD (1994a: 73–74) refers to several arguments in favour of labour protection, notably that stable employment relationships may encourage acceptance of technological change and internal mobility, reduce social costs and frictional unemployment, provide macroeconomic stabilizers by containing spirals of declining demand as a result of adverse economic shocks, and prevent growth of the underground economy (ibid.: 73–75).

---

4 Access to well-educated labour was strongly positively ranked (69 percent); productivity and quality were neutral (61 percent) or positive (33 percent); know-how and competence neutral (59 percent) or positive (50 percent); while relative wage costs were considered neutral (42 percent) or negative (40 percent) (Hødnebø and Stokland, 1994: 130).

The counter-arguments according to OECD are that they benefit powerful and better-paid insiders rather than outsiders, and they may impose undesirable rigidities on firms, lead to immobility by limiting vacancies and the entry of new people, new skills and new ideas, and encourage growth of a dual labour market and fixed-term contracts (ibid.: 75–76).

According to estimates made by Jackman, Layard, and Nickell (1995), there is some evidence in favour of the hypothesis that the speed of adjustment in labour demand is negatively related to the strictness of employment protection and that the persistence of unemployment seems to be positively related to the strictness of protection (ibid.: 14–15). However, the impact on the overall unemployment level is indeterminate, since employment protection tends to reduce flows both into and out of unemployment. There seems to be a negative cross-country correlation between very strict labour protection and employment levels, but it is, according to the OECD, not possible to draw any causal conclusions about the relationship (1994a: 76). (In Chapter 6 Moene et al. suggests a theory that employment regimes with limited hiring and firing actually increase the level of employment.)

With some exceptions, like the highly deregulated labour markets of the UK and the USA, and many Latin countries where labour protection is generally tight, most countries display a complex picture of strict regulation of some features and laxer regulation of other features of employment relationships, causing different modes and sources of labour adjustment. As discussed by Bosch in Chapter 7, Norway seems to fit well into this pattern, suggesting that understanding of the overall impact of regulations cannot be derived from individual provisions but must take account of the whole set of interrelated and often complementary functions of different regulations as well as macroeconomic policies (Emerson, 1988: 805).

Emerson (1988: 779) suggests that employment protection can have different effects over the business cycle. It is also noteworthy that the weak cross-country correlations reflect great variation between single countries, and that alternative sources of adjustment may compensate for inflexibility caused by strict employee protection (Blank, 1993: 181–184): "Individual programs that might appear problematic by themselves, may fit coherently into a web of country-specific institutions" (ibid.: 183). Similarly the European Commission draws attention to the fact that countries with less external mobility (turnover) tend to have greater internal adjustment capacity and that external flexibility does not necessarily imply greater labour market efficiency (European Commission, 1994: 100).

In a recent report of the DG-V of the European Commission, presented in the Social Dialogue, experiences with deregulation of labour markets are discussed, and it is argued that employment performance has not improved since deregulation began; that member states with lower levels of regulation have not had significantly better economic or employment performance relative to others; that other OECD countries with less regulated labour markets have fared no better than more regulated ones, such as Japan and Scandinavia. All this suggests that the employment performance of EU states seems to be largely independent of the labour market regulatory systems in place (European Commission,1996: 2). One factor possibly contributing to this picture might be that deregulation has often been seen as a cost-cutting alternative to other, more expansive policies – notably macroeconomic policies and active manpower policies – rather than a complement (ibid.: 3). Referring to the US example, it is also suggested that deregulation may imply that one mode of regulation – labour law or collective agreement – is replaced by another – civil law, notably contract law (ibid.: 10). A report by McKinsey (1994, in European Commission, 1996: 33), comparing six OECD countries, notes that differences in productivity among leading economies were caused more by differences in competitive intensity in product markets than by differences in labour market flexibility. Work flexibility measured in terms of job creation and job destruction seems to be much the same on both sides of the Atlantic, while labour market factors were seen to have less impact on employment than product market factors in service sectors, with the exception of the European retail industry (ibid.: 33).

All together, most studies seem to support the view that regulation/deregulation of labour markets has less clear-cut effects on employment performance than is often assumed in current political debate and that the employment impact of regulation appears highly contingent on the context of product markets, welfare benefits, and macroeconomic policy in which they are situated.

Norwegian labour regulations in comparative perspective

In Norway it is often argued by employers and conservatives that regulation of employee rights imposes extraordinary constraints on the manpower policies of national employers (NHO, 1995). However, from the somewhat patchy comparative research on cross-national differences in labour standards such as dismissals, temporary work, working time and the like, Norway tends to be ranked in the middle among OECD countries (OECD, 1994b: 152–154; Grubb and Wells, 1993; Emerson, 1988). In international comparison, statutory working time regulations are fairly relaxed as to overtime, pay premiums, period of accounting, and possibilities of exemptions by collective agreement (OECD, 1994b: 143). There are no constraints on the use of part-time work, which is often inhibited by normative constraints in many continental countries, and there are no statutory quotas for handicapped people, which are widespread in other European countries. Statutory regulation of individual dismissal and collective redundancies is internationally ranked among the more flexible (ibid.: 147), granting employers ample room to shed labour for economic or organizational reasons. Moreover, the option of long-lasting (up to 52 weeks) temporary lay-offs on a full-time or part-time basis, publicly financed by unemployment benefits, provides a source of numerical flexibility that in an international perspective is quite generous (NOU, 1993: 19).[5]

As discussed by Naschold (Chapter 9), Norway is one of the few OECD countries that prohibit private placement services, except for certain categories of white-collar employees where public licence is required. A recent amendment of the Work Environment Act (1995), which restricts the circumstances in which temporary employment may be used, represents a constraint on employer personnel policy that is unusual in an international perspective.[6] A fresh empirical study by FAFO estimates the proportion on temporary contracts as 14 percent of all employees, but there is considerable variation between industries and sectors. The proportion of employees on temporary contracts is especially high in the municipal sector, a reminder that normative regulations and actual practice may differ vastly (Nergaard and Stokke, 1996).

As mentioned, cross-country comparison of employment regulation is extremely difficult. Implementation of statutory regulations naturally reflects the balance of power and unformal practices of cooperation between the industrial parties, as well as the labour market situation and court practice (Emerson, 1988: 805). In the Norwegian case, employers often maintain that collective agreements tend to define much stricter regulations, for example as regards working time schemes and dismissal, than is required by law, and that the total dense web of cooperative relations and representative practices in effect inhibits organizational change (NHO, 1995; Reve, 1994). The trade unions, for their part, tend to argue

5 Employers are obliged to pay ordinary wages for the first three days of a full-time layoff. Since the average number of employees on (full/partial) temporary layoff reached 1.3 percent (28 000) of the labour force in 1990, the number was reduced to 0.7 percent in 1992 and has declined further since (NOU 1993: 19).

6 The government has recently proposed an amendment of the act, allowing for exceptions in areas such as sports, culture, and research if agreed upon in a collective agreement.

that there are considerable loopholes and scope for pragmatic adjustment and negotiation of exemptions at workplace level, expressed not least in the vast use of layoffs and overtime in Norwegian companies, the latter corresponding to 70 000 man-years (5 percent of the total) in the private sector in 1995 (Ingebretsen et al., 1996). As to external and numerical flexibility, Salvanes' study of job and labour mobility suggests that the large share of small enterprises provides an important source of labour market adjustment, concluding that "the impact of product market rigidities and a strong welfare state do not appear to have an important impact on the flexibility of the economy" (Salvanes, 1996: 55). The issue of internal, functional flexibility in Norwegian enterprises is discussed in the contribution by Bosch in Chapter 7.

The impact of European labour regulations

Through the European Economic Area (EEA) agreement, Norway is supposed to implement EU directives on labour standards, although a veto option exists. In the struggle over EU and EEA membership, the No coalition argued that Community labour regulations would imply an undue juridification and individualization of Norwegian labour relations and feared that a downward harmonization would emerge (Stueland et al., 1994).

It has been widely assumed that the Norwegian level of protection is generally more stringent than EU/EEA minimum standards, but on certain issues Community regulations have represented an improvement of employee protection, for example in the case of employee consultation on collective redundancies, the right to a written work contract, working time in road transport, transfer of undertakings, information and consultation in transnational companies, and certain health and safety measures (see Dølvik and Olsen, 1994; Holo and Dølvik, 1994: 428–430).[7] The EU directive on working time will be implemented from December 1996, implying somewhat more stringent rules as to daily rest-periods, accounting periods, and ceilings on overtime work.[8]

7 For a more detailed overview of the implementation of Community social legislation in Norway, see Dølvik and Olsen (1994).

8 As to implementation, the Ministry of Labour has proposed that the Labour Inspectorate, authorized to decide on exemptions from working-time rules laid down in the Work Environment Act, shall not be allowed to accept calculated average overtime for more than 6 months (as accounting period, today 1 year), not exceeding 200 hours (today no maximum ceiling), while nightworkers shall be entitled to compulsory, employer-paid health control.

Implementation of EU directives has mainly been pursued through statutory enactment, implying an *erga omnes* effect in several areas previously regulated by collective agreements alone, but in general this has not caused controversy. One exception, however, is the directive on employee rights to information and consultation in transnational companies. The main employer and trade union confederations, NHO and LO, have signed a collective agreement on transposition, integrated into the Basic Agreement, which will be underpinned by a statutory regulation securing generalization of rights. This has caused misgivings among employer and trade union confederations in the service sector (HHS and YS), which argue that the NHO and LO are not representative in their sectors and that this mode of implementation is undemocratic. A similar problematique has emerged in relation to the recent European agreement between the European Trade Union Confederation (ETUC), the European Centre for Public Enterprises (CEEP), and the Union of Industrial and Employers' Confederations of Europe (UNICE) on parental leave, which was supposed to be transformed into an EU directive in June 1996.

Yet, in general it is justified to say that EU adjustment in this field has occurred smoothly, and implied no major change in the regulatory system of labour relations in Norway. Inward labour migration has been very limited and loss of public contracts owing to international competition has so far caused no major problem. However, one important reform has been pursued, notably the adoption of a new law that enables the imposed extension of individual provisions of collective agreements in order to prevent social dumping by foreign workers (see section 7).

Labour market welfare arrangements

If we look at regulation of employee social benefits, Norway is ranked among the most generous states in the OECD area.The universal state social security system covers issues such as medical support, sick leave pay, unemployment benefits, occupational rehabilitation, disablements benefits and old age pensions, which are financed by taxes and excises from employers (0–14.3 percent of wages) and employees (7.8 percent of taxable income). This implies that the indirect labour costs of employers are low in international comparison.

As for maternity leave, Norway has been a pioneer. The Work Environment Act now provides the mother with 12 weeks' leave and the father with 2 weeks' welfare leave in connection with a birth. In 1994 a time account scheme was introduced entitling parents to parental leave for a maximum of 1 year with 80 percent compensation, which can be stretched over three years if taken on a partial basis. As described by Ellingsæter and Rubery (Chapter 4), a paternal quota of four weeks is included, which is lost if not used. The Work Environment Act also secures opportunities of full- or part-time welfare leave (unpaid) and the right to reduced working time for welfare reasons. Child care, however, is expensive: for average-income households it is often nearly NOK 3000 per month/child, implying that almost the whole net wage of low-paid or part-time women workers with two or more children is spent on child care, substantially weakening work incentives for such groups (Kostøl, 1996).

The sick pay scheme is the most generous in the world, providing 100 percent of salary (up to a ceiling of NOK 230 000, corresponding to a good average wage) with no carens days, compared with a compensation rate of 90 percent in Denmark (with a much lower income ceiling) and 75 percent in Sweden (with one carens day). Self-declaration is accepted for four short-term periods of absence and parents are provided with up to four weeks of absence to care for sick children. The employer pays for the first 14 days, while public social security covers further absence. In 1995 sickness absence amounted to 6.7 percent of possible work-days, having dropped from more than 10 percent in 1986, but it has risen again recently. The dominant cause of absence is long-term sickness, often leading to transfer to occupational rehabilitation, labour market schemes, or permanent disability pension (see below).

The public pension system is built on a basic minimum provision and earnings-related supplementary pensions for people with an employment history, corresponding to roughly 55 percent of previous top income up to a certain ceiling (NOK 230 000). The usual retirement age is 67, although a negotiated supplementary scheme agreed between the social partners now allows flexible retirement from the age of 64 (reduced to 63 in 1997 and 62 in 1998). Occupational pensions in the public sector usually secure a compensation level of two-thirds of the previous top wage; such schemes are less prevalent in the private sector, although roughly 50 percent of private sector employees are covered by similar but less generous schemes (Hippe and Pedersen, 1996).

Unemployment benefits, financed by the public social security system, have answered to an average gross compensation rate of 65 percent with a maximum duration of 186 weeks (3.5 years), provided a minimum income of NOK 29 000 has been earned. More stringent rules were approved by parliament in June 1996, basically reducing the maximum duration to three years and raising income thresholds to 50 000. (Unemployment insurance is discussed more in detail in section 6.)

Disability pensions are similar to old age pensions, combining previous and anticipated lost future earnings, implying a compensation level of about two-thirds. During the 1980s the number of disabled people rose rapidly, especially among women, but it has stabilized in recent years. Currently 8.5 percent of people aged 16–65 are disabled, while the rate is 45 percent in the 65–66 age bracket, suggesting that the disability pension has been widely used as a disguised early retirement scheme, providing employers with ample opportunities to shed labour in times of downsizing (Hippe and Pedersen, 1996). Eligibility criteria have thus been tightened in recent years, according to the so-called "working-line".

In international, comparison pension compensation levels are below those in countries such as Germany, France, Belgium, and Italy (OECD, *Economic Surveys*, 1995), but the minimum provisions paid to dependent spouses and the large number of dual-income households mean that total compensation is high in international comparison. According to new living condition surveys, the older population as a whole has fared better than most other social groups in recent years (Dahl, 1996).

The impact of the extensive and fairly generous social security schemes on labour market behaviour is difficult to asses, and reliable comparative research is scarce. As mentioned, Norwegian labour supply appears unusually flexible in international comparison, suggesting that alternative income sources and expansion of the education system have enhanced adjustment and smooth flows in and out of the labour market in accordance with cyclical swings. As indicated, sickness absence is comparatively high, generous parental leave arrangements provide for the permanent absence of a substantial proportion of female employees (and some fathers), while disability schemes presumably have encouraged informal early retirement flows. Still, the share of the population (25–64) out of employment in Norway is low in international comparison, and has decreased by more than 5 percent among women (1982–1992), whereas the share among men has increased by 6–8 percent (OECD, 1994a: 32).

For employers, the extensive schemes of temporary and partial leave for welfare reasons provide a source of staff adjustment but also a continuous need for substitutes and rotation of manpower. This might on the one hand enhance flexibility in labour market participation, on the other hand pose challenges to personnel planning. According to employers, this reinforces the need for a flexible labour supply, which in the view of employers is severely constrained by restrictions on temporary contracts and private manpower services. There is, however, no obstacle to the hiring of temporary replacements, but when labour markets are tight the matching and recruitment of adequate substitutes might naturally be problematic.

Given the long-term ageing of the population and a supposedly declining labour force, which it is assumed will burden the welfare state in the future, a government White Paper on welfare reform has suggested a series of measures to reshape eligibility criteria and the design of welfare provisions to encourage re-employment in order to increase participation, according to the so-called working line (Stortingsmelding 35, 1994–1995). The White Paper expresses government concern that the combined effects of different public income support schemes, e.g. for single mothers, may provide a "welfare trap" that erodes work incentives for certain groups (Ibid).[9] In a situation with few available jobs it appears plausible that such factors may weaken incentives to job search, but a recent study of Statistics Norway concludes that the compensation level for the non-employed in general does not suggest any significant voluntary unemployment (Arneberg, 1996: 22). The average gross compensation rate among the non-employed on social security schemes is 56–57 percent. The level of net compensation is, however, higher. For 20 percent of non-employed and 40 percent of employed, disposable income after tax is in excess of 80 percent of the average wage. Among non-working single mothers, fewer than half achieve 60 percent net compensation and none has more than 80 percent, whereas as much as 50 percent of non-employed in families with children gain over 80 percent (ibid.: 19, 22).[10]

Even though welfare state arrangements have facilitated exit–entry flows of the labour market (Hagen and Hippe, 1993), possibly contributing to keeping open unemployment down, compulsory labour market programmes have contributed to preventing withdrawal from work among the long-term unemployed.

Summary: sources of labour market rigidity and flexibility

All together there can be no doubt that Norwegian labour markets are surrounded by an extensive web of regulations, employment protection, and social welfare schemes that, in an international perspective, grant

9 For a more specific discussion of the impact of employment protection and social security provisions for female employment, see the contribution of Ellingsæter and Rubery in Chapter 4.

10 Despite the fact that the evidence, according to Statistics Norway, does not confirm that distorted incentives have caused voluntary unemployment, alternative calculations, taking account of child-care outlays and the fact that available jobs are often part time and lower paid, might suggest that the benefits of work for certain groups appear less clear-cut. According to OECD (1995a: 36), a net gain from taking a job of only 20–30 percent for low-paid unemployed implies a very high disincentive to work.

Norwegian employees a high level of job security, which presumably has a strong impact on the functioning of labour markets. Some of these schemes may weaken incentives or pressures to work, but also temporarily provide the options of a positive social choice of alternative styles of living. Some of the regulations of employee protection are strict and constrain short-term external adjustment of staff, while others are fairly relaxed and may provide alternative sources of flexibility. The overall effects of this regulatory and institutional framework of Norwegian labour markets are indeed extremely difficult to asses.

The Norwegian Employment Commission (NOU, 1992: 26) suggested that the growth of personal and domestic service employment may have been inhibited by institutional constraints and the impact of a large public sector. In general, however, the internationally high labour force participation and flexibility of labour supply, the prevalence of extensive part-time work (and temporary work) and fairly flexible working hours, together with a middle-range level of job and labour mobility, suggest that there is no strong evidence that institutional rigidities have significantly inhibited external labour market flexibility. As noted in international research, however, strict regulations tend to pose few problems in periods of high labour demand as in Norway in recent years, leaving the question open how labour markets will respond in the future if demand decreases. Thus, it seems plausible to assume, in line with Emerson (1988: 805), that successful macroeconomic stabilization and wage determination are crucial prerequisites for the good functioning of the regulated Norwegian labour markets. Moreover, international studies suggest that skill formation and internal/functional flexibility of enterprise manpower policy might be as important for job growth and competitiveness as external mobility in the long term. These aspects of the Norwegian labour market model are analysed by Bosch in Chapter 7 and touched on in sections 5 and 7 of this chapter.

5. Vocational education and training

A central aim of Norwegian employment policy in recent years has been to strengthen skill formation, partly through educational reform, partly through labour market schemes.

The educational level in the Norwegian labour force is relatively high and steadily rising. In 1992 more than 90 percent of all young people went on to some form of secondary education and since 1994 a right to three years of secondary education has been provided. At present 43 per cent of the population have 12 or more years of education, compared with 32 percent in 1980 (Torp, 1995). Among those who complete secondary school, 48 percent proceed immediately to higher education in colleges or universities, meaning that roughly one-fifth of the population above the age of 19 have received some kind of higher education, placing Norway at the top in international comparison (Pape, 1993).

In recent years the Norwegian educational system has been subject to significant reform and expansion in order to raise skills and reduce unemployment among young people. From 1988 to 1994 the number of places in higher education was increased by 60 percent. The main weakness of the Norwegian educational system, from a labour market point of view, has been a shortage of vocational training capacity. Among those who completed secondary education in 1992, 42 percent were on vocational courses, and only 3.4 percent of 18–24 year olds, compared with over 70 percent of Germans, received apprenticeship contracts in Norway in 1993 (Karlsen, 1991).

To redress the imbalance between technical and academic education, reform of the secondary education system ("Reform-94") aimed at strengthening vocational studies. (For more detailed discussion see Bosch, Chapter 7.) By replacing more than 100 previous secondary school courses with a core curriculum of 13 courses and strengthening apprenticeship training, a dual system similar to the German model was envisaged, although on a smaller scale (Sivesind et al., 1995). A critical factor, however, is the availability and matching of apprenticeship places. Despite a reduction in initial wages of 40 percent and an increase in direct state contributions, a substantial proportion of the first "Reform-94" cohort lacked such a place (August 96), especially many of those searching for apprenticeships in the public sector. In the absence of compulsion, the individual employer voluntarily decides whether to employ an apprentice, causing a free-rider problem.[11]

Norwegian public authorities have had no articulated policy on employer-sponsored skill formation. According to Schøne (1996: 59) roughly one-third of employees aquired formal enterprise training in 1993 (29 percent among those with no secondary education, 38 percent among those with higher education). The chance of attaining such training is lower in large enterprises with high union density, but is generally higher among union members than non-union members (Gulbrandsen, 1995: 177).

11 Different interpretations of this problem prevail: whereas LO and NHO tend to argue that the county educational administrations have not done enough to counteract mismatches between educational supply, pupils' choices, and the needs of working life, others argue that the employers, not least in the public sector, have not responded to their responsibilities.

Reflecting increasing awareness about the importance of continuous training, the main union confederation (LO) has proposed that every employee should be entitled to spend one-eleventh of working time over the life-cycle on training. The idea, envisaged to be realised through cooperation between the social partners and the state, has been well received by the government, which has set up a public commission, and the social partners in the 1996 pay round agreed to start investigating the issue. The implications of such a reform might indeed be far-reaching in terms of labour costs, reduced working time, and increased rotation of job positions, an obvious hurdle being that the educational system offers a poor supply of adequate retraining services.

6. Labour market policies

Since the onset of recession in the late 1980s the Norwegian government has attached increasing importance to pursuing active labour market policies instead of the passive payment of unemployment benefits. The primary goal is to reduce skill mismatches by training the unemployed for ordinary work, thereby reducing the risk of persistently high unemployment and preventing the deleterious consequences of long-term unemployment.

The Ministry of Local Government and Labour is responsible for the framing of labour market policy, while executive responsibility lies with the Labour Market Administration (LMA), consisting of the national Directorate of Labour and a large number of county and district employment offices. The rapid rise in unemployment from 1988 increased pressures related to organizing labour market programmes and administering unemployment benefits, presumably at the expense of the placement service. Under the current recovery, more resources are allocated to strengthen the placement services and improve the service to employers asking for help. The government has stressed the need to improve the efficiency of labour market authorities, and a number of measures have been introduced to upgrade the organization, staffing, and competence of the administration.

Employment placement service

The Labour Market Administration holds a monopoly of placement services. Private, commercial placement services and labour leasing (contracting) are prohibited, according to the Employment Act (art. 26–27). A few private temporary help agencies are however licensed by the LMA, such as Manpower Inc., mainly supplying clerical labour, and some organizations and companies are allowed to organize their own placement services to members on a non-profit basis in cooperation with the LMA. A comparative analysis of the performance and modernization of Norwegian placement services is presented by Naschold and Arnkil (Chapter 9), suggesting that both efficiency and innovative capacity lag behind several other European countries.

The main purpose of the employment offices is to assist firms in filling vacant positions and to help job seekers to find a job. During 1994, 395 000 persons (18 percent of the entire labour force) were registered as "searching for a job", while 283 000 vacant positions were registered at the employment offices (Torp, 1995). Employers are required to report vacant positions to the LMA, but in 1993 approximately 20 per cent of all estimated vacancies were reported directly to the LMA by firms while 32 percent were publicly advertised and then registered by the LMA (Arbeidsdirektoratet, 1994).

Of the total number of vacancies recorded, successful placements were made by the employment offices in 30 percent of cases in 1993. Of these, about 10 percent were matched with an unemployed person (Arbeidsdirektoratet, 1995).[12] According to the Labour Market Administration, the limited number of successful placements reflected skill shortages among the unemployed, but the modest market share of the LMA has triggered discussions about the monopoly of the LMA on placement services. Employers have argued that the official placement service mainly offers low-skilled workers and is not sufficiently oriented to employers' needs for help in filling vacant positions. In this view, efficiency would be enhanced by accepting a supplementary private placement service, a view that gained support from a recent ISF study (Torp and Pettersen, 1989). Apart from allowing more voluntary organizations to set up their own non-profit placement services, the government has countered that commercial agencies would serve only the most lucrative parts of the market and leave the public services with hard-to-employ "rest" categories, reducing both the credibility of the LMA and overall labour market efficiency.

---

12 According to a study by Nordli Hansen (1995) based on a survey of 4000 employees, only 6 percent got their job through the employment offices. The study has, however, been strongly contested by the Directorate of Labour, whose recruitment study in 1993 based on nearly 3700 employer interviews showed that among private employers more than 30 percent of actual recruitments were pursued with the assistance of the employment offices, while the percentage in the public sector was roughly 10 percent (Arbeidsdirektoratet, 1995: 7).

Unemployment benefits

International research documents that the design of unemployment benefits has a strong impact on long-term unemployment (OECD, 1994a). Apart from their desirable social effects, unemployment benefits influence unemployment through two mechanisms, according to Jackman et al. (1995: 4): first, by reducing the terrors of unemployment, they directly increase wage pressure from trade unions and, by reducing the efficiency of unemployed people's job search, employers are encouraged to raise wages; second, the duration of unemployment benefits clearly influences exit-rates from unemployment, thereby increasing both the duration of unemployment and the total stock of people out of work.

In contrast with other Scandinavian countries, where unemployment insurance has been administered by the trade unions (the Ghent system), a compulsory public system of unemployment insurance was introduced by the Labour Party in 1938.[13] In principle, job seekers are obliged to take any "suitable job" regardless of wage and location, or benefits are terminated. How strictly this rule is applied and how it varies with economic cycles is, however, difficult to judge.

Until 1997 the unemployed could receive benefits for two periods, each with a maximum length of 80 weeks. In between the two periods there was a waiting period of 13 weeks, but this could be omitted if no proper job or training had been offered. In the second period the level of reimbursement was 90 percent of the level during the first period. After two periods of 80 weeks on benefits, it is necessary to have a new period of ordinary work or to enrol in a temporary employment programme to meet the income requirements for new periods of unemployment benefit. New entrants are not entitled to unemployment benefits and must rely on means-tested social support.

Today, between 60 and 75 percent of those registered as unemployed

13 In the Scandinavian context the Norwegian unemployment benefit system represents an interesting institutional distinction. As analysed by Rothstein (1992), the design of such systems has represented historical strategic choices with great implications for trade unions, contributing not only to explaining international variation in union density, but also to regulating union control over the conditions of labour supply (through eligibility criteria for receiving benefits). Of the five OECD countries with the highest union density, all have a voluntary system administered by trade unions (the Ghent system), explaining roughly 20 percent of the variation in the union density. In Norway such a system was introduced in 1908, but after some union-driven funds were mismanaged and went bankrupt the whole system was discredited during the 1920s and 1930s and the Labour Party, in cooperation with the liberal (Venstre) and conservative parties (Høire), introduced a compulsory public scheme, seemingly without union protests.

receive compensation, on average around 65 percent of the gross wage. In contrast to, for example, Sweden, there is no means-testing. Among employed persons, average net compensation on job loss is estimated to be 79 percent, while 40 percent receive more than 80 percent (Arneberg, 1996: 18). In 1988, total expenditures on unemployment benefits were NOK 3.2 billion, and by 1994 this had increased to NOK 11.7 billion, reflecting the rise in recipients from 37 000 to 83 000 persons (Torp, 1995).

In order to redress what has been perceived as unintended distortions of incentives, the government in 1996 won parliamentary acceptance for more stringent rules, raising the income threshold to NOK 49 000; shortening the maximum duration from 186 to 150 weeks (75 weeks for people with previous income below 95 000); eliminating the 13-week break after 80 weeks; while keeping compensation at the same level throughout the whole period. This is supposed to be complemented by some guarantee that a proper placement on a labour market programme, in training, or in public employment should be offered before the maximum duration limit is reached, for older unemployed possibly on a permanent basis. If adopted, the reform is expected to strengthen pressures on employment offices and on the long-term unemployed to find a regular job, while the proportion of part-timers with low previous income eligible for benefits will be reduced.

Active labour market measures

A conservative government first introduced active labour market measures in the early 1980s. The programmes were radically extended in 1988 and in the next two years open participation increased by 400 percent while unemployment rose by 90 percent (Torp, 1995). The Norwegian Employment Commission in 1992 suggested a further increase in active labour market measures as an element of structural policy and to give the unemployed a chance to preserve and enhance their human capital.[14]

Active labour market measures and unemployment benefits are organized by the Directorate of Labour, while the local employment offices are responsible for implementation. From 1989 to 1993, total government expenditure on measures to promote employment nearly doubled

14 The follow-up Orskaug Commission (NOU 1993: 6) proposed simplification of the existing plethora of programmes, recommended closer cooperation with local authorities, and improved interaction between private and public agencies to enhance skill formation, and suggested that participation in a job club should be compulsory after three months out of work.

(from ca. NOK 12 billion to ca. NOK 20 billion). Of this, expenditure on unemployment benefits accounted for roughly 54 percent in 1989 and around 60 percent (NOK 12 billion) in 1993 (Statistics Norway, 1994). In 1993, close to 3 percent of the labour force were participating in active labour market programmes (ALMPs). This implies that Norway in international comparison spends a high degree of resources on active labour market measures.

Under the current recovery, enrolment in active labour market programmes has been scaled down, but still more than 1.5 percent of the labour force is included (Fall 1996).

The effects of active labour market policy

The aim of active labour market programmes is to enhance skill formation among the unemployed and thereby improve search efficiency, increase the effective labour force, reduce wage pressures, and improve matching processes (Layard et al., 1991).

It is conventional to classify labour market schemes into two or three types: (a) *demand-oriented* programmes through temporary employment in the public sector or through wage subsidies in private industry; (b) *supply-oriented* programmes improving the skills of the unemployed, through formal education or on-the-job training; (c) *matching-oriented* programmes, notably placement services. Moreover, rehabilitation and quota schemes for labour with health problems or handicaps are sometimes treated as a separate, fourth category. (The main measures in Norway are summarized in Table A.14 in the Appendix).[15]

Internationally, active labour market policies are strongly recommended by, for instance, the OECD and the EU, but the effects of such policies are contested in the research community. Keeping the positive social effects aside, two opposing but not mutually exclusive views dominate economic literature as to the employment effects of ALMPs (Raaum and Wulfsberg, 1995: 2):

15 For registered young unemployed there is a "job guarantee" (16–24 years) which assures an offer of training or a subsidized job if an ordinary job or education is not attainable. Most labour market programmes for this group emphasize the training aspect, but youth unemployment has remained fairly high, youth employment has decreased, and many young employees are increasingly found in low-paid jobs with poor working conditions. Nevertheless, the share of young people not in work or education has shown only a slight increase since 1987 (Statistics Norway, 1996c: 4), reflecting the expansion of education.

(1) The *job competition* argument emphasized by Layard et al. (1991) claims that ALMP have positive effects on re-employment of participants through enhancement of skills, motivation and participation, improving search effectiveness and productivity of not-employed, hereby increasing job competition and reducing real wages.
(2) The *reduced welfare loss* argument put forward by e.g Calmfors and Forslund (1991) implies that the cushioning of the negative social effects of unemployment by ALMPs reduces wage competition and trade union responsiveness to unemployment in wage-setting, causing higher wages and lower employment.

Recent studies, however, suggest that both effects may be present and the total effect is ambiguous (Calmfors and Lang, 1994, in Raaum and Wulfsberg,1995). According to estimates of employment development in OECD countries in 1983–1988 and 1989–1994, made by Jackman et al. (1995: 2–3), ALMP schemes seem to have little impact in the short term but a clear positive effect in the long term.

In recent years a number of attempts have been made to evaluate the effects of individual labour market schemes in Norway, but the overall outcomes are hard to determine definitively, owing to selection bias, the problem of contra-factuality, and the difficulty of aggregating from short-term micro effects to long-term macro effects. Measured against the chance of finding employment or enrolling in further education after finishing a training programme, studies of training programmes have shown that participation increases the probability of starting further education or a permanent job (Try, 1993: 135), but for several courses there were no significant effects 12 months after the end of training (Raaum and Torp, 1993). One of the most comprehensive Norwegian studies, covering a range of training programmes based on data from 1991–1992, concluded that in terms of post-programme job probabilities (after approximately one year) no average employment effect was found, although more disaggregated analysis showed that participants in training that offered formal qualifications experienced positive effects, especially on very popular courses that were extensively rationed and on courses typically leading to qualification for jobs in the public services where job competition presumably was less intense (Raaum et al., 1995: 14–25). The authors, however, emphasize that the positive effects may be underestimated, because many participants take labour marker training courses to qualify for further qualification through labour market training or the ordinary education system (ibid.: 25). A fresh evaluation of training courses based on data from 1994, during the labour market recovery, showed much more positive results (25 percent increased chance of getting a job), suggesting that the effects are strongly influenced by the labour market situation (Arbeidsdirektoratet, 1996). A recent FAFO evaluation of a new youth job-training programme in the private sector shows a positive effect on employment, while young people on a similar public sector job-training programme show a higher chance of enrolling in education than their control group (Eldring and Grøgaard, 1996).

In a recent review of existing evaluations, Try (1996) notes that participation in labour market programmes tends to reduce job search (increasing opportunities for others), but, despite varied results, participation in general appears to enhance short-term chances of getting a job or enrolling in further education and, the more targeted, the better the results of the schemes (ibid.: 17). The studies pinpoint the difficulty of finding adequate criteria for assessing the overall societal effects of ALM programmes. In times of recession with limited access to vacancies results may look meagre, but activation of participants can represent a positive effect in itself, preventing marginalization. For the long-term unemployed this can improve their probability of getting back to work when the recovery starts by interrupting their unemployable status, which in itself tends to reduce competitiveness in labour markets (Hernæs and Strøm, 1994; Colbjørnsen and Larsen, 1995: 5). It has also been suggested that ALM programmes might have a "harassment effect", forcing people to find a job on their own. On the other hand, Naschold and Arnkil (Chapter 9) suggest that preoccupation with administering ALM programmes might inhibit placement efforts.

Despite concern among certain trade unions that ALM programmes could constitute a new type of public secondary labour market, substituting for ordinary jobs, some rotation among groups of potentially marginalized job seekers may have positive unintended effects. Jackman et al. thus maintain that "displacement" effects are greatly exaggerated, stemming from the misconception of a "zero-sum" game, and the effect of improving exit probabilities from unemployment for disadvantaged groups actually contributes to increasing total employment (1995: 5).

Other indirect effects of ALMPs may also be important, as suggested by the study by Raaum and Wulfsberg (1995), who conclude that in the Norwegian case "labour market policy variables as well as total unemployment, seem to be better indicators of downward wage pressure than open unemployment. We find strong evidence that active labour market policies reduce wage pressures" (ibid.: 21). Here Norway is at odds with older results from Sweden, Finland, and Denmark suggesting that ALMPs shift the wage curve upwards (Calmfors and Nymoen, 1990, in Try, 1996: 14). Raaum and Wulfsberg suggest two possible explanations for ALMPs having had opposite effects in Sweden and Norway: first, public relief work (temporary jobs in the public sector) has accounted for a larger fraction in Sweden than in Norway; second, remuneration of programme participants has been significantly higher in Sweden, where, in contrast to in Norway, relief work has been paid according to tariff wages, while participants in training have received higher income than unemployment benefit (1995: 21).[16]

These factors tend to support the argument of Jackman et al. that the institutional design of ALMPs is decisive for outcomes; "what is needed (in most OECD countries) is in fact a change of regime" (1995: 6). Finding that schemes are clearly more effective when they are not optional (voluntary), they argue that participation has to be obligatory and that access has to be guaranteed after a certain spell of unemployment (ibid.: 6), which in fact has been a deliberate aim of Norwegian programmes for the long-term unemployed.

None the less, in Chapter 2 of this book Freeman argues that ALMPs are "not a big gun in the fight against unemployment", while Naschold and Arnkil (Chapter 9) stress the importance of more efficient placement services, especially in a period of recovery.

7. Labour relations and collective bargaining

Since the 1930s the Norwegian model of labour relations has been marked by a cooperative conflict partnership between capital, labour and the state (Müller Jentsch, 1993). Within a regulative order of collective agreements and legislation, centralized concertation has been complemented by local and workplace structures of cooperation (Dølvik and Stokland, 1992). Powerful confederations of trade unions and employers, LO and NAF/NHO, have been key actors in a multi-tiered bargaining system marked by a much stronger state presence than is the case, for example, in Sweden (Wallerstein and Golden, 1996), not least insofar as conflict resolution is concerned. Solidaristic wage policies have been pursued, wage differentials reduced, and, after a spell of neo-liberal ideology in the 1980s, centralized incomes policies have been revitalized in recent years, seemingly with favourable effects on employment and economic performance.

This appears as an interesting paradox in view of the widespread

---

16 According to Try (1996: 14), recent time-series analysis by the OECD (1993) suggests that reduced wage growth is an effect of ALMP in a majority of European countries, whereas employment growth and structural unemployment seem to be positively affected by ALMP.

international predictions of the end of corporatism associated with global integration and technological, structural, and social change (Streeck, 1993; Teague and Grahl, 1992). In contemporary wisdom, corporatist institutions have been perceived as a major cause of the dismal functioning of labour markets, calling for decentralization and deregulation of bargaining institutions (OECD, 1994a).

In this section we describe the main actors and institutions of Norwegian collective bargaining, and summarize the key developments over recent decades. Although the entrenched configuration of centralized institutions and actors has facilitated quite favourable labour market performance recent years, a central question is whether, confronted with ongoing social and labour market transformation, it is sustainable? If so, does the Norwegian example suggest that re-nationalized corporatism actually represents a viable and attractive strategy for coping with increased international competition?

Employers' organizations

Private sector employers in Norway are represented by several associations, of which NHO is the largest, covering 11 430 firms and more than 400 000 employees in 1996. HSH (the Federation of Norwegian Commercial and Service Enterprises) covers roughly 85 000 employees, and the Norwegian Banks Association roughly 25 000 employees.

NHO, which is the product of a merger in 1989 between NAF and two industry and crafts associations, is the most influential of the private employer organizations. NHO is the counterpart of the LO, with which it renegotiates the main Basic Agreement every four years, and commands strong central authority over affiliates as to bargaining strategies and industrial action. The member companies are affiliated to both the confederal organization and the industry branch federations (*landsforeninger*) between which there is a mutual membership. NHO and the industry federations combine the roles of employers' association and industrial interest organization. Despite the fact that more than 90 percent of affiliated companies employ fewer than 100 people, a number of large manufacturing companies, some with considerable state shares, are usually considered to exert strong influence on NHO policy. Membership density increases with firm size and in the early 1990s organized enterprises in total covered more than half of private sector employment and a considerably higher proportion in manufacturing.

In the public sector, there are separate organizations for state and local government. The government is formally the employer in the state sector, and pay negotiations, covering roughly 250 000 employees, are the responsibility of the Ministry of Planning and Coordination. The outcome of negotiations requires formal approval in parliament. In 1993 a new employer organisation for semi-autonomous state enterprises (NAVO) was founded. The local public sector is covered by the Norwegian Association of Local Authorities (KS), which is partly an employers' association, partly a lobby organization on behalf of the interests of the municipalities. Pay negotiations conducted by KS covered roughly 300 000 employees in 1991/92 (Nergaard, 1993: 142). Negotiations in the state and local government sectors are conducted separately, but are coordinated by a joint committee of KS and the Ministry of Planning. Pay negotiations are generally regulated by the Labour Dispute Act, except in the state sector, which is covered by specific legislation. In the state sector, agreements are settled by bargaining cartels of unions from the three union confederations, while the structure in the municipal sector is somewhat more complex.[17]

The structure of employer organization in Norway is marked by a high degree of centralized power, fairly high density rates, and clear demarcations of bargaining areas, inhibiting rivalry and competition. The dominant role of private manufacturing associations, coordinating their policies under the auspices of NHO, has contributed to the institutionalization of an encompassing bargaining structure based on mutual high-trust relations with the LO unions.

Trade unions

Trade union density, which has stabilized around 56–57 percent since 1980, is high in international perspective, but significantly lower than in other Scandinavian countries (Visser, 1991), partly reflecting the fact that unemployment insurance is organized by the state (Rothstein, 1992). Transformation of employment, occupations, and skill structures has caused considerable shifts in organizational patterns (Hernes, 1991).

The Norwegian Confederation of Trade Unions (LO), traditionally organizing blue-collar workers, is still the dominant union force in Norway, owing to its hegemony in core manufacturing industries. LO-affiliated unions covered roughly 54 percent of unionized workers in the labour force in 1994. LO consists of 28 different unions with a total membership of 790 000 members in 1995, of which roughly 73 percent were

17 In practice, the central interlocutors of KS are bargaining cartels of unions from the main confederations and the teachers' association, but individual unions may in principle also be entitled to bargain independently. Moreover, the unions with the bargaining cartels in the municipal sector can break away, whereas cartels in the state sector can bind the individual unions.

occupationally active (Stokke, 1995: 7–8). Nearly 60 percent of LO members are located in private sector, but membership in the public sector is steadily increasing and a growing share of LO membership is women (44 percent).

The two other confederations, AF and YS, which were established in the late 1970s, had 238 000 and 210 000 members, respectively, in 1994 (of which 84 000 were pensioners, students, or self-employed) (Stokke, 1995: 5–7). Together with a number of independent associations, such as teachers, journalists, and policemen, unions outside LO represent roughly one-fourth of employees. Since 1980, LO's share of employees has fallen from 38 to 31 percent (1994), while AF and YS's joint proportion has grown from 10 to 20 percent and the share of independent unions has decreased slowly to about 6 percent in 1994 (Stokke, 1995: 11). About two-thirds of the members of AF and YS are employed in the growing public sector. While AF mainly recruits among academics and well-educated professionals, the membership of YS is based in female-dominated, semi-skilled occupations with low and medium wages in the public sector. LO and AF mainly organize different segments of the labour market, whereas the boundaries between LO and YS in the public sector are blurred, often leading to competition and rivalry. LO-affiliated unions are largely organized on a sectoral and industrial basis, though with some elements of occupational and craft unions. LO has, both formally and in practice, strong central authority with a decisive role in determining the unions' policy as to collective bargaining and industrial action. Strong central power is combined with significant decentralized trade union functions: local bargaining at firm level is integrated into the negotiating system; central agreements usually have to be approved in a ballot of all union members; and local unions play an important role in co-determination and health and safety work at firm level. Thus, as pointed out by Kjellberg (1992), union structure is both more centralized and more decentralized than is the case in most other European countries. This enables articulation and coherence between different levels of union policy (Dølvik and Stokland, 1992; Crouch, 1993).

Declining relative membership, changing occupational and career patterns, and competition from YS and AF have prompted LO debates about organizational reform and coalition building (see Pape, 1994). To the surprise of many observers, in 1993 LO and AF signed a collaboration agreement covering industrial policies, protection of employee rights, research and education, equal rights and family issues, although collective bargaining was not included. As a result, AF has withdrawn from its European confederation, CESI, and achieved membership of the NFS

(Nordic Trade Union Council) and the ETUC (European Trade Union Confederation). There has also been continuous discussion about affiliation of certain unions for semi-skilled health personnel belonging to YS.

The basis of contestation between LO and YS is mainly ideological. YS actively opposes the links between LO and the Labour Party, whereas AF and LO have conflicting views on wage equality and the economic benefits of education.

Political change, increased fluidity of the electorate, and the relative decline of LO membership have led to suggestions that the Labour Party will search for a broader social basis and greater autononomy vis-à-vis LO (Sivesind et al., 1995). Conversely, forces within LO have called for greater independence from the Labour Party. The possibility of collectively affiliating LO members to the Labour Party has been abandoned, but close collaboration and consultation on most policy areas continue. LO is represented on the party executive and on joint committees at every level, and the leaderships of the unions and the Labour Party meet every week for consultation in the so-called Cooperation Committee. This privileged access to the decision-making centres of the state-bearing party has bolstered LO's power and been an important prerequisite for the maintenance of centralized collective bargaining and economic policy concertation. The central role of LO has, however, been increasingly questioned by the unions and political forces being kept on the fringes of these corporatist networks.

Regulative frames of collective bargaining

In international comparison Norway usually ranks highly as regards the degree of centralization, encompassingness, and articulation of collective bargaining (Crouch, 1993; Visser and Ebbinghaus, 1992: 212–213; Traxler, 1994: 175). Negotiations take place at the peak inter-sectoral level, at industry level, and locally at the workplace in the private sector, enhancing vertical and horizontal integration.

Collective agreements are legally binding for the signing parties. The framework of negotiations and institutions for mediation, arbitration, and dispute management is regulated by collective labour law. The National Wage Board, whose representatives are appointed by employers, trade unions, and the state, as well as the National Mediator act as neutral third parties enhancing compromise both between and within collective organizations (Høgsnes, 1995: 6).

The Basic Agreements in the main sectors complement legislation by defining overall aims, principles, and procedural rules. This includes the Peace duty and a broad set of issues such as the rights of shop-stewards, working time, work organization, employee participation, information and consultation, introduction of new technology and training, often substantiating minimum standards set by legislation. Norway has no statutory minimum wage, but the LO–NHO settlements establish income "floors" at branch level. Collective bargaining not only covers pay and working conditions, but often includes issues of social policy such as occupational pension rights, sickness absence and leave arrangements.

Although *erga omnes* procedures for the extension of collective agreements have been unknown in Norwegian labour relations, private employers are bound to apply the terms of collective agreements also to their non-organized employees, in accordance with labour law. In addition, employers not bound by any collective agreements are generally assumed to apply the terms defined by the appropriate settlement, although little research has been conducted on the subject. In the state sector, the terms of collective agreements cover all employees, in accordance with parliamentary decision, while in the municipal sector norms for equal treatment imply that derogations from collective bargaining outcomes are unacceptable. Survey data among employees indicate a level of coverage of collective agreements in the private sector of 60 percent, while coverage is substantially higher in private manufacturing and lower in private services (Hippe and Nergaard, 1992; Traxler, 1994). Although additional research is needed to establish more precisely the coverage rate in the private sector, comparison of survey data from Denmark and Norway suggests remarkable similarities despite the higher union density in Denmark (Olsen, 1995; Scheuer, 1996).

As a response to the internal market and the EEA agreement, trade unions called for legislation allowing generalization of collective agreements. With the purpose of inhibiting "social dumping" by foreign companies, an act enabling the imposed extension of collective agreements was adopted in 1993, allowing signatory parties of an agreement to claim that all employees within a certain area/industry should be covered by its minimum terms (Holo and Dølvik, 1994: 430). The final decision is taken by a Collective Agreement Board appointed by the government and the social partners. So far the provisions have not been tested in practice, but it represents an interesting example of international market deregulation actually causing national re-regulation of labour markets (Traxler and Schmitter, 1994).

Workplace democracy and micro corporatism

Workplace participation and cooperation on productivity issues have been integrated parts of post-war Norwegian labour relations. Through the Cooperation Agreement of 1966 (part of the Basic Agreement between NAF/NHO and LO), cooperation committees, or works councils, were established. Made up of plant management and shop stewards, they are supposed to consult on the financial situation of the enterprise, investments, changes in production systems, product markets, etc. Later on, agreements concerning the introduction of data technology, work organization, training, and consultation in groups were included and in 1996 an agreement on the implementation of the EU directive on "European Works Councils" was added. Inspired by the socio-technical school, experimental schemes for workplace cooperation, employee involvement, and self-determining groups were launched in the metal industry in the 1960s, although with limited dispersion effect (Bakke and Borgen, 1988, 1991). Later the parties set up schemes for promoting projects and competence in negotiated restructuring at company and industry level (HFB) (see Bosch, Chapter 7).

Board-level participation was established under the Joint Stock Company Act of 1973, based on a two-tier system of representation, with employees holding one-third of the seats at each level. The Work Environment Act of 1977 extended existing schemes of employee participation through the working of environment committees and safety delegates.

Unlike the unions in other Nordic countries, unions in Norway have not given priority to economic democracy through worker ownership or wage-earner funds. In contrast to Sweden, the unions in Norway never really challenged employer prerogatives and private ownership, which is presumably part of the explanation of the continued consensus between employers and unions. In recent years, however, the issues of funds, profit-sharing, and employee shares have been raised more frequently in relation to discussions about capital formation and the institutionalization of national ownership structures.

The local foundation of cooperative labour relations, especially in private industry, is important when discussing the future of Norwegian corporatism. Close ties between the local, industrial, and central level might suggest that decentralization drives and a stronger focus on supply-side issues in a "micro-corporatist" fashion may be incorporated into the system without disruptive effects. At the local level, pragmatic collaboration has facilitated large-scale restructuring, although recent studies suggest that labour participation has contributed more by avoiding and containing conflict than by influencing the content of change, which appears to be management driven (Hammer et al., 1994). In the public sector, and in local government in particular, workplace cooperation has proved more difficult owing to the complex politicized employer structure.

It is often argued that the cooperative Norwegian enterprise culture provides a competitive advantage, but in recent years increasing criticism has been voiced by employers and management-oriented scholars (Reve, 1994; NHO, 1995). According to Reve, the Norwegian model of enterprise interest-partnership has undermined the strategic role of ownership and created an inward-oriented culture with a focus on distribution and compromise, thereby inhibiting learning, flexibility, and development of external relations to markets, customers, and suppliers (1994: 582). (The issue of work organization and flexibility is discussed in more depth by Bosch in Chapter 7).

The institutionalization of collective bargaining, 1950–1986

Different models of collective bargaining have been used over the past 50 years.[18] In the early post-war reconstruction, collective bargaining was restrained by state regulations, but during the 1950s industry bargaining developed under tight central control.

Throughout the 1960s the corporatist features of Norwegian labour relations were gradually institutionalized. In 1962 a tripartite Contact Committee between government and the main organizations was set up to serve as a forum for informal discussions about wage negotiations, with purposes similar to the German Concerted Action. The Contact Committee was complemented by the Technical Reporting Committee on Income Settlement of 1967, which plays an important role in defining an authorized and mutually accepted framework of facts and judgements of the economic situation and price and wage developments (Compston, 1995: 107; Fagerberg et al., 1992: 3).[19]

Pay rounds in the 1960s followed a pattern that was later formalized in the so-called "Aukrust model", according to which "responsible" wage growth was determined by the growth of world market prices and productivity in the exposed sectors of the economy (Aukrust, 1977; Fagerberg et al., 1992: 4). Hence national bargainers had to take primary account of the competitiveness of exposed sectors, and negotiations in protected sectors had to stick to that. Normally the export-based iron and metal workers' union started off negotiations, setting the pace for subsequent agreements. According to Colin Crouch's sweeping study of corporatism in Europe, this model is a proto-typical example of how

18 An overview of pay rounds is provided in Appendix Table A.15.

19 Although YS and AF have been included in the Contact Committee, they are not yet part of the Technical Reporting Committee on Income Settlement.

encompassing unions with strong central authority and dominant exposed-industry unions are capable of internalizing product market externalities in their bargaining policies (Crouch, 1993: 19–20).

The high point of Norwegian incomes policies was reached with the so-called "combined" settlements of 1975–1977 in which the Labour government participated directly by providing inter alia tax concessions, transfers, pension contributions, and price subsidies. In the early 1970s, LO redefined the concept of solidaristic wage policies from emphasizing "equal pay for equal work" to giving priority to the aim of reducing wage differentials between all categories of employees, implying an explicit low-wage profile (Hanisch and Høgsnes, 1988, in Høgsnes, 1995: 15). Real pay increased in the mid 1970s by an average of 5 percent per annum, a figure not achieved before or since, and according to Frøland (1992: 57) the state in effect paid for between 40 and 60 percent of the 1974–1978 settlements. This peak era of concertation culminated in compulsory arbitration and a price and wage freeze imposed by the Labour government in 1978 (Høgsnes, 1995: 9).

In 1980, the state pursued tax reform for higher incomes and LO and NAF agreed on a "low-wage guarantee", co-financed by employees and affected employers. This secured upward levelling of wages across sectors through specific pay increases for groups earning less than 85 percent of the average in manufacturing, while LO for its part accepted a ceiling on wage drift. This "deal" became a major source of tension throughout the 1980s.

From 1981 the Labour government made clear that the parties could no longer rely on direct state contributions, and during the subsequent neo-liberal wave under conservative governments (1982–1986) the state withdrew from tripartite concertation. Tendencies to decentralization, wage drift, and leap-frogging triggered erosion of the central bargaining system and wage–price inflation soared. During this phase employers pledged market adaptation of wages and tried to get rid of the "low-wage guarantee", which eventually led to a major confrontation in 1986.

In the 1986 industrial bargaining round, started off by the metal sector, the employers (NAF and MVL) pursued an unprecedented strategy of confrontation. The trade unions demanded equalization of blue- and white-collar working time, whereas the employers claimed abolition of the low-wage guarantee and pledged that only local, market-related wage increases should be awarded. After negotiations quickly reached deadlock, the employers imposed a general lockout, to which the unions responded with massive strike action, before agreement was reached through mediation. The employers, organizationally and politically unprepared for a large-scale conflict, suffered a major defeat, which severely impaired their political credibility. In a situation of overheated labour markets and severe imbalances in the Norwegian economy, owing to falling oil prices, the employers had to accept wage increases and a reduction of the normal working week (to 37.5 hours). Moreover, with some amendments the low-wage guarantee was maintained at branch level, although the parties agreed that the fund should be reduced over a six-year period (NOU, 1987: 26 17–18).

Surprisingly, the neo-liberal wind and state withdrawal (1982–1986) did not lead to increased wage inequalities, according to Høgsnes (1995: 17–18). The trade unions managed to continue the low-wage profile on settlements, leading to increased convergence of agreements both within and across sectors, suggesting that the combined impact of equity norms and institutionalized patterns of coordinated bargaining and dispute management ensured continuity of solidaristic policies, despite decentralization and state non-intervention (Høgsnes, 1995: 19–23).

Dispute resolution and state interventionism

As mentioned, Norway is distinguished by greater state presence in collective bargaining and dispute resolution than is Sweden, reflecting according to some observers a more fragmented organizational structure in Norway (Sivesind et al., 1995). Since the 1970s, Norwegian negotiations have tended to oscillate between central and industry-level negotiations, complemented in some industries by local bargaining, and the form of state intervention has varied with the economic cycle, suggesting that collective bargaining has served as an integrated part of the system of macroeconomic governance in times of crisis. Periods of economic expansion with huge wage drift – as in the mid-1970s and mid-1980s – have been followed by periods of austerity and wage laws, as under the Labour government in the late 1970s and late 1980s. Central "deals" with the main social partners have played a vital role in securing acceptance for such state-imposed solutions.

Another important feature of the state's role in collective bargaining has been dispute management. Industrial action concerning the interpretation, content, or application of a collective agreement (dispute over rights) is unlawful and can be taken to the Labour Court, which is assigned to handle breaches of collective labour law. Industrial action is permitted only in disputes associated with negotiations over the terms of a new or revised agreement (dispute over interest), provided certain rules concerning notification and mediation are followed. In local, company bargaining, usually complementing centrally agreed terms, strikes are prohibited, while "go slows" under certain conditions are allowed.

In a dispute over interest any work stoppage has to be notified to the national mediator, and in practice mediation is obligatory before industrial action is initiated. Voluntary mediation can also be chosen if negotiations are deadlocked. When a bargaining result has been reached or a mediation proposal has been put forward in the bi-annual main negotiations, it is usually voted on by the union members through a ballot.

A distinctive feature of the Norwegian collective bargaining system is the frequent use of compulsory arbitration, where, in accordance with statutory parliamentary decisions, the dispute is transferred to the National Wage Board. Although this is not a new phenomenon, growing militancy among particularist organizations outside the LO–NHO area, especially in the offshore sector, has reinforced such practices in recent years in order to prevent erosion of solidaristic wage policies. This policy has led to numerous claims to the ILO for breaches of international conventions.

The frequent use of compulsory arbitration and mediation presumably contributes to the low degree of overt industrial conflict in Norway. In particular, the authority, legitimacy, and increasing use of the mediator institution enhance compromise and help avoid struggle between the organizations and between leaderships and rank-and-file members (Høgsnes, 1995: 6). As a neutral actor, supposed to protect societal interests and take account of what is conceived as fair outcomes, the mediator is very careful to propose more favourable solutions to groups that are not content with the pattern set by previous agreements (ibid.: 20). The National Wage Board usually behaves similarly — often punishing groups that have initiated conflict – which suggests that these institutions tend to preserve the solidaristic legacy of coordinated pattern bargaining, partly offsetting the advantage of market-based bargaining power for particularistic sections of the workforce.

This pattern of dispute management may have had several consequences. The most evident is the social order function, by preventing external groups from breaking the frameworks set by the main LO–NHO actors. To some degree this could be conceived as a functional equivalent to statutory *erga omnes* procedures in other European countries and a compensatory mechanism for the declining encompassingness of the peak associations. Another possible effect is trade union overbidding and opportunistic behaviour, which can be helpful in accommodating tensions in the unions but might reinforce ritualistic aspects of bargaining and reduce the parties' responsibility for reaching agreement on their own. Whether such features will weaken the credibility of the centralized bargaining system is indeed a central question for the future. A currently proposed reform of the Labour Dispute Act, however, apparently implies a higher threshold for compulsory arbitration, and the resolution of major industrial conflicts in the 1996 pay round without recourse to state intervention may suggest a normalization of Norwegian dispute management.[20]

From crisis to "solidarity pact" – the revival of corporatism since 1986

In the aftermath of the crisis in 1986, trade union leaderships played a committed role in the economic policy shift, leading to wage restraint, incomes policies, and wage laws prohibiting increases beyond the LO–NAF settlements. After a cautious return to normalcy, the employer and LO leaderships have committed themselves to continuing moderate wage policies within the framework of a five-year "solidarity pact" (1993–1997) in order to improve employment and competitiveness.

The interim pay round in 1987 led to the conclusion of an exceptional "no wage increase" agreement between LO and NAF, but local wage drift prevailed (8.5 percent among manufacturing workers).

In the 1988 main bargaining round the LO unions offered pay moderation on condition that no other groups should win excessive settlements. Acting in concordance with LO and NAF, the social democratic government passed a statutory pay freeze prohibiting wage drift, which was approved by parliament. This policy was continued in 1989.

When the income regulation expired in 1990, LO and NHO agreed centrally on a limited across-the-board pay increase with certain measures to help the low paid. Within this framework, local and industry-level bargaining was allowed within fixed time limits and strict guidelines for local wage adjustments from the employer side. LO members finally voted for the settlement after mediation, following an initial grass roots rejection. Thus the 1990 pay round reintroduced multi-tier bar-

---

20 Currently an officially appointed Labour Law Commission has suggested reform of the Labour Dispute Act aimed at reducing the need for compulsory arbitration and thereby complying better with ILO conventions. One reform is a proposal for stricter principles of inderogability, implying that agreements signed by one of the main confederations cannot be deviated from by independent unions (NOU 1996: 14). If adopted this would strengthen the role of confederations, as well as urging stronger internal coordination and more central decision-making power in issues of collective bargaining and industrial action in AF and YS, presumably reducing the scope for independent unions in areas with a confederal presence. In the municipal sector it is suggested that the votes of individual unions can be coupled within each confederation, as in the state sector. As opposition is signalled from both unions outside LO and several parties, it is, however, difficult to judge whether the proposals will be enacted. In any case they reflect the desire of the main actors to bolster the position of the confederations in order to avoid wage competition and maintain solidaristic wage policies.

gaining, combining strict central control with limited decentralization.

This marked a careful return to normalcy, and the two sides of industry confirmed their commitment to continue along the path of wage moderation. The following pay rounds in 1991, 1992, and 1993, stuck to this pattern, maintaining low nominal wage increases and a low-wage profile. This applied also to the 1994 bargaining round, for the first time since 1986 conducted at industry level, although under tight supervision by the peak associations. During the revival of incomes policies, the state has contributed to collective bargaining directly through co-financing negotiated schemes for early retirement, and indirectly by increasing parental leave and introducing a time-account system for parents and public measures to reduce unemployment.

Due to these joint efforts, relative wage costs were brought down considerably in 1988–1994 and the competitiveness of Norwegian manufacturing has been improved.

The "solidarity alternative"

In 1991 the Labour government appointed an Employment Commission with representatives from all political parties, LO, and NHO, supplemented by professional economists and ministerial experts. The Commission, chaired by Per Kleppe, former Norwegian Minister of Finance and General Secretary of EFTA, submitted its report in 1992, entitled "A national strategy for increased employment in the 1990s" (Norwegian Employment Commission, 1992).[121]

In order to bring unemployment down to around 3.0–3.5 percent, a five-year social pact, the so-called "solidarity alternative", was proposed, comprising the following main elements:

- A programme for *wage formation and incomes policy cooperation* whereby cost competitiveness should be improved by about 10 percent during the five years from 1993 to 1997, though securing some real wage increases.[22]

21 A short version in English is available (Norwegian Employment Commission, 1992).

22 The focus on nominal wage moderation binding all societal groups partly reflected Norway's poor productivity growth (Norwegian Employment Commission, 1992: 43): "The best we can hope for in the 1990s may be a productivity performance broadly in line with that of competitor countries." To ensure appropriate wage settlements, the Commission proposed that central negotiations should focus on defining frames of total wage growth, while much of the agreed increases could be negotiated at the local level, in accordance with strict principles agreed between the parties, related to the companies' economic situation, results, productivity, prospects, and competitiveness (ibid.: 46).

- A review of the *composition of public expenditure* with a view to reducing transfer payments, thus creating scope for active measures to increase employment.
- *Structural policy measures*, including an examination of the legal and institutional framework of labour markets, industrial policy, and measures in the areas of labour, social security, and education, aimed at reducing the equilibrium rate of unemployment and preventing labour market exclusion.
- *Active labour market policy* to reduce actual unemployment and enhance skill formation.
- *Macroeconomic* foundations in line with current orthodoxy, assuming fixed-exchange-rate policies, low inflation, and sound budgetary policies. In short, the formula was that monetary policy should stabilize the exchange rate, fiscal policy economic activity, while incomes policies should control inflation. Supplementary reports argued for a strengthening of the so-called *"working-line"* in social policies and cuts of transfers.

The "solidarity alternative" was a strong expression of the broad national consensus and commitment of the main social partners to continuing cooperation within the framework of a "re-nationalized corporatist" approach (Dølvik, 1994). In line with a strategy of "political exchange", the increased value of trade unions' capacity to deliver wage restraint has been skilfully exploited by LO to obtain ambitious labour market policies and a guarantee that major welfare schemes (e.g. the sick pay system) will be maintained. Up to 1995 the main partners stuck to their commitments and by 1996 the results in terms of employment were over-fullfilled, facilitated by growth rates far beyond the Commission's assumptions. However, devaluations and wage restraint in other European countries have made improved cost competitiveness harder to achieve (it has actually declined since 1994) and there are signs of growing dissatisfaction from unions outside LO and from the political opposition, complaining that the "solidarity alternative" grants LO a too powerful position.

Owing to wage moderation and depreciation of the Norwegian currency until 1994, cost competitiveness was substantially improved. Because of declining interest rates and inflation, workers have still benefited from growing real wages. Since 1988 the gap in relative manufacturing wage costs between Norway and its main trading partners decreased steadily from 25 percent to 7 percent in 1994, but increased 2 percent in 1995 partly owing to currency appreciation (NOU 1996:4: 44). Reflecting the public social security system, indirect labour costs are comparatively low in Norway (under 30 percent of total wage costs). Adding that international comparison of relative wage costs does not include functionary wages – which are low in Norway – the Technical Reporting Committee assumes that total wage costs in Norwegian manufacturing largely correspond to those of itsmain trading partners (ibid.: 68).[23] Measured in relative wage costs per produced unit (RLPE), however, the competitiveness of Norwegian manufacturing improved less (2.5 percent) in 1988–1994, reflecting weaker productivity growth than achieved by its trade partners, whereas in 1995 RLPE rose significantly (ibid.: 43).[24] RLPE is, however, an increasingly contested indicator of competitiveness. Measured in export market shares, Norwegian competitiveness improved significantly in 1988–1994, increasing by some 10 percent, whereas domestic market shares have continued to decline, which seems to be a general international trend accompanying economic integration (NOU 1996:4: 38–39).

8. Prospects for continuity and change

The macroeconomic turnaround and the revival of centralized concertation since the late 1980s have parallels with the post-war national reconstruction. The labour movement took responsibility for handling a national crisis and demonstrated its capacity to govern, manage the economy, and generate loyalty, despite its shrinking constituencies. This led to vitalization of a traditional deed of the Norwegian model, notably the primacy of internationally exposed traded goods sectors within a framework of solidaristic wage policies.

The Norwegian policy turn lends support to Katzenstein's thesis that "small states" with corporatist systems of governance benefit from comparative advantages through their flexibility in tackling external imbalances and competitive pressures in an internationalized economy

23 In 1995, the total wage costs of Norwegian manufacturing measured in Norwegian currency (NOK 148 per hour) were similar to costs in the Netherlands and Denmark. Germany, West (193), Switzerland (175), Belgium (162), and Austria (153) had higher costs, while Sweden (133), the USA (121), and the UK (96) had substantially lower total wage costs (NOU 1996:4: 69).

24 According to NOU (1996:4), the sluggish manufacturing productivity growth (estimated at 10 percent lower than that of its trade partners) to a large extent reflects variations in measurement methods rather than real differences (ibid.: 65). Freeman (Chapter 2) refers to OECD data suggesting that development of Norwegian manufacturing productivity has grown at a rate between the EU and the US average since the early 1980s.

(Katzenstein, 1985).[25] It also fits with comparative research suggesting that wage flexibility and economic adjustment capacity is best in countries with either a highly decentralized (USA) or a highly centralized bargaining system (see e.g. Calmfors and Driffill,1988). In the Norwegian case, a plausible hypothesis could be that the trade unions' capacity to contain wage–price inflation has more than compensated for the possible lack of labour market flexibility, which according to OECD wisdom should prompt inflation. If so, the corporatist bargaining system serves as a functional alternative to labour market deregulation.

Another implication is that, contrary to the widespread assumption that internationalization and monetary integration will undermine national "corporatisms" (Streeck, 1991, 1993), the Norwegian example might suggest that "re-nationalized" cooperative practices can be a viable strategy for coping with such pressures (Traxler and Schmitter, 1994). Although market integration is generally assumed to weaken unions, the increased attractiveness of wage restraint may conversely improve unions bargaining power in political exchange.

Instead of the predicted convergence and Europeanization of labour relations, such mechanisms may propel diversity and entrenchment of the social partnership within the confines of the nation-state. The positional thrust of such a logic of competitive national corporatisms may, however, encourage beggar-thy-neighbour policies, reinforcing international constraints on collective bargaining. Hence, national solidarity can intensify international competition (Dølvik, 1992, 1993; Mahnkopf and Altvater, 1995).

Still, from a national point of view, a key question for the future is whether or not national corporatist institutions and practices are sustainable. Internationalization might make them more attractive, but also more difficult to preserve. As noted by Wallerstein and Golden (1996), fiercer international competition, together with technological and occupational change, has been widely assumed to increase pressures towards decentralization of collective bargaining and differentiation of pay structures according to international cost structures, while reduced scope for macroeconomic policy and protection of national industries may limit

25 In a comment on Katzenstein's flexible adjustment thesis, Midttun (1990) draws attention to the effects of the specific sectoral structure in Norway. According to Midttun, the dominant "ground-rent"-based export sectors have allowed maintenance of a dual economy where large parts have actually been sheltered from foreign competition, partly bolstering a kind of super-corporatism, partly harming adjustment in non-ground-rent-based exposed sectors, suggesting that Katzenstein's thesis needs modification in order to grasp Norwegian dynamics.

the state's capacity to provide full employment as an input in political exchange (Notermans, 1995).

Recent comparative research, however, does not lend much support to the universal decentralization thesis (see e.g. Ferner and Hyman, 1992; Wallerstein and Golden, 1996: 4; Traxler, 1994: 186). Decentralization has occurred in some countries, most notably in the UK and the USA, while centralized bargaining prevails in most OECD countries and has even become more entrenched in some countries (Traxler, 1994: 186). It seems that the radical decentralization in the USA and UK was the outcome of the political agendas of government, rather than of structural change in working life (Wallerstein and Golden, 1996: 31). In the Nordic context, where pressures towards decentralization presumably should be most visible, substantial decentralization has occurred only in Sweden and not in the other Nordic countries (ibid.: 4). In the Swedish case it was the confederal employers' association (SAF) that withdrew from collective bargaining, although it should be noted that sectoral bargaining continues. Several studies suggest that this change was due to unique Swedish conditions (ibid.: 30; Martin, 1994). First, there was a strong employer desire to undermine the political strength of LO, the only Nordic trade union confederation that had seriously challenged managerial prerogatives.[26] Second, the driving force behind SAF's withdrawal was apparently the large and powerful Swedish multinational companies. In Norway such companies are few and often partly state owned.

In the Norwegian case several factors may facilitate the continuity of established institutions and practices. First, the Norwegian economy has for long been highly internationalized, the export/import ratio has in fact been fairly stable since the 1950s, and it is questionable how much the single market actually adds to already existing competition. Given the adjustments pursued since 1986, a plausible hypothesis might be that the Norwegian system of labour relations is already well accustomed to coping with the "new international circumstances".

Second, the Norwegian system of collective bargaining is embedded in a dense web of formal and informal relations between the main actors, institutions, and social surroundings, suggesting that norms of conduct and justice enhance continuity rather than change (Høgsnes, 1995: 3). The relative success, mutual interdependency, trust, and personal attachments of key organized actors suggest that none of the main organiza-

26 By promoting a concept of wage-earner funds eventually providing organized labour with majority ownership of all large companies, the Swedish LO, in contrast to its Norwegian counterpart, seemed to break with the legacy of class compromise.

tions has strong incentives to defect from current cooperation, and the costs of withdrawal might be considerable. The corporatist institutions, furthermore, effectively constrain tendencies to free-ride or exit from the existing order by groups benefiting from market-based power (Høgsnes, 1995: 20).

Third, strong public finances provide incentives for organized actors to continue corporatist cooperation with the state. Fourth, despite Norway's comparatively compressed wage structures (OECD, 1995a; Kahn, 1996) and proclaimed tendencies of increased individualization and group identification, opinion polls have suggested that the solidaristic legacy based on wage moderation has enjoyed quite broad public support. Before the 1996 pay round, 54 percent supported continued wage moderation, while 28 percent disagreed (Opinion, 1996). Nearly 63 percent of the adult population thought that wage differentials between top leaders and ordinary employees were too big, while 24 percent found them appropriate (Opinion, 1995).[27]

There are, however, factors that might point in other directions. First, in recent pay rounds professional groups have campaigned for realignment of relative pay structures claimed to disadvantage semi- and high-skilled occupations in the public sector. An AF strike in 1995, stalled by compulsory arbitration, caused acrimonious rifts between the AF and LO leaderships, with the AF accusing LO of illegitimate use of power and reference to the "solidarity alternative" to constrain outside unions' "right to free bargaining". Such events, reinforced by AF's determination to break with wage moderation and the low-wage profile during the main bargaining round in 1996, partly supported by YS, have raised the temperature and suggest that solidaristic wage policies might be more seriously challenged in the years ahead. As indicated, in recent years pursuit of wage moderation has required some use of force to discipline outside unions (Høgsnes, 1995: 10), leading LO and NHO to call for restrictions on who is allowed to take industrial action in order to curb free-riders. Even though AF public unions have limited conflict power and LO commands superior bargaining strength, the legitimacy and ability of LO and NHO to mastermind wage determination may be subject to erosion.

A second uncertain factor is the loyalty of business in supporting the employer leadership's commitment to the "solidarity alternative". Employers face the dilemma of, on the one hand, taking wages out of

27 In a recent poll by Opinion (June 1996), as much as 79 percent of the electorate supported continued wage moderation and, ranking different demands for collective bargaining, only 14 percent wanted higher wages, while 46 percent preferred reduced retirement age and 15 percent retraining and education (Opinion, 1996).

competition and obtaining cost control by means of centralized agreements. On the other hand, shortages of skilled labour and wishes to increase flexibility and differentiate wages as part of company human resource management, may strengthen pressures for more relaxed frameworks and decentralized bargaining within the employer camp. Improved profitability and soaring exports in recent years may also tend to reduce employer concerns with labour costs in favour of securing stable production and eliminating regulatory obstacles to labour utilization. In this respect the "solidarity alternative" might be seen as an uncomfortable straightjacket.

In recent years employers have repeatedly called for the abolition of low-wage guarantees, more relaxed regulations on the disposal of labour, and flexibilization of working time, without success. On the other hand, NHO has pursued strict control of local bargaining to avoid undue wage drift. Still, although employers, after their humiliating defeat and loss of credibility in 1986 and subsequent scandals,[28] had obvious interests in joining forces with the Labour government and union leaderships during the turbulent period of economic adjustment and EU membership struggle, it seems more uncertain whether they have equally strong incentives to continue along this path under the current recovery.

In a recent NHO discussion document on future labour relations in the era of internationalization, drafted by a fairly high-ranking NHO working group, the Norwegian system of labour regulations and collective bargaining is heavily criticized (NHO, 1995). According to the document the current tariff system is "an inherently conservationary force", inhibiting adequate human resource policies, encouraging free-riding, constraining working-time flexibility, and raising costs; and in general enhancing compromise and labour peace to the detriment of required change that might imply conflict. Accordingly, a fundamental overhaul of labour law and the collective bargaining system is recommended, emphasizing thorough decentralization to enterprise level; individualization of pay systems; increased scope for individually or collectively negotiated derogations from agreements; while the central sectoral and confederal agencies should delimit their role to draw up broad framework agreements on overriding principles and serve as competence centres providing support to enterprise actors. It does not seem very likely that

28 Under the pay round of 1992 it was revealed that, during the period of strict wage control, NHO had granted its fired managing director an unprecedented "golden parachute", severely harming the public credibility of the association. In 1996 it was revealed that the NHO President Schnitler had achieved a lucrative option deal in his company, again harming the credibility of NHO's plea for wage moderation.

such a radical approach will gain support in the executive NHO bodies in the immediate term, but the document clearly signals that diverging views are evolving inside the employer camp. The 1996 pay round pursued at industry level, with work stoppages in a situation of high demand, may have strengthened forces favouring decentralization of bargaining to company level. If trade unions cannot any longer deliver centralized wage restraint, the commitment of NHO leaderships to the "solidarity alternative" is likely to wither.

Third, on the trade union side, LO has been committed to maintaining wage moderation and giving priority to qualitative social reforms associated with rights to early retirement, vocational training, reduced working time and the like, combined with a lifting of low-paid groups, with particular focus on women. There are, however, developments that might indicate adjustment of policies. As the result of a long-standing strive for organizational reform, the LO unions, as in Denmark, have embarked upon a process of cartelization, implying that a number of tasks will be transferred from LO to sectoral bodies. The purpose is *inter alia* to become more responsive to the occupational and qualitative concerns of the memberships, enhance recruitment, and possibly also facilitate coalition-building with outside unions (Pape, 1994). Although the principal aim of bargaining will be settled at confederal level, an increased role for sectoral cartels in negotiations may encourage some decentralization and differentiation of bargaining. Accumulated needs to modernize agreements, adjust pay structures, bolster the role of individual union leaderships, and improve recruitment attractivity might pull in the same direction. A more critical interpretation is therefore that cartelization might reinforce sectoral rivalry and weaken the authority of LO in bargaining coordination (Fennefoss, 1994). Owing to impatience among the rank-and-file of the largest manufacturing union (Fellesforbundet), centralized cross-sectoral bargaining could not be sustained in the main 1996 pay round, which consequently was conducted at industry level, though within centrally coordinated frameworks.

A fourth factor causing uncertainty is the impact of the strong recovery of the Norwegian economy. Although Norwegian wage policy has always built on a concept of "solidarity within one class", rather than redistribution between wages and profits, the acceptance of wage moderation in recent years was facilitated by economic downturn and unacceptable levels of unemployment. From 1988 to 1995, however, capital's share of GDP increased substantially. With a prospering economy, soaring company profits, golden "option deals" for top leaders, rising surpluses on public budgets, and recovering labour markets, the willingness of trade unions to persist with moderate wage policies might easily evaporate.

The 1996 pay round, started off by the metal sector, brought a number of industrial conflicts in the private sector, leading to the largest growth in real wages since the 1970s, on average 2.25–2.75 percent according to the Ministry of Finance (Stortingsmelding 2, 1995–1996: 50). In the metal sector, an agreement reached by mediation and recommended by the parties[29] was rejected by union members in a ballot, prompting the most far-reaching private sector strike since the 1930s. The strike demonstrated the increased effectiveness and international impact of industrial action in a context of transnational just-in-time production. According to employer sources, cancellation of Norwegian deliveries rapidly threatened to damage parts of the European car industry. Concerned about loss of contracts, company management seemed unprepared for conflict and the industry employers' association also appeared uncomfortable with the stance of the confederal employers' association, which refused further concessions, possibly hoping for government intervention. The unions got support from the German IG-Metal, which promised it would see to it that Norwegian companies did not lose their contract status, apparently weakening the case for government intervention. Still, the unions were unprepared for lasting conflict and a new compromise was rapidly struck after mediation, leading to some modest improvements in *inter alia* shift bonuses and pension reform (reducing the flexible retirement age from 63 to 62 in 1998 and softening the eligibility criteria), while no specific restrictions were imposed on local bargaining. The metal union leadership and the compromise outcome came under strong fire from rank-and-file militants, but the agreement was eventually ratified by membership ballot.

The grassroots rejection of the initial settlement, considered to be the most favourable since the mid-1970s, reflected accumulated disaffection with wage moderation among the metal workers. During the phase of centralized incomes policies, they had several times voted against agreements, but been bogged down by a majority in private sector LO unions. Golden management "options" and a call for higher management wages during the conflict fuelled discontent. Furthermore, the state and the municipal sector had granted their employees a generous flat pay rise of NOK 6000 (roughly 4 percent) with considerable scope for additional

29 The recommended agreement provided for: a flat pay rise of NOK 1.50, which, together with "overhang" and local bargaining (not covering all), was estimated to provide a total wage rise of some 3 percent for LO members; reduced flexible retirement age from 64 to 63 years, paid for by employers, for strictly specified groups; and agreement to start discussion over reform of life-long training. Employer demands for the abolition of the low-wage gurantee and extended frameworks of the normal working day from 17.00 to 21.00 were not successful.

central and local adjustments, which was celebrated by public sector unions as a principal breakthrough in the improvement of their relative wages. In the service industry, hotel and restaurant workers had pursued a successful strike leading to an almost equally good agreement. Thus a dynamic of rising expectations and comparison of relative wage increases across sectors had been unleashed, whereas the traditional pace-setting role of the traded goods sector seemed challenged by the agreements in the public sector and private services.[30]

The 1996 pay round thus deviated from past policies of centralized wage moderation. Trade unions, coordinating claims across sectors, won through with central social demands such as a reduced flexible pension age and the principle of life-long training, on top of substantial real wage growth, especially for low-paid groups. Whether the 1996 pay round represents a one-year exception to release accumulated tension among unions and employees or represents a turn towards tougher union wage policies remains to be seen. The pay increases indeed went far beyond the criteria of the "solidarity alternative", but compared with recent growth in the economy and the profitability of Norwegian companies a one-off 4 percent pay rise should presumably not present any major problem.

A striking feature of the 1996 pay round was that the government itself apparently acknowledged the need to let off steam among public sector unions and employees. By recognizing their demand to catch up with private sector and offer ample scope for adjusting pay structures in local bargaining, the growing dissatisfaction and rivalry of public sector unions were replaced by unitary celebration. Adding that the main private sector strikes were settled without damaging effects and state intervention, the 1996 pay round can be interpreted as a necessary adjustment mechanism to stabilize the Norwegian system of labour relations (Høgsnes, 1996). Such collectively accepted one-year exceptions might be regarded as a functional prerequisite for the maintenance of the otherwise overly rigid centralized bargaining system. An opposite interpretation, however, is that the 1996 pay round demonstrates the inability of trade unions to sustain wage moderation in times of recovery, suggesting that the "solidarity alternative" will fall apart in coming years (Skånland, 1996). Considering also the tight labour markets, the increas-

30 Eventually, local bargaining in the metal industry led to average additional pay increases per hour around 2.50 (on top of a 1.50 basic increase), in total amounting to *ca.* NOK 8000 (more than 4 percent), thus surpassing the general public sector pay rise. Specific groups in the public sector, particularly professional categories in the health sector, however, achieved additional pay rises in central and local adjustment negotiations which many doubled the basic public sector pay increase.

ingly strong currency and reduced interest rates, the government has pleged fiscal restraint and continued wage moderation to avoid inflation and overheating of the Norwegian economy.

LO still seems committed to moderate and solidaristic wage policies but, faced with growing pressures to achieve a larger share of the cake from the membership and outside unions, the task will not be easy. The strategic response of employers will presumably be contingent on LO's policy choices, but the 1996 experiences with industry bargaining seem likely to trigger internal debate over the future employer approach. It is plausible that increased tension between confederal actors inclined to call for re-centralization and corporate advocates of decentralization will evolve.

Thus, even though the Norwegian system of labour relations has gone through a process of stabilization in recent years, there are clear signs of strain. Tensions between the traded and non-traded goods sectors, between well-educated and poorly qualified groups, between men and women, betweenpublic and private sector, accentuating conflicts between production-oriented and distribution oriented union forces, are clearly visible. The class configuration anchored in the welfare state legacy does not easily fit with the legacy of the post-war "productionist" class compromise. Such tensions are not limited to relations between LO, YS, and AF, but cut across the memberships of LO unions and cause diverse views among employers' associations as well. Controversy over issues of legitimacy and principles of justice and distribution therefore seems likely to gain in importance. A key question for the future, thus, is whether trade unions can succeed in bridging the cleavages between sector interests, occupational identification, and class solidarity, or, borrowing from Crouch, "whether the unions can succeed to replace the crumbling hegemony of exposed, manual workers' unions with something more truly encompassing of the late twentieth-century workforce" (ibid.: 291).

If not, a possible scenario could be an upsurge of inter-union rivalry and disruption of centralized cooperation, unleashing a dynamic of competing wage claims, inflation, and distributional conflict, and probably encouraging employer demands for labour market deregulation. None the less, a scenario of radical change or dismantling of the Norwegian system of labour relations does not appear likely in the near future. One of the long-standing features of the Norwegian system is the high degree of integration and close ties between central, industrial, and local levels, which have enabled considerable adaptability. Despite employer misgivings, the solid local foundation of cooperation, incorporating qualitative, supply-side issues, suggests that a relaxation of the recent centralized grip would not necessarily cause disruption of the system and might, if required, be reversed at a later stage. Even if employers turned to a more autonomous approach, it seems unlikely that they will break with the cooperative tradition and adopt a radical unilateral agenda for decentralization and conflict, such as the Swedish SAF pursued.

Furthermore, contrary to predictions of growing union rivalry and fragmentation, it could plausibly be asked whether the Norwegian system of labour relations has actually shown signs of becoming more integrated in recent years. The strengthened authority of the confederal level in AF, the cooperation agreement between LO and AF, incorporating AF into a common Nordic and European trade union framework, and the commitment of LO to integrating new "female" demands and qualitative social issues onto its agenda may signal a certain inter-union convergence. The increased strength of public sector unions in LO and the changing balance of power between the main union confederations may, as suggested by the 1996 pay round, facilitate cooperation and the negotiated realignment of pay structures and principles of distribution rather than union cleavages and warfare.

The most likely scenario thus seems to be a cautious adjustment and decentralization, closely controlled by the central corporate actors. To the degree that the Norwegian system of labour relations can demonstrate efficiency in providing collective goods not easily provided by free markets and ensure employee confidence that negotiated change can be risked without the threat of major unemployment, it may turn out to be a cornerstone of Norwegian labour market policies beyond the turn of the century.

Acknowledgements

This article is the product of a collective process in which Jon Erik Dølvik has written the final text on the basis of written input from Mona Bråten (6.), Frode Longva (4. and 5.) and Arild H. Steen (3.). We have benefited from extensive comments by Torgeir Aarvaag Stokke, Per Kleppe, Stein Reegard, and Sverre Try and constructive advice from the international research team.

References

Arbeidsdirektoratet (1995) *Rekrutteringsundersøkelsen 1993*. Oslo: Report 1995: 7.

Arbeidsdirektoratet (1996) *Rekrutteringsundersøkelsen 1995*. Oslo: Report 1996: 2.

Arneberg, M. W. (1996) Lønner det seg å jobbe? Kompensasjonsgrader i den norske velferdsmodellen. *Økonomiske Analyser* 4/96, Statistics Norway, Oslo.

Aronsson, T. and J. R. Walker (1995) Velferdsstatens effekter på arbeidsutbudet. In R. B. Freeman et al. (eds), *Välfärdsstat i omvandling. Amerikansk perspektiv på den svenske modellen.* Stockholm: NBER-rapporten, SNS-forlag.

Aukrust, O. (1977) Inflation in the open economy: A Norwegian model. In L. B. Krause and W. S. Salent (eds), *Worldwide Inflation: Theory and Recent Experience.* Washington DC: Brookings Institution.

Bakke, N. A. and S. O. Borgen (1988) *Samarbeidsorientert bedriftsutvikling i et strategisk perspektiv.* Oslo: FAFO-rapport 79.

Bakke, N. A. and S. O. Borgen (1991) *Fagforeningsstrategier for bedriftsutvikling. Utfordringene.* Oslo: FAFO-rapport 121.

Blank, R. (1993) Does a larger social safety net mean less economic flexibility? In R. B. Freeeman (ed.), *Working under Different Rules.* New York: Russell Sage Foundation.

Bosch, G. (1995a) Die These vom Deutschen Exportschlager Arbeitsplatz ist Unsinn. *Welt am Sonntag*, No. 46.

Bosch, G. (1995b) *Flexibility and Work Organisation.* Follow up to the White Paper Growth, Competitiveness, Employment, Report of Expert Working Group, DG-V, European Commission, Brussels.

Brox, O. (1994) *Norge mot tusenårsskiftet. Arbeid for alle – eller flere rike og ny fattigdom?* Oslo: Gyldendal.

Calmfors, L. and J. Driffil (1988) Bargaining structure, corporativism and macroeconomic performance. *Economic Policy* 6: 13–61.

Calmfors, L. and A. Forslund (1991) Real wage determination and labour market policies: The Swedish experience. *Economic Journal* 101.

Calmfors, L. and H. Lang (1994) *Macroeconomic Effects of Active Labour Market Programmes in a Union Wage-setting Model.* Stockholm: Institute of International Economic Studies.

Calmfors, L. and R. Nymoen (1990) Nordic employment. *Economic Policy* 11.

Cappelen, Å. and N. M. Stølen (1995) *Forecasting Labour Market Imbalances.* Oslo: Research Department, Statistics Norway.

Card, D. and R. B. Freeman (1994) Small differences that matter: Canada vs the United States. In R. B. Freeman (ed.), *Working under Different Rules.* New York: Russell Sage Foundation.

Colbjørnsen, T. and K. A. Larsen (1995) *Arbeidsledighet i en oppgangtid.* Oslo: Arbeidsdirektoratet Rapport 1995: 6.

Compston, H. (1995) Union participation in economic policy-making in Scandinavia 1970–1993. *West European Politics* 18(1).

Crouch, C. (1993) *Industrial Relations and European State Traditions.* Oxford: Clarendon Press.

Crouch, C. (1995) Exit or voice: Two paradigms for European industrial relations after the Keynesian welfare state. *European Journal of Industrial Relations* 1(1).

Dahl, E. (1996) *Ensom og ulykkelig?* Oslo: FAFO-rapport.

Dølvik J. E. (1992) The Nordic trade unions and the dilemmas of European integration. In J. Fagerberg and L. Lundberg (eds), *European Economic Integration: A Nordic Perspective.* Aldershot: Avebury.

Dølvik, J. E. (1993) *Nordic Trade Unions and the Social Dimension of European Integration. Towards Europeanisation or Renationalisation of Trade Union Strategies?* Oslo: FAFO paper.

Dølvik, J. E. (1994) Norwegian trade unions at a cross-roads. In T. Kauppinen and V. Köykkä (eds), *Transformation of European Industrial Relations, Consequences of Integration and Disintegration.* IIRA 4th European Regional Congress, Helsinki.

Dølvik, J. E. and T. Olsen (1994) *Arbeidslivspolitikk og fagorganisering i EØS og EU.* Oslo: FAFO-notat 1994: 8.

Dølvik J. and E., and D. Stokland (1992) The Norwegian model in transition. In A. Ferner and R. Hyman (eds), *Industrial Relations in the New Europe*. Oxford: Basil Blackwell.

Eldring, L. and J. B. Grøgaard (1996) *Evaluering av næringslivets fadderordning og praksisplasstiltaket*. Oslo: FAFO-rapport 194.

Emerson, M. (1988) Regulation and deregulation of the labour market. *European Economic Review* 32: 775–817.

European Commission (1994) *Employment in Europe*. Brussels.

European Commission (1996) *Deregulation and Employment*. Brussels: DG-V, Policy Perspective Group.

Fagerberg, J., Å. Cappelen, and L. Mjøset (1992) *Structural Change and Economic Policy. the Norwegian Model under Pressure*. Oslo: NUPI Working Paper.

Fagerberg, J., Å. Cappelen, L. Mjøset, and R. Skarstein (1990) The decline of state capitalism in Norway. *New Left Review* 181 (May/June).

Fennefoss, A. (1994) *Hvor står YS etter avtalen mellom LO og AF?* Oslo: Foredrag YS, 5.1.1994.

Ferner, A. and R. Hyman (1992) Introduction. In A. Ferner and R. Hyman (eds), *Industrial Relations in the New Europe*. Oxford: Basil Blackwell.

Freeman, R. B. (1993) How labor fares in advanced economies. In R. B. Freeman (ed.), *Working under Different Rules*. New York: Russell Sage Foundation.

Frøland, H. O. (1992) Fem påstander om korporatisme som inntektspolitisk styringsmiddel i LO-NAF-området etter 1945. *Søkelys på arbeidsmarkedet*, No. 9, ISF, Oslo.

Glyn, A. (1995) The assessment: Unemployment and inequality. *Oxford Review of Economic Policy* 11(1).

Goetschy, J. (1995) *The Nordic Social Models Facing Europe*. Brussels: ETUI.

Golombek, R. (1991) *Lønnsomheten i norsk industri*. Oslo: SNF-rapport 28/91.

Grubb, D. and W. Wells (1993) Employment regulation and patterns of work in EC countries. *OECD Economic Studies*, No. 21.

Gulbrandsen, T. (1995) Fagforeninger og opplæring i private bedrifter. *Søkelys på arbeidsmarkedet*, 2/95, ISF, Oslo.

Hagen, K. (1990) *Nasjonalstat, velferdspolitikk og europeisk integrasjon*. Oslo: FAFO-rapport 104.

Hagen, K. and J. M. Hippe (1993) The Norwegian welfare state: From post-war consensus to future conflicts? In A. C. Kiel, and A. Torud, *Continuity and Change. Aspects of Contemporary Norway*. Oslo: Scandinavian University Press.

Hammer, T. H., B. Ingebrigtsen, J. I. Karlsen, and A. Svarva (1994) *Organizational Renewal: Management of Large-Scale Change in Norwegian Firms*. CAHRS Working Paper 94/21, ILR/Cornell.

Hammervold, T. and P. Heum (1993) *De største norske industrikonsernene 1975–1992. Verkst og internasjonalisering*. Oslo: SNF, Arbeidsnotat 94/1993.

Hanisch, T. (1995) En million har stått som arbeidssøkere. *Arbeiderbladet*, 30.8.1996.

Hanisch, T. and G. Høgsnes (1988) *Problemer og motsetninger i norsk inntektspolitikk 1973 til 1985*. Oslo: ISF, Rapport 88: 9.

Hernæs, E. and S. Strøm (1994) Tilbake til jobb. SNF-Bulletin, No. 4, Oslo.

Hernes, G. (1977) *Forhandlingsøkonomi og blandingsadministrasjon*. Oslo: Scandinavian University Press.

Hernes, G. (1991) The dilemmas of social democracies. The case of Norway and Sweden. *Acta Sociologica* 34.

Heum, P. (1995) Norske industriforetak og produksjon i utlandet. *SNF-Bulletin*, No. 3, Oslo.

Heum, P. and D. Stokland (1994) Internasjonalisering og nasjonal næringspolitikk – sammendrag og konklusjoner. In P. Heum and D. Stokland (eds), *Internasjonalisering og nasjonal næringspolitikk*. Oslo: FAFO-rapport 173.

Hippe, J. M. (1996) Bargaining, Politics and solidarity: A different story? A study of employment relations and occupational welfare in Norway. Doctoral thesis submitted to University of Bergen, Fafo, Oslo.

Hippe, J. M. and K. Nergaard (1992) Collective agreements coverage in Norway. Mimeo, Fafo, Oslo.

Hippe, J. M. and A. W. Pedersen (1996) The Labor movement, social policy and occupational welfare in Norway. In M. Shalev (ed.), (1996) *The Privatization of Social Policy? Welfare and the Welfare State in America, Japan and Scandinavia*. Macmillan, London.

Hødnebø, P. E., and D. Stokland (1994) *Hvor attraktivt? – Norge som lokaliseringsområde for investeringer og produksjon*. Oslo: FAFO-rapport.

Høgsnes, G. (1995) Nyliberalisme og fleksibilitet i lønnsdannelsen. *Sosiologi i dag*, No. 4.

Høgsnes, G. (1996) Lønnsoppgjøret 1996 – moderasjonslinjens endelikt? *Bergens Tidende*, kronikk 11.5.1996.

Holo, L. and J. E. Dølvik (1994) Rapport norvégien. In *Social Policies in the Community Legal Order and the European Economic Area*. XIVth Congress, International Federation for European Law, Rome.

Ingebretsen, B., P. Saksvik, and C. Vedi (1966) *Overtidsarbeid innen 11 bransjer i LO/NHO-området*. Trondheim: SINTEF-IFIM-rapport.

Jackman, R., R. Layard, and S. Nickell (1995) Structural aspects of OECD unemployment. Paper presented at OECD Conference, January.

Kahn, L. K. (1996) Against the wind: Bargaining recentralization and wage inequality in Norway 1987–91. Mimeo, Cornell University, Ithaca, NY.

Karlsen, T. K. (1991) *Fagopplæring i arbeidslivet*. Oslo: FAFO-rapport 115.

Katzenstein, P. J. (1985) *Small States in World Markets*. Ithaca, NY: Cornell University Press.

Kjellberg, A. (1992) Sweden: Can the model survive? In A. Ferner and R. Hyman (eds), *Industrial Relations in the New Europe*. Oxford: Basil Blackwell.

Kostøl, E. (1996) Interview, *Arbeiderbladet*, 21.3.96, Oslo.

Kvinge, T. (1994), *Utenlandske oppkjøp og etableringer i norsk industri*. Oslo: FAFO-rapport 162.

Kvinge, T., O. Langeland, and D. Stokland (1992) *Kampen om kapitalen – Investeringer og kapitalbevegelser i internasjonale markeder*. Oslo: FAFO-rapport 138.

Kvinge, T., L. Lindholt, and L. Støle (1996) *Nyskaping i norsk arbeidsliv*. Oslo: FAFO-rapport 191.

Larsen, K. A. (1996) *Kommunenes arbeidskraft og kompetansebehov 1992–2007*. ECON Rapport 109/94.

Larsen, K. A. (1996b) *Aldersbølgen og behovet for en seniorpolitikk i staten*. ECON Rapport 120/95.

Layard, R., S. Nickel, and R. Jackman (1991) *Unemployment*. Oxford: Oxford University Press.

LO (1995) *LO-blikk på arbeidsmarkedet*. November, Oslo.

McKinsey (1994) *Employment Performance*. Washington DC: McKinsey Global Institute.

Mahnkopf, B. and E. Altvater (1995) Transmission belts of transitional competition? Trade unions and collective bargaining in the context of European integration. *European Journal of Industrial Relations* 1(1).

Martin, A. (1994) The transformation of employment relations in Sweden. In T. Kochan, R. Locke, and M. Piore (eds), *Employment Relations in a Changing World Economy*. Boston: MIT Press.

Martin, A. and G. Ross (1995) Labor and Europe: European institutions and the precarious construction of interest representation. Paper, Harvard Center for European Studies, Boston.

Midttun, A. (1990) Norway in the 1980s: Competitive adaption or structural crisis? A comment on Katzenstein's small-state/flexible-adjustment thesis. *Scandinavian Political Studies* 13(4).

Mjøset, L., ed. (1986) *Norden Dagen Derpå*. Oslo: Scandinavian University Press.

Mjøset, L., (1992) The Nordic model never existed, but does it have future? *Scandinavian Studies* 64(4).

Mjøset, L. (1996) Nordic economic policies in the 1980s and 1990s. Paper presented to the 10th International Conference of Europeanists, Chicago, 14–16 March.

Mjøset, L., Å. Cappelen, J. Fagerberg., and B. S. Tranøy (1995) Norway: Changing the model. Særtrykk 95/1 ARENA, Oslo, from P. Anderson and P. Camiller (1994) *Mapping the West European Left*. New Left Review, Verso, London.

Moene, K. O. and M. Wallerstein (1996) Economic integration and unemployment in EFTA countries. In B. Eichengreen, J. Frieden, and J. von Hagen (eds), *Monetary and Fiscal Policy in an Integrated Europe*. Springer Verlag.

Müller-Jentsch, W. (1993) *Konfliktpartnershaft. Akteure und Institutionen der Industrielle Beziehungen*. Munich: Rainer Hamp Verlag.

Nergaard, K. (1993) *Samarbeid og selvstendighet*. Oslo: FAFO-rapport 157.

Nergaard, K. and T. A. Stokke (1996) *Midlertidige ansettelser i norsk arveidsliv. Hvor mange, hvem, hvor og hvorfor?* Oslo: FAFO-rapport 197.

NHO (1995) *Nye driftsformer og tariffpolitikk, framtidens system for lønns-og arbeidsvilkår*. Oslo: NHO, Report from a working group.

NHO (1996) Eksplosjon i investeringer ute. Interview with Knut H. Sørlie, NHO, *Aftenposten*, 31.7.1996.

Norli Hansen, M. (1995) Rekrutteringskanaler i det norske arbeidsmarkedet. *Søkelys på arbeidsmarkedet*, No. 2, ISF, Oslo.

Norwegian Employment Commission (1992) *A National Strategy for Increased Employment in the 1990s*. Oslo: Ministry of Finance.

Notermans, T. (1995) *Social Democracy and External Constraints*. Oslo: ARENA Working Paper 15/95.

NOU 1987: 26. *Om Grunnlaget for inntektsoppgjørene 1987*. Oslo: Forbruker og Administrasjonsdepartementet.

NOU 1992: 26. *En nasjonal strategi for økt sysselsettning i 1990 årene*.

NOU 1993: 6. *Aktiv arbeidsmarkedspolitikk*. Oslo: Kommunal og Arbeidsdepartementet.

NOU 1993: 19. *Erfaringen med lov om lønnsplikt under permittering*. Oslo: Kommunal og Arbeidsdepartmentet.

NOU 1996: 4. *Om grunnlaget for inntektsoppgjørene 1996*. Oslo: Forbruker og Administrasjonsdepartementet.

NOU 1996: 14. *Prinsipper for en ny arbeidstvistlov*. Innstilling avgitt, 21.6.1996.

Odnes, D., A. Hompland, A. Pape, and T. R. Larsen (1990) *Kampen om framtiden. Frontlinjer 2006*. Oslo: FAFO-rapport 98.

OECD (1993) *Employment Outlook.* Paris, July.
OECD (1994a) *Jobs Study. Evidence and Explanations.* Paris.
OECD (1994b) *Employment Outlook.* Paris, July.
OECD (1994c) Labour standards and economic integration. *Employment Outlook,* Paris, July.
OECD (1994d) *Income Distribution in OECD Countries.* Paris: OECD Working Papers Vol. II, No. 64.
OECD (1995a) *Economic Surveys – Norway.* Paris.
OECD (1995b) *Economic Outlook.* Paris, December.
OECD (1996a) *Employment Outlook.* Paris, July.
OECD (1996b) *The OECD Jobs Strategy. Pushing ahead with the Strategy.* Paris.
Olsen, T. (1995) EUs arbeidslivspolitikk: Nasjonale og europeiske utfordringer. *Tidsskrift for Samfunnsforskning* 36(4).
Opinion (1995) Lønnsforskjellene er for store. *Aftenposten,* 28.12. 1996, Oslo.
Opinion (1996) Nei til høye lønnskrav. *Arbeiderbladet,* February, Oslo.
Pape, A. (1993) *Kampen om kompetansen – hva brukte vi utdanningseksplosjonen til?* Oslo: FAFO-rapport 148.
Pape, A. (1994) Trade union structure and the institutional framework for labour relations – Organisational reforms in the Norwegian Confederation og Trade Unions. Paper for the conference on Emerging Union Structure, Institute for Work Research, Stockholm, 11–14 June.
Raaum, O. and H. Torp (1993) *Evaluering av AMO-kurs. Sysselsettingseffekter og seleksjon til kurs.* Oslo: SNF, Center for Research in Economics and Administration.
Raaum, O. and F. Wulfsberg (1995) *Unemployment, Labour Market Programmes and Wages in Norway.* Memorandum No. 24, Department of Economics, University of Oslo.
Raaum, O., H. Torp, and H. Goldstein (1995) *Employment Effects of Labour Market Training in Norway.* Memorandum No. 8, Department of Economics, University of Oslo.
Reve, T. (1994) Skandinavisk organisasjon og ledelse: Fra konkurransefordel til konkurranseulempe? *Tidsskrift for Samfunnsforskning* 35(4).
Rokkan, S. (1987) *Stat, nasjon, klasse.* Oslo: Scandinavian University Press.
Rothstein, B. (1992) Labor-market institutions and working-class strength. In S. Steinmo, K. Thelen, and F. Longstreth (eds), *Structuring Politics: Historical Institutionalism in Comparative Analysis.* Cambridge: Cambridge University Press.
Salvanes, K. G. (1996) *Job Creation and Job Destruction in Norway 1976–1992.* Oslo: Ministry of Finance.
Scheuer, S. (1992) Denmark: Return to decentralization. In Ferner and Hyman (eds.) *Industrial relations in the New Europe.* Oxford: Basil Blackwell.
Scheuer, S. (1996) *Fælles avtale eller egen kontrakt i arbeidslivet.* Copenhagen: Nyt fra Samfundsvidenskapene.
Schøne, P. (1996) Virksomhetsintern opplæring – hvem får opplæring og hva er den verdt? *Søkelys på arbeidsmarket,* 1/96, ISF, Oslo.
Sengenberger, W. (1994) Labour standards in the international economy – Challenges and perspectives. In G. Bosch (ed.), *International Integration and the Regulation of Working Conditions.* Gelsenkirchen: SAMF/Institut Arbeit und Technik.
Singh, A. (1995) Institutional requirements for full employment in advanced economies. *International Labour Review* 134(4–5).

Sivesind, K. H., R. Kalleberg, S. Hovde, and A. Fennefoss (1995) A social democratic order under pressure. Norwegian employment relations in the eighties. In R. Locke, T. Kochan, and M. Piore (eds), *Employment Relations in a Changing World Economy*. Cambridge MA: MIT Press.

Skånland, H. (1996) Solidaritetsalternativets fall og framtid. *Aftenposten*, kronikk, 8.6.1996.

Statistics Norway/SSB (1992) *Offentlig forvaltning i Norge*. Oslo: Report No. 13.

Statistics Norway/SSB (1994) *Arbeidsmarkedsstatistikk/Labour Market Statistics 1993*. Oslo.

Statistics Norway/SSB (1996a) *Statistical Yearbook 1995*. Oslo.

Statistics Norway/SSB (1996b) Endringer i inntektsfordelingen 1986–1994. *Ukens Statistikk* 22, Oslo.

Statistics Norway/SSB (1996c) Levekårsundersøkelsen 1995: Velferdsutviklingen halvveis inn på 1990-tallet. *Samfunnsspeilet* 1996, vol. 1, Oslo.

Stokke, T. A. (1995) *Organisasjonsgraden på arbeidstakersiden 1956–1994*. Oslo: FAFO-paper.

Stokland, D. (1994) Konsernstrategier i en internasjonalisert økonomi. In P. Heum and D. Stokland (eds), *Internasjonalisering og nasjonal næringspolitikk*. Oslo: FAFO-rapport 179.

Stortingsmelding 35 (1994–95) *Velferdsmeldingen*. Oslo: Sosial- og helsedepartementet.

Stortingsmelding 2 (1995–96) *Revidert Nasjonalbudsjett*. Oslo: Finansderpartementet.

Streeck, W. (1991) More uncertainties: German unions facing 1992. *Industrial Relations* 30(3).

Streeck, W. (1992) *Social Institutions and Economic Performance. Studies of Industrial Relations in Advanced Capitalist Economies*. London: Sage.

Streeck, W. (1993) The Rise and decline of neocorporatism. In L. Ulman et al. (eds), *Labor and an Integrated Europe*. Washington DC: The Brookings Institution.

Strøby Jensen, C., Jesper Due, and S. Madsen (1994) The Scandinavian model in Europe. In T. Kauppinen and V. Köykkä (eds), *Transformation of European Industrial Relations. Consequences of Integration and Disintegration*. IIRA 4th European Regional Congress, Helsinki.

Stueland, E., F. E. Thoresen, and P. Østvold (1994) *Norsk fagbevegelse og den europeiske unionen*. Oslo: SME/NTEU.

Teague, P. (1994) Between new Keynesianism and deregulation: Employment policy in the European Union. *Journal of European Public Policy* 1(3).

Teague, P. and J. Grahl (1992) *Industrial Relations and European Integration*. London: Lawrence & Wishart.

Torp, H. (1995) Norway Baseline Study. Oslo: Mimeo, ISF.

Torp, H. and S. M. Pettersen (1989) *Markedet for korttids-arbeidskraft. En utredning om utleie og formidling av arbeidskraft*. Oslo: ISF-Rapport 89/6.

Traxler, F. (1994) Collective bargaining: levels and coverage. *Employment Outlook*, July, Paris.

Traxler, F. and P. C. Schmitter (1994) Prospective thoughts on regional integration, interest politics and policy formulation in the EC/EU. Paper for the International Political Science Asociation XIVth Congress, Berlin.

Try, S. (1993) *Evaluering av arbeidsmarkedstiltak rettet mot ungdom*. Oslo: ISF, Rapport 93: 17.

Try, S. (1996) *Effekter av den aktive arbeidsmarkedspolitikken*. Kommunal og Arbeidsdepartementet, Arbeidsavdelingen, Arbeidsnotatserie No. 1.

Visher, M. and T. Midtsundstad (1993) *Utgang fra arbeidslivet.* Oslo: FAFO-rapport 154.

Visser, J. (1991) Trends in trade union membership. *Employment Outlook*, Paris, July.

Visser, J. and B. Ebbinghaus (1992) Making the most of diversity? European integration and transnational organization of labour. In J. Greenwood, J. Grote, and K. Ronit (eds), *Organized Interests and the European Community.* London: Sage.

Wallerstein, M. and M. Golden (1996) *The Fragmentation of the Bargaining Society? Changes in the Centralization of Wage-Setting in the Nordic Countries 1950–1992.* Los Angeles: UCLA.

Chapter 4

Gender Relations and the Norwegian Labour Market Model

Anne Lise Ellingsæter and Jill Rubery

1. Introduction

Over the past decades the Norwegian labour market has integrated an increasing share of the total population into the labour force – an increase that almost entirely reflects higher employment shares of women. The post-industrial sectoral shift in Norway has been characterized by a slow decline in manufacturing jobs and a massive increase in public sector employment, particularly in local government. In the highly gender segregated Norwegian labour market this has meant increasing job opportunities and increasing time spent in paid work among women, while the demand for the traditional male "core" industrial worker has significantly reduced. The total volume of work has been kept relatively constant, but has been redistributed between men and women, and, accordingly, a kind of unintended "work sharing" between men and women has taken place at the societal level. This redistribution reflects demand shifts, institutionally determined work-time reductions (lower retirement age, longer vacations, shorter working week), and women's high prevalence in part-time work. Thus new employment rationing processes in the labour market have been established, in which gender relations play a major part.

The processes generating this result are complex and partly specific to Norway. The Norwegian labour market and its transforming gender divisions are structured by national economic and social institutions. The purpose of this chapter is to identify the gender order (Connell, 1987; Bruegel and Perrons, 1995) upon which the Norwegian employment model is based and to assess the effect of this model on gender equality and the effects of this gender order on the flexibility of the operation of the Norwegian model. Gender order in this context means the gender relations inherent in the central institutions of the Norwegian labour market model and the complex interactions between these institutions.

We argue that gender relations are an integral part of the future development of the Norwegian model.

2. Towards labour market gender equality in Norway?

Women's position in the Norwegian labour market, compared with other industrialized countries, is characterized by features that are distinct for most Scandinavian countries: high employment rates, high levels of part-time work, continuous work patterns among mothers, high levels of gender segregation, high concentration in the public sector, and moderate gender differences in earnings (Blau and Kahn, 1992).

Rapid growth in Norwegian women's employment has diminished gender differences in labour force participation rates. In 1994, labour force participation rates were 79 percent among women aged 25–54 years, compared with 90 percent among men. In comparison, the rates for women and men in the UK were 74 and 93 percent, in the USA 75 and 92 percent, and in the Netherlands 65 and 92 percent, respectively (OECD, 1995). From 1970 to 1990 there was a 25 percent increase in the number of employed persons, and 90 percent of this growth took place among women (Ellingsæter, 1995b). The volume of work performed ("man-hours" worked) by men fell by 9 percent, while that of women grew by 34 percent. Compared with the other Scandinavian countries, women's employment rates in Norway started to rise later, and still lag somewhat behind, partly owing to the later expansion of the public sector.

In the long period of low unemployment, until 1988, Norwegian women had higher unemployment rates on the average than men. During the recession from 1988 this gender difference was reversed. Men's unemployment rate rose from 1.7 percent in 1987 to a high of 6.5 percent in 1993, compared with women's corresponding rates of 2.5 and 5.2 percent. In the economic recovery since 1993, men's unemployment rate has been declining more rapidly than the women's, but is still above that of women.

Part-time work

The rapid increase in women's employment rates in Norway has been associated with a significant increase in part-time work. Whereas the 1970s and early 1980s were characterized by relatively high and increasing levels of part-time work, there was a slight decline towards the end of the decade. The early 1990s showed a stagnating trend. In

1993, part-time workers in Norway accounted for 26.9 percent of total employment. Of all employed women, 48 percent work part-time, compared with 10 percent among men (Kitterød, 1993). Part-time work has not, however, replaced full-time work among women; the proportions of both part-time and full-time working women increased rapidly in the 1970s, and in the 1980s the proportion of full-time working women grew more rapidly than the proportion of part-time working women (Ellingsæter, 1989).

Part-time work in Norway was "normalized" in the 1980s (Ellingsæter, 1989). The proportion working short hours declined, the proportion with permanent employment contracts increased, as did the proportion who were members of unions. The majority of part-time workers have work contracts and work conditions that are fairly similar to those of full-time workers. A particular problem is that of pensions, however. In general, the low income of many part-timers will result in low pension disbursements, and a significant number of employees, notably in the public sector, have work-time contracts below the required threshold level for pension entitlements. Moreover, there is a significant minority among part-time workers who remain in a marginal position. Young people and students are overrepresented in this group. On the other hand, women form the majority of the high and increasing proportion of part-time workers who are underemployed. From 1988 to 1992 the proportion of underemployed part-time workers increased from 11 to 15 percent, and the high level has continued (Hobæk, 1993; Statistics Norway, 1994).[1]

Working mothers

Norwegian women have developed a "dual strategy" towards employment and family; that is, they do not choose either employment or caring for children, but choose both. High employment rates are accompanied by relatively high fertility rates by European standards. The 1980s was the decade of radical transformation in Norwegian mothers' employment relations. From 1980 to 1990 the labour force participation rates of mothers whose youngest child was under 3 years old grew from 47 to 69 percent, and the corresponding increase in participation among mothers whose youngest child was 3 to 6 years old was from 57 to 74 percent (Kjeldstad, 1991). The majority of mothers now continue to work after the birth of their first child. From the early 1970s until the

1 The underemployed are defined as persons working part time who both want, and have tried to get, longer weekly work-hours and who could start to work longer hours within a month.

late 1980s the proportion of women who were employed one year after the first birth increased from 29 to 62 percent (Ellingsæter and Rønsen, 1996). Continuous employment patterns among mothers are associated with improved reproductive rights. Over the past few years, Norway has instituted relatively extensive parental leave, at high earnings compensation, and has also established the right to leave to care for sick children. The take-up of parental rights shows a clear gendered pattern, which is discussed in more detail in section 7.

However, having children still restricts employment, and having more than one child further lowers employment rates and work-hours among mothers of preschoolers. In the late 1980s nearly half of mothers worked reduced hours one year after first birth (Ellingsæter and Rønsen, 1996). In 1992, the highest full-time rate, 60 percent, was found among mothers with one child of preschool age. This might in part be attributed to the higher level of education of one-child mothers, but longitudinal data show that a second child increases the transition to part-time work (Ellingsæter and Rønsen, 1996). Working-time strategies among a large number of Norwegian mothers with preschool children allow them to be independent of non-parental child care. They work inconvenient hours, when fathers or other relatives may take care of their children (Ellingsæter, 1987). Single mothers, whose employment decreased in the 1980s, have significantly lower employment rates than married mothers (Kjeldstad and Roalsø, 1995). This might be related to the relatively generous social benefits for single mothers, and allocation rules that make part-time work costly. However, there is a political majority in parliament to restrict these rights, in order to strengthen the employment incentives for this group, and a parliamentary bill is likely to be approved in the near future.

Segregated labour markets

As already noted, in international comparison the Norwegian and Scandinavian labour markets appear among the most gender segregated. Rising female employment in Norway has not been followed by a radical shift in women's and men's place in the occupational structure. Horizontal gender segregation – the proportion of women employed in typically female occupations, such as nursing, teaching, clerical work, sales work, and cleaning – in fact increased from the 1970s onwards, although it seems to have declined somewhat towards the end of the 1980s, particularly outside the health and social services sector (Ellingsæter and Iversen, 1984; Hansen, 1992). Nevertheless, in 1992 almost half of all female employees were in occupations where women constituted more than 85 percent of all employees (Hansen, 1995). Women dominate among salaried employees at low or middle levels. Although economic restructuring and expanding services imply that more men are classified as white-collar than as blue-collar workers, 40 percent of men are still categorized as blue-collar workers. Vertical segregation is considerable. Women have fewer chances than men of obtaining a high position within the occupational hierarchy: in 1994, only 11 percent of female employees had a supervisory post, compared with 29 percent among men (Statistics Norway, 1995).

International comparisons also show that highly gender-segregated labour markets are associated with a high level of part-time work and high proportions working in the public sector. Welfare services are labour intensive, with a predominance of traditionally female occupations. Thus a highly gender-segregated labour market is both a cause and an effect of the increasing labour force rates among women. The large public sector in Norway, more than 30 percent in 1994 (see Chapter 3), accounts for a large share of the relatively high gender segregation (Hansen, 1992). In the public sector, women constituted 58 percent of employees in 1990, compared with 36 percent in the private sector (Bjørklund, 1991). The relative difference between the proportion of women working in the two sectors remained constant in the 1980s because the proportion of women among private sector employees also increased.

Welfare state expansion through services located at the municipal level led to an equalization of regional differences in women's employment opportunities in the 1970s and the early 1980s. The present system of economic transfers to the municipalities has probably benefited women in the less urbanized areas the most, resulting in the highest levels of public services in these areas. However, recently a governmental commission (the Rattsø Commission) has suggested reforms that may alter this picture.

Despite the high level of segregation, Norway and the other Scandinavian countries have smaller gender differences in wages than for example the UK and the USA (Barth, 1992; Blau and Kahn, 1992). The lowest gender gap in wages is found in Sweden, followed by Norway, where the female/male wage ratio for all employees was 81 percent in 1991 (Kjeldstad and Lyngstad, 1993).[2] The gender gap is still demonstrated in the proportion receiving what is defined as a low wage: in 1995 about one-third of employed women, compared with only one-

2 Based on data from Statistics Norway (1992).

fifth of men, had hourly wage rates below 85 percent of the average wage in manufacturing industry (Statistics Norway, 1996).[3]

3. The gender order of the Norwegian model

State policy plays a central role in the development of the gender order. Not only do Scandinavian countries have large welfare states, which may provide the basis for a more egalitarian gender order, but they have also, to a large extent, organized these welfare state systems around the principle of a "weak male breadwinner" system of household organization (Lewis, 1992). In contrast to a strong male breadwinner system, where women are treated primarily as dependants, a weak male breadwinner state is based on the assumption that most fit adults will be in work or seeking work. The welfare state system is based less on transfers to families and more on the provision of employment, services, child care, and opportunities for temporary leave from work. This represents an "ideal type" Scandinavian model, and, as we see below, Norway has in practice implemented a welfare system with both strong and weak characteristics. Nevertheless, state policy is a central determinant of the emerging gender order in Norway.

The gendered labour market divisions that we have identified above are generated by the gender relations inherent in the central institutions of the Norwegian labour market model: the industrial system, the system of labour market regulation, the labour market system, and the system of social reproduction (Rubery, 1989; Rubery and Fagan, 1994). The *industrial system* is constituted by the industrial structure and firms' organizational practices. The *system of labour market regulation* provides the legal and administrative regulations and voluntary collective bargaining institutions. The *labour market system* covers movements between non-employment and employment, between training and employment, and between job positions within the labour market. The *system of social reproduction* includes both familial and public systems of child care, systems of support for the unemployed and the inactive, and the social attitudes to employment and family that underpin current arrangements. The processes in each institution are basically autonomous, but there are dynamic interrelationships creating on the

3 Other material rewards from work also show significant gender differences. More than one-third of employed men receive fringe benefits (economic subsidies for car, housing, and/or telephone) from their work, Compared with less than one in ten women (Statistics Norway, 1996).

one hand an interlocked and coherent societal system, but also the potential for tensions and contradictions in the different institutions.

4. The industrial system

Transformations in the Norwegian industrial structure have generated new demands for different kinds of workers. From the late 1960s to the late 1980s the post-industrial sectoral shift was characterized by a slow decline in manufacturing jobs and a massive increase in the service sector, particularly in public sector employment (see also Chapters 3 and 8 in this book). Deindustrialization was speeded up by the recession starting in 1988; from 1987 to 1993 employment in manufacturing industries fell by 17 percent (Statistics Norway, 1994). The significant growth in private services (trade, hotels and restaurants, and other services), which increased by 63 percent from 1970 to 1987, was also halted by the recession; the number of employed decreased by 15 percent from 1987 to 1993. Public sector employment started to grow markedly at the end of the 1960s, and has continued to increase ever since. From 1970 to 1987 the number of employees doubled. Public sector employment, and particularly local state employment, continued to grow during the recent recession: from 1987 to 1993 the number of persons employed in government-producing services increased by 14 percent, and 92 percent of the increase was found in local government services.

Accordingly, the public sector's demand for labour has been a major "employment machine" (Esping-Andersen, 1990), compensating for jobs lost by deindustrialization. The recession starting in 1988 clearly intensified the pressure on government budgets and structural reform, as evidenced in other countries, but these pressures have not had any seriously adverse effect on public employment. In addition to the soaring oil revenues that make Keynesian demand policies feasible in Norway, part of the explanation can also be found in the public budgeting strategy followed by the present social democratic government. In general, reduced growth has been concentrated on subsidies and transfers to individuals, households, and private industries, while spending on government services, such as education, public child care, and care for the elderly, which has the most direct impact on employment, has been expanding significantly.

Public sector jobs belong to the "core" jobs in the Norwegian labour market. In general, gender structures in the private sector reflect less favourable conditions for women. A longitudinal cohort study of women shows that the large majority of highly educated women in the post-war birth cohorts have found the best employment opportunities in the public sector (Ellingsæter et al., 1996). Yet among younger women, born in

1960 or later, a substantially higher proportion of those with high educational levels have been recruited into the private sector, although the majority still work in the public sector.

Particular expectations are directed at the state as employer, and the state has the reputation of being a "good employer" (Esping-Andersen, 1990). There are reasons to believe that state and municipal employers feel more obligated to adjust to public policy measures, whereas gender equality reforms may meet more obstacles and resistance among private sector employers. One example is vertical gender segregation, which is even more resilient to change in the private sector. Whereas there has been a notable increase in women in public sector top jobs, no similar gender-equalizing effect is found in the private sector. This suggests that Norwegian women are excluded not from power over other women in the public sector, but from exercising power over men in the private sector.

Moreover, the public sector has a long tradition of offering part-time jobs and other flexible working schedules as well as improved maternity leave arrangements. It has been argued that the public sector is preferred by women because typically female work patterns are more difficult to practise and are "punished" more in the private sector (Hansen, 1995). The public sector has played an important role in the continuity in women's employment careers: having a job in the public sector is shown to speed up the return to work after birth, all other things being equal (Ellingsæter and Rønsen, 1996). Public sector employees enjoy extra benefits in connection with childbirth and child care (see below). The public sector consists of larger workplaces than the private sector, which is likely to make it easier to implement the high mobility created by parental leave arrangements. The proportion having temporary work contracts is higher in the public than in the private sector, partly a result of the more generous rights of leave of absence creating a demand for substitutes (Torp, 1990).

5. The system of labour market regulation

The system of labour market regulation provides the legal and administrative regulations and voluntary collective bargaining institutions that shape employment relations and influence the standardization of employment conditions. In Norway, as in many other countries, central employment rights are not regulated by law but are settled by collective agreements (see also Chapter 3 in this book).[4]

---

4 In Norway, maximum working hours (40 hours per week) are regulated by law, but according to most collective agreements normal working hours are at present 37.5 hours per week.

The rate of unionization, the degree of centralization, and the unions' participation in corporate systems influence unions' bargaining power and strategies concerning labour market transformations. The Scandinavian countries, with their extensive public welfare policies and the coordinating role of central union and employer federations, have created distinctive patterns of industrial relations. In Norway, a little less than two out of three workers are union members. The expansion of the public sector has clearly favoured the unionization of women (OECD, 1991). In the Scandinavian countries, the difference between men's and women's union density rates is now minor, and the share of union members among part-timers is increasing. In Norway, the main difference in unionization is not between men and women or between full-time and part-time work, but between sectors and industries. More than three out of four in the public sector are union members, compared with less than one in two in the private sector (Ellingsæter, 1995a). Whereas about two out of three in manufacturing are union members, the ratio is less than one in three in trade, restaurants, and hotels.[5] An even higher rate of 88–90 percent is found among full-time public sector employees, and also among women working long part-time hours.

The gender wage gap

The relatively smaller gender wage gap found in Norway and the other Scandinavian countries can first of all be explained by the centralized wage-bargaining system, resulting in overall small wage differences (Asplund et al., 1995). The importance of the general wage structure on the comparatively favourable female/male ratio is illustrated when another indicator of gender difference in wages is examined, that is, the way women are treated in relation to the male wage distribution. The average wage for Norwegian women is greater than the wages earned by 26 percent of male workers, a position that is less favourable than for example in the USA, where the female/male ratio is much lower but women's average wage is higher than the earnings of more than 38 percent of male workers (Blau, 1993). Evidently the existence of an equal pay act in Norway has been insufficient to bring about the elimination of the wage gap.[6]

Looking at the past decade, in the early 1980s an equalization of the

5 Calculated on the basis of the Employee and Firm Survey 1993, Statistics Norway and Institute for Social Research.

6 In Norway the 1978 Equal Status Act §5 provides for equal pay for work of equal value.

Table 4.1. Wage differentials in Norway and the UK using national wage data, 1993

Relative pay of female full-time employees and all full-time employees in selected occupations.

A) Relative to average earnings of male non-manual employees in manufacturing.

	Female earnings Norway	UK	*Total earnings* Norway	UK
Primary and nursery teacher	--	86.6%	76.7%	91.2%
Secondary school teacher	84.2%	91.8%	87.7%	100.3%
Nurse	--	69.4%	70.3%	70.0%
Midwife	--	83.3%	77.9%	83.3%
Auxiliary nurse	--	44.5%	65.2%	44.6%
Shop assistant	52.8%	37.1%	53.8%	39.8%
Clerical worker	--	49.9%	57.9%	50.5%

B) Relative to average earnings of female non-manual employees in manufacturing

	Female earnings Norway	UK	*Total earnings* Norway	UK
Primary and nursery teacher	--	145.6%	101.6%	153.2%
Secondary school teacher	111.6%	154.3%	116.2%	168.6%
Nurse	--	116.7%	93.2%	117.7%
Midwife	--	140.0%	103.2%	140.0%
Auxiliary nurse	--	74.7%	86.4%	74.9%
Shop assistant	70.0%	62.3%	71.3%	67.0%
Clerical worker	--	83.8%	76.6%	84.9%

Note: Total earnings for the UK are calculated by assuming the female share of the occupation reference group in the UK is the same as in Norway. This allows for a better source of comparion for those occupational groups in Noway where wage data by sex is missing.

average wage among women and men took place, and thereafter stabilized. Centralization has helped women on average by raising pay for the lower skilled while holding back wages for the higher skilled or more educated, particularly in the public sector (Høgsnes, 1995). The wage gap is smaller and the equalizing effect seems to be stronger in the public than in the private sector (Barth and Mastekaasa, 1993). Reduction of wage inequalities within the national government sector has meant that relative wages have shifted to the advantage of the low-waged groups, while employees with medium and high wages have lost ground relative to manual workers in the private sector. A significant proportion of national government sector employees with medium-level wages are women (nurses, teachers, etc.). The municipal sector has been more reluctant to accept the principle of wage equalization, so that wage inequalities have remained stable over the past 20 years instead of narrowing as in the national government sector (Høgsnes, 1995). High- and medium-paid employees in the private sector have by and large kept their relative position.

Blau and Kahn's (1992) comparative study of the gender pay gap has confirmed that the main factor in the low gender earnings gap in Norway is the narrow wage dispersion and not the position of women relative to men within the earnings distribution.

To consider the impact of the Norwegian system of wage determination on the structure and relative level of women's pay we have made some comparisons of pay in typically female occupations in Norway and the UK.[7] Despite problems of comparison, the picture that emerges is so clear and in accordance with expectations that it is unlikely that the country differences would disappear if fully comparable information were to be available.[8] What we find is evidence of a much wider spread of earnings for traditional female occupations in Britain than in Norway (see Table

7 We are grateful to Damian Grimshaw for compiling these comparative data.

8 Some qualifications must be made as to the reliability of these comparisons: first the sources of data from the two countries are different, with the Norwegian data derived from official wages statistics, which are themselves a compilation of information derived mainly from employers' associations, whereas the UK data are drawn from a representative sample of full-time employees, the New Earnings Survey; second, there are no average earnings figures for Norway relating to all full-time employees, and thus comparisons have had to be made relative to average earnings for subgroups of employees; and, third, the Norwegian data are not always available by gender and thus total earnings data have to be used. This is not a major problem for female-dominated occupations, but because the precise share of women in an occupation varies between Norway and the UK we have tried to standardize for this effect by using Norwegian weights of males to females within the selected occupations to combine average male and average female earnings within the UK to produce a UK total earnings figure with Norwegian employment weights.

4.1). Moreover, there is more overlap between the earnings of women in traditional female occupations and average earnings of male non-manual workers in manufacturing in the UK than is the case in Norway. This suggests that women professionals in the public sector in Norway are lower paid relative both to less qualified women and to non-manual men in manufacturing than is the case for female professionals in comparable jobs – i.e. teaching and nursing – in the UK. Particularly low relative pay levels are found for the highly feminized occupations of primary and nursery teachers. Perhaps even more marked is the relatively high pay for lower-skilled workers in Norway. For example, auxiliary nurses and shop assistants earn respectively 45 percent and 40 percent of male non-manual employees' average earnings in the UK, wheras in Norway the respective ratios are 65 percent and 54 percent. Moreover, the pay of an average secondary school teacher is two and a half times the pay of an average shop assistant in the UK whereas in Norway the differential is only 1.6.

A study of the wage gap in the private sector shows that gender differences are fairly small when one compares women and men who work in the same position and establishment (Petersen et al., 1994: 189). Controlling for both occupation and establishment, women on average earn 2–6 percent less per hour than men. Occupational segregation is the main factor behind the gap between Norwegian women's and men's wages, while establishment segregation has limited impact. This is in contrast to the USA, for example, where establishment segregation is found to be extensive and important for wage differences between women and men in the private sector, although not as important as occupational segregation (Petersen and Morgan, 1995).

Gender divisions in skill levels are significant: nearly half the women are unskilled white- or blue-collar workers, as compared with less than one-third of men. This is partly due to gender differences in educational levels among older cohorts, but in the feminist literature the conception of skill is increasingly seen as socially constructed, and the systematically lower value placed on women's work tasks compared with men's is a growing concern. The economic return from education is on the average lower for women than for men in Norway, which is primarily due to the suppressed wages and low economic return from education in the public sector. A study of the economic return from different types of education shows that the highest economic return is found among those with higher education of long duration who are employed in the private sector, whereas nurses and auxiliary nurses in the public sector have negative economic return (Pedersen, 1995).

In recent years there has been increased scope for decentralized wage-setting in the public sector. In 1990 a new wage system was introduced in the municipal sector, aimed at giving municipalities and counties more freedom in local wage-setting. The present wage-setting is a mixed system, where the central actors in wage negotiation settle a (fairly large) share of the wage growth before the local negotiations start. A study of how this new system works shows that the extent to which the gender equality principle is laid down in the central bargaining process is of significance for local wage settlements, because the gender effect seems to be reinforced at the local level (Hoel, 1994).

A new wage system was also established in the national government sector in 1991, with a similar aim to that of the municipal sector. A study of wage relations for the state sector in the period 1987–1994, covering the period before and after the new wage system, shows that, contrary to what many would have expected, the new wage system has not led to larger wage differentials (Barth and Yin, 1996). The long-term tendency towards less wage dispersion continues. Gender differences were reduced in the period both before and after the regime shift, whether or not it is controlled for type of job. Working part time has a negative effect on wages. The economic return from education continued to decrease after the change. It is argued that these results might be an effect of the central wage-bargaining process overcompensating for the expected differentiation of local wage increases.

Previous studies of gender differences in wages in the national government sector have shown that women with similar formal qualifications to men more rarely achieved high-level positions, which could indicate that women's career prospects were inferior to those of men. A recent study of career trajectories (promotion) in the state sector suggests, however, that the main explanation of gender differences is that women enter the job hierarchy at lower levels than men do (Barth and Yin, 1995). Women and men develop similar career trajectories, and women even catch up somewhat in relation to men. Also, over time the gender difference in starting position is decreasing.

In conclusion, the comprehensive system of wage determination, together with the solidaristic wage-bargaining principle, has reduced the possibility in Norway of using women as a cheap source of labour; thus Norwegian women fail to act as a labour reserve in two senses, both by being permanent participants in the labour force and by not providing a source of low-wage competition for core workers.

Regulation of employment rights and social benefits

Increasing employment rates among married women in Norway have been paralleled by an increasing legitimacy of women's individual right to work, disconnected from men's traditional prerogative to jobs as breadwinners, weakening women's status as a reserve army of labour. For example, the traditional male breadwinner concern is shown to have a weak legitimacy in a situation of layoffs or workforce reductions. The Work Environment Act (1978) regulating layoffs does not state any criteria to be followed. In collective agreements, seniority is the only principle mentioned, but employers do not have to apply this as the basic principle. Seniority is the most preferred criterion among employees (Engelstad, 1990). There is a potential conflict between the preferences of employees and employers' preferences and judicial practices, where the principle of seniority is much weaker. Among employers, productivity is the most important criterion, and judicial practices also show that this is seen as the most important criterion, with seniority the second most important criterion. However, both employers and trade unions are increasingly sceptical about the criterion of need. This finding supports other research showing that the majority of the population reject men's prerogative to jobs in times of high unemployment (Ellingsæter, 1995b).

The system of social security is based on the principle of universalism, which means that for many social needs all persons are insured independently of their labour market relationship. Individual rights based on citizenship can be regarded as one of the most important characteristics of a "weak breadwinner" welfare state system. Most non-Scandinavian European countries have welfare state systems with rights related to labour force participation, with most women in practice receiving benefits on the basis of derived rights, as dependants of male full-time continuously employed workers (Ginn and Arber, 1994; Lewis, 1992; Rubery et al., 1996). The social security system in Norway is financed by the state, that is, by taxes and employer and employee excise taxes. The main benefits are still income related, but the Norwegian social security system has the least differentiation between employment- and non-employment-related rights. Social rights are entirely independent of working-time thresholds, and there are minimal qualifying conditions concerning the duration of the employment relationship. Unemployment benefits are paid on the basis of individual entitlement for up to three years, in contrast to many European countries, including for example Sweden and Finland, where unemployment benefits become dependent upon household income after one or two years.[9] There are some income threshold levels that must be reached before entitlement in Norway, but these are generally very low. This

9 Out of the 15 EU member states, only Belgium, Denmark, and the Netherlands have entitlement to non-means-tested benefits for three years or longer (Rubery et al., 1996; Grimshaw et al., 1996).

applies for instance to sickness benefits. Unemployment benefits have a somewhat higher threshold level, which has recently been increased.[10]

All citizens receive a relatively adequate basic pension. This type of basic pension system, found primarily in Scandinavian countries, has been shown to be particularly beneficial to women, compared with either pension systems based on the income security principle, found in most European countries, or a state residual pension system, as found for example in the UK (Ginn and Arber, 1994). Supplementary pensions in Norway are based on previous income and do not depend on working hours. As a consequence, however, part-time workers with low annual incomes and long periods outside the labour market will receive low supplementary pensions. None the less, the method of calculating supplementary pensions is more favourable for part-time workers in Norway than in, for example, the UK and Germany (Bjurstrøm, 1993).

National employment legislation and social security systems deal with part-time workers in different ways, leading to different consequences of working part time (Ellingsæter, 1995b). In Norway, national employment legislation, such as regulation of rights related to work contracts, period of notice, etc., does not discriminate between full-time and part-time workers (Bjurstrøm, 1993). As a result of the non-discriminatory institutional practices, combined with a large majority of part-time workers working long hours, part-time work in Norway, as in the other Scandinavian countries, represents an employment relationship with few marginal features. This is in sharp contrast to, for example, the British experience. Here part-time work has evolved within a relatively unregulated labour market and within a fiscal system where there is a strong incentive for employers to create low-paid part-time jobs that are exempt from social security contributions by both employers and employees.

The internationalization of economies is supposed to increase pressures on national employment regulations towards flexibilization and deregulation. The outcome of such pressures depends, however, on the power of labour market actors and political alliances. Some aspects of the work contract of particular relevance to the flexible use of labour are regulated by law in Norway. In 1992 the NHO, the central national employers' organization, proposed a lifting of the restrictions on the use of temporary employees, in connection with the ongoing revisions of the Work Environment Act. The trade unions, in alliance with some political parties, suggested restrictions on current practices, by adding amendments

---

10 Sickness benefits require an annual income of NOK 17 750; unemployment benefits about NOK 50 000 for the first 1.5 years, and about NOK 95 000 for the period beyond this (see Chapter 3).

to the existing text of the act. Paradoxically, the revision of the act ended with a result contrary to all deregulatory trends – a more restricted regulation of temporary labour. Nor was the fairly strict regulation of overtime lifted; rather the enforcement of current regulations was enjoined by the local Directorates of Labour Inspection.

Flexible use of labour does not seem to be a dominant part of new employer strategies, although some examples may be found (Isaksen and Simensen, 1995). The restrictive regulations prevent the use of women as a flexible reserve in precarious jobs, though the pressures towards flexibilization, particularly in private services, should not be underestimated. Some argue that the restrictive practices concerning temporary employment might also have negative effects for other groups in the labour market; they might prevent the long-term unemployed from entering the labour market (Colbjørnsen and Larsen, 1995), thus contributing to a polarization between labour market insiders and outsiders.

Furthermore, the gap between formal rights and regulations, on the one hand, and actual practices, on the other, might increase. Restructuring of the labour market and higher levels of unemployment might have resulted in increasing uncertainty among workers, having a disciplining effect. Workers experience more temporal work pressure, particularly in service jobs (Mastekaasa, 1994). Moreover, both paid and unpaid overtime work is on the increase (Rogstad, 1993), indicating that more effort is demanded, particularly from male workers. The growth in unpaid overtime exemplifies the limited effects that formal regulations may have on practices. Normal work-hours and paid overtime are regulated by law and collective agreements, whereas unpaid overtime work cannot be formally regulated. Changing practices may develop new informal norms, outside the institutionalized framework, about time use in the market. Such norms may strengthen the grip of the market on workers, particularly men, weakening their family relationships and counteracting the intentions of Norwegian family policies.

Affirmative action

The Gender Equality Act (§3) opens up the possibility of the preferential treatment of women in recruitment to jobs, but agreements have to be negotiated at firm level. Preferential treatment agreements are found mainly in the public sector (Teigen and Jensen, 1995), which might help explain the increasing private–public difference in the share of women in top jobs. Whereas gender quotas have promoted the integration of women in Norwegian elite politics, the resistance against such measures in private businesses is striking. Recently, the opportunity for preferential treatment of men applying for jobs involving care work for children was debated in parliament. This change was motivated not by the argument of gender-segregated labour markets but by a concern for the many children growing up in an increasingly feminized environment. Resistance to this change came from women's organizations, which argued that this might result in men taking jobs from women.

A study of female engineers' careers in different types of work organizations suggested, however, that the existence of an affirmative action programme at the firm level may have negligible effects (gender quotas were not central in these programmes) (Kvande and Rasmussen, 1990). It was argued that what matters is the type of work organization; flexible organizations provide better opportunities than static, hierarchical organizations. However, the career opportunities for this particular group of professional women have improved exceptionally in recent years in different types of work organizations. In the private sector, young women engineers are promoted more rapidly than are men.[11] A recent study of traditional bureaucratic work organizations (state ministries, also hiring engineers) shows that being a woman actually enhances the chance of being recruited or promoted, other factors being equal (Teigen and Wiers-Jenssen, 1996). Moreover, although recent studies indicate that increasing organizational functional flexibility might provide better opportunities for women in terms of upskilling and career, it might also result in increasing work intensification (Kvande and Rasmussen, 1995).

Parents' rights of leave of absence to care for children also regulate employment relations, but these are discussed in relation to the system of social reproduction in section 7.

6. The labour market system

The labour market system covers movements between non-employment and employment, between training and employment, and between job positions within the labour market. Here we focus particularly on unemployment and training.

Gender and unemployment

Because of the concentration of women in sectors of the economy that are less sensitive to cycles, female unemployment rates tend to rise less

11 "Fakta om ledere", Dagbladet, 26.4.1995.

quickly in recessions and to decline more slowly in recoveries. This pattern is found in many OECD countries (OECD, 1988) and is evidenced in Norway for prime age women (above 30), although unemployment among younger women fluctuates in line with business cycles. Thus, gender segregation in the labour market makes trends in sectors and occupations the most decisive factor for women's unemployment. In Norway, women's massive job concentration in the public sector protects their position in the labour market. Men's employment rates are more cyclically dependent than women's.

During the recent economic recovery, the decline in registered unemployment from 1993 to 1995 took place almost entirely among men (Arbeidsdirektoratet, 1995b). Women's unemployment rate has declined more slowly than men's.[12] This slower decline cannot, however, be completely explained by cyclical demand factors, as indicated above – labour demand in female-dominated jobs also shows a strong increase. The explanation is that there is now a larger group of women who have been either in education or working at home and registering with the employment offices. Women are overrepresented in labour market programmes, and women are actually more often offered places on such programmes than are men (Torp, 1994).[13] Women's unemployment would have increased by 61 percent in 1994, compared with 43 percent among men, if labour market programme participants had been included. The average probability of re-employment seems to be very similar for women and men (Halvorsen, 1994); however, men get jobs somewhat more rapidly than do women (Hernæs and Strøm, 1994).

Increased levels of unemployment apparently generate a relatively higher "silent reserve" (discouraged workers) among women than among men. But this is concentrated among young women. Young women are more flexible about doing things other than being employed or unemployed, for example educating themselves. Thus, in an economic recession, the state increasingly plays the role of a "buffer" to young women, through labour market programmes and expansion in the educational system. Married women are no more "flexible" than men (Blix

---

12 From the first quarter of 1994 to the first quarter of 1995, registered unemployment decreased by 13 percent among men but increased by 4 percent among women (Arbeidsdirektoratet, 1995a). Since then, the female unemployment rate has also declined.

13 Among women, those in programmes as a proportion of "gross" unemployment (those unemployed plus those in programmes) increased from 12 percent in 1988 to 35 percent in 1993, compared with an increase from 10 to 27 percent among men (Torp, 1994).

and Gulbrandsen, 1992; Torp, 1994); the employment rate among married women in general, and of women with preschool-age children in particular, often thought to be the most mobile part of the labour force, in fact increased slightly during the recent recession (Torp, 1994). A comparison of fathers and mothers with young children found no gender difference in unemployment rates (Blix and Gulbrandsen, 1992); but for both mothers and fathers the risk of unemployment increased among those with low educational resources. Women over 40 years old seem to be the least cyclically affected group. They have steadily increased their employment numbers over the past 15 years, partly as a result of the increasing population in this age group and a more continuous labour market pattern among the new cohorts entering this group (Arbeidsdirektoratet, 1995b). The labour force participation rate among women aged 40–66 was higher than among younger women in 1994, which represents a new trend, making these women a dominating group in the labour market.

Some scholars have claimed that unemployed women in particular might experience a transfer through the process of re-employment from the primary to the secondary labour market, where they are forced to accept poorer working conditions (Davies and Esseveld, 1989).[14] On this point Norwegian evidence is somewhat contradictory. One small-scale survey found that it was more often women than men who re-entered temporary jobs (Kaul and Kvande, 1986), whereas a more recent study based on representative survey data shows that the proportions re-employed on permanent work contracts were the same among women and men (54 and 53 percent, respectively) (Halvorsen, 1994). Yet the proportion on permanent contracts among the re-employed is much lower than the average among the employed, which is almost 90 percent.

Increasing unemployment, however, is associated with growth in involuntary part-time work, which affects women more than men.[15] In 1993, 3.4 percent of the labour force, or 73 000 persons (two out of three of them women), were registered as partially unemployed (Arbeidsdirektoratet, 1994). The proportion of underemployed part-time

---

14 Davies and Esseveld's qualitative study suggests that women are marginalized through unemployment and re-employment. These are, however, women with low skills, and the findings may illustrate processes that are occurring to particular segments of the female labour force.

15 The underemployed are defined as persons working part time who both want and have tried to get longer weekly work-hours, and who can start to work longer hours within a month (Hobæk, 1993).

workers in the total female labour force increased from 4.8 percent in 1989 to 6.9 percent in 1993. A similar trend is also found among men, although the level is substantially lower.[16] However, whereas a majority of the underemployed men want full-time work, this applies to only a minority among the women (Hobæk, 1993).

The risks of the Norwegian post-industrial labour market are structured primarily by class and mediated by low education. Men in traditional working-class occupations have been the most severely affected by deindustrialization and unemployment: 36 percent of all those registered as unemployed in 1993 came from manufacturing and construction work. In comparison, these occupations accounted for only 19 percent of all those in employment (Statistics Norway, 1994: Tables 38 and 76). In the early 1990s more than a third of the unemployed had only primary education, compared with only 15 percent in the employed population (Arbeidsdirektoratet, 1995c). Increased long-term unemployment suggests that there is a structural problem in the labour market, reflecting a mismatch between the qualifications of many unemployed and the qualifications demanded in vacant jobs. Most long-term unemployed have work experience in sectors other than those in which job expansion occurs (Colbjørnsen and Larsen, 1995).

Gender, education, and training

Equal access to secondary and higher education independently of gender, socioeconomic background, and geographical location has been an explicit political goal in post-war Norway. Inadequacies in the system of secondary education, particularly within vocational education, recently prompted a new educational reform, "Reform 94". General problems included inefficient flows through the system and a decline in apprenticeships in recent years. The latter was mainly due to the declining demand for workers in building and construction, because apprentice contracts within social services were reported to have increased (Jørgensen, 1993). Women are overrepresented in streams giving general competencies, whereas men are overrepresented in vocational training. In 1989, 39 percent of male students aged 19–24 years were in apprenticeships, compared with only 14 percent of women (Jørgensen, 1993: 134).

The significance of gender, and geographical location, in access to

16 The corresponding increase in underemployed male part-time workers was from 1.1 to 1.9 percent.

higher education has been greatly reduced, but socioeconomic background still operates as a selection mechanism (Hansen and Rogg, 1991). The high proportion of women acquiring general study competence in secondary education is reflected in recruitment to higher education. In 1991, 54 percent of all students in higher educational institutions were women (Jørgensen, 1993), and in 1993 women for the first time were in a majority among the candidates passing higher-level university exams (Statistics Norway, 1994). The rising proportions of women in higher education might improve their labour market opportunities but also make them more vulnerable to the problem of overqualification – the mismatch between educational credentials and the qualifications required for the available jobs.[17]

The educational expansion among women in very different occupations has created differentiation in the wage-bargaining strategies for improving women's wages. For example, Hoel (1995) argues that the increasing proportion of female doctors explains the recent wage strategy among doctors for raising the basic salary. Previously, doctors' fairly high incomes had been obtained through complex compensation for work performed in addition to the normal hours-of-work contract. It will be more difficult for young women who are also mothers to put in the extra time required. Nurses, in contrast, have increased their wage levels by establishing internal hierarchies. The nurses' strategy reflects one solution to the difficulty of lifting wages for numerically large groups in the public sector, which may however be effective only when there is a shortage of the group in question, as is the case with nurses.

In conclusion, low education seems to increase the labour market risk factor in the same way for women as for men, but responses to unemployment may generate gender-specific patterns in different stages of the life course. Polarization among different groups of women may be on the increase, probably between young, unskilled women and the well-educated prime-age groups, as well as between young, well-educated entrants and their less qualified older colleagues. Differing interests among women may result in sharper conflicts between different unions' wage-bargaining strategies.

7. The system of social reproduction

The system of social reproduction includes both familial and state systems of child care, support for the unemployed and the inactive, and the

17 "Overkvalifiserte får underbetalte jobber", Aftenposten, 24.10.95.

social attitudes to employment and the family that underpin current arrangements.

Norway is a society of dual-income families: by 1989 the proportion of dual-income families among married couples was 85 percent (Lyngstad and Strand, 1992). The proportion of single providers is increasing, and accounts for about one in five of all families with children (Kjeldstad and Roalsø, 1995). Women's contribution to the family's total gross earned income is 34 percent; which is high by international comparison. Women's contribution is lowest in families with children, but the difference between couples without and with children is decreasing (Skrede, 1989). Although men in one-income couples earn more than men in dual-income couples, there is an increasing differential between one-income and two-income families (Lyngstad and Strand, 1992). Perhaps surprisingly, the Norwegian tax system is based on joint taxation for spouses, in contrast to the individualized taxation associated with most "weak breadwinner" welfare states. However, spouses have the right to separate taxation of income from wages (NOU, 1976) and, after a major tax reform in 1992 reduced the marginal rate of tax, the disincentive effects of the tax system on women's employment were minimized.

The high proportion of working mothers has made the dilemma of working parents a public issue. Facilitating the combination of employment and parenthood has been defined as its main gender equality policy by the social democratic government (Stortingsmelding 70, 1992). Together with a continued expansion of public child care, the extension of parents' leave of absence to care for childrenand flexible and reduced work-hours are the main political measures.

Today public child care is an important factor in the everyday lives of Norwegian families with young children. However, the notion of an interventionist state leading Norwegian mothers to the market is substantially overstated (Leira, 1992), because mothers entered the labour market long before the supply of public day care had expanded sufficiently to affect their employment decisions. Moreover, supply is short of demand, and child care is expensive for parents with average incomes or above. Coverage rates in publicly funded child care are 14 percent for children under 2 years old and 60 percent for children aged 3–6 (1991) – much lower rates than those found in Sweden and Denmark. Here again, as with the taxation system, the Norwegian welfare state is found to depart from the ideal Scandinavian or "weak breadwinner" model of welfare. From 1997 children will start school when they are 6 years old (previously 7). Daily school hours are short, however, creating a demand for child care after school hours; such care is also in short supply relative to demand.

However, parents' rights to leave of absence to care for children are generous by international and even Scandinavian standards, with Norway now enjoying the highest rate of compensation for parental leave.[18] There is a basic parental leave of absence in connection with childbirth of 52 weeks with 80 percent earnings compensation.[19] This leave includes a maternal quota, altogether nine weeks before and after birth, which is directed at protecting biological motherhood. There is also a paternal quota of four weeks, which is lost to the parents if not taken by the father.[20] The rest of the leave may be shared between the parents as they prefer. An important element is that the leave can be taken according to a time-account system, which in principle gives a high degree of time flexibility. In addition there are two weeks of unpaid "daddy leave" in connection with the birth, which aims at establishing the social father–child relationship as early as possible. Parents have the right to return to work when the leave is over. Parents with children younger than 3 have the right to reduced work-hours without compensation if this is not disadvantageous to the employer (the Work Environment Act (1977)). Moreover, parents have the right to paid leave of absence to care for sick children – ten days for each parent per year. Public sector employees have full income compensation in high-income brackets when on parental leave, two hours off per day for breastfeeding without loss of salary, and extra unpaid leave (a maximum of three years) before the child is 12 years old. Generally, fathers' benefits have been tied to the rights of their partners, which might now be changed to strengthen men's incentives to take leave. For example, the EU's new social partner agreement on parental leave, which is supposed to be implemented in Norway via the European Economic Agreement (EEA), provides an individual right to parental leave for both mothers and fathers.

The social democratic gender equality policy is directed primarily at changing the institutional structures of parenthood, not just of motherhood, and at putting the question of political fatherhood on the agenda. The underlying idea is partly a family policy concern – to strengthen the father–child relationship – and partly a gender equality policy concern –

---

18 Sweden used to pay 90 percent of earnings to those on parental leave but this has been reduced to 75 pecent; similarly the maximum replacement rate in Finland has been reduced to 66 percent, and in Denmark only 80 percent of unemployment benefits is paid. Most other EU countries do not have paid parental leave, or the pay is at a very low level and/or means tested on household income (Rubery et al., 1996).

19 Or 42 weeks with 100 percent compensation.

20 The paternal quota can be taken by single mothers.

mothers' expanding involvement in the labour market needs to be followed by changes in men's family involvement. This policy is based on a model of a symmetrical family, in which time together with children has a high priority among both mothers and fathers.

Fathers together with their children have become part of the new image of masculinity, and meet private and public approval. Several male top politicians gladly let their private role as fathers on parenthood leave attach to their public role. But the paternal quota is based on the assumption that, in order to change the practices of men, they have to be subjected to structural "coercion". That this reform alone, which makes fairly limited claims on fathers' time, will have profound and rapidly visible effects on the domestic gender division of labour is questionable. Before the "paternal quota" was introduced in 1994, less than 4 percent of all fathers took some of the parental leave (Brandth and Kvande, 1992). A main explanation of fathers taking up leave was mothers' relation to employment. The right to share parents' leave of absence occurred primarily among couples with equal and high levels of income and education. In 1994 the proportion of fathers on leave had increased to one-third, and figures for 1995 indicate a further rise to a high of 70 percent. Coercion seems to be working.[21]

On the other hand, the proportion of fathers working excessively long hours increased simultaneously with mothers' increasing employment rates in the 1980s (Ellingsæter, 1990). This trend might be reversed in the 1990s, because there was a decline in long hours between 1991 and 1994 (Kitterød and Roalsø, 1996). Fathers in the private sector are more likely to work long hours than are men in the public sector, other things being "equal" (Ellingsæter, 1990). Fathers in typical career jobs work longer hours than other men do. Fathers' leave of absence and their work-hours seem to be influenced by different factors. The conflict between the company's temporal claim on the worker and the child's temporal claim on its father seems to be less acute in relation to a limited number of weeks away from the job than in relation to usual work-hours. Absences of short duration apparently do not bring a man's job commitment into question in the same way as reduced hours over longer periods.

Working mothers have been a controversial issue in Norwegian poli-

---

21 There are reasons to believe that there might be differences between the private and the public sector. Fathers in the private sector are compensated financially up to a certain threshold, and compensation beyond this level depends on the goodwill of the employer. Full economic compensation eventually has to be negotiated in the local workplace.

tics, surrounded by considerable ambivalence. Reforms have been brought forward by a series of political compromises and not by the strong consensus across political parties found in the other Scandinavian countries. For example, the main argument in favour of expanding public child care in Denmark and Sweden was concern for working mothers, whereas it was the benefit to children that for a long time was the political rationale of public child care in Norway (Leira, 1992). The family policy field is still loaded with controversies, and there is continuous conservative pressure against publicly subsidized child care. Instead the conservative bloc wants to pay parents cash and leave the choice of child-care arrangements to the parents. Recently, the paternal quota has been the most politically controversial issue. One of the fundamental ideas behind the opposition is to redefine the boundaries between the state and the market. Liberals argue that the state is invading the family and distorting the family's freedom of individual choice.

Ambivalence about working mothers is reflected in the population's attitudes. One survey indicates that only 10 percent of the population aged 26–40 years think it is desirable for women with young children to have full-time work.[22] Expectations toward women are contradictory. In some areas, such as the right to free choice of education irrespective of women's later role as mothers and women's right to a job independent of men's demand for jobs, gender-neutral norms seem to have been established (Ellingsæter et al., 1993; Ellingsæter, 1995b). On the other hand, it is a paradox that, although it is accepted that women do or should "invest" as much in education as a man, many expect that women will not use their education in the same way as men in the labour market when they become mothers. Among women, positive attitudes towards gender equality are generated particularly by access to higher education (Ellingsæter et al., 1994). Many of the conventional gender equality measures have particular impact on the situation of well-educated women, such as preferential treatment in job recruitment and public full-time child-care places.

Thus, one of the most serious problems for women's position in the labour market is if the rights to leave of absence in connection with children and to flexible or reduced work-hours become "mother only" practices, such that female employees become identified as a group with "restrictions". Over-generous schemes utilized by women may serve only as a boomerang, "pricing" women out of the labour market and out of career jobs. The demands from work life, particularly on fathers, obviously conflict with the social democratic symmetrical family ideal.

---

22 Norwegian Social Science Data Services, 1994.

8. The impact of the Norwegian labour market model on gender equality

Gender inequality in the labour market is usually explained by three factors: gender differences in time, in pay, and in skills.

Gender differences in pay and in time derive at least in part from household organization – from the breadwinner model of household provision and from inequality in the gender division of domestic tasks. Nevertheless, the translation of these differences in household position into differences in labour market position depends on both the state of gender relations in the social sphere and the set of labour market institutions, particularly those that regulate pay and working time. Where wage-determination systems, as in Norway, reduce wage dispersion between job categories and between establishments, one of the incentives for gender differentiation and segmentation is removed or at least blunted. There is not the same incentive for employers to segregate male and female workers to facilitate the payment of different wages, and men are less excluded from female job areas on grounds of low wages.

Working-time regulation can also in principle reduce the extent of gender inequality and segregation. Restrictions on the length of full-time work can facilitate women's access to full-time work and at the same time provide a basis for a more equal sharing of domestic work. Where shorter full-time work coincides with opportunities for part-time work, the effects on equality may be diminished, as a consequence of gender segregation between full- and part-time employment. However, rights to reduced hours – that is, to remain in the same job but at reduced hours – can also lessen gender inequality and segregation by providing opportunities for continuous employment in the same occupation even with no change in the traditional domestic division of labour. *Thus the characteristics of the Norwegian labour market model, including low wage dispersion, regulation of working time, leave programmes, and rights to reduced hours, should in principle provide a strong basis for the development of an integrated labour market system.*

The actual degree of integration will nevertheless depend not only on the actual impact of wage and working-time regulations, but also on gender differences in skills and in particular on what determines those gender differences. Gender segregation is not necessarily incompatible with gender equality. On the one hand, gender differences in skills may be regarded as social constructs, serving to reinforce women's social roles as carers and their social subordination to men, and at the same time facilitating employer exploitation of women in the labour market by providing the opportunity to structure conditions of employment for these jobs on terms that are acceptable only to second-income earners (Siltanen, 1995; Craig et al., 1985). Under these conditions moves towards gender equality should involve the integration of occupations and the ending of segregation.

Yet at the same time there is a case for maintaining gender difference. Orientations and aptitudes that are regarded as feminine may currently be excluded from male – and thus high-level – job areas and admitted only within female job areas. Under the difference argument, individual women are not necessarily regarded as having predominantly feminine orientations, but the possibility that certain skills are not currently fully appreciated in work is recognized (Gray, 1994; Gilligan, 1982; Rosener, 1990; Hammond. 1992). From this approach, gender equality may be compatible with continuing segregation, and gender equality is not equated with sameness. However, the consequence of full gender equality would be a restructuring of the system of labour organization to give equal weight to feminine as well as to masculine orientations, thus reducing, for example, the extent and form of hierarchy that currently reflects masculine orientations and male power (Cockburn, 1991). Thus equality under the difference principle would also, for example, involve giving weight to feminine notions of cooperation and teamworking within work organization.

The low wage dispersion and the relatively short full-time working hours within the Norwegian labour market model do not seem to have provided the necessary stimulus for the development of a fully integrated and flexible labour market. Despite relative gender pay equality, there has been little evidence of men moving into traditional female occupations. Moreover, differences between public and private sector wages, especially for higher-qualified workers, have remained relatively important and reinforce gender divisions within the Norwegian model.

Restrictions on working time, although in principle in place, do not seem to have been effective in reducing the share of men working very long hours or in changing the basic domestic division of labour, despite the increased take-up of parental leave by fathers (see above). Working-time restrictions may still have facilitated the increase in women working full time, albeit mainly in female-segregated sectors. Opportunities to work part time are also likely to have increased the share of women following continuous employment careers, thereby reducing the risk of occupational downgrading associated with discontinuous employment patterns (Dex and Shaw, 1986; Dex et al., 1993).

Nor is there evidence – in fact quite the contrary – that the Norwegian model has reduced the degree of gender segregation or taken the opportunity to transform work relations into a more functionally flexible, cooperative, and less hierarchical system. Such systems of work organization could be argued in principle to have major potential benefits for current competitive conditions. Countries that have avoided the structural trappings of hierarchy – such as high pay – that are difficult to remove could in principle be in a better position to implement new systems of work organization involving, for example, flatter hierarchies, teamwork systems, and more flexible, less job-demarcated systems of labour division. In the UK, the prevailing "gender order" has been implicated in the persistence of a low-skill economy, trapped in outmoded systems of work organization, and resulting in underutilization of productive capacities (Bruegel and Perrons, 1995). In addition, the relatively low pay attached to higher-skilled work in Norway could mean in principle that the country could move to a high-skill-based system of work organization without a significant increase in labour costs.

Yet, although Norway has avoided the low-pay trap and also has a strong record on the education of both women and men, it is not yet clear that the Norwegian gender order has unleashed the latent productive potential of its labour force. In the persistence of both horizontal and vertical segregation we perhaps see evidence that the full potential that could be derived from a transformation of gender relations has yet to be realized. As yet there is little research on this topic in Norway, but the absence of discussion may in itself be revealing. One indication that Norway may try to capitalize more effectively on its opportunities to develop new, more productive modes of work organization is found in the training reform, where the reduction in the number of training courses and the extension of the apprenticeship system to cover a wider number of areas and a larger number of people at least in principle suggest a determination to move to a higher-skilled and more flexible system of work organization. How successful this policy will be is as yet unknown.

9. The costs and benefits of the gender equality policy

With little evidence at present of the transformation of Norwegian production and work organization systems, it may be the case that the long-term potential of the equality model has yet to be realized. In Norway, as in all societies, short-term economic calculations may be used to challenge the economic viability of equal opportunities policies. This risk applies even though equality policies can and do generate short-term benefits, and the practices of calculating short-term costs and benefits can be shown to be impregnated with gendered notions of what even constitutes an economic cost or benefit (Holtermann, 1995; Humphries and Rubery, 1995). Nevertheless, the longer-term benefits can be expected to be greater than the short-term returns. If a country's comparative advantage derives ultimately from the capacities of its people, then excluding women from the full development of their capacities must indeed undermine a country's longer-term comparative advantage. This economic argument is in addition to and not a substitute for more basic ethical and social arguments.

Even so, one of the major arguments against the Norwegian model, both internally and externally, is that it is too expensive, to be afforded only by an oil-rich cohesive state where transfers between agents are more socially acceptable and less painful – because of higher income – than would be the case in more "normal" economies. Identifying whether the gender equality dimension of the Norwegian model is an expensive luxury or a model with the potential to be transferred at least in part to non-oil-rich or non-cohesive societies has to be one of the tasks of this assessment.

The costs that may be identified with a gender equality model of labour market organization include:

- relatively high costs of public and private services owing to both high wage costs for lower-skilled work and high levels of provision;
- relatively high welfare benefit costs owing to the individualization of rights to benefits and consequently less targeting of benefits on the most needy households;
- costs to both the state and organizations of parental leave systems, including costs of leave payments, costs of disruption, and costs of finding and training replacements; and costs of rights to reduced hours where employers would prefer full-time work;
- potential erosion of international competitiveness as a consequence of shorter working time in traded sectors;
- the lack of an effective flexible reserve army, such that in periods of high employment migrant labour may have to fill the gap (bringing with it the risk of greater social problems than if women provided the flexible reserve), whereas in periods of low labour demand young people, older workers, and indeed men in general may be exposed to a higher risk of unemployment than if women absorbed the fluctuations in labour demand;
- potential long-term problems of access to employment for younger

and older workers because of the larger size of the prime-age population in work;

- the danger of ever-increasing reliance on credentials and qualifications to ration employment, resulting in overexpenditure on education, underemployment of the educated, and very bleak employment opportunities for educational failures;
- deterioration in the quality of life if the result of gender equality is longer work-hours for all or the substitution of inferior social provision of services for higher-quality family provision.

The potential and realized benefits from a gender equality model include:

- the opportunity for women as well as men to use their capacities to the full – including their innate capacities but also their acquired skills and education – in contrast to labour markets where women either do not participate after childbirth or face occupational downgrading if they take time out for child care;
- the opportunity for firms to retain their skilled female labour forces even over the childrearing phase;
- the development of comparative advantage in high-skill areas owing to the large supply of highly educated labour available at relatively low costs (in part because the educated lose bargaining power when education is not a scarce commodity);
- the sharing of the costs of marital breakdown, instead of the concentration of the costs on women who have "specialized" in domestic work;
- increased opportunities for men to participate in family life as a consequence of the lifting of the burden of being the sole provider, the opportunity to work fewer hours, and the provision of parental leave;
- the opportunity, in principle, to adjust more rapidly, and with lower risks of social exclusion and long-term unemployment, to industrial and occupational change, because the narrower range of wage levels should in theory facilitate occupational and inter-firm mobility;
- a lower share of the population not in employment and who therefore risk social exclusion and/or becoming a burden on the state;

- greater equality of access to social welfare, thereby reducing the incidence of poverty in old age or as a result of family breakdown;

- reduced family risk of social exclusion, as a result of both parents having established links to the labour market so that unemployment for one parent does not result in the household losing all links to wage employment;

- a redistribution in favour of families with young children, which should enhance the material welfare of children and allow preferences for the use of child-care facilities and other forms of socialized care to be realized (where care is funded out of current resources, serious underprovision of care facilities may result because the need for care may coincide with periods of extreme budget constraint);

- enhanced well-being and sense of social justice, particularly amongst women.

Although as many arguments can be made about the benefits as about the costs of equality labour market models, gender equality policy debates often start from a defensive position. In part this defensiveness arises out of a deep-seated uncertainty about how to regard the role of services within an economy. This issue needs discussion before we can enter into an assessment of the balance sheet between benefits and costs in the Norwegian model.

Can service sector employment actually be regarded as contributing to output or is it more appropriately regarded as a cost of production? And how should domestic labour be treated – as contributing to national income or as an invisible activity? And, if invisible, how should we react to the socialization of domestic labour through the growth of public or private sector services?

The tendency amongst economists to regard services, especially public services, as unproductive and to consider domestic labour to be an efficient means of organizing social reproduction is summed up by Sherwin Rosen's argument that in Sweden there are too many women employed in the production of household goods and services and too few in the material goods sector.

> If Swedish women take care of each other's parents in exchange for taking care of each other's children, how much extra real output comes of it? (Rosen, 1995).

The use of public resources as the source of funding for substitutes for domestic labour is regarded as particularly suspect by economists; it is notable perhaps that Rosen does not ask what extra output comes of American fast food chains staffed by women providing a substitute for domestic production of food. Because public services tend to be free at the point of delivery, or at least subsidized, the argument is made that there is no real evidence that consumers would purchase these services if they were given choices. In contrast, fast food consumption derives legitimacy from the fact that it is purchased; it is assumed to add to the nation's wealth, even if at the expense of the nation's health. Public services apparently distort the goods markets through their effects on the level of taxation and may crowd out more productive private sector expenditure. Moreover, free or heavily subsidized public services are believed to distort the "market for care" by inducing families to choose lower-quality provision than would be available through either family or private provision. Some parts of this argument need to be taken seriously, in particular that the right not to work and to provide care within the family should be recognized alongside the right to work. Such rights are, however, arguably greater under the Swedish and Norwegian parental leave and other care leave systems than in the USA, for example, where opting out of the labour market to care for a short period of time may jeopardize lifetime career prospects. Parental leave systems extend choices by reducing the high penalties imposed for time out of the labour market.

The argument against public provision relies on two further questionable assumptions: first that there are no benefits in terms of either efficiency or quality in favour of collective care, despite evidence of the benefits to children from early education; and second that domestic labour is available for free so why subsidize it and socialize it? Rosen is influenced by the Lindbeck statement that Sweden has "nationalized the family", which must, according to the way this is quoted, necessarily be a regrettable development. In this approach, there is no explicit consideration of the different assessments of the costs and benefits of socialized care from a woman's perspective; household utility and male and female utility are assumed to be equivalent.

Even more importantly still, the argument fails to address the question of how both employment and households will be organized in the future. The changes taking place in women's social and economic roles in all societies are redefining and indeed undermining the male breadwinner model of household organization, which is simply assumed as a constant in the Rosen argument. This restructuring of the family economy is not solely or mainly dependent upon the provision of public services but is occurring in countries such as the UK and the USA where there is very limited public provision of care. Moreover, as many writers have pointed out, the male breadwinner model involves high state transfers to male breadwinner households and high wage costs to maintain a breadwinner wage (Esping-Andersen, 1995; Maier, 1995; Schmid, 1994). This pattern is also not sustainable. The American model offers an alternative system where domestic services are replaced by market services (both consumption and social services) rendered affordable by low wages, but which are then not available to that part of the population providing the low-wage labour. Esping-Andersen (1995) has suggested that the best way forward is to develop two-income-earner family systems based on minimal self-provisioning; this system is best for employment and best for protection against poverty, as well as, importantly, matching women's aspirations. Esping-Andersen and others foresee problems with the Scandinavian model, particularly with respect to the cost of funding these services, which are not subject to major productivity growth. Some modifications to the Scandinavian model may be proposed, such as, in Esping-Andersen's case, the creation of low-wage jobs for groups at certain points of their life cycles, particularly young people, but few consider a return to domestic labour based around the male breadwinner nuclear household as either a realistic or a desirable alternative.

It may be less essential to reconcile these issues within the Norwegian economy than within the Swedish economy because there is some consensus that Norway can at least afford public services provision and has made a conscious social choice to socialize parts of, but by no means all, domestic labour. Moreover, the costs of child care in Norway are still to a significant extent passed on to the parents. Even though Norway can be considered to have adopted a more modest version of the gender equality Scandinavian model than, for example, Sweden has, it may still be difficult in many non-Scandinavian countries to establish the degree of social consensus to "invest" in a gender equality model. Thus the issue of the transferability of the Norwegian model hinges as much on political and social attitudes as on the question of affordability. A social consensus may be more likely to emerge if it can be argued that men would benefit as well as women. In this case more evidence needs to be found on the impact of the Norwegian system on income distribution between types of households – by age and by presence or otherwise of young children, for example. Research in the UK has recently found that young people are finding it more difficult to make the transition to economic independence and to establish their own households (Irwin, 1995), but these problems may be greatest in societies where there is a continuation of the principle of the male provider in a context where young men in practice are unable to fulfil this role. Problems intensify where more of the costs of children are being privatized onto families. The issue of "Who pays for the kids?" (Folbre, 1994) may provide a basis for solidarity between men and women and for learning from Norwegian experience.

One issue that is not fully clear in the Norwegian system is whether the system of wage determination actually increases or decreases the relative cost of public service work. As we saw earlier, the main effect is to raise pay for the lower skilled but to reduce it for the higher skilled. Because nursing and teaching absorb a high share of public sector employment, the net result for the public services on costs may not be as high as might be imagined. What will be higher will be the costs of lower-skilled work in both public and private services, resulting perhaps in a lower share of market services where low-skilled work predominates. What is clear from the data is that higher-educated women are bearing quite a high degree of the burden of moderating the costs of public service provision. This may not be a stable situation even in the Norwegian context (as we discuss above and below), but certainly it may be a particularly difficult approach to sell to other countries where women professionals are already higher paid in relative terms than Norwegian women professionals but who still have a case for higher pay on the basis of equal pay for work of equal value.

The claim that Norway has a gender equality model may need to be modified because it may achieve equality more for women on average than between comparable groups of women and men. The overall Norwegian model could be regarded as an example of "solidarity within one class", but when we look at the case of women we find the notion of solidarity to be taken one stage further – women are expected to show sisterhood in pursuing their economic interests as a group. This reliance on sisterhood between women, both in the national interest – in the sense of keeping a lid on wage inflation – and in the interests of women as a whole, is itself a form of gender discrimination that is prevalent in all societies.

This approach can be found in employers' attitudes to skill pay differentials for women, where women are expected first of all to be less concerned about receiving a fair reward for effort, and secondly to compare their pay primarily with other women workers (Armstrong, 1982; Craig et al., 1985). Women may also be expected, particularly in professional jobs, to be motivated more by intrinsic than by extrinsic rewards. Feminist writers may have contributed to the emphasis on sisterhood by developing the notion that the long agenda for equal opportunities involves more egalitarian pay structures, flatter hierarchies, and less authoritarian and more cooperative modes of work behaviour (Cockburn, 1991). Implicitly, more advantaged women are expected not to pursue the goal of higher pay and labour market power, in order to foster new and more egalitarian systems of work organization and also possibly to maximize the employment opportunities for women. However, abstaining from competition for pay, privileges, and power may still prove insufficient, in Norway and elsewhere, for bringing about this transformation. Women do share a joint interest in maintaining and developing the welfare state services, but they also have divergent interests and opportunities. Women professionals may have an interest not only in pressing for higher pay for themselves but also in opportunities to use cheap private sector services, both of which imply a breakdown of wage solidarity. Tensions thus exist between women's interests as a group and the interests of particular groups of women.

At the political level, women still support public provision of services more strongly than do men, although both men and women employed in the public sector support the welfare model more strongly than do those in the private sector (Bratterud, 1995). Feminist orientation is also strongly related to support for the welfare state. Thus, although more women professionals can be regarded as "disadvantaged" by the low wages in the public sector, it remains an open question whether the strongest challenges to the wage solidarity policy will come from women or from men.

10. Gender relations and the future prospects for the Norwegian labour market model

The Norwegian government is very conscious of its distinctive model for employment and has published several documents that outline the Norwegian model, its key features, and the critical conditions for future development. However, no explicit mention is made of the role of the gender order in structuring the current model or defining future prospects (see, for example, the pamphlet Put Europe to Work: A Solidarity Alternative for Increased Growth, Competitiveness and Performance published by the Royal Norwegian Ministry of Finance, 1995). It could perhaps be regarded as a truism of labour market analysis that the most distinctive features of any country's labour market tends to be taken for granted within that country. Yet the future prospects for the Norwegian model can be argued to depend to a significant extent on gender issues. Likewise the future shaping of gender relations in Norway will be influenced by – but not fully determined by – the development and adjustment of the Norwegian labour market model.

To explore future prospects further we have identified a set of six possible critical points, which in some cases reflect "worst case" conditions, where gender issues may surface to affect the development of the Norwegian labour market model. These include:

- challenges to the solidarity wage policy;
- a brake on the growth of public services;
- pressure for the reconstitution of a low-paid domestic service labour market;
- problems associated with high and/or recurrent unemployment for young males;
- rejection by women of the part-time employment path and demand for more full-time work opportunities;
- further rejection of the equality model by private sector employers.

These developments are chosen to highlight some of the critical conditions for the continuation of the Norwegian equality model; there is no presumption that all or any of these developments are unavoidable or even probable. However, by identifying these critical points, it may be possible to suggest ways in which policy intervention at an early stage might facilitate a positive evolution of the Norwegian model and prevent the development of strong inconsistencies and incompatibilities between the basic elements of the model and the expectations and desires of both employers and employees.

The first example – major challenges to the solidarity wage policy – would appear to be most likely to result from discontent among public sector professionals, particularly women but also men. Some evidence of the discontent is found in the tendency for more highly educated younger women to enter the private sector. This situation would be more likely to be avoided if there was some commitment to an evolution of the relative pay structure within the public sector, so that low overall pay increases did not necessarily imply a freezing of the existing structure. This evolution may require commitments to change differentials over a reasonably long period of time, involving both increasing and decreasing real wages for jobs where the pay level is not appropriate to the skill involved.

If the result of a modification of the solidarity wage policy is an increase in the wage bill for the public sector, especially the municipalities, a social choice will have to be made about whether these higher costs will be funded. If these are not funded, the higher wages for professionals may well be funded by lower aggregate employment opportunities, particularly for women. One problem, therefore, may be that improvements for some women appear to deprive other women, with this conflict between women's interests disguising the fact that men still hold on, even in Norway, to a higher share of available resources. Women are unlikely to return willingly to the home and instead may compete more actively for jobs in the private sector.

One solution to the high costs of public services, which may be favoured by men and indeed some women, may be to reconstitute a cheap domestic and private service labour market, perhaps based on student labour or immigrants. However, the relative homogeneity of the Norwegian social structure is likely to limit the supply of labour to such a sector, thereby reducing its viability as an alternative to public sector services.

The fourth situation – that of young men facing a disproportionate risk of unemployment or recurrent unemployment – could in fact result from the failure of the Norwegian model to use its solidaristic wage policy to break down the system of gender segregation. Unemployment for less educated men in particular may become an increasing problem. Jobs for which less qualified men have traditionally trained have been declining over the long period and are subject to strong cyclical fluctuations – e.g. in construction. Considerable thought perhaps needs to be given to the new apprenticeship system to ensure that the jobs for which both young men and young women are being trained offer some chance of continuous employment over at least the medium term, and this may imply some modification of the gender division of labour among the vocationally trained. Opening up areas that are currently dominated by women will not necessarily be regarded positively by either sex. However, the problem could be eased by simultaneously adopting policies to move women up the occupational job hierarchy to reduce the long-term underemployment of women, while aiming to reduce segregation and gender stereotyping among young people, especially the less well qualified. In the past, most effort has been placed on encouraging women to enter traditional male manual occupations, but future policies, including the new apprenticeship system, may need to encourage flexibility in both directions. One important constraint on the ability of training schemes to decrease segregation may be the attitudes of employers, who in effect choose the apprentice and thus can impose their view of the appropriate gender of the recruit. This is a difficult problem to solve because training often increases its labour market value where employers are actively involved in the training.

However, it has been suggested that, although a shortage of low-qualified jobs, especially for young men, is predicted in most European countries, in Norway the rise in the educational level of the youth population may outstrip the decline in jobs for the less educated. This could be considered as either a very optimistic interpretation of Norwegian employment prospects, or alternatively a prognosis of structural unemployment, where Norwegians will increasingly become overqualified for the jobs available.

Rejection of part-time work by an increasing share of prime-age women is already evident in the cohort analysis. Anticipatory action to offset the effects of such changes in behaviour could include a reduction in full-time work-hours to avoid a situation where access to work is monopolized by prime-age men and women. This group is in a particularly strong position to monopolize work. By prime age most have found access to employment and have acquired skills and are unlikely to lose their jobs except through redundancy. This applies to women as well as to men with the development of maternity and parental leave and the right to reduced working hours. This prime-age group is thus in effect the insider group in the labour market, and the outsider group consists of those who have not already obtained access to work (i.e. the young), the minority of prime-age workers who are made redundant, and older workers who may be squeezed out of employment. Previously the outsiders used to include women returners, but now the concentration of worklessness falls more on both men and women at different stages in the life cycle. The breakdown of the old rationing system of employment – women doing without work or making do with partial work – needs to be explicitly recognized and a new rationing system devised and introduced. The high participation rates of women and the low wage dispersion may put Norway in a strong position in theory to contemplate reductions in working hours without full earnings compensation for male full-timers as their partners move from part-time to full-time work at relatively similar rates of pay. A further solution to the problem may be found if men, as is in some sense the aim of Norwegian family policy, begin to change their working-time and work patterns, moving more towards the female model at the same time as women move towards the male model. How far public policy can be influential in moving the model in the direction of more flexible and more equal working-time patterns by gender will be constrained by the willingness of private sector companies to adopt the gender equality model. The Norwegian economy is relatively protected from multinationals, with their belief in textbook human resource management practice, and thus Norway has perhaps more freedom than others to impose its own socially accepted equality model. However, even in Norway there are some examples of attempts to "import" flexibility models of employment – for example the attempt to introduce flexible working into the SAS hotel chain (Dølvik, 1995). Moreover there is already some evidence that private companies are less willing to hire women and bear the costs of the equality model, including parental leave, than is the case in the public sector. If private sector companies were to increase resistance, Norwegian women, who up to now have maintained a high fertility rate, may be faced more frequently with a choice between careers or families, or alternatively accept increased segregation in the public sector.

Gender issues are thus likely to emerge as key factors in the evolution of the Norwegian labour market model. To some extent the pattern of development in gender relations will itself be influenced by the path taken in employment, wage, and family policy, but evidence from all advanced countries has also suggested that the process of female integration into the wage economy and the associated changes in family gender relations are not processes that can be put into reverse by labour market policy. Labour market policy and institutions can of course still influence and shape gender relations, and particularly influence the quality of both men's and women's experience in the labour market, but countries cannot any longer necessarily choose between different models – the strong or the weak breadwinner model for example. The displacement of the strong breadwinner model by a modified breadwinner model in Norway (or by conditional equality – Ellingsæter, 1995b) is thus a permanent development, and restraining public services will not reverse the processes of integration induced by the initial expansion of public services. All of the potential problems that gender relations poses for the Norwegian model thus require solutions that do not overstate the scope for public policy to influence gender and familial relations or to impose a return to a breadwinner model of society. However, the major statements on the Norwegian labour market model fail even to discuss gender relations as an integral part of the Norwegian model, let alone as a significant continuing constraint and influence on public policy choices.

Consequently there is little awareness of the advantages that could accrue to Norway from having already made the transition to a dual-breadwinner system, based around relatively low wages but high education levels. Norway is in a strong position to exploit a comparative advantage as a high-skill, low-labour-cost country. Those countries still organized around a single-breadwinner model face potentially much greater problems of transition to a new gender order, requiring a redistribution not only of work but also of earnings if dual-earner systems are not to lead to much wider household income inequalities. Wage compression in Norway has been associated not with decreasing but with rising skill and educational levels. It has yet to be seen whether Norway can harness these advantages and deliver innovative and competitive industries and services, but the likelihood of success is greater if policy-makers recognize that the more equal gender order represents more an asset for than a constraint on future economic development.

References

Arbeidsdirektoratet (1994) *Delvis sysselsatte arbeidssøkere.* Oslo: Rapport 1994:3.

Arbeidsdirektoratet (1995a) *Kvartalsrapport om arbeidsmarkedet.* Oslo: 2/1995.

Arbeidsdirektoratet (1995b) *Kvartalsrapport om arbeidsmarkedet.* Oslo: 4/1995.

Arbeidsdirektoratet (1995c) *Månedsstatistikk for arbeidsmarkedet.* Oslo: 8/1995.

Armstrong, P. (1982) If it's only women it doesn't matter so much. In J. West (ed.), *Work, Women and the Labour Market.* London: Routledge.

Asplund, R. et al. (1995) The male–female wage gap in the Nordic countries. In N. Westergaard-Nielsen (ed.), *Wage Differentials in the Nordic Countries.* Amsterdam: North Holland.

Barth, E. (1992) *Lønnsforskjeller mellom kvinner og menn i Norge.* Oslo: Institutt for samfunnsforskning.

Barth, E. and A. Mastekaasa (1993) Lønnsforskjeller mellom kvinner og menn 1980–1991: Hvilken betydning har utdanningsnivået? *Søkelys på arbeidsmarkedet* 10: 77–82.

Barth, E. and H. Yin (1995) Promotions, career profiles and the gender wage gap. Paper presented at the EALE 1995 Conference, Lyon.

Barth, E. and H. Yin (1996) *Lønnsforskjeller og lønnssystem i staten.* Oslo: Institutt for samfunnsforskning.

Bjørklund, T. (1991) Sysselsettingen i offentlig sektor 1960–1990. Noen hovedlinjer i utviklingen. *Søkelys på arbeidsmarkedet* 8: 107–113.

Bjurstrøm, H. (1993) *Deltidsansattes rettigheter. En komparativ studie av Danmark, England, Norge og Tyskland.* Oslo: Institutt for samfunnsforskning.

Blau, F. (1993) Gender and economic outcomes: The role of wage structure. *Labour* 7: 73–92.

Blau, F. and L. Kahn (1992) The gender earnings gap: Learning from international comparisons. *American Economic Review*, May: 533–538.

Blix, W.-K. and L. Gulbrandsen (1992) Småbarnsmødre er ikke noe B-lag på arbeidsmarkedet. *Søkelys på arbeidsmarkedet* 9: 17–21.

Brandth, B. and E. Kvande (1992) Fedres arbeidsvilkår og omsorgspermisjoner. *Søkelys på arbeidsmarkedet* 9: 158–166.

Bratterud, Å. (1995) Blir kvinner velferdsstatens støttespillere? In A. T. Jensen and W. Martinussen (eds), *Velferdsstaten i våre hjerter.* Oslo: Ad Notam.

Bruegel, I. and D. Perrons (1995) Where do the costs of unequal treatment for women fall? An analysis of the incidence of the costs of unequal pay and sex discrimination in the UK. In J. Humphries and J. Rubery (eds), *The Economics of Equal Opportunities.* Manchester: Equal Opportunities Commission.

Cockburn, C. (1991) *In the Way of Women: Men's Resistance to Sex Equality in Organizations.* London: Macmillan.

Colbjørnsen, T. and K. A. Larsen (1995) *Arbeidsløshet i en oppgangstid.* Oslo: Arbeidsdirektoratet.

Connell, R. (1989) *Gender and Power.* Cambridge: Polity Press.

Craig,C., E. Garnsey, and J. Rubery (1985) *Payment Structures in Smaller Firms – Women's Employment in Segmented Labour Markets.* Department of Employment Research Paper No. 48. London: Employment Department.

Davies, K. and J. Esseveld (1989) Factory women, redundancy and the search for work: Toward a reconceptualisation of employment and unemployment. *Sociological Review* 37: 219–252.

Dex, S. and L. Shaw (1986) *British and American Women at Work: Do Equal Opportunities Policies Matter?* London: Macmillan.

Dex, S., P. Walters, and D. Alden (1993) *French and British Mothers at Work.* London: Macmillan.

Dølvik, J.E. (1995) *Striden ved SAS-hotellet.* En oppsummering av høring 30.8.1995 arrangert av LO og Hotell- og restaurantarbeiderforbundet. Oslo: FAFO notat 1995:11.

Ellingsæter, A. L. (1987) *Ulikhet i arbeidstidsmønstre.* In NOU 1987:9b Vedlegg til Arbeidstidsutvalgets utredning. Oslo. Universitetsforlaget.

Ellingsæter, A. L. (1989) *Normalisering av deltidsarbeidet.* Oslo: Statistisk sentralbyrå.

Ellingsæter, A. L. (1990) *Fathers Working Long Hours. Trends, Causes and Consequences.* Oslo: Institute for Social Research.

Ellingsæter, A. L. (1995a) Kjønn, deltid og fleksibilitet i arbeidsmarkedet. Det norske eksemplet. In D. Olberg (ed.), *Endringer i arbeidslivets organisering.* Oslo: FAFO.

Ellingsæter, A. L. (1995b) *Gender, Work and Social Change. Beyond Dualistic Thinking.* Oslo: Institute for Social Research.

Ellingsæter, A. L. and G. Iversen (1984) *Endringer i kvinners arbeidsmarkedstilpasninger.* Oslo: Statistisk sentralbyrå.

Ellingsæter, A. L. and M. Rønsen (1996) The dual strategy: Motherhood and the work contract in Scandinavia. *Tidsskrift for samfunnsforskning*, no. 3.

Ellingsæter, A. L, T. Noack, and M. Rønsen (1993) Utdanning, arbeid og inntekt – hvor likestilte er kvinner og menn blitt? *Samfunnsspeilet* 7: 2–9.

Ellingsæter, A. L., T. Noack, and M. Rønsen (1994) Likestilling – et ideal for velutdannede kvinner? *Samfunnsspeilet* 8: 7–10.

Ellingsæter, A. L., T. Noack, and M. Rønsen (1997) Sosial ulikhet blant kvinner: Polarisering, utjevning eller status quo? *Tidsskrift for samfunnsforskning*, no. 1.

Engelstad, F. (1990) Oppsigelser ved driftsinnskrenkninger. *Tidsskrift for samfunnsforskning* 31: 319–339.

Esping-Andersen, G. (1990) *The Three Worlds of Welfare Capitalism.* Cambridge: Polity Press.

Esping-Andersen, G. (1995) *Europe's welfare states at the end of the century: Frozen Fordism or postindustrial adaptation?.* Paper presented at the 17th conference of the International Working Party on Labour Market Segmentation, University of Sienna, July.

Folbre, N. (1994) *Who Pays for the Kids? Gender and the Structures of Constraint.* London: Routledge.

Gilligan, C. (1982) *In a Different Voice: Psychological Theory and Women's Development.* Cambridge, MA: Harvard University Press.

Ginn, J. and Arber, S. (1994) Gender and pensions in Europe: Current trends in women's pension acquisition. In P. Brown and R. Crompton (eds), *A New Europe? Economic Restructuring and Social Exclusion.* Canterbury: UCL Press.

Gray, B. (1994) Women-only management training – a past and present. In M. Tanton (ed.), *Women in Management: A Developing Presence.* London: Routledge.

Grimshaw, D., Rubery, J., and Smith, M. (1996) Unemployment and systems of unemployment compensation: A reassessment drawing on evidence from EU member states. Paper presented at International Working Party on Labour Market Segmentation Conference on Employment Systems and Welfare States, Tampere, Finland, July.

Halvorsen, K. (1994) *Arbeidsløshet og arbeidsmarginalisering.* Oslo: Universitetsforlaget.

Hammond, V. (1992) Gender: What does the research tell us? *Management Development Review* 5(1): 6–7.

Hansen, M. N. (1992) Kjønnssegregering i det norske arbeidsmarkedet. *Søkelys på arbeidsmarkedet* 9: 85–92.

Hansen, M. N. (1995) *Sex Segregation and the Welfare State.* Oslo: Institute for Social Research.

Hansen, M. N. and E. Rogg (1991) Høyere utdanning i Norge. Rekruttering, finansiering og omfordeling. *Tidsskrift for samfunnsforskning* 32: 387–416.

Hernæs, E. and S. Strøm (1994) Tilbake til jobb. *Søkelys på arbeidsmarkedet* 11: 109–112.

Hobæk, T. (1993) Skjult ledighet: Undersysselsetting. *Samfunnsspeilet* 7: 5–7.

Hoel, M. (1994) *Lønns- og personalpolitiske virkemidler i kommunesektoren.* Oslo: Institute for Social Research.

Hoel, M. (1995) Differensiering i arbeidsmarkedet og kvinners lønn. Lecture for the Dr. philos. degree, University of Oslo, 4 May.

Høgsnes, G. (1995) Wage determination and the male–female wage gap: The case of Norway. *Comparative Social Research* 15: 167–186.

Holtermann, S. (1995) The costs and benefits to British employers of measures to promote equality of opportunity. In J. Humphries and J. Rubery (eds), *The Economics of Equal Opportunities.* Manchester: Equal Opportunities Commission.

Humphries, J. and J. Rubery, eds (1995) *The Economics of Equal Opportunities.* Manchester: Equal Opportunities Commission.

Irwin, S. (1995) Rights of Passage: *Social Change and the Transition from Youth to Adulthood.* London: UCL Press.

Isaksen, A. and M. Simensen (1995) *Mot et mer fleksibelt arbeidsmarked?* Oslo: Arbeidsdirektoratet.

Jørgensen, T. (1993) Utdanning. In *Sosialt utsyn* 1993. Oslo: Statistics Norway.

Kaul, H. and E. Kvande (1986) *Mestring av arbeidsledighet.* Trondheim: IFIM.

Kitterød, H. (1993) *Fullt og helt eller stykkevis og delt? Deltidsarbeid i Norge og EF -omfang og endring.* Oslo: Institutt for samfunnsforskning.

Kitterød, H. and K.-M. Roalsø (1996) Arbeidstid og arbeidsønsker blant foreldre. *Samfunnsspeilet* 10: 12–23.

Kjeldstad, R. (1991) 1980-årene: Småbarnsmødrenes tiår på arbeidsmarkedet. *Samfunnsspeilet* 5: 16–19.

Kjeldstad, R. and J. Lyngstad (1993) *Arbeid, lønn og likestilling.* Oslo: Universitetsforlaget.

Kjeldstad, R. and K.-M. Roalsø (1995) Enslige forsørgere – trygd, arbeid eller begge deler? *Samfunnsspeilet* 9: 33–39.

Kvande, E. and B. Rasmussen (1990) *Nye kvinneliv. Kvinner i menns organisasjoner.* Oslo: Ad Notam.

Kvande, E. and B. Rasmussen (1995) Intensification through decentralization. Paper to the second European Conference of Sociology, Budapest, 30 August – 2 September.

Leira, A. (1992) *Welfare States and Working Mothers.* Cambridge: Cambridge University Press.

Lewis, J. (1992) Gender and the development of welfare regimes. *Journal of European Social Policy* 2: 159–173.

Lyngstad, J. and B. Strand (1992) Gifte kvinner: Fra forsørget til forsørger? *Samfunnsspeilet* 6: 34–36.

Maier, F. (1995) Skill formation and equal opportunity – A comparative perspective. In J. Humphries and J. Rubery (eds), *The Economics of Equal Opportunities.* Manchester: Equal Opportunities Commission.

Mastekaasa, A. (1994) Dårligere arbeidsmiljø? *Søkelys på arbeidsmarkedet* 11: 159–165.

NOU (1976) *Familiebeskatning.* NOU 1976:12. Oslo: Universitetsforlaget.

OECD (1988) *Employment Outlook* 1988. Paris.

OECD (1991) *Employment Outlook* 1991. Paris.

OECD (1995) *Employment Outlook* 1995. Paris.

Pedersen, P.A. (1995) *Investering i utdanning.* Bergen: SNF.

Petersen, T. and L. Morgan (1995) Separate and unequal: Occupational-establishment sex segregation and the gender wage gap. *American Journal of Sociology* 101: 329–365.

Petersen, T., L.-E. Becken, and V. Snartland (1994) Lønnsforskjeller mellom kvinner og menn i privat sektor. *Tidsskrift for samfunnsforskning* 35: 155–189.

Rogstad, J. (1993) *Overtidsarbeid blant lønnstakere.* Oslo: Institutt for samfunnsforskning.

Rosen, S. (1995) *Public employment and the welfare state in Sweden.* Occasional Paper No. 61. NBER/SNS project, Reforming the Welfare State. Stockholm: Centre for Business and Policy Studies, January.

Rosener, J. (1990) Ways women lead. *Harvard Business Review* November/December: 119–125.

Royal Norwegian Ministry of Finance (1995) *Put Europe to Work: A Solidarity Alternative for Increased Growth, Competitiveness and Employment.* Oslo.

Rubery, J. (1989) Labour market flexibility in Britain. In F. Green (ed.), *The Restructuring of the UK Economy.* Brighton: Harvester Wheatsheaf.

Rubery, J. and C. Fagan (1994) Does feminization mean a flexible labour force? In R. Hyman and A. Ferner (eds), *New Frontiers in European Industrial Relations.* Oxford: Blackwell.

Rubery, J., M. Smith, C. Fagan, and D. Grimshaw (1996) *Women and the European Employment Rate: The Causes and Consequences of Variations in Female Activity and Employment Patterns in the European Union.* Report for the European Network on the Situation of Women in the Labour Market. Brussels: DG-V, Equal Opportunities Unit.

Schmid, G. (1994) *Cooperation and competition between the sexes: Institutional alternatives for justice and efficiency in labour markets.* Paper presented at the 6th International Conference of the Society for the Advancement of Socio-Economics. HEC School of Management, Jouy-en-Josas, Paris, July.

Siltanen, J. (1995) *Locating Gender.* London: UCL Press.

Skrede, K. (1989) *Work, Family and Life-cycle Squeezes: The Need for a Social and Economic Policy for the Reproductive Sphere.* Oslo: INAS.

Statistics Norway (1993) *Labour Market Statistics* 1992. Oslo.
Statistics Norway (1994) *Labour Market Statistics* 1993. Oslo.
Statistics Norway (1995) *Labour Market Statistics* 1994. Oslo.
Statistics Norway (1992) *Survey of Level of Living* 1991. Oslo.
Statistics Norway (1996) *Survey of Level of Living* 1995. Oslo.
Stortingsmelding 70 (1992) *Likestillingspolitikk for 1990-åra.* Oslo: Barne- og familiedepartementet.
Teigen, M. and R. S. Jensen (1995) *Kjønnskvotering i utdanning og arbeidsliv.* Oslo: Institutt for samfunnsforskning.
Teigen, M. and J. Wiers-Jenssen (1996) Ansettelser til stillinger i sentralforvaltningen. Mimeo.
Torp, H. (1990) Fleksibel arbeidskraft. In H. Torp and K. Skollerud (eds), *Organisasjon, arbeidsmiljø og mobilitet.* Oslo: Institute for Social Research.
Torp, H. (1994) Arbeidsløsheten og kvinners yrkesaktivitet. 11: 29–31.

Chapter 5

Why Has Unemployment Been so Low in Norway? On the Potential of Macroeconomic Explanations

Asbjørn Rødseth

1. Introduction

Compared to the European average the Norwegian unemployment performance looks impressive (Figure 1). Massive increases in European unemployment followed the two oil price shocks in 1973 and 1979. Norwegian unemployment increased only slightly, and quickly returned to the old level. In the mid-1980s Norwegian unemployment set out on a path of its own, increasing rapidly in 1987–1990 when unemployment fell in the rest of Europe. This article is an attempt to assess the role played by macroeconomic factors (fiscal and monetary policy, oil revenues, etc.) in making the Norwegian unemployment history so different from the rest of Europe.

Norway's unemployment history is not unique. Sweden is an example of a country with a broadly similar development, although the last increase in unemployment started three years later there (Figure 1). In discussions of European unemployment the former EFTA countries (Norway, Sweden, Finland, Iceland, Austria, Switzerland) are often lumped together as countries with a similar story.[1] At its peak in 1993 unemployment in Norway was for a brief period at roughly the same level as in Germany, the Netherlands and Portugal, but since then a gap in Norway's favour has arisen again.

A large number of international studies have emphasized *institutional factors* like centralized wage bargaining and short duration of unemployment benefits (Bruno and Sachs, 1985; Layard, Nickell, and Jackman, 1991). It is claimed that Norwegian institutions have produced low real wage rigidity, which again has led to low unemployment.

---

1 There have been notable differences between them, though. Finland had relatively high unemployment in the late 1970s. After having had low unemployment throughout most of the 1980s, it had the second highest unemployment rate in Europe in the early 1990s.

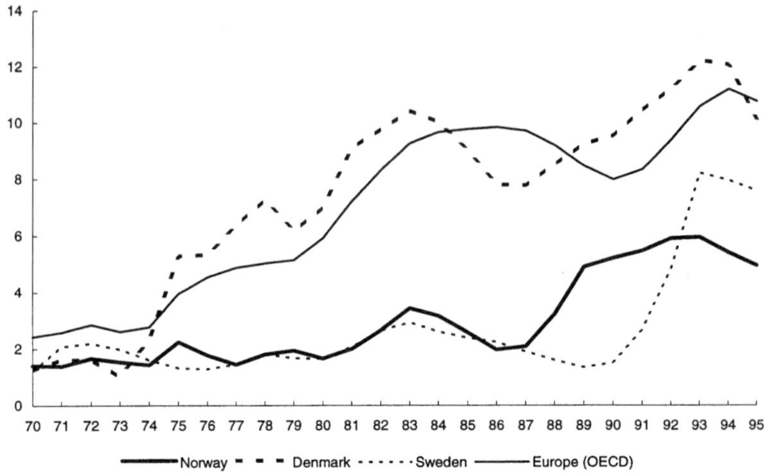

Figure 5.1 Unemployment rates 1970-1995

Source: OECD Economic Outlook (Statistical Compendium 1996/1)

As an antithesis, a study by Eika (1996) attributes most of the difference to *North-Sea oil* and the effect this has had on aggregate demand both directly and through the government budget. According to Eika, unemployment in Norway would have increased substantially both in the mid-1970s and in the early 1980s if it were not for the oil discoveries. Around 1990 it would have exceeded the European average.

Sweden and Denmark have similar institutions (trade unions, welfare provisions) as Norway. Therefore, if one attempts institutional explanations of the Norwegian story, it is intriguing why Denmark had so much higher unemployment (Figure 5.1). If one attempts to explain the Norwegian story by oil revenues, it is intriguing why Sweden behaved the same way as Norway.

Section 2 is a brief overview of macroeconomic developments since 1970 in Norway and in OECD Europe. In Section 3 we discuss the role of institutional versus macroeconomic explanations. Section 4 is devoted to a more detailed account of the episodes where the macroeconomic history of Norway deviates from that of the rest of Europe. Section 5 contains a brief comparison to Sweden and Denmark. Section 6 concludes with some brief remarks about the future.

2. A brief overview of macroeconomic developments

Output and employment growth

Yearly GDP growth in Norway between 1970 and 1995 was 0.8% higher than the European average (Table 1). The high growth must to a large extent be attributed to the discovery of oil on the Norwegian continental shelf in the late 1960s. However, it is remarkable that even if we exclude the oil industry the Norwegian growth rate was only slightly below the European average, and higher than the growth rates of Sweden and Denmark. The oil industry in the first half of the 1990s made up around 15% of GDP and more than 30% of exports. The PPP figures (Table 2) show that Norway's GDP was below average in 1970 and well above average in 1993. Employment, measured in numbers, grew significantly faster in Norway than in Europe as a whole (0.9% against 0.2%) and faster than in the two neighbouring countries (Table 1). Even at the end of the period the oil industry had no more than 1% of total employment. Thus, the direct employment in the oil industry plays only a small part in employment growth. In 1973 the labour force participation of Norwegian women was above the European average, but more than 10 percentage points lower than in Sweden and Denmark (Table 2). In 1994 this had increased by 21 percentage points and was only slightly below the participation rates in Sweden and Denmark. The

Table 1 Average yearly growth rates 1970–1995 (percent)[1]

	Norway		Denmark		Sweden		Europe[2]	(OECD)
GDP	3.5	(1.9)	2.2	(1.9)	1.8	(2.0)	2.7	(2.4)
GDP exclusive of oil (70–94)	2.5	(2.1)						
Consumer prices (70–94)	7.2	(3.1)	6.8	(3.7)	7.7	(2.9)	7.6	(3.9)
Wage rates (71–95)	8.0	(3.5)	8.2	(4.1)	8.0	(2.8)	9.0	(4.8)
Employment	0.9	(1.5)	0.3	(1.3)	0.1	(1.9)	0.2	(2.1)
Government consumption	4.0	(1.8)	2.6	(3.8)	2.1	(1.9)	2.8	(2.3)
Unemployment level 1970–1995	3.0		7.4		2.7		7.0	

1 Standard diviations in parentheses.

2 Average growth rates are weighted with GDP, standard deviations are unweighted averages of the standard deviations for each country.

Table 2 Average yearly growth rates 1970–1995 (percent)[1]

		Norway	Denmark	Sweden	Europe[1] (OECD)
GDP US$ per head	1970	3161	3209	4186	2144
	1994	28434	28182	22389	17742
GDP $PPP per head	1970	2974	3551	3837	3194
	1993	21328	19154	16772	17296
Consumer price inflation, per cent	1970	10.3	5.8	7.0	4.8
	1994	1.5	2.0	2.2	3.0
Government consumption, per cent of GDP	1970	16.5	20.0	21.3	14.8
	1994	21.3	25.3	27.3	19.0
Net government debt, per cent of GDP	1970	-0.9	...	-22.0	14.4
	1994	-21.5	...	23.5	52.9
Labour force participation rates: Men	1973	86.5	89.6	88.1	88.7
	1994	82.3	84.2	78.1	79.0
Women	1973	50.6	61.9	62.6	44.7
	1994	71.3	73.8	74.4	54.5
Labour force participation rates: Men 25-54	1994	86.3	85.7	82.8	83.4
General government financial balances	1971	4.3	3.9	5.3	...
	1994	-0.2	-3.9	-10.4	-5.7

1 Weighted average of the countries for which data were available.

participation rates of men have fallen everywhere, but less in Norway than in other countries.

The OECD, Jobs Study (OECD, 1994) emphasizes the difference between the US and the EU in the evolution of employment and producer real wages (Figure 5.2, panel a).[2] Europe has had strong real wage growth and almost no growth in employment. America has had strong employment growth and almost no growth in real wages. The suggestion is that there is a causal connection: If real wages in Europe had not grown so much, employment would have been higher.

It is then interesting to note in panel b that real wages in Norway followed broadly the same pattern as in the EU.[3] Until 1987 the Norwegian employment path resembled more that of the US. This does not support the view that greater real wage flexibility explains why Norway is different. Real wages in Sweden and Denmark grew markedly less than the European average, while average employment growth was no better. However, the Swedish pattern until 1990 looks like a middle way between the EU and the US. Only during the 1990s did Sweden's employment path fall back towards the European average.

The share of government consumption in GDP was smaller in Norway

2 Employment is measured in numbers and real wages are measured as wage costs per employee divided by the GDP deflator. There are severe problems in comparing the figures, especially since working hours per employee have evolved differently.

3 We have deflated nominal wages by the price index for non-oil GDP because direct employment in the oil industry is so small. If we had not excluded the oil industry, the series would have been dominated by the fluctuations in the oil price.

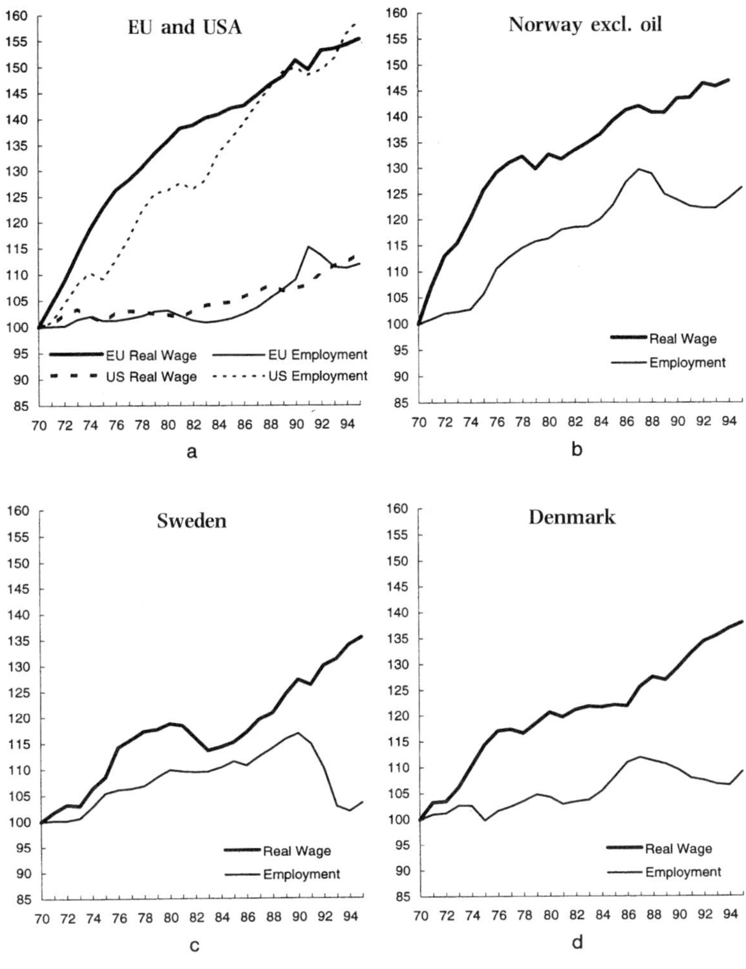

Figure 5.2 Development of real wages and employment in the Nordic countries, the EU, and the USA

than in Sweden and Denmark in 1970, and remained so in 1995. The growth of government consumption was extraordinarily high in Norway (4.0% against 2.8% for OECD Europe), but this was to a large extent off-set by stronger GDP growth.

Cyclical patterns

Developments between 1970 and 1995 have not been even. The law of large numbers means that one should expect more volatility in real variables in small countries. It is then surprising to find that output and employment growth has been somewhat less volatile from year-to-year in Scandinavia than in the average European country (Table 1).

The cyclical behaviour of GDP in Norway has differed considerably from that of Europe at large (Figure 5.3). After the first oil shock the majority of OECD countries had a short and unusually sharp recession in 1974–1975. In Norway the recession was mild and only affected 1975. The recession in the early 1980s, after the second oil shock, was more prolonged. This time the difference between Norway and the rest of Europe was less pronounced. After 1983 Europe had a long period of relatively slow recovery, which lasted until the beginning of the 1990s. In Norway the recovery was much faster and culminated in an extreme boom in 1985–1986. After that we had a period with negative GDP growth. In fact it took 6 years before non-oil GDP reached the 1987 level again. Among the OECD countries few have experienced comparably long periods with GDP below the previous peak. Until recently New Zealand was the only other example. Finland and Sweden may perhaps join the list when we get their figures for 1996. Most OECD countries suffered from a recession in the early 1990s. Norway started the recovery in 1992, when most European countries were in the depth of recession.

The pattern of employment growth in Norway followed that of non-oil GDP fairly closely (compare Figures 5.2 and 5.3). Notice, however, the unusually fast employment growth in 1975–1978, when employment in

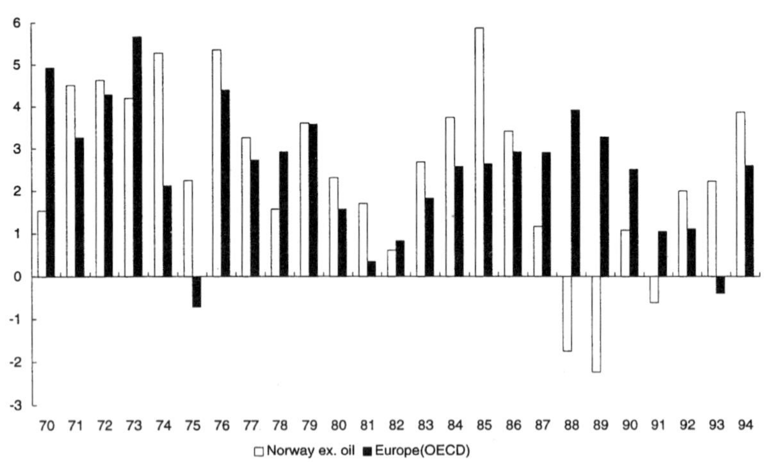

Figure 5.3 Growth rates in Gross Domestic Product (per cent)

Source: OECD Economic Outlook (Statistical Compendium 1996/1) and Statistics Norway

OECD Europe first fell and then stagnated. In the recession of the early 1980s, employment in Norway continued to grow (although just barely so in 1983) while employment in the rest of Europe fell year by year. Thus, until 1987 Norway, unlike most other OECD countries, had not experienced any episodes where employment actually fell. However, between 1987 and 1992 employment in Norway fell by 6 percent.

Inflation

On average, inflation in Norway was slightly below that of OECD Europe (Table 1). Over time the two inflation rates followed a similar pattern (Figures 5.4 and 5.5). In the 1970s inflation was high and variable; since then inflation has fallen gradually. It may seem that Norway started with relatively high inflation (Figure 5.4). However, 1970 was exceptional because of the introduction of VAT. If we leave aside the net effect of this, which was a rise in prices by 5.6 percent, inflation in Norway was at the same level as elsewhere.

In the 1970s, inflation in Norway tended to be somewhat lower than in the rest of Europe. The low wage and price inflation in Norway in 1978–1979 was due to legal restriction on wage and price increases. The disinflation in the 1980s came to a temporary halt in Norway towards the end of the boom in 1986 and 1987. The rest of Europe also had a short peak in inflation when the recovery there culminated around

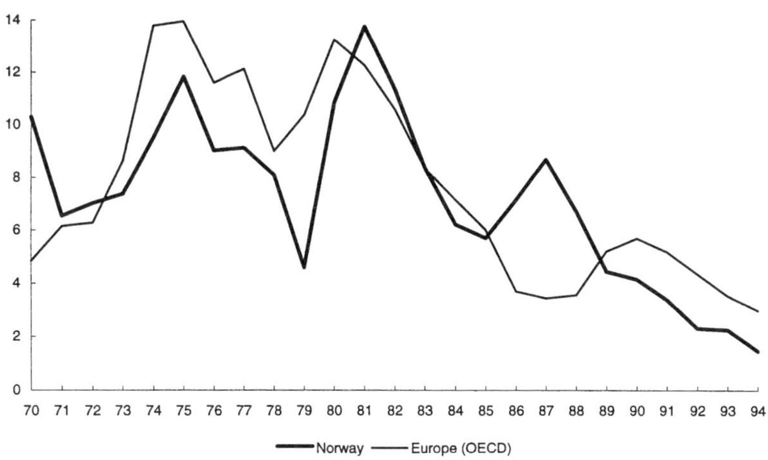

Figure 5.4 Annual growth in Consumer Price Index

Source: OECD Economic Outlook (Statistical Compendium 1996/1)

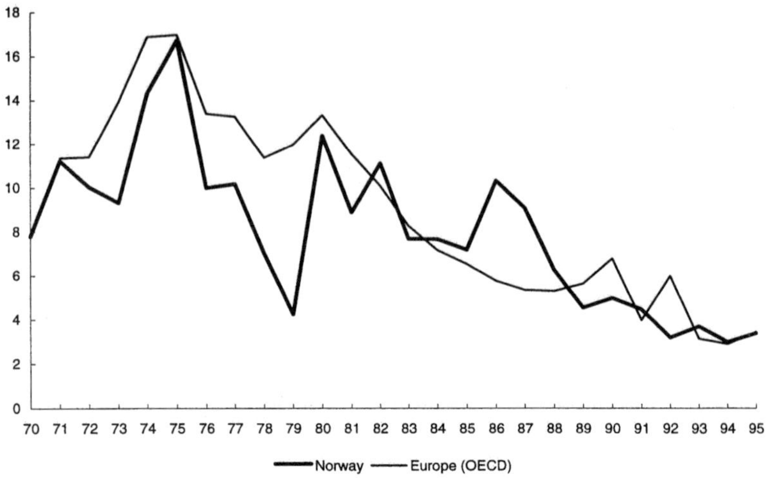

Figure 5.5 Annual growth in Wage Rate

Source: OECD Economic Outlook (Statistical Compendium 1996/1)

1990. In Norway special laws were again used to limit wage increases in 1988 and 1989.

After a short period of floating in 1971, Norway had a fixed exchange rate from 1972 to 1992. The basket of currencies used for defining the central parity changed several times. However, the average inflation rates of the currency "partners" or basket countries have been below the average European inflation rates. Figure 5.6 shows that until 1989 inflation in Norway tended to be *above* "basket inflation"; i.e., the average inflation rate of the countries which the exchange rate was fixed towards. The exception is the wages and prices freeze in 1978–1979.

The ambition to keep down inflation in the early 1970s was marked by a 5% revaluation in 1973. The dotted line shows that relative to this ambition the excess inflation in Norway was even higher. The failure to reach the inflation targets implicit in the exchange rate policy led to two series of devaluations, in 1977–1978 and in 1982–1986. If we take the whole period from 1972 to 1989, the devaluations roughly made up for the excess inflation. Since 1989, our inflation rate has consistently been lower than basket inflation.

A comparison with basket *wage* inflation would give a similar picture, although with a somewhat stronger tendency to excess inflation in Norway until 1988. Thus, until 1988 there was also a tendency to a steady loss of international cost competitiveness, mitigated only by the occasional devaluations and the wage and price freeze.

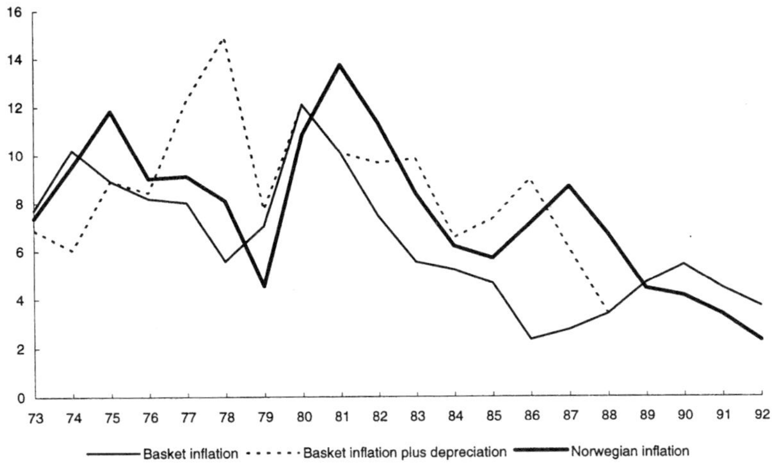

Figure 5.6 Norwegian and basket inflation per cent 1973-1992

Source: OECD Economic Outlook (Statistical Compendium 1996/1)

3. Institutions or aggregate demand?

The institutional hypothesis

As mentioned in the Introduction, Norway's unemployment performance has been explained by high real wage flexibility possibly due to centralized wage bargaining and short duration of unemployment benefits. By real wage flexibility, different authors have meant different things. However, common practice now is to take an estimated wage equation as the starting point and define real wage flexibility as the long-run elasticity of the real wage with respect to unemployment. There are several reasons for being sceptical about explanations of the low Norwegian unemployment that gives all credit to real wage flexibility. In Figure 2 we saw that the producer real wage has followed a similar path both in Norway and in OECD Europe. The econometric evidence for high real wage flexibility is not convincing. Røisland (1993) surveys nine comparative studies of wage formation. Estimates of real wage flexibility in Norway vary greatly and are lower than the OECD averages in several of them.[4]

4 Layard, Nickell and Jackman (1991) actually got a fairly low estimate of real wage flexibility in Norway. However, in the main text of their book, and in their analysis of institutional factors, they use an average of their own estimate and that of Alogoskoufis and Manning (1988). The survey by Røisland shows that the latter estimate is an extreme outlier.

Although the formal duration of unemployment benefits has been relatively short in Norway, the unemployed have often been able to obtain support for much longer periods by alternating between unemployment benefits, training programmes and cash benefits. Furthermore, the short formal duration seems to have been a consequence of the low incidence of long-term unemployment. As long-term unemployment has increased, so has benefit duration.[5]

A general difficulty with explanations that rely solely on institutional factors is that over time unemployment in Europe has changed more than institutions. In the last 15 years institutional change in several countries has gone in the direction of less support to the unemployed and more flexible labour markets (Britain being one example), which according to the theory should have produced less unemployment. It is barely possible to link the increase in employment in Europe with *changes* in institutions. Thus, the story has been that countries with different institutions respond differently to the same shocks. However, the difference between Norway and OECD Europe may be due not to different institutions but to a different history of shocks.

Oil revenues

Eika (1996) used a large macroeconometric model (KVARTS) to simulate the course that the Norwegian economy would have taken had we not discovered oil. The model cumulates the experience from a vast amount of econometric work, and is used regularly for forecasting by the research department of Statistics Norway.

Eika estimates that without oil Norway's unemployment rate in 1993 rather than 6.0% would have been 10.5 percent. In other words, unemployment in 1993 would have been at the same level as in the European Union. Over the whole period 1973–93 the unemployment rate would have been on average 3.2% higher without oil. Unemployment would have started to increase already in the mid-1970s, but it would still have remained below the EU level until 1989.

Constructing a counterfactual path for a period of more than 20 years requires some heroic assumptions. A difficult part is economic policy. In the path without oil, Eika adjusted government expenditures downwards so that they would constitute the same share of GDP as in the actual

---

5 In an ironical twist more definite limits to the duration of unemployment benefits have just been set. The decision was based on analyses showing that countries with low duration had low unemployment, and where low duration and low unemployment in Norway formed part of the evidence.

path. Taxes were kept at a level which in 1993 would have resulted in a government debt of 44% of GDP. The time path of the exchange rate was not changed in the counterfactual path. One could argue endlessly about these assumptions and about the adequacy of the model.

According to Eika, without oil GDP growth in Norway would have been only 1.1% per year in the period 1973-93 against 2.3% in the EU. The estimated growth rate of GDP is less than half of the actual growth rate of non-oil GDP. Thus, the oil industry has "crowded in" rather than crowded out other industries, which is contrary to assumptions. Perhaps the model underestimates the amount of investment that would have gone into other industries if oil had not been discovered. A lot of talent and effort went into the oil industry. Econometric equations estimated mainly on data from after the discovery of oil can hardly capture all the different ways in which oil investments have crowded out other investments. There are also other reasons for suspecting that the model exaggerates the quantitative importance of oil.[6]

It is possible to have different views on the importance of oil. However, it is interesting to note that KVARTS allows Eika to attribute the whole difference in unemployment between Norway and the EU in 1993 to the cumulated effects of what is essentially demand side variables. According to KVARTS, Norwegian institutions would not have been able to prevent high unemployment if the development of aggregate demand had been less favourable.

The scope for aggregate demand effects

The first root of the belief that the low unemployment in Norway must have been caused by institutional factors, not aggregate demand, seems to be the natural rate hypothesis. This indicates that there is a *unique* equilibrium rate of unemployment. If high aggregate demand keeps unemployment below this natural rate, inflation increases without limit. In the long run it will be impossible to keep unemployment below the natural rate. Since inflation in Norway has been below the European average, and has not increased indefinitely, and since unemployment stayed low for so long, the equilibrium unemployment rate must have been lower than in other countries.

6 Economies of scale in some industries in KVARTS make slower demand growth lead to lower productivity growth. It is difficult to believe in such a connection between aggregate demand and productivity lasting for 20 years. Also, price elasticities of Norwegian exports are estimated to be quite low in spite of raw materials and semi-finished goods making up a large share of the traditional exports.

Even if one subscribes to the theory of the natural rate, however, one need not come to the conclusion that the equilibrium unemployment rate has been particularly low. Norway had a fixed exchange rate. If the exchange rate is fixed, unemployment below the natural rate does not lead to steadily increasing inflation. Instead we get an inflation rate which is somewhat higher than "basket inflation"; i.e., higher than the inflation rate in the countries to which the exchange rate is fixed. Basket inflation serves as an anchor which prevents domestic inflation from drifting too far away. However, since inflation is higher than in the other countries, there will be a gradual erosion of our cost competitiveness. This fits well with the description of Norwegian inflation in Section 2. The exchange rate *was* fixed to countries with relatively low inflation. Norway *tended* to lose international competitiveness until 1987. This record is compatible with Norway having had unemployment below its equilibrium rate until the dramatic increase in unemployment in 1988. Since then, unemployment in Norway seems to have been above equilibrium. In fact it has been common to define the equilibrium unemployment rate as the unemployment rate which makes wage growth compatible with unchanged international cost competitiveness.

In recent years the natural rate theory has largely been replaced by *bargaining theories of wage formation.*[7] These theories replace the unique natural rate of unemployment with a "wage curve", which is a downward sloping relation between the level of real wages and the equilibrium *unemployment* rate. Alternatively, the same relation can be drawn as an *upward* sloping relation between the level of real wages and the equilibrium *employment* rate, as in Figure 5.7. The higher the initial real wage, the higher the equilibrium employment rate and the lower the equilibrium *un*employment rate. The reason is that the outcome of wage bargaining depends on both the state of the labour market, as measured by the (un)employment rate, and on the profitability of firms. A high real wage means low profitability and this has a moderating influence on wage increases. Thus, wage increases consistent with constant international cost competitiveness can be achieved either by high unemployment combined with high profitability or low unemployment combined with low profitability.

Empirical studies of wage formation in Norway (and other countries) strongly support the hypothesis that there is a wage curve.[8] It implies

---

7 See e.g. Oswald (1985) or Layard, Nickell and Jackman (1991).

8 See e.g. Blanchflower and Oswald (1990) for international evidence and Nymoen (1989, 1990) and Johansen (1995) for Norwegian evidence. Stølen (1994) presents more mixed results, but does not reject the hypothesis of a wage curve.

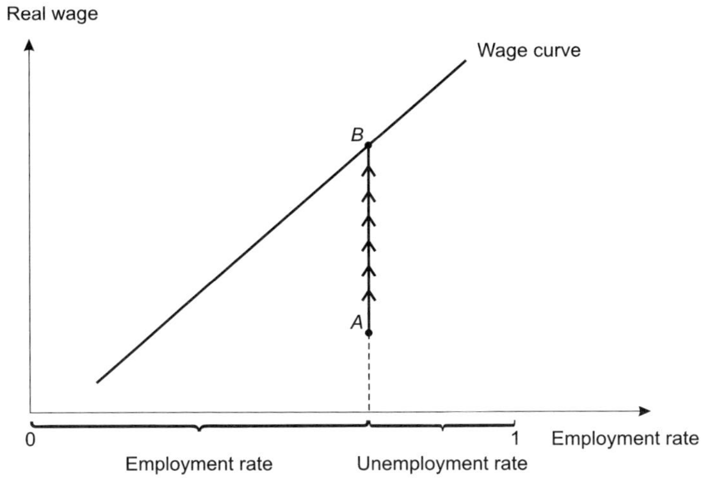

Figure 5.7 The wage curve

that if unemployment is kept at a low level by high aggregate demand, real wages increase and competitiveness deteriorates to begin with. This development is depicted in Figure 5.7 as the upward path starting from point A. Profitability declines gradually. This dampens the tendency to excessive wage increases. After a while, wages have grown to the degree that the economy reaches the wage curve as in point B. The deterioration of competitiveness then stops. The actual unemployment rate has become the equilibrium unemployment rate because of the increase in the real wage. Thus, the loss in competitiveness which results from keeping aggregate demand at a high level is limited in magnitude. If the exchange rate is fixed, inflation at home exceeds inflation abroad only temporarily. We end up with higher prices and higher production costs, but not permanently higher wage and price inflation.

The position and shape of the wage curve is believed to depend on the nature of bargaining institutions, on the characteristics of the unemployment insurance system, on tax rates and on other institutional and structural characteristics of the economy. The demand for labour determines towards which point along the wage curve we shall move. Usually a higher real wage means lower demand for labour and more unemployment. Thus, we have the picture in Figure 5.8 of a downward sloping relation between the real wage and employment. The intersection between this and the wage curve (point B) is the equilibrium employment rate which the economy is heading towards in the short run.

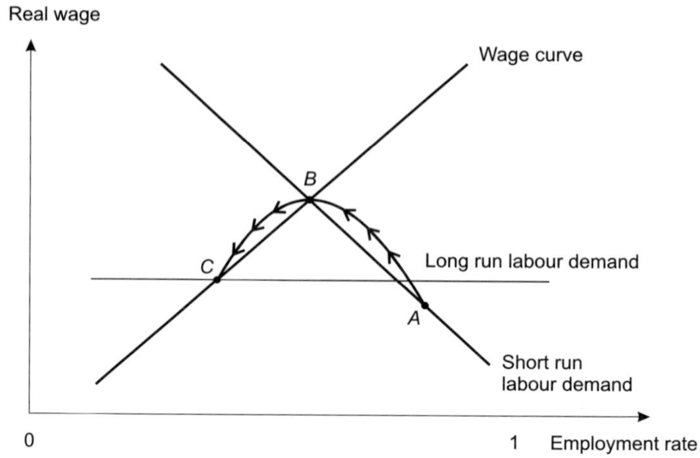

Figure 5.8 Labour market equilibrium

Since capital is internationally mobile, investments in our country must pay the going international rate of return. If the rate of return is lower, there will be too little investment, and in the end there will be no demand for labour. If the rate of return is higher, then there is no limit to the amount of investment which can be attracted and the demand for labour will increase beyond all limits. Thus, the long run labour demand can be represented by a horizontal line at the real wage which is just high enough to give capital the international rate of return. Where this line intersects with the wage curve (point C in Figure 5.8) is where the economy must move in the long run. Only one level of unemployment is consistent with unchanged international competitiveness when profitability is at the internationally competitive level. Thus, in the long run there is a unique equilibrium rate of unemployment in a small open economy with high capital mobility. However, investment (and disinvestment) is a slow process. The long run we speak of here may be decades into the future.

Suppose that an expansion of aggregate demand, e.g. an expansionary fiscal policy, has brought low unemployment as in point A in Figure 5.8. Because the economy is below the wage curve, real wages grow and international competitiveness deteriorates. This means reduced output and employment. After a while (when point B is reached) the deterioration of competitiveness stops, but profitability is then so low that there is little investment in new jobs. This means a further gradual decline of output and employment, and unemployment goes up. This has a dampening effect on wage increases. The real wage declines. After a while the economy approaches a state where real wages are just high enough to give the international return on capital (point C). It is then profitable to maintain the existing capital stock and level of employment. Note that the long run equilibrium unemployment (point C) is independent of the level of aggregate demand that we start with. In the very long run domestic demand has no effect on unemployment.

The process described above may be delayed by expanding for example government employment to compensate for the loss of employment which results from increased real wages and reduced investment. Every time private sector employment declines, a further fiscal expansion is then needed. However, such a policy is bound to lead to unsustainable current account and government deficits.

To this picture we should add the phenomenon of hysteresis or path-dependence. One interpretation of this is: The higher unemployment has been in the past, the higher is the equilibrium unemployment rate today for any given wage level. The explanations given for this phenomenon are among other things that the long-term unemployed lose skills, search less effectively for new jobs, and have less influence in wage bargaining. An important question is whether the increase in equilibrium unemployment due to path dependence is permanent, or whether it fades over time, e.g. because old discouraged and deskilled job seekers are replaced by new entrants from the school system. Personally, I find it hard to believe that the effect is permanent. If it is not, there is still a unique equilibrium unemployment rate in the long run.

The long run may be far ahead, though. Wage adjustments are not instantaneous, and the existing capital stock and the effects of past unemployment may take a long time to wear out. In the meantime the combination of high domestic demand and high production costs at home will lead to large current account deficits. In the early post-war period, when international capital mobility was limited, countries with large current account deficits soon experienced a shortage of foreign currency. The authorities would then have to take measures to curb domestic demand. With the highly developed and liberalized international financial markets of the 1980s and 1990s the financing of current account deficits is less of a problem provided the financial markets are convinced that the country's economic policies are sustainable in the long run. However, a country which runs a large fiscal deficit in order to boost domestic demand may quickly run into credibility problems. The choice is then between raising interest rates and cutting the fiscal deficit. Both alternatives mean reduced domestic demand.

The conclusion is that in principle a continued high level of domestic demand is able to keep unemployment low for a long time without rising inflation. In practice, foreign exchange constraints and credibility problems caused by unsustainable deficits may force governments to take contractionary measures long before the potential employment effect of high domestic demand has worn out. The crucial factor is the sustainability of current account and government defits. The discovery of North-Sea oil obviously meant that these constraints became less severe for Norway, and that we could sustain a high level of aggregate demand longer than other countries.

Institutions again

As will be recalled, Layard, Nickell and Jackman (1991) explained the low Norwegian unemployment by a high degree of real wage flexibility. High real flexibility by their definition is the same as a steep wage curve. This means that shifts in labour demand will lead to large changes in real wages and small changes in equilibrium unemployment. Changes in taxes, terms of trade, unemployment benefits and various other variables which affect wage setting in similar ways can also be shown to have small effects on unemployment when real wage flexibility is high.

However, in the long run it is the position of wage curve which is important, not its slope. The further to the left the wage curve in Figure 8 is, the more unemployment we shall have at the internationally competitive wage. This is true even if the slope of the wage curve is always the same. Institutions may make a difference for the position of the wage curve, not just for its slope. Unfortunately, while there has been plenty of empirical research on institutions and wage flexibility, there has been less systematic research on the relationship between institutions and the position of the wage curve.[9] We shall discuss one possible cause of differences in long-run equilibrium unemployment rates when we compare Norway to Denmark in Section 5.

Another institutional feature which is not captured by the slope of the wage curve is the kind of government intervention in wage formation which took place in 1978–1979 and 1988–1989, and to which we return in Section 4.

4. The historical evidence

As pointed out in Sections 1 and 2, Norway avoided the sharp increase

9 Layard et al (1991) do not even report the constant terms of their wage equations.

in unemployment which other countries experienced in the 1970s. Norway did not avoid increased unemployment in connection with the disinflation of the early 1980s, but the increase was smaller than elsewhere. Since 1983, however, unemployment and the business cycle in Norway has been completely out of pace with that in the rest of Europe. In Section 3 we discussed from a theoretical point of view the potential role of aggregate demand. In the present section we look more closely at the actual developments on the demand side, with the main emphasis on the two episodes where Norway has been most idiosyncratic; i.e., the periods 1974–1977 and 1983–1990. We also look briefly at the two episodes where legal restrictions were used to curb wage increases; i.e. 1978–1979 and 1988–1989.

Against the cycle 1974–1977

In 1975 employment in Europe fell by 0.8 percent, while in Norway it rose by 2.8 percent. In 1976, employment growth in Norway was even higher, 4.6 percent, while in Europe growth was negligible.

In 1974 and 1975 real total domestic demand in OECD Europe grew respectively by 1.4 and -1.4 percent, and in Norway by 7.0 and 5.9 percent. The domestic demand growth continued to be above the European average in 1976 and 1977. The slow growth of demand in Europe had at least two causes. The rapid increase in inflation in the early 1970s had prompted most OECD countries to take contractionary measures, especially in the monetary area. There is reason to believe that even without OPEC the OECD area would have gone into a recession in 1974–1975. The oil price increase transferred purchasing power from oil consumers (Europe) to oil producers (OPEC). The latter were not prepared to spend the money immediately and this reduced world demand.

In addition, the increased oil prices lowered consumer real wages relative to producer real wages. According to Bruno and Sachs (1985) and Layard et al. (1991) and others this put an extra upward pressure on wages (shifted the wage curve upwards) which was bound to increase unemployment.

Norway had also taken some measures to curb domestic demand in 1973–1974 (slower growth in government consumption, a restrictive credit policy which calmed housing investment). However, these measures were fairly weak and accompanied by tax reductions working in the opposite direction. The main weapon used against inflation was instead a 5% revaluation in November 1973. The government also offered tax concessions in return for wage moderation in "tripartite" wage negotiations. Whether these tax concessions actually worked is disputed.

Norway was still a net importer of oil. Thus, the immediate effect of the oil price increase was qualitatively the same as elsewhere in Europe. However, the quantitative impact was smaller because of the domestic oil production, and also because all electricity was produced from hydropower. But there were other factors working towards increased demand in 1974–1975:

- Norway was lagging behind in the business cycle. Rapid export growth in 1973 and 1974 had resulted in high profits in manufacturing. This led to higher investment (Figure 5.11) and higher real wages in 1974 and 1975. Higher real wages promoted consumption growth.

- Offshore investment in oil production increased (Figure 5.9). This was a result of earlier decisions and discoveries, not of the oil price increase.

- One oil refinery (Mongstad) and one petrochemical plant (Rafnes) were under construction. In a country with only 4 million inhabitants, individual projects like these are of macroeconomic significance.

In spite of this, Norway was not unaffected by the international recession of 1975 (Figure 5.3). The number of unemployed manufacturing workers tripled, and the number of registered unemployed hit its highest level since 1959. There were obvious employment problems in the most internationally oriented part of the economy. The rapid expansion of employment was concentrated in the non-traded industries and in government services.

The labour force participation rate of women increased by 7 percentage points from 1974 to 1977, with no increase in female unemployment. This was parallelled by a rapid increase in government supply of child care, old age care and other social services. While increased government consumption was probably a precondition for increased female labour supply, increased private consumption demand was an integral part of it. Women went to work so that the families could buy more goods and services and better housing. The average yearly growth rate of private consumption was above 6% from 1974 to 1977. In this expansion, increased real wages and tax reductions also played a role. The consumption boom was driven entirely by increased household disposable income with no decline in the savings rate.

Increased female participation goes a long way towards explaining the

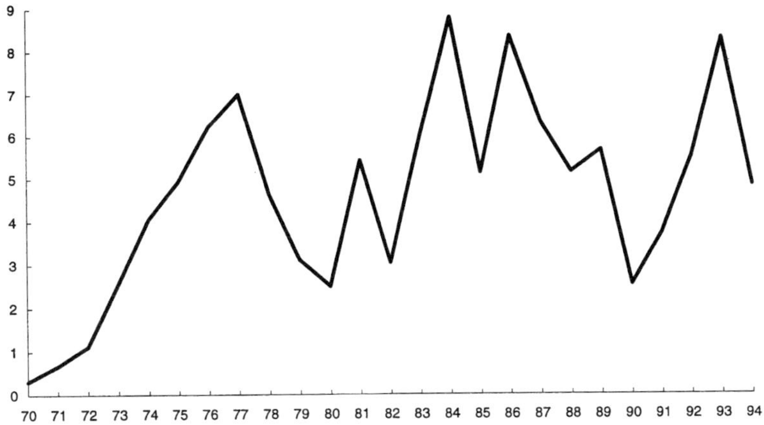

Figure 5.9 Oil investment Norway 1970-1994 billion 1970-kroner

Source: Statistics Norway, National Accounts Statistics

rapid increase in employment in Norway. The net effect on the official unemployment figures of the increased labour supply and the accompanying increase in government services is difficult to assess. The overall effect may have been expansionary, which was lucky timing.

The rapid increase in unemployment in 1975 shocked the OECD countries, and led to a dramatic policy shift towards more expansion of demand. Towards the end of the year the Norwegian authorities also switched in this direction. Excluding oil revenues, government net borrowing increased by more than 6% of GDP from 1974 to 1977. This happened, it should be recalled, at a time when the unemployment rate was virtually constant and when GDP was growing rapidly. The expansion included increased government consumption, tax cuts and a rapid increase in all kinds of transfers to the private sector. This fiscal expansion was unparalleled in the OECD, where the expansionism soon gave way to a more contractionary policy. The reason was that inflation continued to be a problem, and that several countries also felt a need to restrain their current account deficits.

Attempts at consolidation 1977–1979

In 1977 and 1978 there was a dramatic turnaround in policy in Norway. A combination of several factors lead to the conclusion that the policies pursued until then were not sustainable:

The high current account deficits (14% of GDP in 1977); the continuing high inflation (9% in 1977); the loss of international competitiveness; the continuing employment problems in some traditional industries; the realization that the problems of many traditional industries were structural, not cyclic; cost overruns in the oil industry. In fact, many people came to the opinion that Norway was heading towards some kind of economic disaster. An increase in the household savings rate by 3.7 percentage points in 1978 (Figure 5.10) may in part have been a result of this mood.

A devaluation in April 1977 started a series of devaluations. Prior to December 1978, through four parity adjustments, the Norwegian krone had been devalued by 16–18% within the snake. Then Norway left the snake and fixed the krone to a currency basket based on trade weights.

During 1977 and 1978 increasingly strict measures were used to curb the growth of domestic credit. The government budget for 1978 contained several contractionary measures (tax increases on households, less money to local government). The intention to curb domestic demand was clear, but transfer payments and government consumption were still growing rapidly. The final figures leave little doubt that fiscal policy was still expansionary in 1978. However, attempts at fiscal consolidation continued in 1979 and 1980.

The devaluation renewed inflationary pressures, the government attempting to control them by regulatory measures. First there were

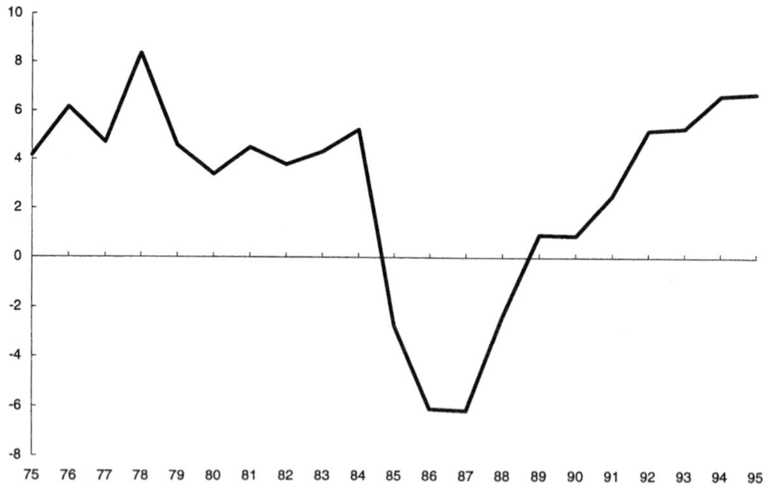

Figure 5.10 Household savings ratio Norway 1975-1995 Source: OECD Economic Outlook (Statistical Compendium 1996/1)

price controls. In May 1978, tripartite wage negotiations failed, and wages were determined by compulsory arbitration, after the government had driven a special law through parliament. In September of the same year the government decreed a general wages and prices freeze for the period until 1 January 1980. Econometric studies are unanimous in finding that the wage freeze reduced wage increases. Point estimates set the effect to between 3 and 14 percent.[10] In relation to Figure 5.8 the effect was to move the real wage down from somewhere near B to a point similar to A. Thus, after 1979 the process of increasing wages and declining competitiveness started again. The long run equilibrium was not changed. In this sense the wage freeze gave only temporary relief, but there was no immediate catch-up.

The wage freeze was accepted without significant unrest among organized labour. The general sense of national emergency was probably important. So also was the structure of the main trade union, LO, which was still dominated by workers in the traded goods industries. The threat of unemployment was real to them. The law appealed to them because it forced workers and firms in other parts of the economy to show moderation too.

Employment growth in Norway declined in this period. Relatively slow growth in private consumption and investment and slow GDP growth in 1978 (Figure 5.3) indicate that the restrictive credit policy worked. When unemployment increased only slightly, it was partly because of the upturn in the international business cycle in 1978. As a result of this and improved competitiveness the traded goods industries did fairly well.

The first disinflation

From 1979 to 1983 the unemployment rate increased by 3.5% in Europe and by 1.5% in Norway. Employment continued to grow in Norway, although at slower rates than in the 1970s, while employment in OECD Europe fell. Until 1985 the decline in inflation in both areas was similar (Figure 5.4). According to Ball (1996), who presents some empirical evidence, the increase in unemployment in the 1980 was a result of the tight monetary policy used to fight inflation. Countries with larger decreases in inflation and longer disinflationary periods had larger increases in unemployment.

---

10 Stølen (1994) and Calmfors and Nymoen (1990) provide estimates in the upper part of the range; Johansen (1995), Ch. 3 and Rødseth and Holden in Calmfors (1990) in the lower half.

The Norwegian recession was mainly a reflection of the international recession of the same years. It was reinforced by cuts in industrial subsidies. However, monetary policy may have been less resolute than in some other countries. Market interest rates were comparable to those abroad (although not among the highest), but credit was also available at lower regulated and subsidized rates. There were some attempts at fiscal contraction, but they were not very resolute either.

When inflation came down relatively easily, the main reason seems to have been the credibility of the exchange rate policy. Inflationary expectations dropped more or less in line with inflation abroad. (The wage and prices freeze in 1978–1979 seems not to have broken inflationary expectations.) The exchange rate peg gained credibility from the high oil prices, which produced huge current account and government surpluses (respectively 3.8 and 4.7% of GDP in 1981), and from the improvement in cost competitiveness which remained after the consolidation in 1977–1979. The devaluations of 1977–1978 were not too much of a burden on credibility, because the previous peg to the German mark through the "snake" had been replaced by the less ambitious national basket. However, the history from the 1970s repeated itself. Inflation, although at about the European average, was higher than the average in the currency basket, and there was again a tendency to deteriorating competitiveness.[11]

The credit boom 1984–1987[12]

The rapid expansion of employment in Norway in 1984–1985 can also be related to domestic demand. True enough, however, the expansion began with impulses from abroad where a slow recovery had started in 1983. Increased profits in leading export industries contributed in 1984 to higher manufacturing investment (up 29.2% in export manufacturing) and handsome real wage increases. However, these impulses were soon joined by others. Just as in the mid-1970s there was a strong increase in oil investments both offshore and onshore (extension of the refinery at Mongstad, the gas processing plant at Kårstø). There was also a consumption boom. In 1985 private consumption grew by 9.9 percent, in 1986 by 5.6 percent. Business investment in the more sheltered

---

11 After 1982 the tendency to deteriorating competitiveness was taken care of by several minor exchange rate adjustments camouflaged as technical adjustments. In the long run this might have undermined the anti-inflation policy, but within the period we look at it probably had minor effects.

12 I have discussed this and the following period in more detail in Rødseth (1994).

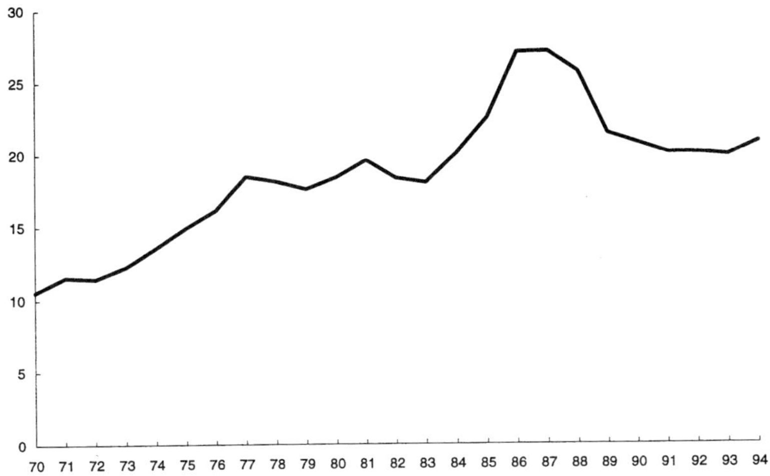

Figure 5.11 Maniland business fixed investment Norway 1970-1994, billion 1970-kroner

Source: Statistics Norway, National Accounts Statistics

industries followed suit. On-shore business investment in fixed capital increased by 50% from 1983 to 1986 (Figure 5.11). Fiscal policy played a less active role than in the mid-1970s. The 1985 budget (an election year) is usually regarded as more expansionary than its predecessors, but in 1986 tax increases and other measures were taken to curb domestic demand.

The most remarkable fact about the boom was the precipitous fall in the household savings rate—by 10% in just two years from 1984 to 1986 (Figure 5.10). This drop in the savings rate and the tremendous increase in investment would not have been possible without liberal access to credit. The most important move towards liberalization of the Norwegian credit market was taken in November 1978. Since then Norwegian banks have had relatively free access to the international credit markets, and, thus, have been less dependent on the Norwegian Central Bank for liquidity supply. After this first move, credit was liberalized in several steps. In January 1984 certain ceilings on bank lending were removed. From then on the old system of quantitative restrictions was in practice abandoned.

One question is whether deregulation of the financial markets gave a direct positive impulse to the boom in private consumption and investment. Then there must have been a queue of borrowers who were held back in their spending plans because of credit rationing. A queue existed, but the scant evidence that there is seems to indicate that the queue was not very long. After all, there had just been a recession. Until the second quarter of 1983 the credit ceilings were either lifted or ineffective for most banks. There were also several channels for credit outside the banks, and there is no indication that the pressure on these was very strong.

There may have been a more indirect impulse from deregulation. Several observers have noted that the marketing of loans became more aggressive and that less attention was paid to credit risk. This could have been a result of the increased competition that went with deregulation. Unfortunately there is no quantitative information which can indicate the size of this effect.

Although there probably was a direct impulse from financial deregulation to increased consumption and investment, it was more important that the quantitative regulations no longer acted as brakes on the expansion that came from other sources. When consumers perceived that their permanent income had increased, they could go out and buy a new car and a new house right away. They did not have to save first as in earlier expansions. Firms relied less on financing from retained profits, and could more quickly exploit perceived new profit opportunities.

In principle increased interest rates could play the same role as quantitative restrictions in dampening an expansion. However, Norway had a fixed exchange rate and relatively free capital movements. Until the last months of 1985, oil prices were high, the current account had a huge surplus and inflation was still declining. Investing in Norwegian kroner seemed to be relatively safe. Money market interest rates were kept higher than abroad, and this resulted in a large capital inflow. Thus, the exchange rate policy prevented a more active use of the interest rate to curb the expansion before 1986. After oil prices fell, confidence in the Norwegian currency evaporated quickly. Interest rates rose, but they might well have increased. There was also a half-hearted attempt at reintroducing some of the old regulations. In general monetary policy in these years was marked by a struggle between those who favoured the old regime and those who favoured the the new, with the result that neither quantitative restrictions nor the interest rate were used with enough force.

In conclusion, the main impulses behind the expansion were probably the international upswing and the increased oil investments. Deregulation, fiscal expansion in 1985 and the general optimism due to high oil prices also contributed. The extraordinary strength of the expansion was made possible by the absence of quantitative constraints on credit and the inability and unwillingness to raise interest rates sufficiently.

The end of full employment

That Norway was heading for an economic downturn seemed obvious to many observers as early as 1986. Although employment continued its rapid growth in 1987 (1.9 percent) the turnaround in economic activity was already evident in several areas. The real crisis came in 1988 and 1989, when mainland GDP fell by respectively 1.7 and 2.9 percent. Employment fell each year from 1988 to 1992. The worst year was 1989 with a fall in employment of 3 percent.

The signal which released the downturn was the fall in oil prices in 1986. Expectations suddenly became more pessimistic. This was underlined by increasing money market interest rates as speculation against the krone escalated, and by a fiscal contraction. Low oil prices and high domestic demand combined to produce a current account deficit of 4.5% of GDP in 1986. But even if oil prices had not fallen, the bubble would have burst sooner or later. The household savings rate, which was negative, would have had to return to more normal levels. Business investment would have had to come down again, if for no other reason than that there are limits to how much office and shopping space 4 million people can use. The whole private sector was going into debt at a rate which was clearly unsustainable. Some consolidation would have had to take place sooner or later. Actually, the savings rate rose almost as quickly as it had fallen; by 7.1% from 1987 to 1989. Business fixed investments in the mainland industries fell by more than 30 percent. It was important that several big investment projects came to an end in this period: The development of some North-Sea oil fields, the oil refinery at Mongstad, some large hydropower developments.

New wage laws 1988–1989

As in the mid-1970s, the overheating of the Norwegian economy in the mid-1980s resulted in wage increases which far exceeded the increases in the countries to which the currency had been fixed. In the 1986 wage round the employers tried a lockout, but their tactics failed, and the result was wage increases agreed in 1986 for 1986 and 1987 which were clearly in excess of what they expected abroad.

In the mid-1970s Norway had been able to continue a hard currency policy for several years in spite of worsening competitiveness and widening current account deficits. In May 1986, with increased capital mobility, a devaluation was forced upon Norway as soon as it was clear in what direction the wage agreements would go, and before the wage round was completed. The earlier fall in the price of oil and political infighting over a tax increase, which resulted in a change of government in the middle of the crisis, contributed to the speculation against the exchange rate.

The devaluation (officially 12 percent) was not sufficient to prevent a deterioration of competitiveness, which contributed to the later fall in employment. It was unfortunate that the devaluation happened when the labour market was overheated, but it probably still had some effect into the late 1980s.

As in the 1970s, the government went into talks with the LO and NHO with the aim of securing wage moderation. This resulted in fairly moderate wage agreements between the LO and NHO in 1988 and 1989, and limits on local bargaining. The main contribution of the government was to extend these agreements by law to the rest of the labour market. Nobody could get more than the workers in the LO had got from the NHO. This was not a complete wage freeze as 10 years earlier, but it came quite close. Econometric estimates indicate that the incomes policy reduced wages with between 4 and 8 percent.[13]

In other respects the situation was totally different. The wage moderation was now being supported by a much higher level of unemployment. Although fiscal policy was changed in a more expansionary direction from the summer of 1988, it was a far cry from the "countercyclical" policy of the 1970s. Interest rates were high, because the foreign exchange market feared a new devaluation. There was no price freeze. Thus, when the wage laws expired in 1990, there was no spurt in price inflation.

Inflation came down at a time when it was increasing in the rest of Europe, and international competitiveness improved. The current account went into surplus again in 1989. All this boosted the credibility of the fixed exchange rate, and the interest rate differential towards the basket currencies was diminished to virtually zero in 1990.

The early 1990s

In the spring of 1990 there were many signs of renewed growth in Norway. Private consumption was growing again. Oil investments were growing, and the decline in mainland business investment was less steep than before.

Just as things seemed to be going better, Norway was hit by the international recession of the early 1990s, and in particular by the downturn

---

13 Stølen (1994), Johansen (1995), ch. 3.

in our largest export market, Sweden. In 1991 the export volume of traditional goods fell by 2.7 percent, in spite of improved competitiveness.

The reduction in the interest rate differential between NOK and the basket currencies had not resulted in lower real interest rates in Norway, the reason being that other countries increased their interest rates to combat the tendency to rising inflation in the late 1980s. In 1990 Norway changed from pegging to a national basket to pegging to the ECU. This meant that real interest rates continued to be high even after the recession had hit most of Europe. The reason was the unique position of Germany within the EMS. For Norwegian consumers real after tax interest rates rose as a result of a tax reform in 1992.

In December 1992, as a result of the turmoil in the ERM, the Norwegian authorities had to give up the peg to ECU. This resulted in a minor depreciation. More importantly, it made possible a substantial reduction in interest rates. A softening of German monetary policy cleared the way for further interest rate reductions. Moreover, firms and households had been reducing their debts substantially since 1987. This, together with increasing oil investments, a more and more expansionary fiscal policy, and some positive impulses from abroad contributed to rapid output growth towards 1995. It also seemed that international competitiveness was good after several years of low wage increases. For the first time in the period under study here, Norwegian firms were gaining market shares, and manufacturing employment was increasing. At last total employment began to grow again, and unemployment started to fall.

5. Some comparisons to Sweden and Denmark[14]

Oil revenues have been important for the low Norwegian unemployment. How did Sweden manage then? Part of the answer is that Sweden started with extremely good public finances. In 1970 Sweden had a government surplus of 5.3% of GDP and net government assets of 22% of GDP. In the 1970s these played the same role as the Norwegian oil reserves and permitted an extraordinary fiscal expansion. Sweden in fact carried on with its expansionary policies longer than Norway, but there too it ended with loss of competitiveness and huge government and current account deficits (respectively 7.0 and 3.6 of GDP in 1982).

Sweden's way out was to devalue the currency by altogether 28% in

---

14 For more information on Sweden and Denmark, see Jensen (1996) on Denmark, Calmfors (1993) on Sweden and the chapters in Calmfors (1990) by Andersen and Risager on Denmark and Calmfors and Forslund on Sweden.

1981 and 1982, and to combine this with more restrictive fiscal policies. Workers did not get compensation, and real wages were kept down (Figure 2). There were no legal restrictions on wage increases, but, as in Norway four years earlier, there seems to have been a sense of national emergency. There was an understanding between the new Social Democratic government and the trade unions about the need for wage restraint.[15] The extraordinary character of the event is perhaps best illustrated by the fact that the index regulations that pensioners were entitled to were abolished by parliament with only minor protests.

Sweden, like Norway, had a deregulation boom after 1985. Since Sweden was not negatively affected by the fall in the oil price, the boom lasted longer there. In the following recession, concerns about government debt prevented Sweden from pursuing the same expansionary fiscal policy as Norway, and, thus, the rise in unemployment was greater there.

In one sense the history of Sweden as told above supports the view that aggregate demand and the oil industry were important for Norway. However, in both countries it has been possible to take extraordinary measures to reduce real wages and improve international competitiveness. In Norway the main instrument was wage laws (following devaluations), in Sweden aggressive devaluations without wage compensation. In both countries the precondition for the success of these measures was a consensus based on a sense of national emergency among the public, and on that the measures would be applied equally to everybody. It is quite possible that if oil had not been discovered in Norway, devaluations could have been used in the same aggressive way as Sweden in 1982, and with the same positive results.

Denmark had a current account problem even before the first oil shock, the country depending entirely on fossil fuels for its electricity production. Thus, the increased oil prices hit harder there than in Norway and Sweden. Denmark also had higher inflation rates in the early 1970s. Thus, the Danish government was not in a position to stimulate aggregate demand to the same extent as the governments of Norway and Sweden. This goes some way towards explaining why unemployment in Denmark increased more in the late 1970s.

When unemployment was first allowed to increase, there was probably also an extraordinary fall in the demand for labour due to reduced labour hoarding in firms (see Moene, Nymoen and Wallerstein in this

15 Sweden had also devalued in 1977 by 10 percent. However, there was not the same degree of wage moderation then. Sweden had a non-socialist government from 1976 to 1982.

volume) or other productivity effects of increased unemployment (compare efficiency wage theories). In fact, productivity figures for manufacturing indicate that some of this may have happened in Denmark after 1974, in Norway after 1988 and in Sweden after 1990.

The debt problems accumulated in the 1970s meant that Danish fiscal policy was fairly contractionary throughout the 1980s. Denmark also had a "deregulation" boom at the same time as Norway. In the Danish case deregulation of international capital movements combined with increased credibility for the fixed exchange rate policy led to a dramatic fall in interest rates. In Denmark there has been much focus on the boom having increased wage inflation. It is noteworthy, though, that the increase in wage inflation was much smaller there than in Norway and Sweden. As in Norway and Sweden, the boom was followed by a downturn where unemployment increased again (Figure 5.1). In the decade after 1982 efforts to cut the government budget deficit must have exerted a considerable downward pull on employment in Denmark.

Denmark never had the kind of extraordinary improvements of international competitiveness which Norway and Sweden had. Why this was so seems to be more a question of politics than of economics. At any rate, Denmark had to improve competitiveness the hard way, by unemployment exerting downward pressure on wages. In the end though Denmark has had slower growth in real wages than both neighbours (Figure 5.2). Relative to its equilibrium level, unemployment in Denmark must on average have been higher than in Norway and Sweden.

However, the difference between Denmark and Norway is smaller if we look at employment/population ratios for core groups rather than average unemployment rates. In 1994 the employment/population ratio for men 25–54 years old was 85.7% in Denmark and 86.3% in Norway (OECD Employment Outlook, 1996, Table 4.2). Because of higher labour force participation in Denmark, the difference in unemployment rates for the same group was somewhat higher, 2 percent. For women in the same age group, the difference in the employment/population ratio was 1.5 percent, in the unemployment rate 5.5 percent.

In the Norwegian labour force surveys there are large groups, especially of women, which regard themselves as unemployed, but are not counted as such, since they have not searched actively for work during the last two weeks. In Denmark these groups almost do not exist (Nesheim and Drevdal, 1995). The main reason is probably that Danish statistics apply a weaker (and non-standard) job search criterion. Danes may also have more incentive to register as unemployed, as support for the unemployed has been more generous there. An additional reason may be that in less densely populated Norway it often takes more than two weeks between each local job opening which an unemployed person can apply for.

Thus, it appears that towards the end of the period the real difference between Norway and Denmark was smaller than the commonly used unemployment figures indicate. Comparable figures for 1983 seem to show that there was a better correspondence between the differences in employment and unemployment rates then.

The comparison with Denmark seems to indicate that different statistical methods and different incentives for registering as unemployed may be responsible for some of the difference between Norway and Europe. (This would be one way in which the equilibrium unemployment rates could differ for the same real wage.) Unfortunately there is little research on this. We do know, however, that Denmark is an outlier in both its statistical practices and its generosity in supporting the unemployed. The problem in comparing Norway and other European countries is likely to be smaller. However, it is indicative that the OECD (1994) Jobs Study finds a stronger response of the labour force to employment in Norway than in most other European countries. If this is due to a discouraged worker effect, employment in Norway may have varied proportionally more over time than the headline figures suggest. However, reverse causation cannot be excluded. A country which is able to create many new jobs when the labour force increases, as Norway did in the 1970s, would also get a high coefficient.[16]

6. Lessons from history

The questions we started with were: Why has unemployment in Norway been so low compared to the European average? Why has the time profile of unemployment been so different? In my view it should be clear from the history told above that a large part of the explanation is related to aggregate demand. Strong domestic demand prevented a rise in unemployment in the mid-1970s. Strong domestic demand also brought unemployment down to a low level in the mid-1980s. During most of

16 The large increase in the number of full-time students in Norway after 1988 is sometimes pointed to as evidence of an increase in hidden unemployment. However, many students are counted as unemployed in the Labour Force Surveys and this is contrary to practices in some other countries. The increased number of people who received disability pensions after 1988 was partly a result of problems in the labour market. However, many of these claimants would have received old age pensions in other countries. If anything, early retirement for labour market reasons seems to be more common in other countries than in Norway.

the period from 1970 to 1987 the unemployment rate in Norway seems to have been below its equilibrium level.

When inflation in Norway did not exceed the European average, the main reason was an ambitious exchange rate policy. The results did not measure up to the ambitions. There was a constant tendency to higher inflation than the exchange rate policy gave room for, and to declining international competitiveness. There were occasional devaluations in the decade from 1977 to 1986. However, the policy still succeeded in keeping inflation below the European average. The credibility of the exchange rate policy rested on high oil prices most of the time.

When the loss of international competitiveness did not reach the intolerable level, it was mainly because of the two "wage freezes" of 1978–1979 and 1988–1989, following the two "major" devaluations of 1977 and 1986. In these two episodes the economy showed a kind of real wage flexibility which cannot easily be captured by the coefficient in front of unemployment in a wage equation. If we had not had the oil, we might have had more wage moderation of this kind.

After 1990 Norway managed to keep inflation low, with unemployment considerably below the European average. This may be explained by the absence of hysteresis effects. Because of its better unemployment history, Norway probably still had lower equilibrium unemployment, especially in the first few years.

Will Norway be able to keep unemployment lower than in other countries also in the future too? With oil revenues at a new peak and the surpluses on both the current account and the government budget likely to exceed 5% of GDP, Norway is clearly in a position where it can pursue a more expansionary fiscal policy for some years. It would be simple to recreate the booms of the mid-1970s and mid-1980s driven by domestic demand. Whether we can afterwards repeat the wage moderation and wage laws of 1978–1979 and 1988–1989 is more questionable. We almost certainly cannot use exchange rate policy the same way as before.

It may be difficult to declare a national emergency every ten years. Power over the trade unions may be moving from workers in the traded goods industries to those who work in government services and other sheltered industries. If foreign exchange speculators expect that the boom ends with a devaluation as in 1977–1978 and 1986, they will wreck any attempt at pursuing a strong exchange rate policy. Not even high oil revenues can prevent this. Responding to tensions which build up gradually over the years by recurring large devaluations is not an option today. It would require extremely high interest rates to keep the speculators at bay while waiting for a sense of national emergency to penetrate public opinion.

As pointed out in Section 3, the long run equilibrium level of unemployment is independent of aggregate demand. If we try to push employment below this level through an expansionary fiscal policy, and if we cannot replay the corrective actions taken in the past, we shall have to pay with a period of higher employment in the future. This will be necessary in order to restore international competitiveness and to break inflationary expectations. This problem is aggravated by the fact that petroleum production is expected to start declining already five years from now. There is also great uncertainty about petroleum prices. The risks are high that a fiscal expansion would soon have to be reversed.

In the end it is only a low long-run equilibrium rate of unemployment which can ensure that we have lower unemployment than other countries. This article has attempted to show that the difference in the time paths of unemployment in Norway and in Europe at large *may* be explained without recourse to differences in the long-run equilibrium rate of unemployment. However, the possibility that Norway has a lower equilibrium unemployment rate is still open. More research is needed to determine this. We gained competitiveness in the early 1990s with unemployment considerably below the European average. We do not know how much of this achievement should be attributed to low hysteresis effects due to low unemployment in the past, and how much should be attributed to lower equilibrium unemployment. Fortunately, both alternatives give us the prospects of some years with unemployment below the European average.

One possible explanation for the difference between the US and the EU is that there is less hysteresis in the US because the short duration of unemployment and less social support means that people cannot afford to stay unemployed for long. For different reasons there may also be smaller hysteresis effects in Norway than in other European countries. That so many unemployed are educated either in labour market programmes or in the regular education system may mean that it is easier to get them back to work when employment expands again. Central bargaining may also mean that the insider–outsider distinction is less relevant. This remains to be seen. Wage increases in the next few years will give some clues as to what level of unemployment the Norwegian economy can sustain in the long run.

Notes

I am grateful for excellent research assistance from Sveinung Skjesol and for financial support from the Research Council of Norway. Data are mainly drawn from the OECD Statistical compendium 1996:1. Data on the oil industry and "mainland Norway" are from the Central Bureau of Statistics (National Accounts). Other sources are indicated in the text. The Norwegian National Accounts underwent a major revision in 1995. This study is based on the old national accounts from before the revision, because that was the only way to get comparable figures for the whole period. Growth rates from the new accounts are occasionally used to prolong a series to 1995.

References

Alogoskoufis, G. S. and Manning, A. (1988) On the persistence of unemployment, *Economic Policy* 7: 427–69.

Ball, L. (1996) Disinflation and the NAIRU. *National Bureau of Economic Research*, Working Paper 5520.

Blanchflower, D. G. and Oswald A. J. (1990) The wage curve, *Scandinavian Journal of Economics* 95, 45–48.

Bruno, M. and Sachs J. (1985) *Economics of Worldwide Stagflation*. Oxford: Basil Blackwell.

Calmfors, L. (ed.) (1990) *Wage Formation and Macroeconomic Policy in the Nordic Countries*. Oxford: Oxford University Press.

Calmfors, L. (1993) Lessons from the macroeconomic experience of Sweden, *European Journal of Political Economy* 9, 25–72.

Calmfors, L. and R. Nymoen (1990) Real wage adjustment and employment policies in the Nordic countries, *Economic Policy* 5:2, 397–448.

Eika, T. (1996) Petroleumsvirksomheten og norsk økonomi (The petroleum activity and the Norwegian economy), *Økonomiske analyser* 15:5, 26–33.

Jensen, S. and E. Hougaard (1996) Recent developments in the Danish economy: problems, politics and prospects, *Economic Policy Research Unit*, Copenhagen Business School, EPRU Analyse 13.

Johansen, K. (1995) *Real Wage Responsiveness to Unemployment and Insider Forces: The Norwegian Experience*. Doctoral dissertation, University of Trondheim.

Layard, R., Nickell S. and Jackman R. (1991) *Unemployment: Macroeconomic Performance and the Labour Market*. Cambridge: Cambridge University Press.

Moene, K., Nymoen R. and Wallerstein M. (1997) This volume.

Nesheim, H. and Drevdal, S. (1995) Utviklingen i sysselsetting, ledighet og yrkespassivitet i de nordiske land (The development of employment, unemployment and non-participation in the Nordic countries), *Økonomiske Analyser 14:1*.

Nymoen, R. (1989) Modelling wages in the small open economy: an error-correction model of Norwegian manufacturing wages, *Oxford Bulletin of Economics and Statistics* 51, 239–258.

Nymoen, R. (1990) *Empirical Modelling of Wage-Price Inflation and Employment Using Norwegian Quarterly Data*. University of Oslo: Økonomiske doktoravhandlinger 3.

OECD (1994) *The OECD Jobs Study: Evidence and Explanations*. Paris: OECD.

Oswald, A. J. (1985) The economic theory of trade unions: an introductory survey, *Scandinavian Journal of Economics 87*, 160–193.

Rødseth, A. (1994) Vegen til høg arbeidsløyse (The road to high unemployment), pp. 61–89 in A. Sandmo (ed.): *Perspektiver på arbeidsledigheten*, SNF-Årbok 1994. Bergen: Fagbokforlaget.

Røisland, Ø. (1993) Komparative studier av lønnsdanning (Comparative studies of wage formation), *Stiftelsen for samfunns- og næringslivsforskning*, Arbeidsnotat 73.

Stølen, N. M. (1994) *Wage Formation and the Macroeconomic Functioning of the Norwegian Labour Market*. University of Oslo: Økonomiske doktoravhandlinger 18.

Chapter 6

Labor Market Friction and Unemployment

Karl Ove Moene, Ragnar Nymoen, and Michael Wallerstein

1. Introduction

One of the primary objectives of social democratic governments and unions in the postwar period has been the maintenance of full employment. Like the Democratic Party in the US, the Social Democratic parties in Northern Europe came to power near the peak of unemployment during the Great Depression and established a long-lasting parliamentary majority by presiding over an economic recovery and the achievement of full employment. Throughout the postwar period, social democrats successfully appealed for votes on the basis of their record as guardians of full employment.

The basis for the identification of social democracy with full employment can be seen in Figure 6.1.[1] In the 1960s and early 1970s, the macroeconomic performance of Norway and Sweden was not particularly distinctive. Full employment was achieved throughout Western Europe in the period between the recovery from the Second World War and the first oil price shock. In most of Western Europe, however, the era of full employment ended abruptly in the mid-1970s. By the early 1980s, the average rate of unemployment in the European Community exceeded 10%. Even as growth resumed in the mid-1980s, unemployment in the European Union remained high in comparison to the 1970s, let alone in comparison to the full employment of the 1960s. Yet, throughout the 1970s and most of the 1980s, unemployment in Norway and Sweden remained low. As late as 1987 in Norway (and 1990 in Sweden) the unemployment rate was not much above 2%.

The paper is part of the project "Unemployment, Institutions and Policies" at SNF, Oslo. Financial support from the Research Council of Norway is gratefully acknowledged. We are also grateful to Sveinung Skjesol for excellent assistance.

1 The data for all countries except Denmark refer to the OECD standardized unemployment rate. In the case of Denmark, where standardized unemployment figures are unavailable, we used the unstandardized rate.

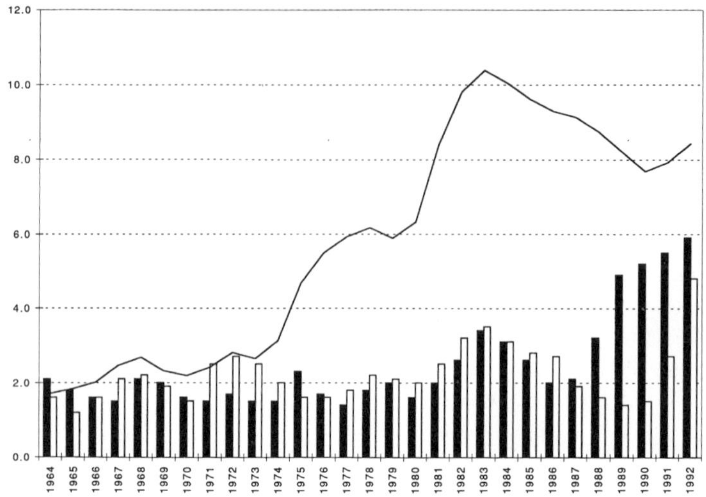

Figure 6.1 Unemployment in Norway, Sweden and seven EU countries, 1964-92. Norway is solid black column, Sweden is the outlined column. The line is the unweighted average of Italy, France, Germany, UK, Belgium, the Netherlands and Denmark.

Today, the difference between Norway and Sweden and the rest of Europe in terms of unemployment has been reduced as unemployment rates have risen sharply. In Norway, unemployment rose from below 2% in 1987 to over 6% by 1993. In Sweden the rise in unemployment came later but faster. In fact, the decline of production and employment in Sweden in the early 1990s is worse than the decline that occurred during the 1930s (Rødseth 1994). In 1990, unemployment in Sweden was still below 2%. By 1992 Swedish unemployment had risen above 5%. In 1993 the Swedish unemployment rate reached 8.5%. Unemployment in Finland rose from 3.5% in 1990 to 15% by the end of 1992. Moreover, standard unemployment figures do not include the participants in active labor market policies. Including workers enrolled in active labor market programs would increase the current rate of unemployment to 8% in Norway and 12% in Sweden in 1993.

There is substantial consensus today on at least some of the causes of the initial rise in unemployment in Europe. Although scholars differ on the relative weights to attach to different shocks, most believe that the large oil price increases of 1973 and 1979 and the deflationary policies and high real interest rates of the early 1980s contributed significantly to the rise in unemployment (Bean 1994). The more recent rise of mass unemployment in the Nordic countries can be explained by a sharp contraction of domestic consumption as a boom in housing and other asset prices came to a sudden end (Rødseth 1994, King 1994).

Two aspects of the European unemployment experience are more difficult to understand, however. First, the failure of unemployment to fall again as the initial shocks passed is hard to explain. High unemployment in Europe has persisted for far longer than can plausibly be explained by the factors that seem to account for its initial increase. The second puzzle is why the unemployment rate in countries like Norway and Sweden remained low for many years, in striking contrast to most other European countries.

A second, related aspect of worsening labor market performance is the increase in unemployment–vacancy for a given vacancy rate. Since the 1970s, the rate of unemployment that coexists with a given rate of job vacancies has roughly tripled in Western Europe (Bean, 1994: 591). A similar shift has occurred in Norway, as well, but with a lag. This is often taken as evidence of increased mismatch between the types of workers looking for work and the types of workers demanded by employers. Direct measures of mismatch, however, do not show significant change since the 1970s (Jackman and Roper, 1987; Stølen, 1993; Manning, Wadsworth and Wilkinson, 1995).

In this paper, we describe a mechanism and present some empirical evidence from Norway concerning the interaction of labor market friction and unemployment that may provide an understanding of the persistence of both high unemployment and full employment. Labor market friction, particularly friction associated with government imposed regulations concerning wages, working conditions and layoffs, is frequently blamed for the persistence of high unemployment in Europe. Our treatment of friction is different in two significant ways. First, we concentrate on friction that is an endogenous consequence of the process whereby unemployment workers are matched with job vacancies. Second, we show that the interaction of friction and unemployment potentially explains the persistence of full employment as well as the persistence of high unemployment. In fact, high levels of friction in our model, and in the Norwegian data, are associated with low levels of unemployment and vice versa.

The friction we study arises from the cost of finding and training workers. It is widely recognized that raising the cost of laying off workers inhibits firms from hiring. Less appreciated is the reverse point: The greater the cost of filling vacancies, the fewer workers will be laid off when demand falls but is expected to rise again in the future.[2] While hiring costs may take

2 See Bean (1994) and Røed (1996) for surveys of the literature on the persistence of unemployment in Europe.

many different forms, from the cost of interviewing applicants to the costs of training in firm-specific skills, in this paper we present a simplified exposition that includes only the costs associated with the time it takes to fill a vacancy. Under conditions of full employment, labor is scarce and vacancies are difficult to fill. When vacancies are difficult to fill, employers are reluctant to reduce their work force when demand falls, provided the fall in demand is perceived as temporary. The more employers refrain from laying off their workers when the price of their output is low, the smaller is the pool of unemployed workers and the harder it is to fill vacancies. The more employers hoard labor, in other words, the more likely is labor-hoarding to be an optimal response by the firm to a period of low prices. Conversely, when unemployment is high, vacancies are readily filled and the implicit costs of layoffs decline. In this way, high unemployment can reduce the demand for labor associated with a given array of wages and output prices.

The result can be the presence of two, locally stable, equilibria, one with high level unemployment and low friction and the other with low unemployment and high friction. As long as unemployment remains below a threshold, temporary increases in unemployment are followed by a return to the previous level when demand recovers, as occurred in Norway and Sweden in the early 1980s. In this way, government policies of demand management in combination with union policies of nominal wage restraint can have lasting effects. Once unemployment crosses the threshold, however, unemployment may remain high even when demand and real labor costs return to the levels previously associated with full employment.

The main body of this paper is divided into two parts. In the first, we provide a more detailed account of our argument and contrast it with other explanations for the persistence of unemployment. In the second part, we present some empirical evidence that the Norwegian experience since 1974 fits our explanation of persistence in key respects. We conclude with a brief discussion of some of the macroeconomic implications of our findings.

2. Persistence of High and Low Unemployment

Several different explanations of the persistence of high levels of unemployment in Europe have been suggested in recent years. Perhaps the most well-known is the insider–outsider model, developed by Lindbeck and Snower (1988) and Blanchard and Summers (1990). According to the insider–outsider model, unions represent the interests of insiders, or employed workers. When unemployment is low, the number of insiders is high and the union is concerned with maintaining a large number of jobs. When layoffs occur, however, the number of union members is reduced. When demand picks up again, the remaining insiders prefer to have their wages increased rather than have employment restored. Once the unemployed have lost their insider status, the argument goes, they are ignored by the union in the wage-setting process.

Other authors have emphasized the effect of low demand on the stock of capital in the economy. Soskice and Carlin (1989) emphasize the decline in physical capital as firms reduce investment when demand is low. Others, notably Layard, Nickell and Jackman (1991), emphasize the decline in human capital. The longer workers have been out of work, the more their skills deteriorate. When demand increases, employers may compete over the already employed workers, bidding up their wages, rather than fill vacancies with workers who have been out of employment for a long period of time.

None of these explanations is entirely convincing in the Nordic context. Local union leaders primarily represent the interests of employed union members, as suggested in the insider–outside model, but wage bargaining in the Nordic countries is dominated on the labor side by either the national unions or the central union confederations. There is little evidence that the national union leaders show less concern for unemployed workers than those who remain employed.[3] Neither do the approaches that emphasize the decline in physical and human capital appear to capture the entire story. Evidence of hysteresis remains even after controlling for the stock of physical capital, as we discuss in our empirical work. The decline in human capital may have an impact, but all of the Nordic countries employ an extensive set of active labor market policies designed to upgrade the skills of those without work.

The cost of filling vacancies

Our alternative approach to understanding the persistence of both high unemployment and full employment is based on the mutual dependence of employers' choice of employment policies, the tightness of the labor market and friction in the labor market. A labor market with friction is a labor market in which unemployed workers may fail to be matched with available job vacancies. Friction implies that excess supply and excess demand for labor may exist simultaneously.

3 In Sweden, unemployed workers remain union members since the unions administer the unemployment insurance system. In Norway, the central negotiators don't have sufficient information to distinguish the unemployment of union members from unemployment in general.

For concreteness consider the probability that a firm can fill a vacancy within a given time period. In general, the probability of filling a vacancy is less than one, even when there are unemployed workers, since the process whereby unemployed workers are matched with appropriate job vacancies takes time and resources. The likelihood of filling vacancies depends on many factors, including the wage offered, the firm's expenditures to fill job openings and the aggregate number of workers searching for work relative to the total number of employers searching for employees. To simplify our exposition, we focus on a stylized environment where the wage is set in centralized negotiations, and where expenditure advertising vacancies and screening applicants is negligible.[4] In this case, the probability of filling a vacancy is exogenous from the point of view of an individual firm.

Although the wage is set over the contract period, the price of output may fluctuate. Let the price of the value-added produced by the worker in each period be an independently and identically distributed random variable and consider a position that is currently filled. The firm's employment strategy, in this context, consists of a cut-off price. If the realized price falls below the cut-off price, the firm lays off the worker. If the price is higher than or equal to the cut-off price, the firm continues to hire the current employee. Since we have not included any training costs or redundancy payments, it is clear that the optimal thresholds for hiring and firing will be the same. In a more complete analysis with turnover costs, the threshold price would differ.

In Moene, Nymoen and Wallerstein (1995), we show that the profit-maximizing choice of the cut-off price is independent of whether or not the position is currently open or filled. In addition, we show that the optimal cut-off price satisfies the simple condition that expresses the terms of the trade-off faced by the firm in setting its employment policy. On the one hand, the firm suffers a loss in the current period if the price of what a worker can produce falls below the cost of labor and the firm does not lay-off its work force. On the other hand, a firm that does lay-off its workers whenever the value added per worker falls below the cost of labor may be unable to hire as many workers as it would like if demand increases. The optimality condition states that the firm should set the cut-off price at the level where the immediate cost of maintaining the firm's work force intact is just equal to the expected profits that will be lost due to possible labor shortages in the future. In an environ-

4 For a discussion of lay-offs and labor hoarding with endogenous wages, see Moene and Wallerstein (1995).

ment where it is not always possible to fill vacancies immediately, the marginal cost of labor is less than the wage.

We can derive the response of employers' strategy to a variety of changes in the economic environment.[5] An exogenous reduction in the probability of filling a vacancy (that is, an increase in friction) lowers the optimal cut-off price since an increase in friction increases the importance of having a secure labor supply. In addition, the cut-off price, increases as the interest rate rises, since the more the future is discounted the less the possibility of future labor shortages affects the decision to lay-off workers in the present. A wage increase of one unit raises the optimal cut-off price by more than one unit. At a higher wage, the cost the firm is willing to incur before laying off workers is reduced. A downward shift in the price distribution has a similar effect. Thus, when the mean of the price distribution falls, workers face increased prospects of unemployment for two reasons. First, the price is more likely to fall below the threshold, holding the threshold constant. Second, firms raise the threshold at which workers are laid off. When the distribution of prices is perceived to have shifted downward, firms will lay-off workers at price levels that would not have prompted lay-offs previously.

Equilibrium

From a single firm's point of view, the likelihood of finding a suitable worker within a given time period is exogenous, at least if the firm's wage offers are constrained by an industry or higher-level wage agreement. But, in aggregate, the likelihood of filling a vacancy depends on the number of unemployed workers who are searching for work and the number of other firms that have vacancies to fill, which in turn depends on firms' choices of employment policy.

The interaction of the macroeconomic environment and the microeconomic adjustment of employers' employment strategies is illustrated in Figure 6.2, in which we assume that there is a fixed number of identical firms that face independent firm-specific price shocks, each with one unit of labor. The four quadrants represent: (i) the impact of the anticipated ease of filling vacancies on firms' cut-off price, (ii) the effect of the cut-off price on the slackness of the labor market, (iii) the effect of the slackness of the labor market on the number of successful matches of unemployed workers and job openings, and (iv) the effect of the number of successful matches on the expected ease of filling vacancies. None of the steps is trivial.

5 See Moene, Nymoen and Wallerstein (1995) for details.

The effect of the anticipated ease of filling vacancies on firms' choice of cut-off price, quadrant (i), has already been discussed in the previous section. Consider, then, the second quadrant, where we illustrate the effect of firms' cut-off price on the slackness of the labor market. Labor market slackness is defined as the number of unemployed workers per job vacancy, or the unemployment–vacancy ratio. Note that, since all firms face the same price distribution, all choose the same cut-off price. Realized prices, however, vary for each firm depending on the luck of the

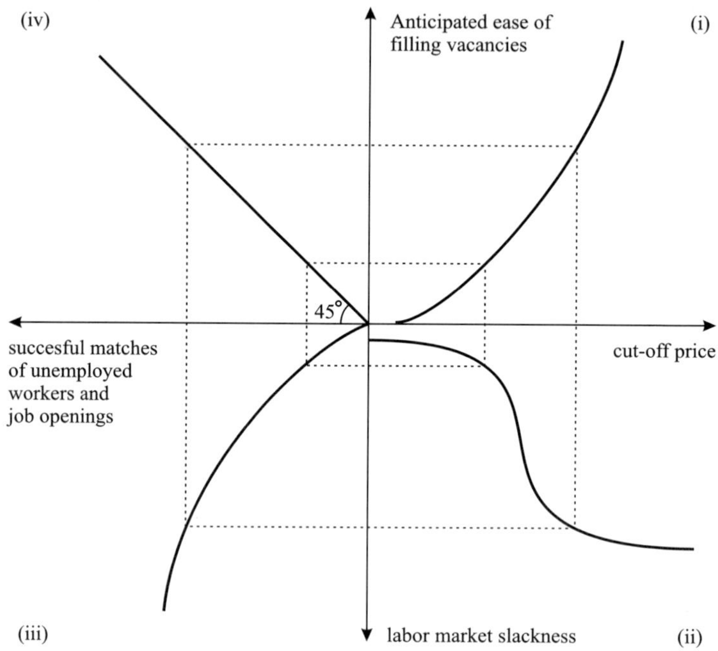

Figure 6.2 The interaction between employment strategies and labor market tightness.

draw. At the beginning of each period, positions are either filled or unfilled. After prices are realized, a fraction, say $F(x)$, of firms with workers receive such a low price that the workers are laid off, while the fraction $1\text{-}F(x)$ of firms with unfilled positions receive prices high enough to seek to fill their vacancies. Here x is the cut-off price, and $F(x)$ is the function that describes the probability that the realized price will be less than or equal to x. If we assume that there are the same number of positions and workers, the number of unemployed workers equals the number of unfilled positions. The number of vacancies equals the fraction $1\text{-}F(x)$ of the number of unfilled positions. Thus, the number of unemployed workers per vacancy is given by $1/[1\text{-}F(x)]$. Since $F(x)$ is an increasing function (the higher the cut-off price, the greater the probability that the realized price will be less than or equal to the cut-off price), the unemployment–vacancy ratio is an increasing function of the cut-off price. Quadrant (ii) illustrates the shape of $1/[1\text{-}F(x)]$ for a typical bell-shaped cumulative density function.

The third quadrant illustrates the relationship between the slackness of the labor market and the probability of successfully filling an empty position. It has become standard practice in labor economics to conceptualize the matching of unemployed workers with vacant jobs as an outcome that requires searching by both employers and workers (Mortensen, 1986, Pissarides, 1990). It is common to describe the number of successful matches that occur per job vacancy as an increasing function of the number of workers searching for work relative to the number of employers searching for a worker. In a tight labor market where there are few unemployed workers per vacancy, the number of successful matches per vacancy is also small. In a slack labor market with many unemployed workers per vacancy, the ratio of successful matches per vacancy is close to one.

The fourth quadrant completes the circle by equating the number of matches per vacancy with the anticipated ease of filling vacancies. This is a steady-state condition. In a steady-state equilibrium, employers' anticipated ease of filling vacancies must equal the current ease of filling vacancies, which is the same as the number of matches per vacancy.

Quadrants (iv) and (i) describe how the macroeconomic environment affects firms' choice of employment strategy, while quadrants (ii) and (iii) illustrate how firms' choice of employment strategy alters the macroeconomic environment. This interaction of microeconomic and macroeconomic effects creates the possibility of multiple equilibria, as indicated in Figure 6.2 by the two dotted lines. In Moene, Nymoen and Wallerstein (1995), we prove that there may be either one or two stable equilibria for a given wage rate and price distribution or level of aggregate demand. If two stable equilibria exist, the equilibrium with the higher cut-off price yields (a) the highest unemployment, (b) the shortest average duration of employment, (c) the longest duration of unemployment, and (d) the highest level of expected profits.

The low unemployment equilibrium has more friction in the labor market and fewer lay-offs than the high unemployment equilibrium. With more friction, job vacancies are filled with greater difficulty. The difficulty of filling vacancies causes firms to hold onto their workers over a broader range of price fluctuations. Expected profits go down for both reasons. Employment, however, becomes less sensitive to price variations, which implies that the average duration of jobs increases. Greater friction in the labor market is more than compensated by the choice of a lower cut-off price by employers. Accordingly, there are fewer unemployed workers per vacancy and less unemployment overall. Less competition for jobs among the unemployed implies that the average duration of unemployment declines.

Figure 6.3 illustrates the relationship between the level of aggregate demand (or the mean of the price distribution) and employment, holding the wage fixed. Holding the wage constant, an increase in aggregate demand will induce employers to reduce the cut-off price, decreasing the number of lay-offs and increasing employment. At a sufficiently high level of demand (the region above D1 in the figure), only the low unemployment equilibrium exists. If the level of demand is sufficiently low (below D2), only the high unemployment equilibrium exists. At levels of demand between D1 and D2 in the figure, two equilibria exist. In this region, there are two levels of employment that are compatible with a given level of demand.

The figure illustrates two potentially important aspects of the relationship between aggregate demand and employment. The first is that the relationship is potentially discontinuous. In general, a small change in aggregate demand has a small impact on employment. However, a small decline in demand from just above D2 to just below D2 when the economy is at the low unemployment equilibrium will cause a large decline in employment as the economy shifts to the high unemployment equilibrium. Secondly, there is a ratchet effect or hysteresis in the labor mar-

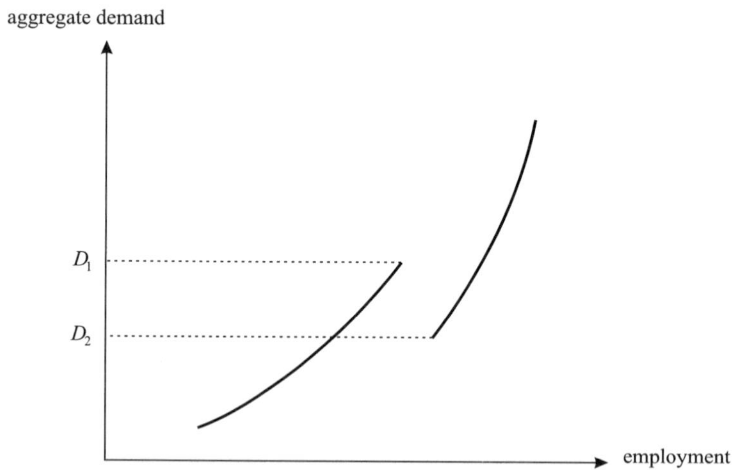

Figure 6.3 The discontinuity of the labor demnad.

ket in the sense that a reversion back to the initial level of demand just above D2 is not enough to induce a shift back to full employment. To induce a shift to the low unemployment equilibrium once the economy has adjusted to high unemployment, it is necessary to raise aggregate demand above D1.

Figure 6.4 illustrates the same points with regard to changes in the wage level holding demand constant. An increase in the wage level causes employers to raise the cut-off price, increasing the likelihood of layoffs and decreasing aggregate employment. A wage increase from just below *w*1 to just above *w*1 could cause a discontinuous jump in unemployment, in which case a reduction of the wage back to its previous level would not be enough for the lost employmentto be regained. Once the economy is stuck in the high unemployment equilibrium, the wage must be reduced below *w*2 for full employment to be restored.

3. Empirical Evidence

Our argument suggests that changes in the cost of hoarding labor is an important mechanism of persistence of both tight and slack labor markets. Negative demand shocks of a sufficient magnitude can make firms appear permanently less willing to take on labor. We cannot test the existence of multiple equilibria with our data, since Norway has shifted from a low unemployment regime to a higher unemployment regime but not back again in the sample period. We can, however, test the model's

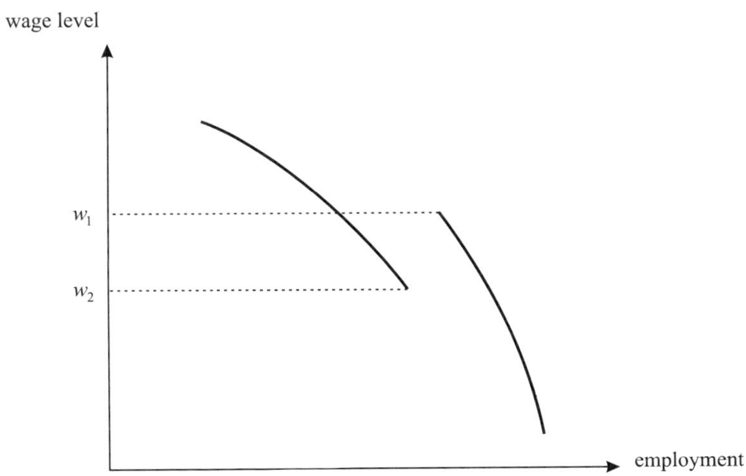

Figure 6.4 The discontinuity of the employment as a function of the wage level.

implication that there should remain a separate effect of friction, even after one includes all "conventional" explanatory variables, such as wage costs, product demand, capital stock, occupational mismatch and search intensity in estimates of the demand for labor or the unemployment–vacancy ratio. In this section, we test the null hypothesis that indicators of labor market friction have no explanatory power in estimates of labor demand or the unemployment–vacancy ratio once conventional explanatory variables are included in the equation.

There are two important issues that we address in our empirical tests. The first concerns the stability of the estimated coefficients across a change in regime from low to high unemployment, such as occurred in Norway in 1988–1990. The second issue is that friction is an endogenous variable in our model. How can we know that causality runs from expected labor shortages to a higher demand for labor and not (only) from labor demand to expected labor shortages? As we discuss below, the two issues are related in that the stability of estimates provides evidence regarding the direction of causality.

The unemployment–vacancy relationship

The Norwegian unemployment–vacancy ratio for the period 1970.1–1993.3 is illustrated in Figure 6.5. The total period is split in to four intervals of six years each. As seen from the figure, the unemployment–vacancy curve shifts outwards in the 1980s and 1990s implying that a given vacancy rate corresponds to increasingly higher unemployment rates. There is also some indication of a vertical movement in the 1990s. Overall, the shifts in the Norwegian unemployment–vacancy curve correspond closely with changes that have occurred in the unemployment–vacancy curve throughout Western Europe (Layard, Nickell and Jackman, 1991).

The two traditional explanations given for the outward shift in the unemployment–vacancy curve are increased mismatch, e.g. regional or occupational imbalances between supply and demand of labor, and reduced search intensity among the unemployed. Our argument suggests a third mechanism. Quadrant (ii) in Figure 6.2 indicates that the unemployment–vacancy ratio is an increasing function of firms' cut-off price. While the cut-off price is not observable, we have argued that it is dependent on labor market friction, the rate of interest, the wage and product demand. We would not want to assume that the cut-off price adjusts immediately to changes in (expected) costs, demand and friction, however. The relationship between the unemployment–vacancy ratio and

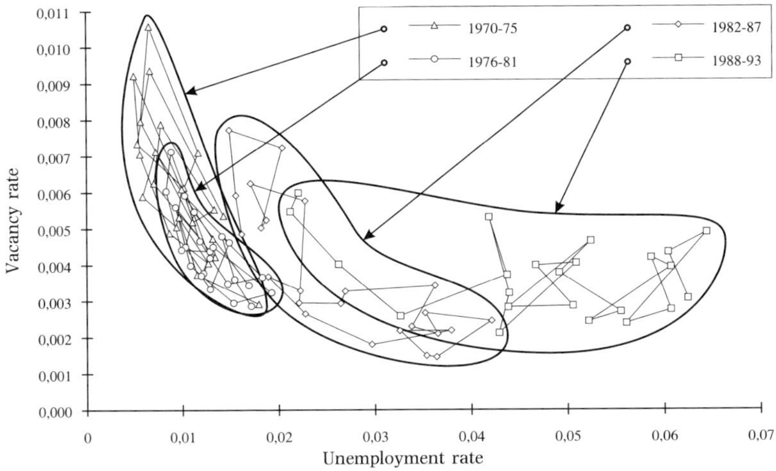

Figure 6.5 The Norwegian *u*/*v*-curve, 1970-1993

the cut-off price is a steady-state relationship that is best estimated using the error–correction model.

We use the fraction of firms experiencing labor shortage, denoted LSH, as a proxy for the perceived difficulty in filling vacancies. The data on friction are taken from the business survey series collected by Statistics Norway. The interest rate variable is a 'short' interest rate and is denoted IR. The wage-cost data, WCP, is for the manufacturing and construction industries. Product demand, D, is based on final expenditures in fixed (1991) prices. One might argue that in the present context it is not the level of demand itself that is important, but rather demand relative to capacity. Hence, the demand variable used below is D/K, where K denotes the capital stock. To capture the possibility that reduced search intensity among the long-term unemployed can account for the observed shift in unemployment–vacancy ratio, we have also included a measure of long-term unemployment, lu, on the right hand side. Finally, for labor market mismatch we have combined an annual occupational mismatch series due to Stølen (1993: 35), with the seasonal pattern of a five-sector occupational mismatch series. The details regarding the data sources are given in the appendix. Three additive seasonal dummy variables were also included but are not reported here.

Based on the above information, set with quarterly data from 1974 through 1993, we estimated the following log-linear equation where conventional "t-values" are in parentheses:

(1)

$$\widehat{\Delta \ln(u/v)_t} = -\underset{(3.097)}{0.6771} - \underset{(10.635)}{0.7897}\, \Delta \ln (u/v)_{t-2} - \underset{(7.479)}{0.2376}\, \Delta \ln(u/v)_{t-3}$$

$$- \underset{(2.888)}{0.4593} \ln(D/K)_{t-1} + \underset{(8.248)}{1.693}\, \Delta \ln(lu)_{t-1} + \underset{(2.482)}{1.477}\, \Delta \ln(WCP)_{t-3}$$

$$+ \underset{(3.546)}{3.111}(IR)_{t-3} - \underset{(2.948)}{.01848}\,(LSH)$$

$$DW = 2.07$$
$$R^2 = 0.881$$

The lagged differences in $\ln(u/v)$ were included to whiten the residuals. Without the lagged differences in $\ln(u/v)$, there is large negative autocorrelation. Differences in the dates of the independent variables were set to allow for differences in the speed of adjustment. We assume, for example, that u/v responds more quickly to LSH than to wages or interest rates. Below equation (1) we report the Durbin Watson statistic (DW). We show in Moene, Nymoen and Wallerstein (1995) that equation (1) passes a variety of misspecification tests.

Note the highly significant coefficient of the change in long-term unemployment, $\Delta \ln (lu)_{t1}$. In contrast, lagged levels terms of lu are never significant in this specification. Over the sample, the composition of unemployment has only exerted a transitory effect on the u/v ratio. The estimates show that the same is true for wage costs. Therefore neither long-term unemployment nor wage costs are included in the following static, long-run solution (steady-state) of (1):

(2)

$$\Delta \ln(u/v)_t = \text{constant} - \underset{(3.32)}{1.894} \ln(D/K) + \underset{(3.19)}{12.59}\,(IR) - \underset{(3.90)}{8.197}\,(LSH/100)$$

Equation (2) shows that friction, as captured by LSH, affects u/v in the predicted way for given levels of demand relative to capacity and the interest rate. The approximate "t-values" of the long-run coefficients suggest statistical significance of all three right-hand side variables in (2).[6] Evaluated at sample means, the estimated effect of a unit increase in LSH

6 The coefficients and t-values in the long-run equation are derived from the estimated dynamic equation (1). See Bårdsen (1989).

is on a par with the effect of a (sustained) 1% increase in demand relative to capacity, and is only moderately smaller than a 1% reduction in the interest rate.

Mismatch is conspicuously absent from our estimated equations. The reason is that we were unable to establish a sensible long-run effect. Moreover, including a measure of mismatch does not influence the other coefficients a great deal. It is unlikely that this finding depends crucially on our particular mismatch index. Stølen (1993, ch. 2.2) calculates indices by region, gender and age, as well as occupation. Overall, mismatch appears to have been just as high in the 1970s as in the late 1980s. For this reason, it is unlikely that mismatch can explain much of the large shifts in *u*/*v* that have occurred since the 1970s.

Given the large shifts in *u*/*v* shown in Figure 6.5, the stability of any model of *u*/*v* must be open to doubt. The standard errors of the residuals of equation (1) are stable over the sample. In addition, none of the 'break-point' Chow statistics for the sequence {1970(3)–1993(3), ..., 1993(2)–1993(3),1993(3)}, are significant at the 5% level. In Figure 6.6 we show the numerical value of the coefficient on LSHt from (1), together with plus or minus twice their sequentially estimated standard errors (denoted β_t) and $\beta_t \pm 2 \cdot SE_t$ in the graphs). The variation in the coefficient is only a fraction of the standard error. The standard errors imply that the LSH coefficient is significant for all sample sizes beyond the late 1970s.[7]

Labor demand and unemployment

According to our argument, the demand for labor increases as the ease of filling vacancies declines, holding other determinants of the labor demand such as wages and product demand constant. In this section, we use an alternative measure based on aggregate unemployment. This is partly motivated by a concern for robustness. The results shouldn't depend critically on the exact measure of friction since there are multiple possible measures. Secondly, an employment-based measure would facilitate the application of our results to improve the empirical models actually used for policy analysis and forecasting. The prediction that

7 Despite the apparent stability of the model in equation (1) one might argue that the estimates are affected by simultaneity bias. To test this, we re-estimated (1) with instrumental variables for LSH where the instruments for LSH are lagged LSH, lagged expected LSH, the lagged short-term unemployment rate, the log of lagged short-term unemployment, the lagged change new vacancies and the lagged growth rate of product market demand. For the all coefficients, the changes are minor. See Moene, Nymoen and Wallerstein (1995) for details.

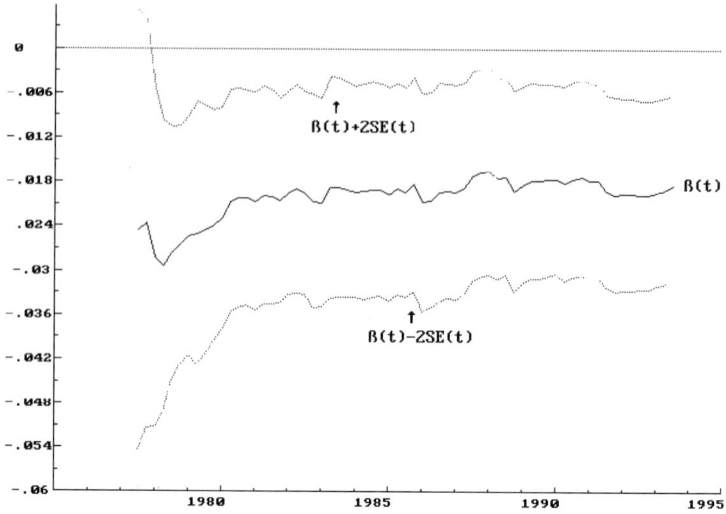

Figure 6.6 Equation 1: Recursive estimates of the coefficient of LSH, with +/-2 estimated standard errors.

expected friction matters is not confined to total employment but is equally relevant for sectoral labor demand. Thus we base the test on a model of labor demand in manufacturing and construction, comprising some 30% of all employed wage earners in Norway.

The relationship between expected unemployment to firms' cut-off price and labor demand is likely to be non-linear. At very low levels of unemployment, the difficulty of filling vacancies is likely to fall rapidly as unemployment increases. At higher levels of unemployment, however, further increases may have a smaller effect on the ease with which vacancies are filled. To accommodate non-linearities we have adopted a logistic transformation of the expected rate of total unemployment, denoted STU, where the exact parameterization was based on calibration using business–survey data. We assumed, in addition, that the expected future rate of unemployment is equal to current rate of unemployment plus a seasonal adjustment. Finally, we use total unemployment, i.e. open unemployment plus the number of people active in labor market programmes as we are interested in the total number of people who are available for employment.[8]

Equation (3) shows a labor demand function for the Norwegian manufacturing and construction sector from 1974 through 1992. The number of wage earners Nt is explained by growth in product demand D_t, the

8 Labor market programs accommodated around 30% of total unemployment in 1992.

level of demand relative to capacity D/K_t, the length of the working day H_t, price competitiveness P_t^*/P_t, where P_t^* is an index of import prices of competing products, the wage-share of value added WSHt and the logistic transformation of expected unemployment STU_t.[9]

(3)

$$\Delta \ln(N)_t = \underset{(4.30)}{1.44} + \underset{(14.65)}{0.76} \ln(N)_{t-1} + \underset{(3.30)}{0.05}\, \Delta \ln(D)_t$$

$$+ \underset{(3.90)}{0.07} \ln(D/K)_{t-1} - \underset{(3.37)}{0.15} \ln(H)_t + \underset{(3.92)}{0.07} \ln(P^*/P)_{t-1}$$

$$- \underset{(2.40)}{0.02} \sum_{i=1}^{4} \ln(WSH)_{t-i} - \underset{(4.17)}{0.03}\, STU_t - \underset{(3.87)}{0.043}\, D8lql_t + \epsilon_t$$

$$DW = 2.07$$

Increases in STU_t indicate increased unemployment or less labor market friction. According to our estimate, an increase in *STU* from 0 to 1, roughly what occurred in 1989, causes a short-run decline in employment of 3%, while the long-run response (where $\ln(N)_t = \ln(N)_{t-1}$) is a reduction of 12% (0.03/0.25). As an illustration of the order of magnitude of the friction effect, note that in order to fully accommodate an exogenous negative shock to employment of this order, the real exchange rate P*/P would have to depreciate by 41%, or the wage share would have to fall by 33%.

The overall fit of (3) is illustrated in Figure 6.7, which shows the actual, fitted and forecast values of $\ln(nw)_t$ estimated over the sample 1974(4)–1984(4). The lower panel zooms in on the ex post forecast period, adding a band of ± twice the forecast standard error (denoted $\pm 2\sigma$ in the graph). Moreover, estimates of the *STU* coefficient are empirically stable for any sample ending after 1984. (There is not much information in the sample before 1984, as friction was constant.) In the light of the huge fluctuations in labor shortage (friction), the within sample stability of the *STU* parameter provides support for the existence of a causal relationship between friction and labor demand.[10]

---

9 The variable $d81q1$ is a dummy variable for the first quarter of 1981, which is an outlier in our sample. Removing $d81q1$ from the right-hand side of (3) doesn't change the results significantly.

10 To see why this is true, let $\hat{\beta}$ denote the *OLS* estimate in the regression of y on x (as in $y = \alpha+\beta x$ + error term), while the *OLS* estimate of the reverse regression (x on y) is denoted $\hat{\beta}'$. Then $\hat{\beta}\hat{\beta}' = r^2$ where r is the correlation coefficient between x and y. Therefore, if r changes over the sample size, and if $\hat{\beta}$ is stable then $\hat{\beta}'$ cannot also be stable.

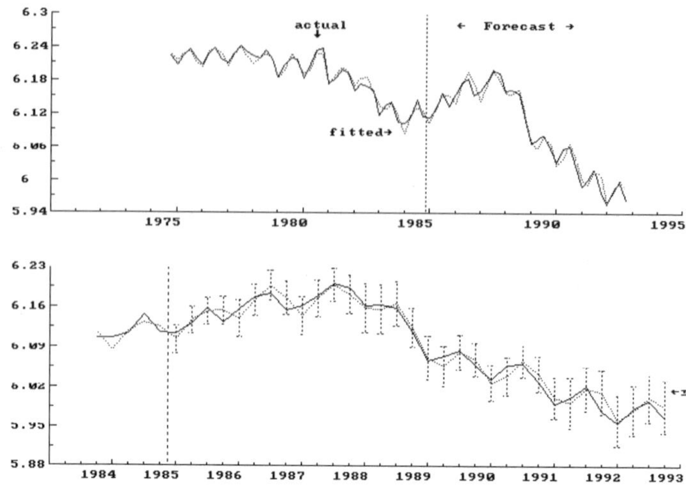

Figure 6.7 Equation(3): Upper panel: Actual, fitted and forcast values of ln (N), based on re-estimation of the model over 1974(4)-1984(4). Lower panel: One step ahead forecasts of ln (N), with +/-2 forecasts standard errors.

The growth in product demand ($\Delta \ln(D_t)$) and the length of the working week ($\ln (H)_t$) may be regarded as endogenous variables, in which case the parameter estimates in (3) are biased. Instrumental variables estimation yields an almost identical estimate of the coefficient of STU_t.[11] We also note that the main results conveyed by (3) are not critically dependent on the exact shape of the transformation of expected unemployment. We have experimented with several specifications of the logistic transition function without much loss in explanatory power. Another check of robustness is to use LSH_t itself instead of STU_t as a measure of friction. Compared to (3), WSH_t becomes insignificant, but all the other coefficients remain significant, and the coefficient of LSH_t gets a t-value of 3.6.

4. Conclusions

During periods of slack demand, firms face a trade-off between reducing costs through lay-offs and maintaining a work force large enough to increase output rapidly when demand picks up. The cost of lay-offs to the firm depends on the anticipated difficulty of filling vacancies when the firm wants to expand. The difficulty of filling vacancies because other

11 Our instruments are $\Delta \ln D_{t-j}$ (j = 1, 2, 3, 4), $\ln H_{t-4}$ and a variable $\ln NH_t$, where *NH* is the normal length of the working week.

firms are hoarding labor is a friction in the labor market, a friction that was prominent in Norway and Sweden until recently. When labor markets are tight, the delay in filling vacancies increases and labor hoarding increases which, in turn, further increases the tightness of the labor market. When labor markets are slack, vacancies are easily filled and labor hoarding disappears. This feedback from labor market tightness to the extent of labor hoarding creates the possibility of multiple equilibria in the labor market.

Our argument runs directly counter to the conventional view that labor market friction reduces employment growth. There is an important difference, however, between friction that emerges endogenously from a tight labor market and labor market friction that is due to government regulation of hiring and firing practices. Our results indicate that the difficulty of filling vacancies encourages firms to retain their work force intact, even when current revenues are below labor costs. Our argument does not imply that employment can be increased by raising the direct cost of lay-offs.

The possible existence of multiple equilibria has significant consequences for macroeconomic policy and the unions' wage policy. In order to understand the potential importance of the social democratic commitment to full employment, it must be recalled that the low unemployment equilibrium is only locally stable. A negative demand shock of sufficiently high magnitude would easily shift the economy to a new equilibrium with a high level of unemployment. For this reason, temporary government interventions to counter negative shocks and stabilize demand may have lasting consequences for employment if countercyclical policy prevents a shift from a low unemployment equilibrium to a high unemployment equilibrium. The possible existence of multiple equilibria makes demand management policies particularly important.

The same is true of union wage restraint. If full employment leads unions to raise wages, the low unemployment equilibrium may easily be eroded. There is a level of profitability of enterprises that is necessary for employers to a cut-off price that is compatible with a full employment equilibrium. Here the Nordic experience speaks against the view that the stronger the unions the worse the economy. Precisely because unions in Norway and Sweden were strong institutions in the sense of being large relative to the work force, highly centralized and closely allied with a party that was often in government, they accepted much responsibility for national economic performance.

Rødseth (this volume) discusses the events that ended the period of full employment in Norway. With multiple equilibria in the labor market, as argued above, the effect of a change in demand on unemployment may be discontinuous. If the labor market is initially at the low unemployment equilibrium, a small shift downward in the level of demand (around which the prices fluctuate) will not increase unemployment much. But a larger decline in demand may cause the low unemployment equilibrium to cease to exist. In this case, the labor market would move quickly to the equilibrium where most firms choose flexible employment and unemployment stays high.

A subsequent recovery in which the level of demand is returned to its original position would not, by itself, move the labor market back to the low unemployment equilibrium. Peer Gynt in Ibsen's play was wrong: back and forth is not the same distance. To go back to the initial equilibrium requires that most firms change their employment strategy. The existence of multiple equilibria, however, means that once the economy has converged to high unemployment it is profitable to maintain a high cut-off price that sustains this equilibrium as long as most of the other firms do the same. In fact, to try to move back to the initial low unemployment equilibrium may be excessively risky in terms of the danger of overheating the economy. In addition, it may be politically difficult to obtain the required wage restraint on the part of unions as the mutual gift exchange between unions and the government is broken by government's failure to guarantee full employment as its part of the exchange.

Data definitions

Unless otherwise stated, all variables are taken from the database of the Bank of Norway quarterly macroeconometric model. All data are available on request.

D: Product demand at fixed 1991 market prices.

d81q1: Dummy variable equal to 1 in 1981.1 and zero otherwise.

K: Capital stock in the industrial sector (manufacturing and construction) at fixed 1991 prices.

WCP: Hourly industrial wage cost in NOK.

LSH: The employment weighted percentage of manufacturing firms reporting labor shortages. Source: Business survey; Statistics Norway.

lu: Long-term unemployment rate (>26 weeks).

N: The number of employed wage earners in the industrial sector (manufacturing and construction), 1000 persons.

P: Value added deflator, manufacturing and construction. Factor prices. 1991=1.

P*: Index of competing prices. 1991=1.

u: Registered unemployment rate.

tu: Total unemployment rate, i.e. including persons on labor market programs.

v: Registered vacancy rate.

IR: "Real interest rate" calculated as nominal short-term interest rate -.25ln(Pt / Pt-4).

References

Bean, C. R. (1994) European Unemployment: A Survey. *Journal of Economic Literature*, 32: 573–619.

Blanchard, O. J. and Summers, L. H. (1987) Hysteresis in Unemployment. *European Economic Review*, 31: 288–295.

Bårdsen, G. (1989) Estimation of Long-run Coefficients in Error-correction Models. *Oxford Bulletin of Economics and Statistics*, 51: 345–350.

Jackman, R. and Roper, S. (1987) Structural Unemployment. *Oxford Bulletin of Economics and Statistics*, 49: 9–36.

King, M. (1994) Debt Deflation: Theory and Evidence. *European Economic Review*, 38: 419–445.

Layard, R., Nickell, S., and Jackman, R. (1991) *Unemployment*. Oxford: Oxford University Press.

Lindbeck, A. and Snower, D. J. (1988) *The Insider-Outsider Theory of Employment and Unemployment*. Cambridge, MA: MIT Press.

Manning, A., Wadsworth, J. and Wilkinson, D. (1995) Making Your Mind Up: Skill Mismatch in the UK. Paper presented at the Conference in Honor of Asar Lindbeck, Stockholm, June 16–18.

Moene, K. O. and Wallerstein, M. (1995) Full Employment as a Worker Discipline Device. In J. Roemer, ed., *Property Rights, Incentives and Welfare*. London: Macmillan.

Moene, K. O., Nymoen, R. and Wallerstein, M. (1995) The Persistence of Slack and Tight Labor Markets. Northwestern University: Center for Urban Affairs and Policy Research Working Paper 95-7 and the University of Oslo: Department of Economics Memorandum.

Mortensen, D. (1986) Job Search and Labor Market Analysis. In O. Ashenfelter, and R. Layard, eds., *Handbook of Labor Economics, Volume 2*. Amsterdam: North Holland.

Pissarides, C. A. (1990) *Equilibrium Unemployment Theory*. Oxford: Basil Blackwell.

Rødseth, A. (1994) Vegen til Høg Arbeidsløyse. In A. Sandmo, ed., *SNF Årbok 1994: Perspektiv på arbeidsledigheten*. Bergen: Fagbokforlaget.

Røed, Knut. (1996) Hysteresis in Unemployment. A Survey. *Journal of Economic Surveys*, forthcoming.

Soskice, D. and Carlin, W. (1989) Medium-run Keynesianism: Hysteresis and Capital Scrapping. In P. Davidson and J. Kregel, eds., *Macroeconomic Problems and Policies of Income Distribution*. Edward Elgar Press.

Stølen, N. M. (1993) *Wage Formation and the Macroeconometric Functioning of the Norwegian Labor Market*. Ph.D. thesis, University of Oslo.

Chapter 7

Flexibility in the Norwegian Labour Market in a Comparative Perspective

Gerhard Bosch

1. Flexibility and the Norwegian passion for equality

Conventional economic theory is characterised by a passion for inequality. Unemployment is regarded essentially as a consequence of excessively high wages and overly generous protective regulations. From this perspective, the remedy for unemployment is greater wage differentiation and the removal of protective regulations. The creation of inequality is seen as one of the mechanisms responsible for the success of the American job machine. The social cost of such defensive flexibility is high. As income differentials widen, society becomes increasingly polarised and the potential for conflict mounts.

In recent years, Norway has taken a different path. At a time when income differentials have widened in virtually all OECD countries, they have narrowed considerably in Norway (Kahn 1995), to such an extent in fact that income differentials there are now the narrowest in the OECD (Table A10 in the annex). And while dismissal protection has been restricted in virtually all other industrialised countries, the use of fixed-term contracts has been made more difficult in Norway, in order to limit the degree of polarisation in the labour market between permanent and temporary employees. In short, it can be said that, "Norwegian culture is characterised by a passion for equality," (Sivesind et al. 1995). This raises the question of whether the social standards necessary for the creation of equality "are 'luxury goods' whose consumption becomes too costly in periods of economic turbulence" (Cambell, Sengenberger 1994: 421-422). Critics of the Norwegian model complain that it allows firms to be excessively inward-looking, insufficiently customer-oriented and unable to adapt to changed market conditions (Reve 1994).

In what follows, it is our intention to investigate whether equality in the Norwegian labour market reduces economic efficiency and innovation or has a positive effect. Theoretical arguments can be constructed to support both points of view: efficiency and equality might be regarded as mutually contradictory or complementary. Narrow income differentials, for example, might facilitate inter-firm mobility, since workers changing firms are unlikely to have to take a significant pay cut. Moreover, the narrowing of the social gap between various categories of employees may improve cooperation based on trust and motivation. On the other hand, it can be argued that inadequate financial incentives lead to underinvestment in training and a lack of motivation for employees to exert themselves at work. Whether the positive or negative effects of equality prevail depends on the overall structure of Norwegian labour standards. Clearly, the general package needs to contain a high proportion of proactive or offensive forms of flexibility (Boyer 1987), which tend to foster those aspects of flexibility that help to increase efficiency. Rigid regulations and inflexible institutions quickly lose legitimacy and efficiency in a rapidly changing environment, which is why the offensive forms of flexibility have constantly to be evolving and developing. This requires a high level of receptiveness to new ideas among the principal actors in the labour markets and those able to influence the pace and direction of reform. This dynamic aspect is particularly important in highly regulated countries such as Norway. What is, to an outsider, the astonishingly high degree of consensus between the social partners, and the equally great influence they exert over policy, cannot be sustained in the long term by invoking a glorious past but only by implementing successful new projects, through which they can prove, both to their own members and to the wider society, their ability to shape events. Offensive flexibility requires just such innovative abilities. It is surprising how much the Norwegian industrial relations literature relies in its prediction of the future crisis of the Norwegian system on quantitative indicators such as the changing structure of the economically active population, the declining share of LO in trade union members and not on the capacity for actively shaping future change. The capacity for innovation indicates the extent to which future problems in the Norwegian labour market are susceptible of resolution through a forward-looking policy. In an environment in which innovation is possible (though not necessarily welcome), crises and problems are not the harbinger of decline but rather a signal for action.

In periods of radical change, one of the attractions of the neoclassical model of the labour market lies in the implicit promise that the market itself will solve all problems and that policy-makers will be relieved of the difficult task of building consensus. In countries in which institutional learning processes have become locked up, even former advocates of the welfare state can become persuaded that deregulation is perhaps not the desirable but probably the only path to be taken. However, the consequent "depoliticisation of the economy" means that the ability to influence events in many other spheres is renounced as well. In Norway, other objectives are being followed, such as promoting the reconciliation of paid employment and family responsibilities through the system of parental leave or the narrowing of social differences through the solidaristic wage and social policy. In deregulated labour markets, such objectives are very difficult to achieve. Another attraction of the neoclassical model is that firms have a great deal of room for manoeuvre in adjusting their organisational structures to an increasingly turbulent environment. There is no doubt that it is increasingly difficult to control many of the parameters of company activity, such as the structuring of payment systems or working and operating hours, through centrally determined standards. One of the challenges of the future is whether traditionally centralised welfare states, of which Norway is one, will succeed in integrating the trend towards the decentralisation of company activity into its institutional framework or whether decentralisation will remain alien or even become a disruptive element.

A part from the risks of a "depoliticised economy" and the problems caused by a break with tradition, there are two further reasons why reregulation rather than deregulation seems a sensible policy for Norway. Firstly, the Norwegian economy is dominated by small and medium-sized firms (cf. Table 7.1); as is well known, such firms have few resources of their own to spare for planning functions and are particularly dependent on the wider environment for the training and further training of their work forces and for innovative processes. Secondly, Norway is very sparsely populated, which makes it difficult for mutually supportive and stimulating clusters of firms to develop properly (Porter 1990). Moreover, the relatively low level of demand means that enough institutions of the quality required for innovation processes at firm level are unlikely to evolve through the action of free competition. This applies to private training providers, for example. In more densely populated countries, such as Germany, the larger cities, such as Hamburg or Dortmund, now have several hundred private training providers; comparable structures do not exist in Norway, so the state has to intervene in a regulatory capacity. This is particularly so if all Norwegians in all parts of the country are to be offered the same opportunities.

There is no doubt that macro-economic and social innovations are easier to implement in smaller countries (measured in terms of population rather than surface area), with their more homogeneous interest structures and less convoluted circle of actors, than in larger countries. To

Table 7.1: Breakdown of employment by size of establishment in manufacturing industry (in %)

Number of employees	Norway	USA [1]
1 - 99	47.0	24.6
100 - 500	33.9	34.7
> 500	19.1	40.7

[1] Plants with fewer than 5 employees not included
Source: Salvanes, 1996

that extent at least, the conditions in Norway are favourable to innovation. However, there are sufficient examples of smaller countries that have been unable to exploit this comparative advantage in innovative capacity. This may be due to the dominance of obdurate, unyielding elements, which also exist in Norway. It is true that new hi-tech industries have developed in Norway, not least because of the rapid expansion of higher education. For example, Norway is now a net exporter of software and a world leader in offshore technology. Nevertheless, the Norwegian manufacturing sector remains dominated by industries such as wood, paper and energy, in which little research is needed. None of the developed OECD countries has such a low share of employees in high technology manufacturing as Norway (Figure 7.1). And since most of them are also employed in small and medium-sized firms, this means that manufacturing industry has generated relatively little impetus for the development of the wider social environment, particularly in the spheres of research and training. The traditionally dominant industries in Norway also have a high share of unskilled and semi-skilled employees. The climate in many firms is often one of indifference to training, and a traditional workerist mentality tends to prevail. Although in material terms there are actually few differences between the various social classes, a higher proportion of Norwegians consider themselves working class than their counterparts in comparable firms in Germany (Sivesind, 1995).

In what follows, I intend to tackle the issue of internal and external flexibility in the Norwegian labour market[1]. In a country with so many small and medium-sized firms, a certain level of external flexibility is required since, on the one hand, firms are unable to solve all employment problems internally and, on the other, a change of firm is often the only path to promotion for many employees. External flexibility is the

1 The following analysis is based on some 20 interviews with Norwegian experts and representatives of the social partners, and on case studies of firms. The available literature in English and German has also been evaluated.

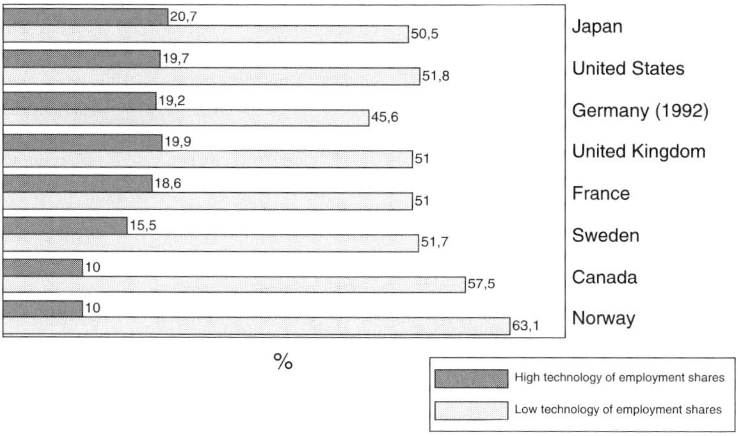

Figure 7.1: High and Low Technology Manufacturing 1994
Source: OECD 1996:246

subject of section II. The following three sections deal with various aspects of internal flexibility. Section III investigates how the industrial relations system influences internal flexibility.

In recent decades, the trade unions have been granted considerable rights of participation in that system. We suspect that, for institutional reasons, there are no universal recipes for a successful management style, and in consequence we ask whether a distinctively Norwegian management style has emerged and what potential for both innovation and problems it contains (section IV). Average working time in Norway is one of the lowest in the world. Section V investigates the extent to which more flexible working time has helped to increase internal flexibility. In the 1970s, Norway still had a very high share of low-skill workers. Educational standards have been raised more quickly than in many other OECD countries (OECD 1996: 250), the vocational training system has recently been completely reorganised. This reform and its possible effects on internal and external flexibility will be the subject of section VI. In section VII, the most important results will be summarised and some conclusions drawn.

2. External flexibility

The available data indicate, that in international comparative terms, the Norwegian labour market enjoys a considerable degree of external flexibility. In the case of manufacturing, Salvanes found a gross job reallocation rate of 16.8% (1977-1992), while the rate in the US and

Canada is about 20% (Salvanes, 1996: 23). The dominant source of job reallocation is within industries and regions, differs considerably between sectors and far exceeds what is necessary to accommodate net changes in job positions (ibid: 53, 56). Internal migration between regions has remained stable since the mid-1970s and is among the highest in the OECD countries. In 1987, 2.6% of the Norwegian population moved to another region, compared with 1.1% in Germany and Great Britain (1986) and 2.8% in the USA (OECD 1994: 66). Monthly flows into and out of employment are considerably above the average for countries with protected internal labour markets, such as Japan, Italy, France or Spain, but lower than in countries in which there is little dismissal protection, such as the USA (OECD, 1995a: 28). The Norwegian universal pension system also implies lower barriers to external mobility than in countries that rely more on occupational and firm-internal welfare (Hippe and Pedersen, 1993)

In terms of the strictness of employment protection legislation, Norway lies roughly midway between deregulated labour markets such as those in the USA, Canada or New Zealand and the highly regulated labour markets of Southern Europe (OECD 1994: 74). The regulatory apparatus is designed to foster internal labour markets. So firms have to find internal solutions to the employment problem. Redundancies for economic reasons are accepted only if no other suitable work can be offered in the plant.[2] The length of notice that is required makes redundancy sufficiently difficult that alternative solutions, such as training, working time reductions, temporary lay-offs or internal transfers become financially attractive for firms. In order to terminate indefinite contracts, employers have to give notice of between 1 (less than 5 years' service) and 6 months (for workers aged over 60 and with more than 10 years' service). However, once the opportunities for internal adjustment have been exhausted, redundancies are permitted without restrictions as a last resort. In such cases, there are no statutory provisions for severance pay.

Firms have limited room for manoeuvre in the selection of workers for redundancy. In selecting candidates for dismissal, the accepted custom, for workers with the same qualifications and skill levels, is "last in, first out". If there are any departures from this practice, they may be challenged by employee representatives. The scope for employers to decide unilaterally on dismissals is further restricted by the strict regulation of fixed-term contracts, which cannot be used unless there are "objective"

2 A new reform has recently been proposed which would, among other things, oblige corporate groups to offer, wherever possible, alternative jobs within the group to workers made redundant in a particular plant (NOU, 1996: 6).

reasons to do so[3]. In accordance with the "passion for equality", therefore, employers have only limited scope for dividing the workforce into core and peripheral employees. The regulations that make dismissals for personal reasons more difficult also fit into this pattern[4]. The state provides support for temporary lay-offs. Workers laid off temporarily may receive unemployment benefits for up to 52 weeks. The relatively generous support for temporary lay-offs is, as it were, the counterpart of the restrictions on the use of fixed-term contracts, since it reduces the risks incurred by employers when they make permanent appointments.

In practice, however, there is a higher degree of external flexibility than might be expected simply from an analysis of employment protection legislation. This is because of the high percentage of small and medium-sized plants in Norway that cannot develop internal labour markets. Even fixed-term contracts are in widespread use (see chapter 3: section 4), since one of the accepted "objective" reasons is the replacement of absent workers. Two per cent of people in employment are on parental

Table 7.2. Gross percentage of firms claiming that use of temporary / casual employees has increased over the past three years.

	Norway		Denmark		Germany		France UK			
	91	*95*	*91*	*95*	*91*	*95*	*91*	*95*	*91*	*95*
Temporary *Increased*	36.3	24.4	23.9	39.8	46.7	38.5	46.6	36.3	47.4	60.0
or casual *Same*	35.7	43.8	56.5	50.6	36.6	46.2	36.8	46.7	38.7	33.5
employees *Decreased*	28.1	31.9	19.6	9.7	16.7	15.4	16.6	17.0	13.9	6.4
N=	171	160	301	259	593	247	734	300	1176	793

Source: Price Waterhouse Cranfield Project, 1995.

3 Such "objective" reasons include apprentices, trainees, substitutes (for a specific person on leave), participants in labour market programmes, and if the work by its genuine character is temporary. In 1995 the actual wording of the law was made even more stringent to exclude any "soft" interpretation of the term "genuine character"». Still, in 1995 13.6 per cent of all Norwegian employees were temporary employed. Temporary contracts was most pronounced in the public sector, and of less importance in private manufactoring (Neergaard and Stokke, 1996). For further information on these regulations, see chapter 3.

4 Until 1995, regulations in this respect were excessive. Employers had to give reasons for dismissals during the probationary period. Employees had a right to object and could remain in their jobs until the case was decided, which sometimes took up to three years. As a result, the probationary period was no longer a probationary period. Since the beginning of 1995, however, all restrictions on dismissals during the probationary period were removed.

leave at any one time, which gives companies plenty of scope for using fixed-term contracts. This applies particularly to firms that employ a high proportion of women (public service and service sector). In 1995, however, almost one third of the Norwegian firms surveyed in the Price Waterhouse Cranfield study claimed they were hiring fewer fixed-term or casual workers than in the previous three years. The figure for Great Britain was only 6.4% (Table 7.2).

Norwegian legislation on employment protection makes it difficult for firms to separate off simple, standardised activities, allocate marginal workers to such jobs and to adjust to changing market conditions with simple numerical flexibility (hiring and firing). Such strategies prevail in Great Britain and Japan, for example, where firms make extensive use of peripheral workers. Firms in these countries make little effort to integrate and train peripheral workers. Norwegian firms will have to attach much greater importance to developing functional flexibility throughout the entire workforce, rather than regarding it as a privilege for core employees.

3. Industrial relations and internal flexibility

Aggregate wage moderation, a solidaristic pay policy, the reconciliation of paid work and family life and comparable living conditions in all parts of the country – all these objectives require a highly centralised system of bargaining between the social partners. The many small and medium-sized firms in Norway are dependent on external stimuli if they are to modernise. This raises the question of the extent to which the social partners, in their centralised negotiations, go beyond the traditional distribution issues in order to face this challenge. At the same time, production structures are changing; the "flexible firm" can be achieved only if it has greater freedom of action at a decentralised level. Thus at both levels, the social partners have to have the capacity to innovate, and a mix of centralised and decentralised bargaining is required. Both levels are traditionally well developed in Norway[5].

The trade unions and the employers' organisations are highly centralised, and their head offices have sufficient power and authority to facilitate bargaining at central level[6]. Unlike the DGB in Germany or the TUC in Great Britain and the corresponding employers' associations, LO

5 In the public service and the service sector, pay bargaining takes place mainly at central level. The additional, decentralised bargaining level is a "privilege" enjoyed mainly by export industries. In recent years, experiments with local adjustment bargaining have spread within municipalities once in the state sector as well.

6 For further discussions on the centralisation of the collective bargaining and the oscillation between central and local bargaining, see chapter 3 and chapter 8.

and NHO can also conclude collective agreements and make extensive use of this power. The state also makes frequent interventions. Tripartite negotiations have proved useful, since not only wages but also many other questions "which in most countries are lumped together under the label of 'welfare state' arrangements", are dealt with (Høgsnes, 1994: 23).

The rapid growth of the AF and YS white-collar unions has caused the LO to lose its representative monopoly in recent years, perhaps leading to a more fragmented trade union side the years ahead. In contrast to Sweden, there has been no general agreement between the trade union federations as to which groups of workers they are to represent. While AF and LO represent different groups, LO and YS are competing with each other for members rather than avoiding conflict through "institutionalised fragmentation" (Flanegan et al. 1983: 167). In manufacturing industry and its export industries, which are the main focus of this report, the LO is still the dominant union and is solely responsible, with the employers, for negotiating the so-called "Basic Agreement", which determines industrial relations at the workplace. However, AF (as well as LO and, to some extent YS) represents some occupational groups in manufacturing industries, including engineers, foremen, master craftsmen and middle managers.

Thus the micro-structure of the Norwegian trade unions is astonishingly baroque. Some parts of the trade unions are organised according to the industrial principle, other parts according to the craft principle and yet others by status (middle managers' and foremen's union). There is a striking contradiction between these structures and those in the wider society, which are highly egalitarian and less concerned with status. Nevertheless, a high degree of centralisation and the consolidation of individual trade unions into four cartels in 1994 have placed LO in a position to coordinate the pay negotiations conducted by its unions. And viewed superficially at least, the Norwegian trade union structure does not have all the negative consequences that can be observed in similar situations, such as that in Great Britain, for example. Among such negative consequences I would include the militant representation of sectional interests and the impeding of flexibility through job control and formalised job demarcation, which reduce the scope for internal flexibility.

However, more detailed analysis of the micro-structures of the Norwegian trade unions reveals the existence at many points of strong sectional interests and inter-union rivalry over membership that are a direct consequence of these outdated structures. For example, one public service union pushed through a particular training course for cooks in the public service (which included a few more modules for diet cooks) just so that they could represent them; when all cooks received the same training, they came under the aegis of another union. Separate training courses for electricians in the engineering industry and those in other industries developed for the same reason. A proposed flattening of company management structures was also opposed because it would lead to the loss of middle management jobs. There are a number of similar examples[7]. LO's preoccupation with collective bargaining at the central level has meant that the organisational reforms that have been discussed since the 1920s have still been only partially implemented.

"In contrast to the labour side, the structure of the employers' side has become less fragmented. NHO (the Confederation of Norwegian Business and Trade), which is LO's counterpart in private-sector wage negotiations, is the result of a merger of three employer associations in 1989. It has streamlined its organisational structure by reducing the number of member trade organisations from 150 to 30, and it now presents a more coordinated policy than before." (Sivesind, 1994: 30). Thus the employer's associations in Norway have been a stabilising element in the central bargaining system, in contrast to many other countries, where employers' associations are tending rather to fragment. Moene/Wallerstein even see them as the leading proponents of centralised bargaining, since "with decentralised bargaining, the cost of declining demand would be concentrated, at least initially, on employers and workers in the export industries. In gaining control over the wage demands of workers in the non-traded goods sector, metalworkers and their employers were able to force all workers to share the burden of lowering wage costs in the export sector" (1995: 189).

When the central wage negotiations have been concluded, bargaining on additional pay rises takes place at firm level in the manufacturing sector. The central agreements can lay down upper limits for company agreements, to ensure that wage drift can be controlled and the agreed wage moderation is not contradicted. Yet in what follows we wish to focus on another aspect. In the view of the social partners, firm-level bargaining should not be confined to pay alone but have its own separate agenda, including safety and work environment, work organisation, the development of company organisational structures and the introduction of new technologies.

In order for this agenda to be pursued, employee representative struc-

---

7 A representative of NHO said in an interview: "It proved to be difficult to place skilled trades in vacancies for similar but not identical occupations. The unions defended the right of certain occupations to fill certain vacancies".

tures at firm level have been consolidated and strengthened over the past 30 years. After the Second World War, production committees were set up; in 1966, they became part of the Main Agreement between LO and N.A.F (later NHO) and were renamed works councils (*bedriftsutvalg*). These works councils are really consultative bodies. The Work Environment Act of 1977 made work environment committees compulsory in all plants; they have wide-ranging powers, including the right to stop dangerous work. The most important role at plant level is played by shop stewards, whose position is established not by legislation but by collective agreement. The Main Agreement lays down regulations on the election of shop stewards and their release from work, as well as defining not only their rights but also their obligations (they are required, for example, "to do their best to maintain smooth and peaceful cooperation at the place of work § 6-5"). Plant-level bargaining on pay and working time, for example, are conducted between management and shop stewards and not the works councils. The membership of employee representatives on boards has been regulated since 1973 by the Joint Stock Company Act. One third of board members are elected by employees.

Equally as important as the development of formal representative structures is the attempt to give them real content. In this respect, the Main Agreement is full of declarations of good intent, and reads in part like an exposition of the philosophy of the modern, participation-oriented firm – with one difference: employees' rights are firmly enshrined in the agreement and can survive crises. The common interest of both parties in high-trust organisations is emphasised: "LO and NHO agree on the need for good and trusting relationships between enterprise and employees. For individual employees and the workforce as a whole a strong feeling of unity between enterprise and employees is of the greatest importance. It is also a necessary basis for efficient production... Developing forms of codetermination and a better working environment in the enterprise will necessitate extensive decentralisation and delegation of decision-making powers within the enterprise, so that those who work in each department or working group are allowed a greater right to make their own decisions in their daily work" (Main Agreement § 9-1 and § 9-2). However, not only about 1990 was "productivity" written into the agreement as an objective (Qvale 1995). The social partners have further agreed that enterprise development measures should be jointly financed (Supplementary Agreement: Enterprise Development, which in 1982 produced the Joint Enterprise Development Programme, or HF-B).

The first programmes on work organisation and the introduction of autonomous work groups jointly financed by LO and NHO were implemented as early as the 1960s, and from them sprung the ideas behind the Work Environment and Joint Stock Company Act. By 1992, projects in about 500 plants had been supported through the HF-B. This represents about 7.5% of the 6,685 Norwegian firms with more than 5 employees. In the metal and engineering industries, 15% of firms have completed an HF-B project[8] (Sivesind et al., 1995: 309). In the past, the purpose of company reorganisation projects tended to be the improvement of working conditions; nowadays, however, the state-supported "Enterprise Development 2000 Programme" leans more heavily towards encouraging improvements in competitiveness "by utilisation of Norwegian traditions of cooperation". Firms facing direct international competition are being particularly targeted. The plan is that this programme should provide support for projects in 80-100 firms between 1995 and the year 2000.

Thus in this area, LO, NHO and the state have assumed joint responsibility for stimulating the further development of company organisational structures in private industry (NHO and LO, no date). In doing so, they have succeeded in involving a remarkably high proportion of Norwegian firms in jointly managed projects. For a German observer, it is striking how much the trade unions encourage direct participation at the workplace, of which the German unions have to date been very suspicious, having tended to focus rather on representative structures. It can be inferred from this that the unions have a high degree of institutional security and that there is a high degree of mutual trust that prevents trade union representative structures being annulled in this way. We are not in a position to assess the effects of all these programmes in detail. From a critical point of view, we would suggest that insufficient efforts have been made to diffuse the experiences gained from individual projects throughout the economy as a whole and that it has taken far too long for competitiveness, productivity and customer-orientation to be accepted as objectives. On the positive side of the balance sheet, it is not only formal, plant-level representative structures that have been strengthened in recent decades; a great deal of support has also been provided in a variety of ways for the continuing development of company organisational structures (i.e. for offensive strategies). To overstate the case somewhat, it can be concluded that, while firms in other countries expend a great deal of effort in building up company cultures, Norwegian firms are able to exploit the cultural conditions that exist in their own society. We shall turn our attention in the next section to the experience of plant-level representation in Norway and its effects on management styles.

8 HF-b projects are to be evaluated in 1997.

4. Plant-level cooperation and management style

To judge solely from its formal structures, the Norwegian system of interest representation seems to be excessively complex. The social partners are well aware of this problem. Thus the Main Agreement makes express reference to the merger of the works councils and the working environment committees. In the absence of such a merger, the Agreement states that: "A practical division of work must be arranged if both councils are maintained". The fact that several unions exist side by side at plant level increases the complexity still further. In a different, low-trust industrial relations environment this could lead to a nightmare of marathon meetings and nerve-racking duplication of work in committees. In a more positive environment, however, it can lead to a high level of information and participation and highly integrated organisations that can function only with openness and honesty. The high level of information and participation may be due to the fact that a large number of people in Norway are involved in one way or another in the representation of workers' interests. "The ABU survey shows that 13-14% of the workforce have been representatives on work environment committees," (Sivesind et al., 1995: 319); in Germany, in contrast, only a relatively small group of often quasi-professionals represent workers' interests on works councils.

Nerve-racking marathon meetings were far from unknown in the two plants we visited[9]. *The personnel manager of one of the firms had previously been in local government, where he had successfully conducted joint pay negotiations with 16 different trade unions. In the manufacturing firm where he is currently employed, success in this respect has eluded him. True, most issues are discussed at monthly meetings with the shop stewards from the various trade unions, as provided for in the Main Agreement (§9 – 3). However, pay negotiations are conducted separately, although the result is the same. The personnel manager of the other firm described a similar situation; he also has to conduct 10 separate rounds of pay negotiations with different trade unions at different sites, although the outcome of the negotiations is virtually the same in all the plants.*

In other respects, the unions obviously cooperate closely with each other at plant level. *The LO representative in one of the firms we visited said that LO did not like "yellow" unions, but that within the plant the unions cooperated closely with each other. Branch chairmen held meetings one or*

9 We conducted interviews with the personnel managers and trade union representatives in two Norwegian firms belonging to multinational groups.

twice a month. Since the LO representative had been released from work, he saw it as his duty to help the other unions. All the unions, he said, were concerned to see the company thrive. They had to join forces in order to fight to keep the plant's production capacity in Norway. The key to this, he said, was to understand what customers in other countries expected of the company's products and services. The crucial factor in the successful management of change was to provide full information at an early stage. Frequent informal contact was necessary for this, he said. It was management's responsibility to formulate company strategy. If workers were able to understand the reasons underlying company strategy, then they would be willing to accept change. The unions received all their information from the company's senior management. There were problems, he said, with middle management.

Both firms were recently broken up into product divisions in order to get closer to customers. The restructuring of both firms is being supported by projects from the "Enterprise Development 2000 Programme", both of which are intended to improve cooperation between management and unions as a means of increasing competitiveness. *In one firm, the "department works councils" provided for in the Main Agreement (§ 13) have been set up in the various divisions. Both the personnel manager and the unions were agreed that the representatives on the central works council "had slept most of the time and no important questions had been discussed". There was also a feeling that employee representatives should have to deal more directly with the challenges posed by both competitors and customers.* There was clearly a recognition in both firms that employee representatives had been too preoccupied in the past with internal problems and had as a result underestimated the need to adjust to changes in the external environment.

The unions adopted different approaches to the organisation of the representative bodies. In one of the companies, the works council and the working environment committee were merged in order to reduce the time spent in meetings. In the other company, both committees remained separate, so that it would be possible to appoint outside experts, such as doctors or safety specialists, to working environment committees, although without voting rights. In both companies, however, the shop stewards were the most important employee representatives. This probably applies more generally. Taking on other duties is less prestigious. If the shop stewards do not support the work environment committees, then they are of little significance in practice. This considerably reduces the complexity of the representative bodies. There is in fact no competition between them, but a clearly defined power centre. This power centre is maintained by cooperation between the various unions.

In their dealings with management, workforce representatives do not

Table 7.3: Organisational commitment measures

	Norway	United States
Organisation commitment scale[a] (*n* = 4383, Norway; 398, US)	3.09 (0.61)	2.78 (0.51)**
EFFORT: I am willing to work harder than I have to in order to help this organisation to succeed.	3.51 (0.72)	3.19 (0.67)**
PROUD: I am proud to be working for this organisation	3.21 (0.86)	3.08 (0.62)*
LOYALTY: I feel very little loyalty to this organisation (reflected).	3.38 (0.89)	3.15 (0.76)**
STAY WITH ORGANISATION: I would turn down another job at comparable pay in another organisation.	3.16 (1.11)	2.24 (0.87)**
ANY JOB: I would take any job to keep working for this organisation	2.17 (1.07)	2.23 (0.77)
COEFFICIENT ALPHA	0.65	0.72

[a] Response categories for each item: 1 = Strongly Disagree, to 4 = Strongly Agree.
** t-test for differences between Norway and US means is significant at $p < 0.001$;
* t-test significant at $p < 0.01$ (2-tail tests)
Kalleberg and Mastekaasa (1994: 276)

exploit these representative structures to the fullest extent possible but manage them pragmatically, with good understanding between the various parties. Despite all the formalised representative structures, Norwegian firms are characterised by a "high degree of informal communication" (Sivesind et al. 1995) that goes far beyond the communication between unions and management. Social distances between the two sides are small, and there are few visible signs of hierarchical attitudes, such as separate dining facilities for management or particular forms of address. Management has to adopt a democratic leadership style. They have to keep workers informed, justify their decisions and demonstrate superior expertise; they cannot simply rely on their formal positions. (Table 7.3)

In a comparative study of the USA and Norway, Kalleberg/Mastekaasa (1994) established that Norway's egalitarian tradition is associated with a considerably higher level of organisational commitment in firms than exists in the USA (Table 7.3), which has beneficial effects on productivity. It may well be that the close cooperation between employees and management in Norway is one of the country's most important sources of flexibility, since many of the demands placed upon the organisational structures of modern firms are deeply rooted in the wider society and do not have to be introduced laboriously from firm to firm[10] as in many other countries, particularly the USA, with its Taylorist, low-trust culture.

In management research, which is heavily influenced by the traditions of the English-speaking world, employers are generally assumed to enjoy a high degree of autonomy in implementing the personnel strategies they consider necessary. Negotiations with trade unions and works council have no place in this literature and are frequently treated simply as disruptive factors, despite the fact that in many countries they influence styles of personnel management that have been very successful. Thus there are no universal management strategies; rather, those strategies are shaped by institutions. This is acknowledged in more recent management research, and has led to a series of international comparisons of management styles (Godderham et al., 1996; Brunstein 1995; Brewster/Hegewisch, 1994). There is, therefore, no toolbox of instruments with which the same results – a highly motivated workforce, for example – can be achieved in all countries.

In their assessment of an international comparative study[11], Gooderham et al. (1996) observe striking differences among various European countries (Norway, Germany, UK and Denmark) in the use of certain personnel policy instruments in 1992 and 1995. The results can be summarised as follows:

- In Norway, Denmark and Germany, trade union influence at plant level has actually increased in recent years, while managers in the UK consider such influence to have declined drastically.
- Norway is the only country in which the use of fixed-term employment contracts has declined. At the other extreme, in Great Britain the use of such contracts increased most.
- Norway has far and away the highest share of firms that formally brief employees about their strategy, and this applies to all categories of employees (management, professionals/technicians, clerical and manual workers). In this respect, German firms lag behind even their British counterparts. This is interpreted as an indication that works councils assume these briefing functions.

---

10 A study carried out by International Survey Research, in which 20,000 people in Europe and the USA were surveyed, showed that Norwegian employees demonstrate a higher than average level of satisfaction with their work and felt themselves well managed; the lowest values were recorded in the UK, which also has the most strained relationships within firms (Financial Time, February 1, 1995).

11 The study in question is based on data from the Price Waterhouse project 1995.

- Performance appraisals and individual award systems are much more common in Great Britain than in Germany. They are least widely used in Norway.

These results are consistent with other, more qualitative comparisons of management strategies. It is clear that the influence of the trade unions has been drastically reduced in Great Britain and that firms have adopted a core-periphery strategy. At the same time, British firms have been able to exploit their regained autonomy in order to introduce individual incentive schemes. In Germany, payment systems are regulated by collective agreements, which leaves management little scope for exerting its own influence. The system of co-determination, the importance of which has actually increased in recent years[12], is highly formalised (Wächter/Stengelhofen, 1995). Works councils act as intermediaries between workers and management and are sceptical of any forms of direct communication between the two sides. In Norway, contacts between management, trade unions and employees are much more informal, so that many of the new management instruments can also be used at the workplace, since they are consistent with the tradition of Norwegian co-determination at the workplace. "Direct participation appeared to be a supplement to, not a replacement for, representative participation" (Hammer et al., 1994: 30). However, individual incentive schemes, which are least widely used in Norway, run counter to the tradition of egalitarian wage policies.

Thus the particular challenge for Norwegian firms is to motivate employees without any direct material incentives. They have clearly been successful in doing this in the past (cf. Table 7.3), but now seem to have come up against the limits of their traditional strategy. In order to accelerate the pace of change, an increasing number of firms are now experimenting with new payment systems, in which a certain proportion of total pay is dependent on company results, skill and the ability to work in a team. Approximately 10% of firms in the private sector claim to have introduced some kind of performance-related pay scheme, i.e. profit-sharing, performance bonuses etc. (Langeland, 1995). In the new system introduced by the key manufacturer Trioving, described by the

12 A panel study of the implementation of the German Law on Labour Relations at the Workplace, amended in 1972, that compared the way in which the legislation was put into practice in 1974/5 and 1989/90, concluded that the participation of works councils in company decision-making processes had increased dramatically. In particular, it would seem that difficult situations, such as major reorganisation and redundancy programmes, tended to bring management and works councils closer together (Kotthoff 1994).

employers' association as exemplary, 5% of total pay is dependent on department and company results, and payments vary further according to competence, initiative, job difficulty and commitment (NHO, no date).

There are many indications that one of the biggest problems for Norwegian management is a sort of consensual easy-goingness, which is both widespread and an obstacle to innovation. In a report by the International Institute for Management Development, Norwegian managers are ranked almost bottom for innovation and entrepreneurship. Sivesind, who compared two plants in the aluminium and chemical industry in Germany and in Norway, concluded that supervisors tried to sidestep conflict in order "to avoid being on bad terms with subordinates by any means possible" (Sivesind, 1995: 87). The American management consultant George Kenning, who has worked for a long time in Norway, is well known there for saying over and over again to Norwegian managers, "You must not be ashamed to be the boss" (Kalleberg, 1991). In Germany, which has its own problems because of its markedly hierarchical organisational structures and its particular concern with status, the decisions of supervisors tend to be accepted. They have considerably greater scope for making unpopular decisions. One problem seems to be the often inadequate level of vocational training among supervisors in Norway. They have usually been promoted within the firm and have less formal training than their German counterparts. There is no training for supervisors in Norway that compares with the German master craftsman's diploma (*Meisterbrief*). Moreover, Norwegian supervisors have a wider span of control than their German counterparts. This certainly gives Norwegian workers greater room for manoeuvre in performing their tasks, but they are not able to learn so much from their supervisors[13]. Compared to German industry, with larger market shares in competence-intensive manufacturing, demand for highly skilled labour in Norway is much lower. Norwegian manufacturing, as already mentioned, consists of a large number of locally based, small and medium-sized enterprises and a few larger export-intensive enterprises mainly involved in the extraction of raw material and in primary production. Moreover, in Norway, manufacturing qualifications are traditionally created by on-the-job training (Sivesind, 1995: 61).

The clear weaknesses of the Norwegian style of management lie mainly in the weak decision-making capacities and inadequate training of supervisors and in organisational structures that allow little scope for

13 The mere absence of supervisors does not increase the autonomy and the possibilities for self-realisation if the operator lacks information and insight (Sivesind, 1995: 58).

learning processes. In future, it will probably be necessary to provide not only better training for workers and supervisors (section VI) but also more financial incentives in order to create the basic conditions on which efficient firms depend, which include, among other things, the ability to do several jobs, good work quality, successful teamwork and readiness to undertake further training. This could be one of the instruments for overcoming the disadvantages of the easy-going, consensual style of management that exists in Norwegian firms.[14]

5. Reduction and flexibilisation of working time

In 1986, employers and unions in the metal industry concluded an agreement that reduced standard working time from 40 to 37.5 hours per week. The centralised collective bargaining system made it possible to extend this reduction to the whole of the economy. As a result, Norway now has the shortest standard working week in the world. The reduction in working time was not accompanied by agreement on a policy of wage moderation, so that, unlike in Germany (Bosch 1990), additional financial burdens were placed on firms. Like their German counterparts, Norwegian employers demanded that working time be made more flexible in return for the reduction in the working week. They proposed that working hours be adjusted more closely to demand by distributing them more flexibly over the entire duration of the standard working day, which under the provisions of the Work Environment Act starts at 6 a.m. and ends at 9 p.m. Normal working time hitherto had been between 7 a.m. and 5 p.m. The employers also wanted to improve machine utilisation times by introducing flexible breaks and eliminating those that had not been enshrined in collective agreements.

The collective agreement left it up to the social partners at plant level to implement the working time reduction and to negotiate the flexibilisation of working time. The working time legislation and the collective agreements allowed a great deal of scope for making working time more flexible. However, if no agreement could be reached, then the old regulations remained in force; in many cases, employers had to pay a high price for changes. A study of the implementation of the 37.5-hour week

14 Employees generally have an overwhelmingly positive attitude to economic incentives. A large majority of employees also agree (in part or in full) with the statements that economic incentives will increase employees' business awareness (78%), encourage cooperation (80%), make employees work harder (80%) and reduce turnover (71%) (Langeland, 1995).

Table 7.4: Percentage of organisations with a change in the use of flexible working hours/time over the last three years

	Finland	Denmark	France	Germany (West)	Italy	Ireland	Norway	Netherlands	Sweden	United Kingdom
Increased	62	16	19	55	32	25	23	43	35	30
Same	24	53	46	27	22	27	59	38	52	31
Decreased	0	1	1	1	0	1	1	0	1	1
Not Used	12	25	24	14	36	31	10	14	10	32

Source: Price Waterhouse Cranfield Project 1995

in 220 plants in the engineering industry showed that 90% of management proposals for more flexible working time came to nothing. All that was agreed was a more flexible system for organising breaks in order to improve machine utilisation times (Karlsen, 1989). Moreover, the employers' associations had failed to support their members in their attempts to introduce more flexible working time by offering advice and developing actual models for them to implement. Only recently did NHO compile a survey of the various forms of flexible working time.

Thus the reduction in working time was not the starting signal for a reorganisation of working time at plant level. Norway lags a considerable way behind other countries in the introduction of flexible working time (Table 7.4). As a result, opportunities for innovation have remained unexploited. In Germany, the reduction in working time did provide the impetus for innovative behaviour on the part of firms, albeit with a certain time lag. Firms initially reacted conservatively to the working time reductions of the 1980s in the belief that it would be sufficient to change just one element in their work organisation, i.e. working time. This proved to be a costly mistake. What was actually needed was a rethink of the entire system of work organisation (Bosch 1995). Among other things, workers had to be trained in order that they could cover for each other more satisfactorily, the fine-tuning of working time was delegated to work groups and pay incentives had to be developed in order to encourage workers to adjust their working time to the company's needs. The real revolution, which has taken place largely out of the public gaze, is that firms are controlling actual attendance time less and less and turning their attention rather to monitoring outcomes and the way in which functions are performed (including internal duties such as group discussions). In exchange, employees are being offered attractive options such as blocks of time off and more individual control over working hours.

Trade unions and workers have put forward good arguments against the flexibilisation of working time, on the grounds that it makes working time less predictable, thereby making it more difficult for individuals to plan ahead. However, structural changes in the economy have made the reorganisation of working time inevitable. Because of the increasing range of variants they now have to produce, manufacturing firms are less and less able to rely on stocks and have to react at short notice to fluctuations in demand. As a result, it is human beings who are becoming the buffer in the production system. In the long term, supply-side restrictions on the flexibility of working time are likely to emerge in Norway. Rising participation rates among women mean that part-time workers can be regarded less and less solely as a flexible reserve of labour. If, under such conditions, working time organisation remains unchanged, then the only way of achieving flexibility is through the use of overtime and temporary lay-offs. In many cases, the conservatism of Norwegian working time organisation is the reason why overtime has increased in recent years. Such a traditional form of working time flexibilisation hardly helps individuals to plan ahead either.

If overtime is to be restricted, working time will have to become very much more flexible. Rigid restrictions on overtime could wreak a great deal of economic havoc, so necessary overtime will have to be offset by extra time off in lieu. Researchers on working time regard agreements on time taken off in lieu of overtime as a precursor of annualised working time (Bosch 1996a and b). Thus it is not possible to argue against annualised working time while at the same time demanding restrictions on overtime. However, employers will not be able to demand of workers complete subordination to the rigours of the market; rather, they must give them greater freedom to organise their own working time by devolving greater decision-making powers to work groups. It is apparent that the social partners have not yet really got to grips with these new challenges. In the long term, this may prove to be particularly problematic for the trade unions. If they do not initiate a debate on the organisation of flexible working hours and develop their own proposals on the subject, they run the risk of seeing collectively agreed and statutory working time standards weakened by an unregulated approach to flexibilisation.

Table 7.5: Youth unemployment relative to general unemployment in 1993

	Unemployment rate		Ratio of (2) : (1)	Youth unemployment in % of population 15 - 24 years (1992)
	All persons (1)	Youth 1 (2)		
USA	6.7	13.3	1.0	8.9
Japan	2.5	5.1	2.0	2.0
France	11.6	24.6	2.1	7.1
Germany	5.8	4.9	0.8	3.3
Italy	10.2	30.6	3.0	14.6
Spain	22.4	43.2	1.9	16.6
Sweden	8.1	18.4	2.3	6.3
Norway	6.0	13.5	2.3	7.8
OECD	7.8	15.1	1.9	

1 under-25s

Source: OECD 1994: 14; OECD 1995: 42

6. General and Vocational Training

If we accept Robert Reich's thesis that capital has become increasingly mobile and that the focus of economic and labour market policy should now be the development of human resources (Reich 1991), then the defensive flexibility (aggregate wage moderation) that is already an element of Norwegian economic policy will have to be supplemented by offensive flexibility (raising of skill levels and institutional modernisation). A solidaristic pay policy needs to be accompanied by measures to improve productivity, which has to be high enough for wages to be really "earned". This in turn requires improvements in skill levels and work organisation.

Education standards have risen considerably in Norway in recent years. In 1972, 64.5% of the Norwegian labour force had a low level of education (primary education only), compared with only 16.3% in 1993. At the same time, the proportion of the population with a university degree has risen from 9.9 to 26.2%. The general level of education and training has risen more rapidly in Norway than in most other OECD countries (OECD, 1996: 250). In 1992, direct public expenditures for educational institutions in Norway accounted for 7.6% of GDP, one of the highest values in the OECD (OECD, 1995b: 76).[15]

Such improvements could hardly have been made without structural changes to the education system. This applies particularly to a country like Norway, with its small, sparsely scattered population. Unlike in Germany, the state cannot continue to finance the various kinds of school in a differentiated education system (secondary modern, vocational and grammar schools) when pupil numbers shift dramatically. In recent decades, therefore, the trend has been towards the integration of hitherto separate educational paths. The primary and lower secondary stages of the Norwegian education system have always been integrated in a single, unified state system. Private schools are the exception. In 1966, grammar and secondary modern schools were merged. In 1974 (with implementation in 1976), virtually all upper secondary education, both general and vocational, was brought together into one comprehensive system.[16] General and vocational studies exist side by side in the same school and can even be combined within a course (Education in Norway, 1990: 19). In the 1970 and 1980s, the integration of the education sys-

15 International studies, however, indicate that the content of many courses is not sufficiently well adapted to the demands of technical change and changed markets (Kvinge et al., 1996: 53).

16 Some vocational schools were retained.

tem gradually became a physical reality as new, integrated school buldings were constructed (Skinningsrud T., Bjørnavold J., 1994: 7).

The high degree of interchangeability between the various parts of the education system led to an extraordinary increase in demand for university places, which has clearly not been slowed down by the introduction of selection or high tuition fees, as in the USA or Japan (Windolf, 1994). The increase in the supply of academically well-qualified workers meant that the labour market was decreasingly accessible to young people without the upper secondary school leaving certificate. In 1975, one third of the 17-19 age cohort were in employment. In 1992, only 4.7% did not remain in the education system (Skinningsrud T., Bjørnavold J., 1994: 11). Even for academically well-qualified young people, the transition from school to employment has become increasingly difficult. In 1993, the youth unemployment rate was 2.3 times higher than the general unemployment rate (Table 7.5) and it was feared that the situation would deteriorate further, since the Norwegian vocational training system was being increasingly eroded.[17] The number of training places in firms was declining. Of the 64,932 young people aged 16 in 1988, 0.3% had a training place by the autumn of 1988, 1.5% by the autumn of the 1989 and 4% by the autumn of 1990. In 1992/3, 55.9% of all journeyman's examinations were taken by adults aged 25 or over who had taken a theoretical course while they were working and prepared themselves for the examination primarily through on-the-job experience (Skinningsrud T., Bjørnavold J., 1994: 25). Thus vocational training was increasingly turning into further training for adults.

The main reasons for the erosion of the youth training system were:

- The increasing reluctance of firms to provide training: the excessively high wages paid to apprentices, included in training costs, have been put forward as a cause. In internationally traded sectors, for example, apprentices were paid about 90% of the wage of a skilled worker.
- The inefficiency of the vocational school system: many young people who had begun a full-time training course[18] were not being offered

---

17 Doubts are often expressed about the meaningfulness of youth unemployment figures, since many young people are still receiving education or training. However, the unemployment rate among economically active young people aged between 15 and 25 is considerably higher in Norway than in Germany and Japan, for example (Table 6), which indicates that the labour market is less able to absorb young people.

18 Various forms of vocational training existed side by side. A small proportion of trainees received a combination of in-plant and vocational training running parallel to each other, as in the German dual system, while most courses consisted of a variable period of school-based training followed by in-plant practical training.

> more advanced courses in the same subject in their second and third years, with the result that they were shunted aimlessly from one foundation course to another (Skinningsrud T., Bjørnavold J., 1994: 22). Thus of the 20% of young people who had begun a foundation course in industry/craft in 1988, only 3% ended up in the advanced course II in the same subject. Moreover, excessive specialisation meant that local authorities lacked the means to put on the number of courses required.

Thus Norway was on the way to an education and training system in which educational institutions provided most of the specialist skills used at work. Dertouzos et al. (1989) describe this as Pattern A, a category that includes the United States. Pattern B countries (such as Germany) rely heavily on company-sponsored training. According to Dertouzos, Pattern B countries have greater flexibility; furthermore, young people can be more easily integrated into the world of work. In our view, this greater flexibility, is produced only if young people are also given an adequate theoretical grounding by attending courses at vocational school.

The inadequate number of training places was considered by the Norwegian Employment Commission to be the greatest weakness of the Norwegian training system. They recommended stronger links between schools and working life and an expansion of vocational training, in order to "reduce youth unemployment, which is high in Norway, but also to reduce the shortage of qualified labour, which in turn can reduce equilibrium unemployment and inflationary pressures" (Norwegian Employment Commission, 1992: 65). A parliamentary committee on education published a white paper entitled "Knowledge and Competence. On certain aspects of upper secondary education", which laid the foundations for a programme of reform (Skinningsrud T., Bjørnavold J., 1994: 38-39).

In the reform of 1994, the state, LO and NHO agreed on such an expansion of the vocational training system as a means of reversing Norway's development into a Pattern A country. The main elements of this reform are:

- The state undertakes to offer every young person a course of education at upper secondary level.
- One third of each age cohort are to be offered an apprenticeship. The social partners have committed themselves to joint efforts to achieve this goal.
- The first two years of vocational training take place in schools. This is followed by one year of training in a firm or two years of training combined with productive work.

- Firms' training costs have been reduced. The social partners agreed to reduce apprentices' wages to about 50% of those of a skilled worker. The basis for this agreement was the assumption that young people spend half of their time in firms being trained and the other half working productively. In addition, firms receive a subsidy of 53,000 kroner per training year.
- The number of occupational specialisations has been reduced. In the first year, the number of different basic courses has been reduced from 109 to 13, and in the second from 140 to about 85. Moreover, vocational training is to be offered in completely new areas, such as office work and the caring professions. The ability of the social partners to impose additional specialisations in the pursuit of sectional interests (cf. section III) has been restricted.
- The previously diverse forms of vocational training have been homogenised. All courses, irrespective of future occupation, now consist of two years' school-based training followed by two years' training in firms.
- Some of the responsibility for vocational training has been devolved to local government. If the local authorities are unable to find young people a position as an apprentice, they must finance further school-based courses.
- Training courses have been modularised. This is intended to facilitate further vocational training. It is now easier for adults to establish their skill levels and to complete any modules they may not have done before.
- Young people who have successfully completed a vocational training programme can take continuation or extension courses and eventually gain the equivalent of the upper secondary school leaving certificate required for university entrance.

The advantages of this educational reform lie in the fact that it seeks to promote internal and external mobility in equal measure. Improved training will not only enhance internal mobility but also make it possible to extend the range of tasks performed by semi-autonomous groups within the plant. As a result, there is a chance that the already high level of informal cooperation in Norwegian firms will be further enhanced by training and become more efficiency-oriented. At the same time, the existence of recognised vocational qualifications will lead to the development of occupational labour markets that will facilitate inter-firm mobility (Bosch 1992: 20).

There are few countries in the world that have the capacity to undertake such a thoroughgoing reform of their education and training system. It is true that the reform aroused interest in all quarters. All the actors were in favour of expanding the supply of skilled workers and reducing youth unemployment. At the same time, the reforms were intended to reduce the traditionally high degree of specialisation, which obstructed labour market mobility and reduced the level of interchangeability between the various parts of the education and training system by creating too many blind alleys. However, those who have experienced the inertia of education and training systems in other countries will know that such rational arguments are in no way sufficient to make reform possible. Education systems are one of the means by which social status and earnings opportunities are distributed. The more unequal the earnings opportunities in a society are, the more differentiated the education system will tend to be in order to select out the next generation of high-earners at an early stage. In particular, those who benefit from the differentiated structures will bitterly resist any attempt at reform. Thus in Germany, for example, the establishment of a comprehensive school system failed largely because of resistance from middle-class parents who feared their children would be disadvantaged by the break-up of the grammar schools. The education committee of the state parliament of North Rhine Westphalia, with the support of prominent industrialists on the committee, recently proposed a more circumspect reform, namely an increase in the time all children spend in non-selective primary schools from four to six years, on the grounds that early selection does not allow all pupils to reach their full potential and social inequality is reinforced as a result (Bildungskommission NRW, 1995). However, remembering the "school battles" that erupted in Germany in the 1970s, the ruling SDP immediately declared that it would change nothing.

So how were the Norwegian reforms pushed through? Certainly subjective factors, such as the vision and drive of a few individuals, played a decisive role. In looking for structural explanations, I return once again to the centralisation and ability to act of the main actors, the NHO and LO, the relatively small number of actors in a country like Norway and, finally, the country's egalitarian tradition. When social differences and pay differentials are relatively small, the educational privileges of particular social groups do not have to be defended so vigorously. Finally, earlier reforms had already paved the way for the most recent reform. General education had already been integrated, so new facilities could not be created. Moreover, because a high proportion of vocational training is school-based, most of the costs fall to the state, which helped to gain acceptance for the reforms in the business community. The social partners took it in turns to put pressure on the other side to act, thereby helping the process along – perfectly possible if both sides are strong.

On both sides there were long-established corporate structures and traditions, and it was only by pointing to the demands and intransigence of the other side that they could be broken down. As a result, the reform seems to be more thoroughgoing than the revision of occupational profiles in Germany, where the organisational structures on the employers' side, divided into chambers of industry and commerce on the one hand and chambers of crafts on the other, meant there was a great deal of resistance to too much uniformity and a lot of unsuitable compromises had to be reached (Streeck et al., 1987).

The differences between the Norwegian system and the German dual system are clear. School-based and in-firm training take place consecutively in Norway rather than simultaneously. General educational courses have a greater academic content in Norway than in Germany, because the school-based components last longer. Young Norwegians are on average younger than their German counterparts when they go into firms, since many young Germans finish their general education before entering vocational training. The state assumes a greater share of the costs of training. Mismatch problems become apparent at a later stage in Norway, after the second school-based year, while they can be detected in Germany right at the beginning. One weakness of the German system is undoubtedly the poor quality of the training provided in many firms. As far as long-term flexibility in the labour market is concerned, the higher share of general education in the Norwegian system will undoubtedly be advantageous if the system can be successfully implemented.

One impressive characteristic of the 1994 reform is its unity and intellectual consistency. The decisive factor in determining the success of this major reform programme will be its implementation. The success, or otherwise, of trade unions, employers and local authorities in persuading firms to make sufficient training places permanently available will be crucial. This is particularly difficult in office work and social services. The other problems that have already become apparent can be summarised as follows:

- There is a mismatch between young people's wishes and the training places on offer. For example, there are not enough young people interested in training for the chemicals and construction industries.
- Many young people, already weary of school, feel themselves overtaxed by the high share of general academic subjects, such as Norwegian, mathematics and English, and failure rates in the compulsory examinations held at the end of each year are rising sharply.
- In other areas, courses have attracted criticism because students are

taught too little of the relevant theory. The electricians' union has managed to make three years' school-based training compulsory in their sphere, so that students can receive a more thorough theoretical grounding.

- Some foundation courses are insufficiently specialised, with the result that some courses include such diverse occupations as printing and hairdressing.

The 1994 reform will have to be further developed in the years to come. The state and the social partners will have to remain in close contact with each other if pragmatic solutions are to be found quickly for the problems that emerge, especially in order to devise ways of persuading employers to take on apprentices. Future changes will undoubtedly tend to introduce a greater degree of differentiation into the system, with an inevitable reduction in its homogeneity. At the upper end (electricians, for example), there will probably be improvements in quality, while at the lower end quality among the disillusioned is likely to decline. It is also likely that the training provided in small firms will not come up to expectations, since such firms have few resources for the provision of quality training. This has certainly been the experience in Germany over recent decades. There is a world of difference between the training provided in large firms that employ full-time training officers and have their own training workshops and that provided in small firms (Bosch, 1993).

In the years to come, the 1994 reform will also highlight other problems in the Norwegian education and training system. On the one hand, the inadequate levels of training among supervisory staff will become more obvious as they are required to show increasingly well-trained subordinates how to do a job. On the other hand, competition may well develop between older and younger workers as well-trained youngsters pour into firms. Studies carried out in Germany in industries such as glass-making, steel and chemicals, where classic on-the-job training was replaced by vocational training in the 1970s, show that firms no longer abide by the old seniority rules in deciding on internal promotions and tend instead to give preference to well-trained, younger workers when deciding on promotions to more demanding and supervisory positions. Works councils, the members of which were themselves often semi-skilled workers, initially opposed in-firm vocational training (Drexel 1980). It was not until firms agreed to train older workers as well that they approved the new training system.

In order to avoid such generational conflicts between younger and older workers, new opportunities will soon have to be provided for older workers to benefit from further training. The Norwegian Employment

Commission was right in stating that, "Norway has no unified policy of adult education" (NEC, 1992: 67). The modularisation of the training process may provide a starting point for such opportunities. This will make it possible to diagnose more accurately the gaps in employees' skills and to tailor the further training provided in firms and by the labour market authorities more closely to real needs. The vocational training schools could make available their skills and experience and become regional training centres for adults as well as young people. Thus the 1994 reform has put pressure on the state and the social partners to change the system of further vocational training in the next few years.

7. Conclusions

The question with which we started this paper was whether the Norwegian passion for equality and the social standards that regulate internal and external flexibility in the labour market reduced efficiency or were themselves a source of flexibility.

In investigating employment protection in Norway, we came to the conclusion that an equal balance between employees' interests and firms' needs to adjust had been created. We noted that external flexibility is relatively high in Norway. This is due, firstly, to the relative lack of restrictions on dismissals for economic reasons, secondly, to the small size of the average firm, which means that many firms cannot solve their employment problems internally, thirdly, to the low wage differentials, which make it easier for workers to change firm and, fourthly, to the universal pension system that enhances mobility across firms. The fact that larger firms must first seek to redeploy workers internally is viewed positively by leading members of the business community, even from the point of view of efficiency alone. The former CEO of Scandinavian Airlines System has written that protective legislation has "compelled us to take a hard look at employment security. Perhaps many US business executives would take issue with this legislation, but I think it is a blessing. It provides a basic platform of security which allows the decentralisation of responsibility and encourages risk taking. Surprisingly, in decentralising SAS, we have met with less success in the United States than anywhere else. We like to think of America as the land of the free and the home of the brave, but Americans are actually reluctant to take risks in their daily job. I think this is because most US companies do not offer real job security. Either you keep the boss happy or you don't get paid next week" (Carlzon 1989: 84).

Collective bargaining is highly centralised in Norway, and this has provided the basis for a policy of wage moderation. The employment level has been increased in two ways as a result. On the one hand, international competitiveness has been improved and on the other additional jobs have been created in less productive service industries. In recent decades, the social partners have managed to go beyond such macroeconomic objectives and the perennial questions of distribution to discuss company reorganisation and extend their power to shape events to the micro level. Several generations of state-led reorganisation programmes paved the way for this. The social partners are now running a joint programme on company reorganisation (HF-b) in the private sector, thus providing the impetus for company reorganisation projects. A basic consensus has emerged, now enshrined in the Main Agreement, that co-operation at work, the participation of the workforce in the process of change, the delegation of decision-making and the introduction of group work are desirable and should be encouraged by both sides of industry. Not until a few years ago did the emphasis of the reorganisation programmes run by the state and the social partners shift from an exclusive focus on the improvement of working conditions to a concern with increasing economic efficiency and competitiveness. Such external inducements from the state and the social partners are particularly necessary in Norway, since the proportion of small and medium-sized firms is especially high; they are, moreover, scattered very thinly across the country because of the low population density and therefore find it difficult to form industrial clusters open to innovation.

Thus in Norway, over a period of many years, the foundations have been laid for the high-trust cooperation in the workplace that is the exception rather than the rule in low-trust, Taylorist cultures such as the USA or Great Britain. Thus trade unions are fully integrated into the firm at plant level without having had to give up their influence beyond the plant, as they have in Japan.

Management, trade unions and workers are linked by a dense network of informal and formal relationships. A democratic management style prevails, in which managers have to keep their workforces informed and earn their legitimacy through superior expertise. This results in a considerably higher level of organisational commitment among employees and a higher level of internal flexibility than in the USA, for example.

Considerable efforts have been made in Norway in recent years to supplement defensive flexibility, i.e. the maintenance of international competitiveness through a policy of wage restraint, with offensive elements, namely improvements in skill levels in the labour force. In addition to the substantial expansion of higher education, the thoroughgoing restructuring of the vocational training system, in particular, reflects the capacity for reform of the main actors in the Norwegian labour market.

All parties had to accept compromises. The trade unions agreed to a pay cut for young workers, the employers undertook to offer a training place to one third of each age cohort and the state agreed to finance a high share of training costs. In many other countries, such major social reforms nowadays fall victim to the ideological trench warfare triggered by deregulation. Norway has exploited the comparative advantage enjoyed by small countries in this respect, namely the capacity for reform that results from the relatively small number of actors involved in such countries.

This capacity for reform will be put to the test again in the next few years, when the problems that have emerged during the implementation of the 1994 reform will have to be solved and the further training system will have to be reformed in order to avoid generational conflicts. Improvement to vocational and further training may help to eliminate the hostility to training that exists in many Norwegian firms because of the high share of low-tech manufacturing (see Figure 7.1) and encourage internal and external mobility.

These positive developments have to be offset to some extent by the negative aspects of the Norwegian model, which cannot be overlooked. Norwegian managers are often afraid to take unpopular decisions, which means that a sort of consensual easy-goingness exists in Norwegian firms, which engenders a climate unreceptive to innovation. It is middle management, which plays a central role in the implementation of new organisational structures, that often lacks the professional expertise required to push through unpopular decisions. One of the main reasons for this is their inadequate level of training; for example, there is no separate training for master craftsmen in Norway. Moreover, little use has been made to date of payment systems that offer financial incentives for team work and encourage customer orientation through profit-related bonuses.

It is true that Norway today has the shortest working hours in the world. However, the short working week is coupled with traditional working time arrangements. Unlike in Germany, the 1987 working time reduction did not provide the initial impetus for the introduction of new, more flexible working time arrangements or for innovation processes at plant level. As a consequence of the new working time systems, firms had to rethink their entire system of work organisation. The conservatism of Norwegian working time arrangements is one of the reasons why the volume of overtime has risen in recent years. As a result, opportunities to create jobs by redistributing work and to modernise firms have gone begging.

Furthermore, the structure of employee representation at plant level is too complex. Various representative bodies with similar responsibilities exist alongside each other (shop stewards, works council, work environment committees). This complexity is compounded by an intricate trade union structure, in which various organisational principles (industry, craft and status) coexist. It is true that the various trade unions generally cooperate closely with each other and agree on a pragmatic division of labour between the various bodies. Nevertheless, this not infrequently results in unproductive marathon meetings, particularly during pay negotiations, still the core trade union activity, which in this society of equals confirms the old adage that it is the small differences that are most carefully preserved.

In summarising the strengths and weaknesses of the Norwegian model, we have come to the conclusion that efficiency and equality are not mutually contradictory. The Norwegian labour market has a high level of internal and external flexibility. Low pay differentials facilitate external mobility; they also help to lower social barriers at work and encourage communication and teamwork. The state and the social partners can communicate better with each other and find it easier to agree on reforms than in societies with more sharply polarised income and social structures, in which trade unions are not generally accepted as partners with an equal right to shape events but tend rather to be marginalised.

However, the potential of Norway's "passion for equality" has by no means been exhausted. The survival of the Norwegian model depends on the ability of the most important actors to exploit the productive power of "cooperation" in order to push through new reforms. A failure to forge ahead with such reforms would be fatal in an increasingly turbulent environment. In a highly regulated labour market like that in Norway, the consensus between employers and trade unions would quickly break down and allow neo-liberal ideas to hold sway.

The main objective in future must be to support macro-economic stability and growth more strongly than hitherto by adopting a micro-economic innovation policy that focuses particularly on training, modernisation and product innovation. With such a strategy, the comparative advantage of a relatively egalitarian income distribution lies in, among other things, a plentiful supply of low-cost, high-skill labour. There is no shortage of possible plans for reform. In our analysis, we have listed the following starting-points: resolving the problems that have emerged in the implementation of the 1994 reform (and in particular the development of strategies to increase firms' readiness to offer training), improving the training of master craftsmen and middle managers, the development by the social partners of joint proposals for new payment and flexible working time systems, the development of more customer and innovation-oriented organisational structures in firms, the reform of the trade union structure and a simplification of representative structures at plant level. A successful innovation policy will create more room for manoeuvre within the economy for the pursuit of social objectives, such as the humanisation of work or promoting equality for women in the labour market and the reconciliation of paid work and family life.

References

Bildungskommission NRW (1995) *Zukunft der Bildung – Schule der Zukunft.* Denkschrift der Kommission Zukunft der Bildung – Schule der Zukunft beim Ministerpräsidenten des Landes Nordrhein-Westfalen, Neuwied.

Bjørnavold, J. (1994) *Continuing vocational training (CVT) in Norway.* NORUT Social Science Research, Tromsø.

Blank, R. M. and R. B. Freeman (1994), Evaluating the connection between social protection and economic flexibility. In R. M. Blank (ed.), *Social Protection versus Economic Flexibility. Is there a Trade-Off?* Chicago: University of Chicago Press.

Bosch, G. (1990) From 40 to 35 hours. Reduction and flexibilisation of the working week in the Federal Republic of Germany. *International Labour Review, Vol. 129 no 5:* 611–627.

Bosch, G. (1992) *Retraining – Not Redundancy. Innovative approaches to industrial restructuring in Germany and France,* Geneva: International Institute for Labour Studies.

Bosch, G. (1993) Vocational training and changing patterns of labour relations in Germany. In G. Laflamme and contributors, *Vocational training. International Perspectives.* Geneva, Quebec: International Labour Office and University of Laval, Department of Industrial Relations.

Bosch, G. (1995) Flexibility and work organisation. In *Social Europe,* supplement 1/95, European Commission, Directorate General for Employment, Industrial Relations and Social affairs (in English, French and German).

Bosch, G. (1996a) Jahresarbeitszeiten – Flexibilität auch für Stammbelegschaften. *Journal für Sozialforschung* 3.

Bosch, G. (1996b) Redistribution of work, flexible work organization and creation of jobs. Report – expert group EU DG V, Brussels. To be published in *Social Europe.*

Boyer, R. (1987) *La flexibilité du travail en Europe.* Paris: Édition La Découverte.

Brewster, C. and A. Hegewisch, eds (1994) *Policy and Practice in European Human Resource Management.* London: Kogan Page.

Brunstein, I. ed. (1995) *Human Resource Management in Europe.* Berlin: de Gruyter.

Campbell, D. and W. Sengenberger (1994), Labour standards, economic efficiency and development: Lessons from experience with industrial restructuring. In W. Sengenberger and D. Campbell (eds.), *The Role of Labour Standards in Industrial Restructuring.* Geneva: International Institute for Labour Studies.

Carlzon, J. (1989) *Moment of Truth. New Strategies for Today's Customer-Driven Economy.* New York: Harper & Row.

Dertouzos, M. L., R. K. Lester, R. M. Solow, and the MIT Commission on Industrial Productivity (1989). *Made in America: Regaining the Productive Edge.* Cambridge, MA: MIT.

Dølvik, J. E. (1993) *Nordic Trade Unions and the Social Dimension of European Integration. Towards Europeanisation or renationalisation of trade union strategies?* Oslo: FAFO-Paper.

Dølvik, J. E. (1994) Norwegian trade unionism at a crossroads?. Paper presented to the 4th European Regional Congress of the IIRA, Helsinki.

Dragendorf, R. and W. Heering (1986) *Beschäftigungsdauer, Effizienz und Flexibilität. Ein Beitrag zur Ökonomie des Beschäftigungsvertrags*. Berlin: FSA Print 3/86.

Drexel, I. (1980) Die Krise der Anlernung im Arbeitsprozeß. Betriebliche und gesellschaftliche Ursachen der Trennung von Qualifizierung und Produktion. *Soziale Welt* 3.

Education in Norway (1990) Ministry of Education and Research. Oslo.

Emmery, F. and E. Thorsrud (1976) *Democracy at Work – The report of the Norwegian industrial democracy program*. Leiden: Martinus Nijhoff Social Sciences Division.

Flanegan, R. D., D. W. Soskice, and L. Ulman (1983) *Unionism, Economic Stabilization and Incomes Policy. European Experience.* Washington D.C.: The Brookings Institution.

Fricke, E., G. Notz, and W. Schuchardt (1986) *Arbeitnehmerbeteiligung in Westeuropa. Erfahrungen aus Italien, Norwegen und Schweden.* Frankfurt/New York: Campus Verlag.

Gooderham, P. N., O. A. Kvitastein, and O. Nordhaug (1996) *Management of Human Resources in European Firms: A new institutional perspective.* Department of Organizational Sciences, Norwegian School of Economics and Business Administration, Bergen.

Gustavsen, B. and G. Hunnius (1981) *New patterns of work reform – The case of Norway*. Oslo: Universitetsforlaget.

Hammer, T. H., B. Ingebritsen, J. I. Karlsen, and A. Svarva (1994) Organizational renewal: Management of large-scale change in Norwegian firms. In Center for Advanced Human Resource Studies, Cornell University, Working Paper 94-21.

Hippe, J. M. and A. W. Petersen (1993) The Labour Movement, social policy and occupational welfare in Norway. In M.Shalev (ed.), (1996). *The privatization of Social Policy? Welfare and the welfare state in America, Japan and Scandinavia.* London: Macmillan.

Høgsnes, G. (1994) *Collective Wage Bargaining and the Impact of Norms of Fairness – An analysis based on the Norwegian experience*, 2 vols. Oslo: University of Oslo – Institute for Social Research Report 94: 8.

Kahn, L. M. (1995) Against the wind: Bargaining recentralization and wage inequality in Norway 1982–89. Preliminary draft of a paper, Cornell University.

Kalleberg, R. (1991) Kenning-tradisjonen i norske ledelse. *Nytt norsk tidsskrift* 8(3): 218–241.

Kalleberg, A. L. (1992) *Job training in Norway: Organizational and individual differences*. Bergen: Centre for Research in Economics and Business Administration (SNF), Working Paper No. 29/1992.

Kalleberg, A. L. and A. Mastekaasa (1994) Firm internal labor markets and organizational commitment in Norway and the United States. *Acta Sociologica* 37: 269-286.

Karlsen, T. K. (1989) *Arbeidstid og fleksibilitet i arbeidslivet*. Oslo: FAFO.

Kotthoff, H. (1994) *Betriebsräte und Bürgerstatus. Wandel und Kontinuität betrieblicher Mitbestimmung*. Munich: Mehring.

Kvinge, T. L. Lindholt, and L. Støle (1996) *Nyskaping i norsk næringsliv*. Oslo: FAFO-rapport 191.

Langeland, O. (1995) Alternative belønningsformer og incentivistrukturer i arbeidslivet [Alternative payment systems and incentive structures in the labour market]. In D. Oldberg (ed.), *Endringer i arbeidslivets organisering*. Oslo: FAFO.

Moene, K. O. and M. Wallerstein (1995) How social democracy worked: Labor-market institutions. *Politics and Society* 23(2): 185–211.

Nergaard, K. and T. A. Stokke (1996) *Midlertidige ansettelser i norsk arbeidsliv. Hvor mange, hvem, hvor og hvorfor?* Oslo: FAFO-rapport 197.

Nesheim, T. (1995) *The Norwegian business network programme – content, context and output*. Bergen: Centre for Research in Economics and Business Administration (SNF), Working Paper No. 05/1995.

NHO (n.d.) *Tidsmessige lønnssystemer. Offensive bedrifter*. Oslo: Trio Ving Gruppen.

NHO and LO (n.d.) *Getting across Differences – the Norwegian way. The social partners' joint action programme, developing companies to create values*. Oslo.

NOU (1996) *Arbeitdstakeres stilling i konsernforhold m.v.* Oslo: Kommunal og Arbeidsdepartementet, S.6.

Norwegian Employment Commission (1992) *A National Strategy for Increased Employment in the 1990s*. Oslo.

OECD (1994) *The OECD Jobs Study. Facts, Analysis, Strategies. Unemployment in the OECD Area 1950–1995*. Paris.

OECD (1995a) *Employment Outlook*. Paris.

OECD (1995b) *Bildung Kompakt. OECD-Indikatoren 1995*. Paris.

OECD (1996) *Technology, Productivity and Job Creation. Analytical report*. Paris.

Porter (1990) *The competitive Advantage of Nations*. New York: Free Press..

Qvale, T. U. (1995) Local development and institutional change. Experience from a "fifth generation" national programme for the democratisation of work life, Contribution to the Royal Netherlands Academy of Arts and Sciences and Kurt Lewin symposium in organizational decision making under different economic and political conditions, Amsterdam, Vrije Universiteit, 1–3 June 1994, mimeo.

Reich, R. (1991) *The Work of Nations. Preparing ourselves for 21st-century capitalism*. New York: Random House.

Reve, T. (1994) Scandinavian Management: From competitive advantage to competitive disadvantage. *Tidsskrift for samfunnsforskning*, no. 4.

Salvanes, K. G. (1996) *Job creation and job destruction in Norway 1976–1992*. Oslo: Ministry of Industry and Energy, Ministry of Finance and Ministry of Local Government and Labour.

Sengenberger, W. and D. Campbell, eds (1994) *The Role of Labour Standards in Industrial Restructuring*. Geneva: International Institute for Labour Studies.

Sivesind, K. H. (1994) Bargaining and participation in Norway. *Economic and Labour Relations Review* 5(2): 28-46.

Sivesind, K. H. (1995) The indispensable role of culture. Explaining different understandings of work through a comparison of German and Norwegian factories. *Comparative Social Research* 15: 35–101.

Sivesind, K. H., R. Kalleberg, S. Hovde, and A. Fennefoss (1995) A social democratic order under pressure: Norwegian employment relations in the eighties. In R. Locke, T. Kochan, and M. Piore (eds.), *Employment Relations in a Changing*

World Economy. Cambridge, MA: MIT Press.

Skinningsrud, T. (1994) *Compulsory Education, Initial and Continuing Training and Adult Education as a Continuum*. Tromsø: NORUT Social Science Research.

Skinningsrud, T. and J. Bjørnavold (1994) *A study of Norwegian Policy and Practice on the Prevention of School Failure and Marginalization among Young People in the Transition from Education to Adult and Working Life*. Tromsø: NORUT Social Science Research.

Streeck, W. et. al (1987) *The Role of Social Partners in Vocational Training and Further Training in the Federal Republic of Germany*. Luxemburg: CEDEFOP Document 1987.

Thonstad, K. (1993) *An Example of a Social Contract*. Oslo: LO, Samfunnspolitisk avdeling.

Wächter, H. and T. Stengelhofen (1995) Germany. In I. Brunstein (ed.), *Human resource management in Europe*. Berlin: de Gruyter.

Wever, K. (1995) *Negotiating Competitiveness. Employment relations and organizational innovation in Germany and the United States*. New York: McGraw Hill.

Windolf, P. (1994) Strukturwandel der Hochschulausbildung in Deutschland, Japan und in den USA. In H. Demes and W. Georg (eds), *Gelernte Karriere. Bildung und Berufsverlauf in Japan*. Munich: ludicium Verlag, pp. 123–158.

Chapter 8

Public Sector Labour Markets and Labour Relations in Norway

The Exception from the European Rule

Berndt K. Keller

1. Introduction

In this article I will argue from an institutional perspective and try to integrate the often separated analysis of labour markets and labour relations. In accordance with the general purpose of the entire project I will focus on current trends and some possible future challenges/problems and not elaborate on historical developments that are well documented in the existing literature (Dølvik, 1994: 83–91). The natural (dis)advantage of a foreign and/or comparative perspective is that it cannot be expected to cope with too many legal, institutional, and empirical details but is allowed to concentrate on an overall perspective.

In contrast to and in completion of the other parts of the research project, the present and future status of the public sector will be the main and only subject of this article. I will take for granted that, in contrast to at least some or maybe even the majority of other European countries, the public sector in Norway is an integrated part of the whole welfare state, providing necessary infrastructural preconditions for all kinds of activities in the private sector, especially in harder times with more fierce international competition.

2. Public sector employment: Size and trends

There are of course problems of how exactly to define the public sector for different purposes of international comparisons. Do the postal service, railroads, social security systems, hospitals, and/or the labour market administration, among others, belong to the public sector? We have to be aware of these statistical difficulties in all international comparisons. The percentage of public sector employees in the total labour force is usually taken as the most valid indicator of differences in the importance of the public sector in national economies and its significance for the overall functioning of the labour markets.

The size of the public sector

In Norway (with a total labour force of *ca.* 2.1 million and about 650 000 employed in the public sector) the percentage of public employees is fairly high in comparison with the majority of other industrialized Western democracies, i.e. EU member states and/or OECD countries: official data indicate that in the middle of the 1990s about 31 percent were employed in the public sector. If we count the hours worked, the percentage is (at about 27 percent) a bit lower because of the higher proportion of part-timers in the public sector; but this indicator has not very frequently been used.

If we introduce the frequently used distinction between different levels and the corresponding division of duties and tasks (in the case of Norway, federal and local/municipal, not the regional or federal state level), we find that the vast majority of public employees (about 80 percent) are employed at the local level. The growth rates of the various levels and areas of employment have been quite different though; the focus of employment has been shifting. The central governmental "bureaucracy" is relatively small and has not been growing in the recent past – in contrast to the local level where health and welfare services in particular, but also higher education and research, have increased. The state sector is probably shrinking because of rapid technological change and because of less employment in the defence area.

All in all, Norway fits very well into what could be called the Scandinavian pattern of well-developed, relatively generous, comprehensive welfare states with high public sector employment (both in numbers and as a percentage) as an almost necessary consequence of this political choice (Kolberg, 1992). It might even be that Norway and not, as frequently assumed in the past, Sweden has to be considered the prototypical case – at least for the future. Developments in Norway, which started not only from a low level but also relatively late, have almost reached Swedish standards. But, in contrast to Sweden, the recent situation has been comparatively easy to handle.

The growth of the public sector

From a foreign, "non-native" perspective, there have been some surprising overall aggregate trends in public sector employment over the past, say, three to four decades. Not only was the Norwegian public sector growing considerably in the 1960s and 1970s when there was enormous public sector growth everywhere in the Western world (Rose, 1985) but, in contrast to the vast majority of other European countries, it has continued to grow throughout the 1980s and 1990s when this long-term trend had either come to an end or even been (slightly) reversed in other countries. In that regard, Norway constitutes an exceptional case of a continuing increase (and not just stagnation since the 1980s) in public sector employment.

In comparison with corresponding trends in private industry, it is surprising that growth in the public sector has been more or less steady even in times, i.e. the late 1980s and early 1990s, when employment in private industry decreased. In contrast to the vast majority of other European countries, there has been no major political or serious economic discussion about substantial cutbacks, retrenchment, shrinkage, etc. of the public sector "employment machine". Moreover, despite some downsizing of employment in certain public services, there is next to no large-scale political controversy along the lines of "Can we still afford the welfare state?" or about "rolling back the state", including vigorous demands to restrict pensions, to cut the numbers of replacements, etc.[1]

Quite the contrary. At least from the foreign perspective, there is even a surprisingly high degree of societal consensus that the public sector, or to be more accurate some carefully selected parts of it, should and will continue to grow (in absolute and relative terms) in the foreseeable future. The main, but definitely not the only, reason for this surprising policy mix of selected growth is that additional public services will have to be provided at the local level because of foreseeable demographic developments: the rapidly changing age structure of the population with a larger number of old people implies a public duty to take care of them. Considerable revenues from the state-controlled oil sector not available for the public budgets of other developed countries of course facilitate this broad consensus not only about the sheer quantitative size but also about the indispensable value of the public sector. All in all, Norway faces not a self-perpetuating process of uncontrolled public sector growth but a politically controlled growth of selected parts. It is not only the size but also the content of the public sector that matters.

The characteristics of the public sector

The costs of the wages and salaries of public employees represented about 28 percent of total public expenditure in the early 1990s – and they have not been expanding over recent decades. They are, of course, much higher at the local/municipal level (about 75 percent of total cur-

1 In comparative perspective the present debate about the system of sick leave insurance does not ask questions of principle.

rent expenses). Total current expenditure on the public sector demonstrates not a procyclic pattern but relatively steady increases.

As regards the age structure of public sector employees (within an ageing overall labour force), there is an increasing number (not percentage) of older employees. Even though the level of education is higher in the public sector than in private industry,[2] one of the main aspects of all strategies of manpower planning and development is that the formal education of older employees is relatively low. Therefore the public sector will have to hire not only greater numbers of qualified employees but also highly educated new entrants in the foreseeable future in order to increase its efficiency; because of the enormous recent increase in the number of students these applicants will be available.[3] Generational tension may arise between senior employees inhibiting advancement and better-educated young recruits.

In various countries different forms of atypical employment have been gaining in importance since the 1980s (Delsen, 1995). In Norway, contingent work, i.e. limited contracts or temporary work, plays a more important role than it used to, although, within a system of strict regulation of labour standards, legal requirements are fairly restrictive, forbidding short-term contracts. These different forms are more common in the public sector, especially in local/municipal government (with about 20 percent, but statistics are incomplete – Torp, 1995: 16–17; for details see also Chapter 3). These more recent trends could be interpreted as a characteristic feature of labour market flexibilization in the public sector.[4] The segmentation into core and peripheral segments or between the well-protected and the more marginal groups results in growing inequality.

Comparable recent trends towards flexibilization, which are even more important in the public sector than in private industry, can also be observed in other European countries such as Germany (Keller, 1993: 71–78; Henneberger, 1996). In contrast to widespread public opinion, these labour markets have traditionally been segmented to a considerable degree, and segmentation has even increased since the 1980s; public employers are no longer the "good" or "model" employers they used

2 Because of the tasks they have to fulfil, the educational profile of public sector employees differs significantly from that of the national labour force – the level of education is higher.

3 In quantitative terms the future demand for manpower will consist of two components: substitutes for retiring employees and new entrants for new jobs (such as care for the elderly).

4 Basically I conceive of flexibility in terms of numerical and internal, not functional and external, flexibility.

to be in their heyday (up to the 1970s). The principle of life-long employment or employment stability does not apply to all public employees.[5] Part-time work is not necessarily a form of atypical employment in Norway.

Female participation in the labour force

The rate of female participation in the labour force in general and in the public sector labour force in particular has significantly increased since the 1970s.[6] As in the other Scandinavian countries, this rate (over 60 percent in 1980 and more than 70 percent in 1990) is very high in comparison with the rest of Europe (the major exception being the Netherlands), not to mention the extremely low rates particularly in the Mediterranean countries. Thus, a significantly higher number of people can be employed with the same overall input of hours as in the 1970s, and Norwegian labour markets have been able to absorb a larger share of the labour supply.

This long-term development has not only led to a high overall participation rate but almost by definition resulted in a significant proportion of female part-time employment (almost 50 percent, most of it in municipalities). As in all other countries, the vast majority of part-timers (about 90 percent) are women. This distribution caused a sharp increase in support systems, e.g. kindergartens and other child-care institutions.[7] The rising participation rates of women in the labour market and public sector growth are, of course, intertwined.[8]

The labour market status of women has improved since the 1980s; in Norway women do not provide the flexible "reserve army". Among other trends, there is an increasing but still relatively low number of women in leading/senior executive positions. There is still a gender-specific segregation of the labour market in general and of public sector labour markets in particular: jobs occupied by women are concentrated in specific areas of employment (such as health, child care, primary schools), especially at the local level. *Ceteris paribus* their income is still lower than that of men, despite equal pay provisions and the principle of equal pay for work of equal value. Among the structural reasons for this are the

5 This principle is explained in more detail in Chapter 4.

6 In that regard Sweden and Denmark were a decade ahead of Norway.

7 Maternity leave as a paid leave of absence can extend to one year and can be spread over three years; it has had an impact on part-time employment.

8 Dual-income families not only have different social needs but also provide a certain amount of flexibility.

facts that women are still underrepresented in top positions, that they are segregated into lower-paid groups, and that they have fewer seniority rights because of longer leaves due to childbirth (Friedrich Ebert-Stiftung/EPSC, 1996: 178).

Last but not least, the Gender Equality Act of 1979 prohibits differential treatment of men and women and provides equal employment opportunities.[9]

3. Labour relations in the public sector

The system of labour relations

In a purely formal perspective the system of labour relations is rather fragmented, especially on the union side. There is nothing like a unitary union and mergers are not likely to happen on a large scale. The system of interest representation includes a fairly large number of individual unions belonging to three different confederations of differing size: the old LO, dating back to the end of the 19th century, and two newer organizations, AF and YS, established only in the mid-1970s.[10] The affiliated unions do not necessarily organize completely different strata of the labour force, but compete for members to a certain extent. One important difference, which I will refer to later, is that LO unions organize mainly low-skilled, blue-collar workers, whereas AF members focus more on white-collar employees and professionals.

As in the vast majority of other countries, the general organizational pattern of private industry is mirrored in the public sector: in both sectors the degree of centralization of the bargaining system is fairly high. In private industry, collective bargaining can take place not only at the industry level but even at the central–intersectoral level, thus constituting an exception from the majority of West European countries (Bridgford and Sterling, 1994: 125–129). LO makes more frequent use of the intersectoral option.

The overall density ratio of union membership (i.e. including the public sector) is, at almost 60 percent, rather high in comparative perspective with Western Europe or the OECD countries, although it is significantly lower than in the other Scandinavian countries. This rate has, again in contrast to a considerable number of comparable countries,

9 This important issue of gender-specific labour market segmentation and discrimination is dealt with more extensively in Chapter 4.

10 There are also some independent unions, for example in the oil industry or the Teachers' Union in the public sector, organizing about 10 percent of all union members.

been fairly stable even in turbulent times (Visser, 1990), and there have been no major losses in membership.

The density ratio of the public sector in Norway is, at 80–90 percent, much higher than that of private industry. This pattern is well known and can also be found in most other Western countries (Stieber, 1989: 268; Visser, 1990: 50). The growth of the public sector creates incentives for different unions to organize the newly hired employees, and resistance of public employers scarcely exists.

Last but not least, we have to differentiate between the density ratio and the coverage rate. The latter is very high in comparative perspective with the other OECD countries and is significantly higher in the public sector than in private industry because contracts either are generally binding (in the municipal sector) or can be extended to all employees (by parliamentary decision in the state sector) (see Friedrich Ebert-Stiftung/EPSC, 1996: 92).

The public sector has its own organizational structure that follows the already mentioned distinction between the state and local/municipal levels:

- At the state level, the Ministry of Planning and Coordination is in charge of all employers' interests including wages and pay. The outcome of negotiations requires formal approval in parliament. There is a separate employers' association for the local/municipal and regional levels, the Norwegian Association of Local Authorities (KS) organizing municipalities and county municipality governments and serving as their bargaining agent in centralized negotiations.[11] This organization is independent not only from the Ministry of Planning but also from NHO, the peak organization of private industry. KS is partly an employers' association, partly a lobbying organization – and seems not to be overtly strong.
- On the opposite side there are various unions that are members of all three confederations and organize either only within the public sector or in the public sector as well. A potential source of conflict is created by the fact that the interests of members in both sectors can differ. There are two separate bargaining systems for the state and the local/municipal level. Integration and centralization are much easier at the state level because of the very low number of actors involved and, therefore, of concluded agreements. The local/municipal level is, of course, much more fragmented, with a rather large

11 A separate employers' association (NAVO) has recently been established for state enterprises and semi-autonomous state agencies such as Telenor and the public broadcasting company (NRK).

> number of unions (about 30) of differing size and domain. However, tacit forms of integration also occur within federations/bargaining cartels. Within the public sector, negotiations for both levels are conducted separately but are closely coordinated by a joint committee of KS and the Ministry of Administration (Høgsnes, 1994: chs 14–16). The overall level of coordination seems to be rather high and fairly effective whereas in the majority of other countries both levels are more or less separate from each other.

Confederations not only coordinate the differing views of their member unions on a voluntary informal basis, but also bargain on their behalf and recommend outcomes, despite their members' formal right to bargain individually in the municipal sector.[12] These collective efforts by bargaining cartels are conceived of as being more efficient in the long run than individual attempts at bargaining. All in all, the degree of intense intra- and inter-organizational coordination taking place not only within but also between these peak organizations, before as well as during central negotiations, is surprisingly high on both sides of the bargaining table.

Rather than the more or less open conflict one might expect from a purely formal or legal perspective, this dispersed representational structure does not create a huge amount of competition or fierce rivalry at the workplace level and/or a high degree of open or hidden industrial warfare at the central level. On an informal basis this fragile system of labour relations appears to be fairly integrated – not only within unions belonging to the same confederation and sharing the same ideology but even between different confederations. It is not the sheer number of organizations that is important for overall success but the form of their explicit and implicit cooperation.

In particular, the relationship between LO and AF, organizations not of equal but of comparable size within the public sector, seems to have developed gradually into one of mutual recognition and even closer cooperation. In an official document signed in late 1993, both organizations agreed to cooperate in some selected areas of common interest (education, equality, employees' rights, employment) without, however, neglecting persisting conflicts in other fields (primarily wages and salaries).

Understanding and mutual trust will most likely increase through more and closer cooperation in working groups, and opportunities to

12 Individual unions in YS-Kommune and AF-Kommune retain their individual rights to vote on the outcomes whereas in LO-Kommune internal arrangements inhibit this.

exert political influence will probably grow. A *modus vivendi* for the future has been defined at the top level despite the fact that wages are explicitly excluded from this "agreement of intention". From a macro point of view, this positive-sum game could even stabilize the overall mode of organizing and representing interests. The argument that the agreement might be one-sided and that AF profits more than LO seems to be exaggerated from the macro point of view. "One possible interpretation of the agreement is that LO accepts that AF is the only credible confederation for the academics, and that LO wants to form a pressure group together with AF on issues that concern all types of employees" (Sivesind et al., 1995: 306).

The third confederation, YS, could easily be the loser from this new strategic alliance formed by its opponents. For the YS, which is almost as big as AF, interest representation might be more conflictual and competition for potential members in the public sector might be more difficult to win. For organizational reasons, its main opponents are LO organizations rather than AF members.

Problems of necessary coordination at the macro level are considerably eased by this high degree of centralization, which also implies a concentration of power at the central level of the organizations – more in LO than in AF and YS.

In stark contrast to the situation in other countries, none of the main actors shows a strong interest in a thoroughgoing change in the legal framework, i.e. a profound decentralization of the bargaining system.[13] "Deregulation" and "flexibilization", either of private industry or of the public sector, are not the most prominent political catchwords in Norway. Strong demands for sharp turns in labour relations policies proposed in other countries since the early–mid-1980s play a comparatively minor role. Unions' existence are not threatened by private employers' associations and/or the government, and the established balance of power seems to be fairly stable; change in the whole structure will be rather slow.

There has been a national consensus between the social partners and politicians over wage bargaining, which constitutes an informal, but more or less officially accepted and well-established Norwegian model of pattern-setting and pattern-following linking both sectors. Private industry sets the targets, and not just for "ground rules", and takes the lead, while the public sector is the follower in terms of the timing (date of expiration of previous contracts and beginning of negotiations) and content

13 The UK is at the opposite end of the continuum, while others, like the Netherlands (see Peijpe, 1996), are moving rapidly in the same direction.

(demands and settlement) of collective agreements. According to this general agreement the public sector should not normally have the highest increases. This typical sequence of events is not automatic but might be reversed once in a while with the public sector concluding first; but this change does not negate the overall rules of the game.

Within the municipal sector there seems to be one dominant settlement despite the existence of several different agreements, i.e. the LO contract determines the range of opportunities for all other organizations. This semi-institutional mechanism to control the wage formation process is fairly robust despite the fact that the municipal sector is not monolithically organized and has required some intervention to secure compliance.

Solidaristic wage policies

Like its Scandinavian neighbours, Norway has been following solidaristic wage policies for several decades in private industry and in the public sector in particular, where wage differentials are minimal in comparative perspective. These strategies, reflecting a cultural "egalitarian ethos" and a surprisingly strong legacy, have been successful in the sense that they have sustained a much less dispersed wage structure than occurs in all other European countries, not to mention the USA.[14] So far this "passion for equality", with its persistingly flat wage structure, has not created major conflicts, although some groups not only have made no gains, but have even experienced substantial losses in real wages (Høgsnes, 1995).

Comparisons of wages and incomes between sectors are frequently made – if only for political purposes. But valid comparisons are always difficult for different reasons: there are no (or at least no exact) equivalents in private industry for some groups of public sector jobs, and there are differences in wages within private industry for jobs existing in both sectors. Thus comparisons of average wages can be misleading for at least some groups (Keller, 1993: 164–167 for details).

Norwegian data show that public sector wages are relatively low in relation to those in private industry, although some low-skilled groups, such as bus drivers, are able to make more money in the public sector than in private industry. This fits into the general pattern which can also be detected in other countries that the low skilled earn relatively more in the

14 See Chapter 3 for details.

public sector, whereas the highly skilled are better off in private industry.

One consequence of this rather stable income pattern could be that for some groups of public sector employees (lawyers and engineers, among others) employment opportunities in private industry could become more attractive. All in all, however, mobility between the public sector and private industry seems to be rather low. With the exception of a very few specialists with certain skills for particular jobs, there are no general problems of recruitment for public sector jobs because of manpower shortages. This situation, which was different in the early–mid-1980s, might be changing for some groups (health and social employees).

In general one could argue from the view point of orthodox human capital theory developed in the 1960s that individual rates of return on investments are extremely low in Norway, especially in the public sector. Therefore individual incentives to invest in more education (including apprenticeship and further training) hardly exist. One possible explanation is that other conditions of employment (such as work content and greater flexibility in working time) compensate for lower incomes and make the public sector more attractive as an employer. A more general counter-argument could be that education has a value in itself that cannot, or cannot only, be counted in the rationalistic calculation of the maximation of life-long earnings.

From a macro point of view, a high level of formal education becomes a necessary individual precondition to finding a job, not to maximizing one's long-term income.[15] From the collective perspective it also makes sense to invest in education, especially if it is true that in the future more jobs will require more training and higher skills. Skill formation and development become decisive determinants of competitiveness (see Sivesind et al., 1995, for details).

Dispute settlement

Another significant institution is the Norwegian system of compulsory arbitration of collective disputes over interests, which establishes a peculiar tool for conflict resolution. This type of dispute settlement is rarely found in other liberal democracies, or at least not in private industry, where conciliation and mediation procedures prevail (Adams, 1995: 86–88). For some parts of the public sector at least one could of course repeat the argument

15 This so-called statistical screening function of education is also in line with "job competition theory", which implies that education becomes more urgent only to get access to jobs and career ladders.

well known from equivalent discussions in comparable countries (Ozaki, 1990) that the urgent necessity of providing certain indispensable services to the general public legitimizes even drastic forms of binding intervention, i.e. "undemocratic" restrictions of the right to strike for all public employees or at least for the so-called core groups (such as policemen and firefighters or doctors and nurses).

The mere existence of this peculiar instrument of interest arbitration exerts a significant influence over the system of collective bargaining. Compulsory arbitration by legal enactment, i.e. by a committee of neutrals, provides more than a means of last resort because it can be, and indeed has been, used frequently (especially in the 1980s) as part of encompassing incomes policies. This dispute resolution device guarantees and secures that the same content is achieved in a number of different, formally independent collective agreements for particularistic and independent groups. It can also be exploited for two other purposes: to keep dissenting and/or independent unions in line with the "blueprint" of the main agreement between the LO and NHO, the so-called social order function; or even by union leaders to settle intra-organizational conflicts with dissatisfied member groups without having to go on strike. The instrument prevents or at least shortens labour conflicts occasionally arising from some groups (police and nurses, among others) after the expiration of previous contracts.

In both sectors, compulsory arbitration affects the whole character of free collective bargaining in general and collective labour conflicts in particular, leaving the problem of the right to bargain and the freedom to take strike action open. The question of whether or not this practice, "which involves some interference of parliament 'at a distance' "(van Peijpe, 1996: 38), is compatible with international conventions is difficult to decide. Claims to the ILO have been made.

4. Labour market policies

Active labour market measures

Public expenditure on labour market policies has been rather high in all Scandinavian countries in comparison with others. The so-called active labour market policy in Sweden has long been characterized by strong active measures instead of purely passive support even in times when unemployment was fairly low. Like its Scandinavian neighbour, but with a delayed start, Norway has also introduced different active strategies. In contrast to recent developments in Sweden, however, Norway has managed not only to continue but even to strengthen its active strategies at a rather high level in the 1990s.[16]

A major part of the existing labour supply has always been absorbed by the public sector, without however "crowding out" private industry job creation. The employment function of the public sector is rather high because of its sheer size, but it should not be considered the "employer of last resort". The public sector could also be used as an instrument of labour market policies.

Rates of unemployment increased in the late 1980s and early 1990s and were high by traditional Norwegian standards (although still very low in all possible comparisons with other European countries). This development came as a real surprise and taught lessons for future fiscal and labour market policies. As a concerted reaction Norway has increased the number of students (and of employees in universities and equivalent institutions).[17] This somewhat unexpected labour market strategy has two contradictory effects:

- On the one hand it is an efficient remedy for preventing unemployment or at least keeping it low, especially youth unemployment, which is among the lowest of all industrialized countries. Furthermore, this strategy increases the general human capital, which is, according to general labour market wisdom, urgently needed for economic survival in the era of the second industrial revolution and which creates competitive advantage in the increasing global competition.[18] Nowadays Norway is one of the countries with the highest degree of formal education and training.
- On the other hand, this strategy of "up-skilling" could create new problems or intensify emerging problems for a well-educated society when more graduates with better education seek appropriate jobs in the near future – and have difficulties getting them. It is not at all clear whether or not the public sector, with its steady but rather slow growth in employment, will be able to absorb the higher number of qualified entrants or whether or not private industry will create enough qualified jobs. This is the reason some critics (including private employers) argue that there has been an overinvestment in human capital, causing a waste of scarce public resources. According

16 See Chapter 3 for further details.

17 The same trend of growing universities and shrinking defence can be observed in Sweden (see Swedish Agency for Government Employees, 1996).

18 Thus, the Norwegian "low cost, high skill" economy manoeuvres itself into an advantageous position in comparison with "low cost, low skill" economies.

> to this view, the general shift towards more-skilled jobs takes longer than is generally assumed – or is empirically not justified.

The encompassing system of employment policies is highly integrated. Instruments include training/retraining programmes, wage subsidies for temporary placements in the private or public sector, and public job creation schemes for limited periods of time to be converted into ordinary jobs. The specific target groups for these reoriented public policies include young people, the long-term unemployed, and women. Purely passive transfers and subsidies for the unemployed have been cut back because these strategies have been considered inappropriate for solving the unemployment problem. The general consensus has been that it is important "to bring people (back) to work".[19]

There is a high degree of consensus between unions, the government, and other political actors about the necessity and usefulness of more active strategies in order to improve the level and quality of continuous education.[20] The significant difference between Norway and the majority of other European countries is that massive labour market policies will not be urgent in the immediate future: the level of registered unemployment has decreased and is remarkably low in contrast with other countries (at about 5 percent of the labour force, in comparison with 11 percent as the EU average).[22] The general condition of the labour market not only has been fairly stable in the short run, but has improved since 1993, and further increases in jobs both in private industry and in the public sector are expected in the future. These recent developments are remarkable because the total labour force participation rate is (at around 78 percent) much higher than that in most other European countries.

Privatization

Demands for the privatization of some or nearly all components of the public sector put forward by conservatives, liberals, and private employers, among others, have continued to be a controversial political issue in

19 The system of unemployment insurance is fairly generous despite some recent adjustments, which concerned the duration and not the level of compensation. The provision of sufficient employment opportunities for minorities has created problems, in Norway as well; see Chapter 3 for details on labour market welfare arrangements.

20 As in other countries, private employers occasionally doubt the efficiency of labour market services and monopoly regulation.

21 See Chapter 3 for details.

the vast majority of Western countries since the early–mid-1980s (Martin, 1993). Privatization is a polyvalent concept, though. In its most radical form it means the abolition of the public nature of services followed by private ownership and loss of public control. A more moderate version is the creation of some private competition in the delivery of services without changing the public organization of services. A fairly soft form is the privatization of the rules governing public services (Treu and de Felice, 1990: 69–72).

In comparative perspective, demands for privatization have been less vigorous and less challenging in Norway than in the majority of other countries. Furthermore, they have been targeted at the local/municipal level and at selected parts of the former public sector (mainly railroads, the postal service, and Telecom/Telenor, where technological changes allowed cuts). There are also problems of perception by the public: "Surveys show that there is strong support for a large public sector and there is not a strong support for widespread privatization; in some core areas there is a call for stronger public involvement (e.g. health, education, care for the elderly)" (Royal Norwegian Ministry of Government Administration, 1993: 2). Interestingly enough, the health sector, having been privatized in some other countries (including the USA) but being (with some minor exceptions) part of the public sector in Norway, has not been under serious consideration for privatization! The political decision to keep certain services in the public sector is at any rate remarkable.

The political controversy between government and trade unions does not lead to ideological warfare (as in the UK, not just in the Thatcher years, or in the USA, not just during the Reagan administration). Within a general consensus the crucial question was not *if* certain services should be provided, but who should provide them. The general aim was not to make money by selling the "family silver" because rapidly growing public debts had to be reduced, but to increase the autonomy of public bodies, introduce some sort of competition and more market orientation, and improve productivity and efficiency. The overall economic pressure was less severe than in other countries.[22]

The steps actually taken in the recent past have not followed radical recommendations and have had very moderate results: some large government agencies have been changed into government/state enterprises with a particular public company structure – but not into strictly private

22 Interestingly enough there is even an opposite trend, although not for political reasons: some major banks, formerly private owned, went bankrupt and were nationalized in order to save them.

companies.[23] Because the shares of limited liability companies are still publicly owned, the state in principe continues to exert control over all major decisions of the now semi-private companies. The overall result has been the introduction of some market-like mechanisms instead of strict and complete privatization. Opinions on privatization at the local level (health care is just one example) are more mixed.

Trade unions have been reluctant about this critical issue and argued that their members' interests in terms of rights and wages would be better protected if they kept their status of public employees. The unions' views had an impact far beyond their formal right to discussion with employers because unions were integrated partners in the smooth process of political negotiations about privatization. At least so far, despite downsizing, the actual numbers of layoffs and redundancies have been kept to a minimum and alternative strategies have been applied (early retirement, offer of jobs elsewhere, re-education, among others). All in all, Norway was well advised in being more reluctant than other countries to use privatization as a means of public sector reform: the empirical results of privatization measures in different countries are less positive than one might suppose from the conservative blueprint (Martin, 1993). Moreover, costs would not necessarily be lower after privatization.

Working time

In some European countries there has been ongoing discussion on shortening working time (in most cases on a weekly basis) in order to create more employment opportunitities for the unemployed.[24] Advocates of this view have argued that the public sector should and could easily be included in this overall employment strategy because it would be easier to solve the obvious problem of implementation in the public sector than in private industry, where employers cannot be forced to hire new employees (e.g. replacement ratios create a certain risk).

This whole idea has had little success within the present agenda of the Norwegian system of interest intermediation. The majority of unions are still reluctant, arguing that this option is not the best way to create additional jobs and/or to reduce unemployment. Some unions with large

23 Public enterprises to be found in other comparable countries such as telecommunications, postal services, electricity, and transportation constitute about 20 percent of public employment.

24 France in the early 1980s and Germany in the mid–late 1980s are two prominent examples.

groups of female members, however, have opted for shorter hours and might be able to put the issue on the bargaining agenda in the foreseeable future.[25] Furthermore, working time in Norway is already low in comparison with other OECD countries since it was officially reduced in the mid-1980s to 40 hours per week minus 30 minutes per day for lunch, i.e. to 37.5 hours per week; and the comparatively lower level of unemployment does not, as in other countries such as Germany, create the urgent need to take general immediate action.[26]

The strategy of a shorter working life, i.e. voluntary early retirement, could be conceived as a supplement to a shorter work-week but with similar employment goals. Such demands would face the same objections as the shorter work-week does, and demographic trends would create additional problems. All in all, in contrast to other countries, neither exit option has been a hot political issue in Norway (and the other Scandinavian countries) over the past few years and is unlikely to be in the foreseeable future.

More realistic than a flat general reduction of weekly working hours for everybody could be the gradual flexibilization of working hours by other, more targeted means, e.g. strict limits on widespread overtime work, the extension of parental leave, more sabbaticals, more further training and education. A more disguised way to reduce the size of the labour force can be detected in the high percentage of disabled persons leaving the labour force of private industry well before the official retiring age of 67, which is (with Denmark's) the highest in Europe. This instrument of course increases the financial burden on the pension system.

The European Union

In November 1994, Norway, a member of the European Economic Area (EEA), decided not to join the European Union – in contrast to Sweden and Finland.[27] Nevertheless Norway (like Switzerland, another non-member by referendum) has to adapt its macro politics and its national regulatory standards to all major decisions taken in Brussels

25 Recently, however, the main federation, LO, has adopted a more open stance, inviting debate about reduced working time, not on a general basis but in flexible and targeted ways.

26 A related discussion in other countries focuses on the considerable amount of overtime in both sectors and its reduction in order to create additional employment opportunities.

27 The arguments of the discussion are well known and need not be repeated here.

("autonomous adaptation"). Without being a member, the Norwegian economy is integrated into the single European market.

In contrast to the majority of EU member states, Norway would easily be able to fulfil the strict criteria of convergence for European Monetary Union (EMU) defined in the Maastricht Treaty. But, not being a member, Norway will stay outside – keeping its relative independence (in economic policies), preserving the option of re/devaluation (in response to changing oil prices), and creating no additional problems for collective bargaining (especially in the national public sector).

There has been a common, unrestricted labour market within the Nordic countries since the mid-1950s. Nevertheless, the number of migrants has always been very limited despite the fact that the cultures and languages are very similar, i.e. mobility barriers are not very high.[28] The interpenetration rate of national labour markets is fairly low in general and especially low in public sector labour markets in particular. This situation is the same as the conditions in other countries and will most likely not change in the foreseeable future (Pedersen, 1995: 244).

Freedom of movement within the European Economic Community had already started in the mid-1960s – without, however, creating mass migration from the south to the north, not even in the "golden" labour market age of the late 1960s/early 1970s when unemployment in the Northern member states was extremely low. The small percentage of foreigners in some national labour markets has even been decreasing over the past two decades. This adaptation included some peculiarities within public sector labour markets (Art. 49 of the Treaties of Rome). Formerly restricted access to the vast majority of public jobs had to be opened to citizens of other member states.

The Norwegian government has adapted all national regulation to European requirements, and not just as far as freedom of movement is concerned. The consequences of free and unrestricted movement between EEA and EU labour markets will most probably not be very severe – the aggregate numbers of migrants are and will remain fairly low.[29] Capital is likely to be more mobile than labour.

---

28 There are some differences between countries and foreign labour is highly concentrated in certain industries.

29 An exception could be doctors because their limited numbers in Norway lead to the hiring of foreign doctors. A typical pattern of mobility for professionals could be some sort of temporary employment abroad.

5. Corporatism as an explanation of success

In political science and political sociology, corporatism has been defined as a specific form of interest intermediation. It is different from other, more pluralist–liberal forms of conflict resolution in that the market is replaced by politics as the major mode of regulation. Highly institutionalized and centralized, more or less voluntary forms of concertation between government, unions, and employers' associations try to cope with the central problems of social order. Labour relations in general and incomes policy in particular are frequently used test-cases for the success of the whole arrangement at the macro level.

From a purely formal point of view, Norway does not seem to be a typical example of the corporatist model. But in practice it is a more or less prototypical model of this kind of political experiment (Høgsnes, 1994: ch. 4). Processes of trilateral decision-making within a highly regulated labour market usually include a special relationship between government and federations of unions. The largest confederation, LO, and its affiliated unions enjoy a certain privileged status of a pattern more or less characteristic of corporatist arrangements in different countries. A high degree of centralization of power within and between organizations is another necessary precondition for the successful coordination and integration of policies.

Another common feature is a special relationship, i.e. close cooperation, between unions in general and federations in particular (mainly LO) and the social democratic government. The framework constitutes the so-called solidarity alternative: "reducing unemployment through pay moderation" (EIRR, 1995: 16). In the 1980s, unions even agreed to wage freezes. In the recent past, major unions (especially in the public sector) have been following "responsible" incomes policies, demanding only moderate wage increases. Nevertheless, real disposable incomes have grown to a considerable degree because of consistently low rates of inflation (Royal Norwegian Ministry of Finance, 1995: 13). Furthermore, social improvements have been made. Thus the well-known interplay of "give and take" and its trade-offs can benefit all corporate actors in the long run. To defect in order to pursue short-term interests would turn out to be a very costly alternative within this institutional frame of reference.

The politics of consensus are deeply rooted in the egalitarian Norwegian society and economy – and since the experience of the conservative government in the mid-1980s there has been no viable political alternative. Employers' organizations also act very pragmatically, are not strongly influenced by neo-liberal ideological forces, and accept the existence and the role of unions within a system of tripartite cooperation. Complaints about all kinds of wage formation "rigidities" and the high degree of labour market "regulation" at the macro level are (at least since the conservative interlude of the 1980s) much rarer and less vigorous in Norway than in other European countries.

This general consensus and the resulting tripartite management of major economic conflicts and social problems are extremely valuable assets with some obvious advantages: they have been able to prevent in Norway what social scientists in general and sociologists in particular elsewhere in Europe have kept calling since the early–mid-1980s the trend towards a two-thirds society (or two-tier society), i.e. a sharp and increasing internal separation and a considerable degree of social exclusion of large groups of the population. To a foreign observer, the degree of social homogeneity and social inclusion in an "affluent" society is (still) surprisingly high.

The sheer size of the country seems to be of major importance as an explanatory factor. Because everybody knows and meets everybody else on quite different occasions, within close networks today's opponents can be tomorrow's partners – and vice versa. In an atmosphere of cultural coherence and a high level of confidence, it is always possible to make some sort of compromise that can be sold to the members of associations on both sides.

Or, to put it in the more elegant language of game theory, in this situation of iterated games you cannot defect but have to continue to cooperate in your own well-understood self-interest. If individual or collective actors tried to maximize their short-term payoffs – which would, of course, be the appropriate strategy in a one-shot game – they would most likely hurt their long-term self-interest because the other actors would probably stop cooperating. Being aware of this well-known context, the continuation of cooperation is the optimal long-range strategy ("cooperation pays"). Thus payoffs are stable and outcomes are highly predictable.

The secret of this amazing success has a lot to do with oil revenues. This "manna from heaven" provides stable budgetary conditions, reduced the formerly rather high public debt to zero in 1995, thus preventing growing interest payments, guarantees that given tax burdens will not rise, and creates a solid base for economic policies and the welfare state – for the time being and for the foreseeable future. The basic structure of this rather sophisticated system of interest representation and intermediation had of course been developed before oil revenues began to flow. But this constant source of public revenues establishes not only the necessary but also the sufficient preconditions for the long-term survival of the model because the general consensus is easier to sustain, especially in more difficult times. The crucial question, however, is not only where the manna comes from but how it is used as a policy tool, i.e. how it is spent wisely to the benefit of society.

Thus, the welfare state that makes enormous transfers for different groups possible (not only in agriculture and peripheral districts) will still be affordable in a rich oil country even without increasing the tax burden for the individual citizen and without creating additional political conflict. Therefore Norway can afford to deviate from the mainstream or orthodox textbook and political wisdom as regards economic growth and full employment, which usually includes the political recommendation of a minor role for a smaller public sector, strict deregulation, and flexibilization.

The so-called Nordic model is not just a Swedish model any more. Nowadays it is perhaps more of a Norwegian model. In more or less clear contrast with recent developments in Sweden, Norway has been able not only to keep its mode of interest representation and interest intermediation fairly stable, but also to develop it even further.

6. Future problems as minor challenges: A foreign view

Norway is a "small, peripheral, export-based economy" that is one of the fastest growing economies in Europe. All indicators of macroeconomic performance are developing more or less rapidly in a positive direction. Norway is economically able and politically willing to afford a considerable public sector; one could even argue that it is a "public sector based economy". In contrast to at least some other European countries, there is a general consensus between all relevant political actors and societal groups (including not only unions and employers' associations but also most political parties and the general public) that the public sector is and should be an integrated part not only of the Norwegian welfare state but also of the whole economy – and it should be not only maintained and perpetuated but developed even further.

Because of this strict political priority, serious frontal attacks on the usefulness and size of the public sector would not be an appropriate strategy for politicians hoping to win an election. Furthermore, in terms of the new political economy (or public choice), the mere size of the public sector guarantees some political influence and protection in terms of votes. However, public employees cannot prevent change and reforms of the public sector because they are and will always be a minority of the constituency.

The "Norwegian model of solidarity" represents an exceptional case in Europe and seems to create not only a predictable but also a sustainable alternative. The hot political (not to say ideological) debates in other European countries about the future of the public sector[30] have next to no equivalent in Norway. Even conservatives opt not for a much smaller public sector in general (as their counterparts in all other countries do) but mainly for a more efficient one.

If emerging tendencies towards the decentralization and flexibilization of the collective bargaining system are to gain in importance, they will most likely be of a rather moderate nature; they will try not to abolish the existing system but only to adjust it to changing circumstances. "Negotiated adaptation" could be the Norwegian version of coping with necessary change. To be more precise, within the present frame of collective bargaining there is some, but not too much, room for additional local bargaining in order to suit local and individual needs. This narrow scope for additional compensation will probably have to be widened because of shortages and bottlenecks in some local labour markets (nurses are just one prominent example) and because of emerging tendencies towards more flexibility favoured by some interest associations. Recent experiments with local wage adjustments in municipalities (Ingebrigtsen, 1994) point in that direction.

Therefore the most important problem is not how to cope with the present economic and/or financial situation, which can hardly be called a "crisis", but how to prepare for a possible (although not very likely, in my view) future critical situation if/when oil revenues fade away sometime after the year 2000. Constraints on public budgets could then create a more serious problem than they do today in the "golden age" of oil.

For the time being there seems to be no real need for radical and structural reforms of the public sector. Future problems and challenges are not very pressing, and Norway can afford to be what has been called in another context a "reluctant reformer and slow learner" (Olsen, 1996). What is recommended is gradual change and incremental adaptation and not complete modernization of the whole public sector. Certain strategies discussed or even implemented in other countries (such as decentralization of certain responsibilities) could and should be observed in order to prevent possible welfare losses, to increase the productivity and efficiency of selected, lagging parts of the public sector at the local/municipal level, to rebuff the usual everyday complaints about the poor quality of public services, and to prevent the necessity for major

30 The UK is the most prominent but definitely not the only example; see Winchester and Bach (1995) for details.

abrupt changes in the distant future by making minor smooth adaptations in the near future.[31] It is worth noting that the Norwegian government itself has been aware of the problem of public sector performance for quite some time (Royal Norwegian Ministry of Labour and Government Administration, 1991).

There has been growing discussion about changes in management strategies in almost all other West European countries since the 1980s (Lane, 1993: 124–149; Olsen and Peters, 1994). These strategies include not only general budgetary cutbacks and downsizing but also contracting-out, outsourcing, profit centres, atypical employment, etc. The necessity of restructuring and reorganizing in order to increase efficiency plays a major role in various countries.

"New public management" and human resources management strategies were developed and politically tested in the Anglo-Saxon countries. "Trust in markets and managerialism were key aspects of the doctrine. A concept of public administration emphasizing due processes and rules was declared to be old-fashioned and dysfunctional. It was to be replaced by a 'new public management' emphasizing goals and results and giving private firms an exemplary role in public sector reform" (Olsen and Peters, 1994: 10). In practice, however, there is no homogeneous trend of modernization; different national regimes and trajectories of development prevail.

In Norway, where these concepts are not big issues, new individualized employee relations will not substitute for the old collective labour relations. Despite their relevance, not all of these tools and concepts would be appropriate for all parts of the public sector (although they might be for areas at the municipal level). Particular strategies (maybe chosen instead of further steps towards privatization) would probably increase – for example, decentralization of authority and transfer of tasks, better control of running costs and all available resources, the use of strategic planning instruments, some structural reorganization.

One set of changes could have to do with the introduction of performance-related pay systems, which in historical perspective are fairly rare and unusual in the public sector, where seniority-based systems dominate and prevail, but which are more common in private industry. Nevertheless, they have been under serious consideration in some countries (recently even in Germany; see Keller, 1996) with the aim of increasing efficiency without the need for additional resources (OECD, 1993). Wherever these systems of pay determination have been intro-

31 Chapter 9 elaborates on these different issues of modernization.

duced they have led not only to greater flexibility of wages but also to trends towards the decentralization of collective bargaining. This question is not a central issue in Norway and the unions have decided against it ("a job is a job") because they would be manoeuvred into a precarious position.

However, times might change and political desires for greater efficiency through a change in the system of pay might become stronger. A decisive point would be if there were to be an increase in the overall public sector wage bill, providing additional scope for supplementary benefits based on individual performance, or if the overall amount of available funds were to remain constant, leading to more serious distributional conflicts because some employees would have to face decreasing incomes. Another important problem would be the implementation of these strategies: would the final decision about the allocation of funds and individual pay increases be made unilaterally by (central and/or local) management or would unions have some degree of influence? Because of the Norwegian system of stable corporatism, strong union involvement would be quite likely.[32]

According to widely accepted economic wisdom, the level of wages and salaries in the public sector constitutes a significant determinant of the overall level of employment. One could, of course, repeat the well-known argument that unions bargain not only over wages but also over employment and that cheap qualified labour provides the basis for increased employment opportunities. The well-established strategy of a solidaristic wage policy and wage moderation can, however, go "too far" and might create more militancy or even protracted goal conflicts in the foreseeable future. There have been some dissatisfied (not to say frustrated) groups (such as nurses and employees with university degrees) that will more actively try to challenge the highly centralized bargaining system and narrow wage differentials in order to improve their relative position within the wage structure. One convincing legitimation of their demands is that they have to pay back the state loans they received as students; a reduction in the repayment of these loans would reduce the costs of attending university. Another reason could be that, in times of growing surpluses in public budgets, soaring profits in private industry, and low levels of unemployment, an urgent need for wage modera-

---

32 A related option could be promotion on the basis of individual performance instead of seniority. In some municipalities, experiments with more performance-related supplementary bargaining have been pursued, seemingly with the approval of initially sceptical unions (e.g. Telemark Fylkeskommune).

tion is less obvious from an individual point of view and more difficult to pursue from a collective point of view.

It is not unlikely that these groups of semi-professionals and professionals will be (at least partially) successful in an increasing struggle over distribution. Their unions (mostly affiliated to AF) will be able to attract growing numbers of public employees as members because of the expansion of employment in their organizational domains (mainly education and health). They will therefore be stronger and more powerful in collective bargaining, demanding higher relative wages for the core groups of their membership. The LO confederation and its unions will probably in the long run continue to lose members (at least in relative terms) and therefore tend to lose influence and power, because structural changes in the labour force keep removing jobs from their domains. The above-mentioned groups are even more likely to achieve (some) success because some public (and not just private) employers might also be interested in more differentiated wages and a more dispersed wage structure in order to attract and motivate core personnel.

On the other hand, it might be politically appropriate to keep wage differentials relatively small and to stick to the "passion for equality" for different reasons. It would be easier to employ the increasing number of young professionals leaving university in forthcoming years. Furthermore, the interests of large groups of females who profit from the present structure and would be hurt by major changes could be better protected within the solidaristic framework.

In any event, this latent, and sometimes (as in the 1995 bargaining round) already manifest, long-term conflict will not be easy to mediate. One rather sophisticated, not necessarily stable, but viable option could be a split in the overall bargaining process: the social partners could settle for more or less solidaristic wage increases during the main, fairly centralized bargaining round but allow for some flexible adjustments afterwards and much less visible compensation for certain selected groups at the workplace level.[33] Thus, tensions could be eased and the system of solidarity wages kept in balance. The well-established corporatist system of interest intermediation would support these kinds of arrangements.

---

33 There is a lot of empirical evidence from other countries that changing bargaining levels and leaving some scope for decentralized bargaining do not work for an indefinite period although they do work for quite some time; for Germany, see Keller (1993:202–207). The pattern is, of course, not unknown in some sectors of private industry in Norway and seems to have been applied in adjustment negotiations in the public sector recently.

The ongoing economic and social integration of Western Europe creates pressures in non-member states for major private organizations and also for public authorities "to go Europe". This pressure is usually more important in private industry than in the public sector. Nevertheless international cooperation will have to be intensified and ties will have to be strengthened, not only within Scandinavia. At the peak level, national union confederations such as LO and AF are already members of the European Trade Union Confederation (ETUC); and individual unions have joined the industrial committees affiliated with the ETUC.

The social dialogue as an instrument for the development of European social policy in general and for industrial relations policy in particular can be traced back to the mid-1980s at least. Success in terms of binding agreements signed by the social partners has been – and will most likely continue to be – rather limited.[34] So far, mainly some non-binding statements/points of view have been agreed on by the peak federations; binding agreements do not exist in public sector.

The Social Protocol of the Maastricht Treaty tries to strengthen and to improve this "new machinery" by stressing the principle of subsidiarity and by decentralizing the social dialogue from the peak to the sectoral level, i.e. from the macro to the meso level. The aim is to develop what has frequently been called the social dimension of the internal market. The social partners at the branch or industry level, e.g. the industrial committees and their counterparts on the employers' side, are encouraged to negotiate over a whole range of issues defined in the Social Protocol and to conclude voluntary collective contracts. The decisive question is of course whether or not this revival of the social dialogue and its shift to the meso level could provide an appropriate strategy for the development of social policy – or could even, in the long run, become a functional equivalent to collective bargaining at the national level.

The public sector has, for whatever reasons, not played a major role in European integration. It was not even mentioned in the Treaty of Rome and it is considered, at least for the time being, to be one of the last remaining domains of purely national regulation and without supranational interference.[35] One major difference between private industry and the public sector is that the major industrial relations achievement

---

34 The only exception is the framework agreement on parental leave signed in late 1995, which also covers the public sector. The problem is that national provisions are superior in the majority of member states and contentious issues such as income during parental leave are explicitly not dealt with.

35 General rules of competition and public procurement, however, imply that parts of the public sector become more exposed to national and international competition.

of the recent past, the Directive on European Works Councils, which had to be implemented at the national level by the autumn of 1996, does not apply to the public sector.

Nevertheless, national public sectors will be affected and considerably changed by the ongoing processes of integration – traffic, some state monopolies, communications, and the new European institutions such as the European Central Bank established in the early 1990s are some prominent examples. The fulfilment of the convergence criteria of the Maastricht Treaty and the forthcoming European Monetary Union have already created major strains for the national public sectors because they have led to major budgets cuts and a reduction in employment in some countries.

The public sector constitutes no exception within the lagging social dimension of the internal market, whose future very much hinges on the sectoral social dialogue. On the union side there are two organizations. One is the well-established European Public Service Committee (EPSC), one of the biggest and most important industrial committees of the ETUC; EPSC is what the European Commission calls a representative organization and fully recognized as a social partner. The other is the Confédération Européenne des Syndicats Indépendants (CESI), launched only in the early 1990s and still fighting for formal recognition after having failed the procedure once (Keller and Henneberger, 1995). EPSC faces some internal competition from CESI. The two associations do not cooperate at all, and the structure of their memberships is different. Recently AF changed its membership in the European confederations – leaving CESI and joining the ETUC.

Until now EPSC has had no equivalent on the employers' side as a partner for negotiations within the sectoral social dialogue. Like their counterparts in other countries, public employers' associations have, at least for the time being, been more reluctant to launch European associations than have unions – or have not been able to get organized at the European level.

The sectoral social dialogue will not cover all of the public sector but will presumably be further decentralized according to different levels and/or subjects. It is more likely to get started in highly internationalized parts and not in the core parts of public administration. Issues for the social dialogue and areas of mutual interest will not be wages, salaries, and working hours but are most likely to be so-called qualitative matters such as vocational training, retraining, mobility, and gender issues. Therefore, the sectoral social dialogue will, at least in the foreseeable future, not develop into an equivalent to collective bargaining because almost all the necessary structural requirements are missing.

Yet the development of organizational structures and modes of interest representation at the European level might achieve some important influence over processes of restructuring at the national level.

Last but not least, the ongoing discussion on the use of the so-called petroleum funds will be difficult to resolve. On the one hand, these funds could save something for the future, "for unborn generations", and create a strong financial basis for the period after the oil revenues have declined.[36] On the other hand, the whole project of solid, risk-free investments in foreign capital markets (in order to control domestic prices and wage inflation), which includes some sort of budgetary constraints for the time being, might prove hard to put into practice for political reasons: the instrument could easily be pre-empted because there are and will continue to be strong incentives for politicians to spend all available financial resources now or at least in the immediate future (maybe even for new programmes providing more and better social services for citizens at the municipal level) in order to gain power or be re-elected. The Norwegian experience of the recent past provides at least some empirical evidence for this view, arguing that it proves to be difficult to take long-term interests into consideration in the short term.

References

Adams, R .J. (1995) *Industrial Relations under Liberal Democracy. North America in comparative perspective.* Carolina, SC: University of South Carolina Press.

Bridgford, J. and Stirling, J. (1994) *Employee Relations in Europe.* Oxford: Blackwell.

Delsen, L. (1995) *Atypical Employment: An International Perspective. Causes, Consequences and Policy.* Groningen.

Dølvik, J.-E. (1994) Norwegian trade unionism at a crossroads? Paper presented to the IIRA 4th European Regional Congress, Plenary 1: *Transformation of the Nordic industrial relations in the European context,* Helsinki, pp. 69–116.

EIRR (1995) Norway 1995: The 1995 bargaining round. *European Industrial Relations Review* 260 (September): 15–16.

Friedrich Ebert-Stiftung/EPSC, eds (1996) *Industrial Relations Systems in the Public Sector in Europe.* Oslo.

Henneberger, F. (1996) Arbeitsmärkte und Beschäftigung im öffentlichen Dienst: Eine theoretische und empirische Analyse für die Bundesrepublik Deutschland. Dissertation. Universität Konstanz.

Høgsnes, G. (1994) *Collective Wage Bargaining and the Impact of Norms of Fairness. An Analysis Based on the Norwegian Experience,* 2 vols. Oslo: University of Oslo Institute for Social Research, Report 94:8.

36 Let us assume after the turn of the century or so although there are some realistic hopes that either natural gas could become an equivalent large-scale natural resource to be exploited or that newly discovered oil fields could be exploited by means of some still unknown, improved techniques.

Høgsnes, G. (1995) Wage determination and the male–female wage gap – the case of Norway. *Comparative Social Research.*

Ingebrigtsen, B. (1994) *Wage Negotiations in Norwegian Municipalities. Bargainings Between "Parts of the Firm".* Olso: IFIM-paper 5/94.

Keller, B. (1993) *Arbeitspolitik des öffentlichen Sektors.* Baden-Baden: Nomos Verlagsgesellschaft.

Keller, B. (1996) Between unification and Europeanization. Continuity despite discontinuities in public sector labor relations in Germany. Paper presented at the ARAN Workshop "The Restructuring of Employment Relations in Public Services in Western Europe. A Comparative Analysis", Rome, 25–28 January.

Keller, B. and Henneberger, F. (1995) Europäische Arbeitsbeziehungen im öffentlichen Dienst. Verbandliche Organisation und Vermittlung von Interessen, Industrielle Beziehungen. *Zeitschrift für Arbeit, Organisation und Management* 2: 128–155.

Kolberg, J. E. (ed.) (1992) *Between Work and Social Citizenship.* Armonk and London: Sharpe.

Lane, J. E. (1993) *The Public Sector. Concepts, Models and Approaches.* London: Sage.

Martin, B. (1993) *In the Public Interest? Privatisation and Public Sector Reform.* London: ZED Books.

OECD (ed.) (1993) *Private Pay for Public Work: Performance-related Pay for Public Sector Managers.* Paris.

Olsen, J. P. (1996) *Norway: Reluctant Reformer, Slow Learner – or Another Triumph of the Tortoise?* Bergen: LOS-center Notat 96/37.

Olsen, J. P. and Peters, G. (1994) *Lessons from Experience. Experimental Learning in Administrative Reforms in Eight Countries.* Oslo: ARENA Working Paper No. 3.

Ozaki, M. (1990) Labour relations in the public sector. In R. Blanpain (ed.), *Comparative Labour Law and Industrial Relations in Industrialized Market Economies*, vol. 2, 4th and revised edn. Deventer: Kluwer, pp. 221–244.

Pedersen, P. J. (1995) Intra-Nordic and Nordic–EC labour mobility. In J. Fagerberg and L. Lundberg (eds), *European Economic Integration: A Nordic Perspective.* Aldershot: Avebury, pp. 223–248.

Peijpe,T. van (1996) Public sector collective bargaining in the Netherlands and Nordic countries. *International Journal of Comparative Labour Law and Industrial Relations* 12: 25–41.

Rose, R. ed. (1985) *Public Employment in Western Nations.* Cambridge: Cambridge University Press.

Royal Norwegian Ministry of Finance (1995) *The Revised National Budget 1995.* Oslo.

Royal Norwegian Ministry of Government Administration (1993) *Public Sector Management Reform in Norway – Recent Developments.* Reprint of the Norwegian contribution to the OECD 1993 survey of public sector management developments, Oslo.

Royal Norwegian Ministry of Labour and Government Administration (1991) *Measuring Public Sector Performance in Norway.* Oslo: Report, May.

Sivesind, K., Kalleberg, R., Hovde, S. and Fennefoss, A. (1995) A social-democratic order under pressure: Norwegian employment relations in the eighties. In R. Locke, T. Kochan, and M. Piore (eds), *Employment Relations in a Changing World Economy.* Cambridge, MA and London: MIT Press, pp. 297–324.

Stieber, J. (1989) Introduction: Co-operation and conflict in public service labour relations. In A. Gladstone et al. (eds), *Current Issues in Labor Relations. An International Perspective.* Berlin and New York: De Gruyter, pp. 267–276.

Swedish Agency for Government Employees (1996) *The Central Government Sector in Sweden.* Stockholm.

Torp, H. (1995) *Norway Baseline Study.* Oslo: ISF Ms.

Treu,T. and de Felice, A. (1990) The future of labor relations in the public service. In W. J. Dercksen (ed.) *The Future of Industrial Relations in Europe. Proceedings of a Conference in Honour of Prof. W. Albeda.* The Hague: SDU uitgeverij, pp. 65–75.

Visser, J. (1990) *In Search of Inclusive Unionism.* Deventer: Kluwer.

Winchester, D. and Bach, St (1995) The state: the public sector. In P. Edwards (ed.) *Industrial Relations. Theory and Practice in Britain.* Oxford: Blackwell, pp. 304–334.

Chapter 9

Modernization of the labour market organization

– Scandinavian and anglo-saxon experiences in an international benchmarking perspective

Frieder Naschold and Robert Arnkil

1. Welfare State, Modernization and the Labour Market

Whereas the 1980s were characterised by restructuring of many private-sector industries, in the 1990s scientific and political interest in the OECD countries has increasingly turned towards the restructuring of the public sector. Led by English-speaking countries such as Great Britain and New Zealand, followed by some Scandinavian states, an ever increasing number of European states are now riding the wave of public sector modernization. The spectrum of themes and approaches ranges from traditional cost-cutting, productivity and privatization strategies, to questions of quality assurance and personnel development and the increasingly acute questions of devolving central state responsibilities to civil society.

For Norway the question of the development of the public sector is important if only for the sheer size of it. Norway has one of the biggest and comprehensive public sectors in the world. What makes the issue even more compelling is the fact that in the modern global competition the public and private sectors are more and more interconnected and there is also growing competition between different public sector regimes.

This article seeks to describe and analyse the recent experiences gained during this restructuring process, focusing on the public sector developments in selected OECD-countries – particularly the Nordic countries and Great Britain together with New Zealand – at both central and local government levels.

We are concerned with two fundamental issues in the public sector evaluation: 1) The effectiveness and efficiency[1] of the public sector and

1 Following standard terms of management science and economics by *effectiveness* we refer to the degree of goal achievement and by *efficiency* we refer to input-output ratios.

2) the ability to learn. After Fujimoto (1996) we call these the *productive capability* and the *evolutionary capability* of the public sector.

From the international and Norwegian debate we can identify four scenarios or hypothesis concerning productive and evolutionary capability of the public sector in Norway:

1) The issue is irrelevant for Norway because of "Manna from heaven" (see chapter 2), i.e. the favourable economic situation – in essence the oil revenues – serve as a buffer against a need to concern oneself with public expenditures, productive or evolutionary capabilities.
2) The Norwegian welfare state is big, but also efficient and exhibits good evolutionary capability so there is no need change either path or pace.
3) The Norwegian welfare state is big and inefficient, but is catching up. It is a second mover in modernization, assimilating experiences in a slow, but wise way, like Aesop's tortoise (Olsen, 1996).
4) The Norwegian welfare state is big and inefficient, but is not catching up ("the tortoise is too slow") and thus there would be a need to enhance both productive and evolutionary processes.

---

1) Manna from Heaven – the modernization issues are irrelevant for Norway
2) Welfare State Efficiency – Norwegian public sector has found its recipe
3) Catching up – Norway has been slow but is adequately catching up
4) Welfare State Conservatism – Norwegian public sector is ineffective and not catching up

---

Figure 9.1 Four Scenarios of the Norwegian Welfare State Naschold-Arnkil, 1997

The study places the public sector of Norway and the Norwegian labour market administration in particular in an international comparative context against these scenarios and provides a multi-level quantitative and qualitative benchmarking overview. Concepts, structural assessment and quantitative and qualitative data are used at three levels: overall macro level – Norway in the context of OECD developments – sectorial macro-labour market level – the Norwegian labour market administration compared with other LMA:s in Europe- and sectorial micro-labour market level – a comparative case-study of Norwegian employment offices with employment offices in Europe and New Zealand, with particular interest in the key function of placement service. We proceed in the following way:

In chapter I we analyze the macro level: what are the major trends and issues in public sector in selected OECD-countries and give the first assessment of the position of Norway on the macro level. The databases here are different independent studies.

In chapter II we look at the sectorial level: what are the different governance structures and what is the performance of labour market authorities in selected countries. The findings position the Norway labour market authority in perspective. The databases here are both different independent studies and interviews and data collection by the authors.

In chapter III we look at the local level: the practices of local employment offices and they are benchmarked quantitatively and qualitatively. The main database here is in-depth interviews in the local offices performed conjointly by the authors.

Finally, in chapter IV we return to the four scenarios and assess the modernization of the Norwegian public sector particularly in the light of the labour market authority.

2. Modernization of the Public Sector in the OECD: Trends and Issues – an overall assessment

The traditional, vertically integrated form of public sector organization

Modernization and reform processes always include a critically viewed reference model to be surpassed. In the European context this can be called the Traditional Model of the state and public government.

The inadequacies of the traditional, i.e. bureaucratic, rule-oriented conception of the public sector identified by the New Public Management Movement lead to corresponding demands for change. The most important of these are governance by objective and results, performance management and results budgeting (management by results), contract management of autonomous "results centres", contracting out and the formation of quasi-markets. (figure 9.2).

While the critique of the underlying mechanisms of bureaucratic governance by rule may well be convincing – and at the very least the alternative concepts put forward appear to have lost none of their attraction – neither apologetic studies nor the ideology-critical studies are sufficient to evaluate the development trends of the public sector. What is required in addition is an evaluation of real development trends on the basis of empirical evidence.

Since the beginning or middle of the 1980s, and then even more so from the end of that decade the Scandinavian countries have initiated a process of internal modernization of their public sector under a social-democratic

Traditional model	New Public Management
1. Strong vertical integration: the unity of programming, implementation and financing	Decentralization; more autonomy to result units
2. A wide horizontal range of products (services) (conglomerate structure)	Networks of semiautonomous result units (matrix structure), public-private mix
3. Steering by rules	Management by results/objectives
4. Universal selection criteria	Decentralized criteria
5. Functional and hierarchical organization (high level of vertical and functional division of labour)	Authority delegated to semiautonomous result/ market segment units, central administration downsized, multiskilling
6. Unified and centrally organized personnel and finances -functions	Delegated to the result/ market segment units
7. Internal promotion, incentives and remuneration	Result-payment and incentives

Adapted from Naschold et al., 1996

Figure. 9.2 The Traditional Model of Public Government and New Public Management

hegemony. From the start of the 1990s this process was pushed forward under the influence of conservative parties, which added market-based steering mechanisms. This development came to a slowdown with the swift onset of economic crisis in 1991/92: the urgent questions of the budget deficit and the problem of mass unemployment redefined the societal priorities. The steps implemented until then were subjected to critical reflection. Voices were raised, some calling for an acceleration of the existing transformation dynamics, others favouring more stability and status quo.

The challenges to reform the public sector

Since the 1980s the public sector in many OECD countries has been undergoing far-reaching processes of restructuring. The dynamics and orientation of this restructuring have been determined by the confluence of three factor-complexes: economic crisis, tensions within the institutional framework of the welfare state and party-political mobilisation processes.

The mainstream of public sector modernization is nowadays oriented towards the views and strategies of the New Public Management Movement (Caiden, 1991) (taken here as a combination of public choice theories and managerialism, cf. Aucoin, 1992), whose critique centres on the size and, more importantly, the structure of the public sector, focusing on the prevailing regulatory mechanisms, such as governance by rule, the functional division of labour according to the single-task-related workshop principle, pronounced hierarchy, the lack of process-chain-linked cooperation and the lack of strategic management.

There is a common core to public sector modernization in the OECD countries, one which transcends the convergencies and divergencies of the programmatic level: on the one hand the functional shifts in the strategic role of the government from producer to enabler, on the other a systematic decoupling and recomposition of the programming, realization and financing of service production. These two new constitutive principles open up design options which go beyond traditional bureaucratic forms of task processing. These include a distinction between politics and managerialist steering, leaner and radically decentralised organization structures, the formation of diverse results oriented units with operative autonomy, emphasis on the internal and external competitive environment in ordering and purchasing services, and in particular systematic customer/citizen quality feedback systems. A new best practice model of public sector task fulfilment appears to be forming around these elements.

Since the mid 1980s public sector modernization has also been subjected to two fundamental criticisms: the reform strategies are considered to be a cyclical passing trend within the public administration without a significant increase in efficiency compared with traditional bureaucratic systems; and, in contrast to the first criticism, current modernization strategies are considered to be a danger to democracy and to be dismantling the welfare state. Both criticisms can point to considerable supportive evidence. The reform efforts during the 1970s largely proved to be passing trends with little impact. In a number of OECD countries modernization strategies have indeed involved numerous measures which have restricted democracy and dismantled the welfare state, either for ideological or party political mobilisation reasons or in the form of a cut-back strategy motivated by fiscal policy concerns. It is particularly this latter criticism that has raised doubts in Norway about the feasibility of modernization.

But developments in the OECD countries also exhibit a number of cases in which efforts to reform the public sector have been very successful without negative effects on democracy or redistribution: rising productivity performance by distinguishing between agencies and central government departments; utilisation of the MbR[2] negotiating process as a step towards

2 MbR = Management by Results, MbO = Management by Objectives. In different countries these concepts are used sometimes with different emphasis, but essentially meaning same kinds of developments. MbR emphaisises more the outcomes, MbO (an earlier version) more goals and objectives.

total quality management; utilising MbR systems in the form of interactive co-planning with citizens in technical and social areas; integrating MbR systems with systematic customer/citizen quality feedback systems; distinguishing between programming, financing and implementation in the sense of various forms of the "enabling authority"; interaction between results orientation, regulation and competition in local government services; integration of MbR systems and organizational outsourcing with the aim of stimulating institutional competition; extending the opportunities for employee participation and further development of industrial relations.

All these examples have achieved a successful balance of increased organizational effectiveness and efficiency without negative redistributive effects on product quality and working conditions, whereby organizational design and contextual characteristics can be precisely specified.

At the same time, these examples serve to warn against the promises of easy solutions. The simplistic paths of exclusive internal modernization, privatisation or unilinear social devolution lead astray. The reality is always a complex mixture of government regulation, economic competition and social devolution.

Equally, all the above examples also indicate the ambivalence of public sector modernization. The departure from administrative rule steering renders the state regulatory system both more flexible and more precarious, and is thus conducive both to regressive development paths such as to dismantling the welfare state and restricting democracy, ideological privatisation and new-taylorist work intensification, and to progressive modernization parts involving higher productive and distributive efficiency, greater decentralisation and improved opportunities for participation. Thus the fate of public sector modernization depends on the specific development dynamic of the reform process. This in turn is very largely politically determined.

It is with these thoughts in mind that we want to take a closer look at the developments in some of the OECD-countries.

Public sector reform trends in the OECD: Profiles and processes

Contrary to the official view taken by the OECD as an organization, there is no evidence of a linear homogeneous trend in public sector development. Rather, four regulatory regimes of welfare state modernization can be distinguished within the OECD.[3]

Great Britain and New Zealand have largely followed the logic of the

3 Naschold 1996

private sector, their strategy being based on the three elements of privatisation/reduction in the size of the public sector, market oriented organizational alternatives and neo-taylorist managerialism. Denmark and the Netherlands are on the development path characterised by far-reaching devolution of government activities to civil society together with a broad-based introduction of competitive elements in market-related areas and results steering in the administry areas. In countries such as Sweden, Finland and Norway, the results steering regime is still predominant, increasingly in conjunction with competitive instruments and selective decentralisation and privatization projects. Such heterogeneous countries as Japan, Germany, the USA and Australia have in common the clear predominance of administrative rule steering, having largely rejected results steering (except in the USA) and the selective reduction in the scope of state activity by means of competitive instruments and privatisation programmes.

There is not just one, but rather – as a mixture of international trends and local factors – a limited plurality of development paths of public sector modernization within the OECD. Indeed, as far as future developments are concerned, convergence seems less likely than centrifugal development trends within regulatory models. This is because both the optimality points and the risk areas are very different in a predominantly market regulation system with results steering elements than in a developed system with extended participation by civil society and in systems in which results steering is supplemented by competitive instruments, and of course in classical rule steering with privatisation components. Moreover, contrary to the assumptions made by the OECD, the plurality of regulatory regimes makes it impossible to derive and justify an immanent ranking of these regimes or to presuppose that one specific regime (in particular the anglo-saxon model) is necessarily more efficient than the others.

Norway: Incremental internal modernization

Norway is one of the leading OECD countries with regard to welfare state development: in 4th place in general government spending (1989) and 3rd place regarding public sector employment as a share of total employment (1991). Yet, due to its primary-good-oriented economic structure and the steady deterioration in its terms of trade, the country's productive basis faces the threat of erosion. Due to its North Sea oil output, though, Norway has fared better in terms of macroeconomic performance than its Nordic neighbours prior to and during the recent crisis. Norway is in last place in the OECD ranking with respect to net indebtedness, for instance. To some extent this economic and welfare state structure is reflected in Norwegian public sector reform policies. Compared with the other OECD countries Norway has a very distinct modernization profile, consisting of three characteristic complexes:

- Public sector reform in Norway concentrates almost entirely on internal modernization and involves very little by way of privatization, competitive strategies or reliance on quasi-market mechanisms. In line with the discussion in the Nordic countries, and particularly following the example set by Sweden, internal modernization is taken to mean relatively autonomous agencies with performance management, results budgeting, public corporations and free commune experiments.
– Together with Denmark and the Netherlands, and following a long tradition of its own, the modernization of public management in Norway is complemented with reform of the labour process and human relations issues, although the reforms in these are rather limited in scope.
– Public sector reform in Norway has been incremental in nature, without quantum leaps, decidedly moderate, and lacking a radical design; in many ways it is a policy of "second move": examples of this include governance by results and the budgetary reform begun in 1992/93 which followed developments in Sweden and Finland.

A recent Norwegian study clearly corroborates this picture. In 1993 a comprehensive international comparison on modernization was made by the Bertelsmann Foundation (1993)[4] rating the democracy and efficiency of local government on seven key dimensions in several countries. Using the same evaluation dimensions and criteria the Norwegian study (Baldersheim and Ögård 1996) arrives at the result that in the lead are Phoenix, USA and Nacka, Sweden. The three Norwegian municipalities rank lowest with a German city against the other Bertelsmann cases (see Table 9.1).

The modernization profile of the Norwegian public sector is more readily understood when its development dynamic is taken into account. The ability to cope financially with high welfare state spending and economic disequilibrium by virtue of the wealth of natural resources, the limited hegemony of the ruling party in Norwegian politics (social democratic minority government against a fragmented non-socialist camp), the lack of incentives to pursue a redistribution policy involving social polarisation in view of the social homogeneity of the population structure, absence of a distinct performance crisis, the relatively weak presence of the forces for modernization within the state apparatus (here in the Ministry of Government Administration), without strong support from

4 Carl Bertelsmann Prize 1993

Table 9.1 Norwegian municipalities against Bertelsmann-network cities

	USA	FRG	Finland	Denmark	Sweden	Norway A	Norway B	Norway C
Performance under democratic control	100	56	58	70	78	52	60	52
Citizen and customer orientation	100	54	58	68	56	27	33	17
Cooperation btw. politics and administration	95	45	55	52	87	40	64	56
Decentralised leadership	98	28	64	55	79	26	43	14
Controlling and information systems	93	28	35	32	64	27	21	4
Staff potential	91	33	35	50	51	26	41	21
Innovativeness	86	34	54	60	53	28	35	30
Total/rank	663/1	278/6	359/4	387/3	468/2	226/8	297/5	194/7

Baldersheim and Ögård, 1996

the Cabinet Office and the Ministry of Finance – as in Sweden – and the Ministry of Finance and a permanent ministerial committee – as in Finland permit precisely the type of incremental, moderate internal modernization which Norway has experienced. To say the least: Norway is more a laggard, and definitely not a leader in Public Sector reform within the OECD countries.

3. The Governance of Labour Market Policies – a Sectorial Comparison

Macro-structure and micro processes: A reference model to examine different constellations

We use the following model (see figure 9.3) to describe and evaluate the different constellations in the labour markets and labour market authorities in the countries studied.

In the macro constellation, the developments in the primary market play a decisive role. The long term trend in the labour markets has been towards rising complexity and segmentation combined with difficult employment problems. In the face of these challenges labour administrations in various countries have started to modernize their steering and services. In this development the state and the labour administrations exhibit various degrees of centralization vs. decentralization in the modernization process. In the previous passages we have already seen that Norway has been a rather reluctant reformer.

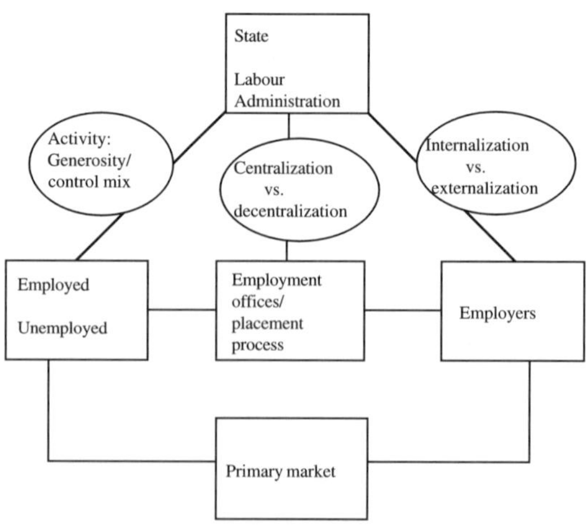

Figure 9.3 The macro-sectorial-micro model Naschold-Arnkil, 1996

On the demand-side (employers) the different countries exhibit different degrees of internalization vs. externalization of the employment/ unemployment problems. Traditionally, the Nordic countries have displayed a high degree of internalization, but in the face of quite different economic situations and pressures, the Nordic scene has begun to diverge to some degree. On the supply side the generosity/ control-mix of benefits differs. In Great Britain, a stringent control approach prevails whereas the Nordic countries exhibit different degrees of a generous regime. In the face of huge public deficits, all other Nordic countries besides Norway have been under pressure on this issue.

Looking at the micro level we can identify the local employment offices of the labour administrations. At the heart of the local office is the placement process, the key function mediating supply and demand in different kinds of labour market and employment contexts. All the aspects mentioned above have their effect on the conditions of the processes on the local level and the different regimes and countries present different solutions to the challenges of modernization also on the local level. Here also the question of public vs. private services plays a role. The micro processes are dealt with in section III.

Generosity-control mix

The countries differ in the generosity/ control scene, although there has been a tendency of increasing control in all of the countries. Still there is a distinct difference in the regimes of Great Britain and the Nordic countries. In Britain, it is the customer who has to prove he is active in finding employment. In the Nordic countries, one could say, it is up to the employment officer to prove to the customer that he/she has been active in finding employment for the customer, or at least has a good plan to do so.

The control element is traditionally strongest in Great Britain and there is presently a new step in introducing even more pressure on the job-seekers (via the so-called job-seekers allowance to be adopted in 1996). This will mean a strict approach to proving one is really available for the labour market and showing evidence for active search for employment. The availability will be tested by giving a job offer more or less straight away at the beginning. The people are called in every two weeks in Britain to give proof of their activity. This is something quite different from the Nordic countries, where one can stay on for months without anybody "bothering" you. The job-seekers allowance will also mean a considerable drop in the level of benefits because mortgage will not be included and the earnings of the spouse are taken into account.

Denmark has traditionally been the most generous on benefits and various schemes, but there, too, discussion on control has been rising. There is societal weariness on the extremely high tax rate and even a new phenomena of people "turning in" each other for misuse of benefits. On the practical level, very little pressure was exercised. After being registered (for benefits) a newcomer would be asked to come for discussions after a month. After that he/ she will be called in only if deemed to belong to a "risk group". A customer can, in practice, spend several years in active labour market programs and maintain a comfortable standard of living.

An international comparison (Blöndahl and Pearson, 1995), taking as its main point the length of benefit entitlements (see definition under Table 9.2) produced a following rank order in generosity of benefits (see Table 9.2): 1) Denmark 2) Netherlands 3) Belgium 4) Norway 5) France 6) Portugal and Spain 7) Austria 8) Sweden and Finland.

So Denmark, Netherlands and Belgium are at the top with Norway rather close. Sweden and Finland occupy the "upper middle ground". In the recent years changes have been taking place in the generosity-levels of several countries, usually towards more stringency. Some measures have been taken in Sweden and Finland to cut down expenditures on benefits, but not much pressure has been put on the customers. One could say that in Britain the customer has to prove to the officials that he/she is doing something and in the Nordic countries it is still vice versa.

The structural profiles: A comparison of labour market authorities[5]

National labour ministries and the labour market authorities subordinate to them are particularly well suited to the purpose of identifying central government development trends from an international comparative perspective. All the labour ministries in the OECD countries selected for analysis are classical central government departments employing the classical instruments of legislation (for the purpose of regulation) and

5 Depending on data availability, the comparison encompasses five to seven countries: Norway, Great Britain, Sweden, Finland, Austria; in some cases Denmark and the Netherlands. The conclusions drawn are based on numerous documents and a large number of interviews conducted with representatives of the national labour ministries and labour market authorities. It was not possible within the scope of this paper to completely standardise the data, thus permitting a full quantitative comparison. Although relatively similar definitions are used in national statistics, the underlying labour market operations are often rather different. For this reason the findings are compared summarily and using ordinal scales and structural profiles.

Table 9.2 Summary Measure of Benefit Entitlements, 1961-1991

	1961	1971	1981	1991	Order/91
Australia	17	14	22	27	10
Austria	20	23	29	31	7
Belgium	42	41	45	43	3
Canada	22	21	25	28	9
Denmark	20	34	54	52	1
Finland	5	8	23	29	8
France	25	24	31	37	5
Germany	30	29	29	28	9
Greece	7	7	7	17	14
Ireland	17	17	28	29	8
Italy	4	2	1	3	17
Japan	12	13	9	9	16
Netherlands	13	48	48	51	2
New Zealand	42	27	27	26	11
Norway	4	5	29	39	4
Portugal	0	0	9	34	6
Spain	9	12	28	34	6
Sweden	4	6	25	29	8
Switzerland	2	1	13	22	12
UK	24	25	24	18	13
US	17	11	15	11	15

Blöndahl & Pearson 1995

Definition. The index is a simple average of *replacement rates for three durations* (first year, second and third year, and *fourth and fifth year*) crossed by *three family situations* (single, *dependent spouse*, and with spouse *at work*) and *two earnings levels* (average earnings and two-thirds average earnings). The worker is 40 years old and has worked without interruptions since age 18. After any UI entitlement is exhausted, it is assumed that the person is entitled to the appropriate rate of benefit in unemployment assistance and guaranteed minimum income programmes. For countries where unemployed insurance is voluntary, the replacement rate is a weighted average for members and non-members of unemployed insurance funds, the weights depending on actual coverage rates. Further details of the construction of the index are given in OECD (1994b), which also discusses the limitations of the index.
SOURCE: OECD Database on Unemployment Benefit Entitlements and Replacement Rates.

money (for the purpose of monetary transfer). At the same time, in formal organizational terms they also have the most highly decentralised subordinate administrative structure in the form of regional and local labour market authorities and administration (employment offices etc.). In view of the specific requirements and organizational structures of the labour ministries, many countries have attempted to combine the rigour of rule steering with the responsiveness of decentralised base units. It is therefore not surprising that in all the OECD countries processes of change are particularly pronounced in the ministries of labour.

The British labour market authority matches perfectly the profile of central government as a whole in the UK compared with that in the other OECD countries. The Employment Department (ED) Group with its

Employment Service Agency is a highly centralised and hierarchical administration with, formally at least, a decentralised network of field offices (see Figure 9.4). Over the years the Employment Service Agency, in particular, has generated a highly developed MbR system in which elements of strategic management (retrograde planning, integration of resources and strategy) play a prominent role. Besides the hierarchical setting of conditions, the main instruments of overall steering include contractual relations between the ministry and agencies and, increasingly, the inclusion of market mechanisms and competitive instruments, especially in the areas of training (notably the Training and Enterprise Councils). Work organization, personnel deployment and skill enhancement are all in line with the labour policy regime of neo-taylorist managerialism mentioned above.

The Swedish labour market authority has a highly decentralised and non-hierarchical process structure. The Labour Market Agency (AMS) operates within the framework of a broadly defined mandate ("mission") and in the context of a loose form of results steering in which programmes are subjected to intense examination in the course of the budgetary process after a three-year period. The most important steering instruments are the contractual relations between the ministry and agency and pronounced self-regulation in provincial and local labour market organizations within a broad contractual and hierarchical framework. The central government has been halved from 800 to 400 in ten years, much more decisively than in the other countries. The regional (district) middle level is very lean and the employment offices did not regard it as particularly influential aspect of their work. A combination of organizational development and TQM is the motor behind a relatively continuous processes of organizational learning in Sweden. The quality work in the Swedish LMA is in a pilot phase using to a large degree the Swedish Quality Award concepts (based largely on the Malcom Balridge award). In their approach the Swedes emphasize self-assessment and a decentralized approach. The central government is rather in the role of a facilitator than setting standards. Private competition has not played a major role in Sweden although it has been allowed since 1993.

The Finnish labour market authority has a relatively highly centralised and hierarchical tradition, being the only case in which the ministry and the labour market authority are fully integrated. This tradition has had a profound influence during the introductory phase of MbR steering and MbO budgeting. More recently an increasing number of decentralised initiatives have made progress: experiments in work organization and skill enhancement, process enhancement measures and attempts to further decentralise the entire organizational structure. These developments have

	Great Britain	Sweden	Finland	Denmark	Norway	Austria
1) Legal status	Agency	Agency	Ministry	Agency	Agency	Agency
2) Relationship politics – administra-tion	Contract within hierarchy	Broad frames and mission	Contract with MbR	Contract with MbO	Hierarchy/contract with MbO	Hierarchy/ contract
3) Delegation - decentralization	Centralized	Decentralized	Centralized with distinct decentraliz -ing tendencies	Centralized with decentralizing tendencies	Centralized with decentralizing tendencies	Centralized
4) Formal integration of labour market policy	No	Yes/no	No	Yes	Yes	Yes
5) Steering system	MbR	MbR	MbR	MbO/frames	MbR/MbO	Rule steering
6) Budgeting system	Advanced result budgeting	Mission/result budgeting	Result budgeting	Result budgeting	Result budgeting	Line item budgeting

Figure 9.4 The Governance of Employment Policy in six European countries

Figure 9.4 continued...

Figure 9.4 The Governance of Employment Policy in six European countries *(continued)*

	Great Britain	Sweden	Finland	Denmark	Norway	Austria
7) Strategic management (development level 1-4)	2-3	2-3	1-2	1-2	1-2	1-2
8) Process qualification	Continuous short-term MbR change cycles	TQM and organi-zation development	Partial TQM and local improvements	Partial TQM and local improvements	Partial TQM and fragmented local improvements	Fragmented local experiments
9) Market/ competition instruments	Privatization/ business-led labour market institution	Marginal privatization under public conditions	Limited privatization and competition instruments	Some privatization	No privatization and competitive instruments	No privatization and competitive instruments
10) Work organization	Neo-taylorism	New forms of organization	Bureaucratic work organization with medium depth new developments	Bureaucratic work organization with medium depth new developments	Bureaucratic work organization with some new developments	Bureaucratic work organization with a few new developments
11) Qualification level of personnel	Low	High/medium	Medium	Medium	Medium/low	Low/medium
12) Trends of debate	Internal debate on decentrali-zation of the system	Further decentralization	Decentralization and local initiatives	Centrally driven reforms and some decentralization	Centrally driven reforms and some decentralization	Internal debate and first steps towards decentralization

Naschold/Arnkil, 1997

produced a question on the real value added by the middle level. The general trend has been to strengthen the local employment offices. In terms of TQM/ quality work a comprehensive customer-feedback system, affording quality analysis down to employment office level, has been introduced. Process control and internal customer developments have played a much lesser role. New unit structures emphasizing customer-segment orientation (demand-supply split) (f.ex. special employer-service units) have been launched all over the country. Private services in employment services were enabled since 1994, but they have not had a major impact so far, largely due to the slump of the economy. Discussions have begun on the further use of market mechanisms. Benchmarking and competitive instruments in terms of comprehensive comparisons of effectiveness, efficiency, performance, quality and economy of both districts and employment offices have been introduced.

The Danish labour market authority adopted their management concept, MbR (called monitoring by goals and frames) from the Swedes but have a clearly more centralized system than Sweden. The central government and the regional (county/ district) are strong leaving the local level to a rather unindependent role. The Ministry decides on the goals and frames and these are discussed in the national and county boards. The general breakdown of resources is done with objective criteria, i.e. rate of unemployment and the like. There is not much negotiable leeway in this. In Denmark there is a considerably high degree of involvement of politicians and interest groups (unions) in the matters. The involvement of the labour market partners and municipalities on the county level is high. In terms of quality work or OD, Denmark has been rather hesitant. Quality work, done here and there in the counties, has concentrated mainly on process standardization, much in the same way as Norway.

The Norwegian labour market administration (LMA) has up till now had a more centralized and hierarchical structure than Finland and especially Sweden. In the last few years, under new leadership modernization reforms have been launched. Nevertheless, the MbR of the Norwegian LMA is more limited in process interaction between the different levels and elaboration of result measurements particularly for the local level than Sweden and Finland. In general the decentralization tendencies are less pronounced than in Finland and particularly Sweden. There are reform programs under way like quality work, which is a centrally driven project with an emphasis on process control. It is more concentrated on internal processes (like also Denmark) whereas the Swedes have a more comprehensive approach and the Finns have focused on outside customer feedback. The customer feedback of Norway is a centrally executed survey which affords aggregate analysis with limited participation and analysis for local levels.

A Norwegian study on the Norwegian LMA ("Arbeidsmarkedsetat-93") corroborates our picture. The report suggests that the Norwegian LMA needs reorganization particularly so that local employment offices would get more power. According to the report, to make LMA more effective, a better system of result steering is needed. The report says that a more decentralized organization is suggested to enhance the capability to adopt to local needs. Resources should be shifted from central administration to lower levels. The organization needs a better system of information so that goals and results can be measured. Although reorganization is needed, the report sees that the LMA needs a three level organization, but the regional level must give the local levels better information and help them to develop their organization and staff. The employment offices need also better cooperation with partners at the local level. A special mention was made of employers and training. It is also noteworthy for the purposes of our analysis on the micro-level that the report does not put any special emphasis on LMA's role in filling vacancies, but rather mentions it as a function among functions.

The Austrian labour market authorities is traditional administrative departments in terms of structure and processes: highly centralised and hierarchical. Although the role of the labour market authority is performed by agencies, the relations between ministry and agency are classically bureaucratic and not contractual. Rule steering systems have retained their predominance together with traditional line-item budgeting. The most important instrument remains legislation and hierarchical command relations as the form of intervention to be used for both general and individual cases.

The aggregate performance: Innovation, effectiveness and process dynamics

Closer analysis of the national profiles enables some initial conclusions to be drawn regarding the three hypotheses underlying the Scandinavian discussion mentioned above (cf. the Scandinavian studies by Henning and Ramström, 1989 and Niklasson and Thomsmark, 1994). The country comparison reveals two distinct modernization constellations: the innovative reform countries Sweden and Great Britain on the one hand, and the "traditionalists" such as to some extent Norway and clearly Austria on the other. Finland is characterised by a parallelism of the old and the new, and is located between the two major constellations with respect to almost all the dimensions of restructuring.

It is also evident that the modernization constellation contains two very different "innovation regimes": Great Britain, with its highly centralised and neo-taylorist steering system, with mass production and continuous rationalisation through rationalisation drives, etc., and Sweden with its highly decentralised system, a high level of local self-regulation, a strategy of flexible specialisation with continuous intra-organizational improvement processes on the other. Thus the international comparison shows that it is not a question of a simple dichotomy between mass production and flexible specialisation. Rather there are three different regulatory regimes within the labour market authorities: the two innovation regimes just mentioned and the traditional regime of centralised rule steering.

What can be said about the effectiveness and efficiency of these various regulatory regimes? An initial insight into this extremely complex question can be gained on the basis of national labour market data and of interviews conducted by the authors with representatives of national authorities (here including Germany and the Netherlands).

As far as workload is concerned, Finland, Austria and Denmark carry the heaviest burdens; Sweden and Norway the lightest, with Great Britain and Germany in between. In terms of efficiency – which is clearly closely linked to workload – Denmark, Great Britain and Germany are in the lead by a long way, followed by Sweden and Finland in the middle ground, ahead of Norway, Austria and the Netherlands. As far as effectiveness is concerned – i.e. with respect to the strategic variables of the filling vacancy ratio and job placement rates – Great Britain, Germany (and probably Denmark, too) lead the group, followed by Sweden and Finland. Austria, Norway and Netherlands bring up the rear. In terms of market share (ratio of placements to all appointments in the economy)[7], Sweden, Great Britain and Germany lead, with Finland, Norway and Denmark in the middle group and Austria and Netherlands in the rear.

Drawing together the results for effectiveness and efficiency in an overall qualitative appraisal, the ranking is approximately as follows:

High Performance: Great Britain, Germany, Denmark
Medium Performance: Sweden, Finland
Low Performance: Norway, Netherlands, Austria

7 The market share figures are from Walwei, 1994 (which uses 1990-1992 data), with Finland (1992) added. Appointment figures are often national estimates. Market share can be calculated in many different ways. In the recent years labour administrations have been using utilization rates, etc. derived from different kinds of surveys.

Table 9.3 Workload, Effectiveness, Efficiency and Market share in six LMAs[6]

Country	Work load			Effectiveness		Efficiency	Market share
	Vacancies/ employee	Job-seekers/ employee	Working population/ employee	Placements/ vacancies (%)	Job-seekers placed/employee	Placements/ employee (%)	Placements/ appointments (%)
Austria	90,1	209,9	1393,5	23,3	9,8	20,4	12
Netherlands	41,0	133,0	879,5	53,1	15,9	21,2	12
Great Britain	64,1	92,2	1139,9	70,7	57,4	46,6	24
Sweden	60,1	61,4	419,2	48,0	67,0	29,4	25
Finland	122,6	205,4	992,2	47	42	38,3	20
Norway	66,8	26,0	480,6	35	20	20	17
Denmark	74,0	446,0	1720,3	70,3	-	52,9	18
Germany	49,4	103,8	636,6	67,6	47,2	50,9	24

(Sources: BMAS 1992 and Walwei 1994, modifications by Naschold and Arnkil)

6 Following standard management science and economics terms by effectiveness we refer to the degree of goal achievement (here interpreted as placements to vacancies) and by efficiency we refer to input-output ratios (here interpreted as placements by employee ratio).

The figure can be interpreted into an ordinal scale:

Figure 9.5

Country	Work load			Effectiveness		Efficiency	Market share
	Vacancies/ employee	Job-seekers/ employee	Working population/ employee	Placements/ vacancies	Job-seekers placed/ employee	Placements/ employee	Placements/ appointments
Austria	High	High	High	Low	Low	Medium	Low
Netherlands	Low	High	Medium	Medium	Low	Low	Low
Great Britain	Medium	Medium	High	High	High	High	High
Sweden	Medium	Low	Low	Medium	High	Medium	High
Finland	High	High	High	Medium	High	High	Medium
Norway	Low	Low	Low	Medium	Low	Medium	Medium
Denmark	Medium	High	High	High	----	High	Medium
Germany	Low	Medium	Medium	High	High	High	High

The findings suggest two surprising conclusions.

– The performance of innovation regimes such as Great Britain and Sweden is not superior, and is to some extent inferior, to that of the traditional regulatory regime in Germany. Thus it can be concluded that, contrary to the initial hypothesis, there is at least one independent third regime – that of flexible qualified mass production[8] – in addition to the bi-polar regimes of mass production and flexible specialisation. This form of production generates a comparable, if not higher, level of performance within the labour market authority than the two other regulatory regimes.

– Moreover, the comparison between the two innovation regimes, Great Britain and Sweden, reveals performance values that contradict a traditional picture of Sweden as a high performer in this field: Great Britain has higher values than Sweden in terms of both efficiency and effectiveness.[9]

– There are also significant differences in performance level between the two "traditionalists", Germany and Austria. Indeed, the differences here are far more pronounced than between the two regime types.

– There is also a substantial degree of variation between the Scandinavian countries. The performance of the Danish labour market authority is one of the best, while Sweden and Finland occupy the middle ground (with Sweden rather closer to the leading group) and Norway behind these.[10]

Scandinavian developments and the strategic position of Norway

The intra-Scandinavian comparison conducted by Naschold (1996, using also ECON 1993 study) comparing workload, working hours, skill

8 This term is derived from the analogous debate in the private sector, particularly in the automobile and engineering industries (cf. Gordon, 1994).

9 The high performance of UK and Germany must be proved on the micro level. As it turns out, in the UK there is a lot of "front end turbulance" and "turndoor effect" related to a forceful control approach and thus producing also ostensible performance. The deeper picture of the German performance has not yet been interpreted.

10 What about the apparent paradox that low unemployment countries seem to pursue an ineffective unemployment policy and vice versa? First it must be noted that the decisive elements depend on the economical factors and labour administrations and employment policy are of relative importance in the matter. Secondly there are deviating cases like Germany and thirdly there are cyclical components where in a good labour market situation (like in Norway), with a lot of vacancies and less job-seekers, it is more difficult to produce good effectiveness figures (placements to vacancies ratio) whereas in a bad situation, with less vacancies and a lot of job-seekers it is easier.

levels of staff and use of computers in the employment offices serves to both confirm and differentiate the results of the OECD comparison given earlier. Let us just summarize the findings here:

– Denmark is confirmed as being characterised by a regulatory regime of effective and efficient mass production analogous to the British system. With a heavy workload and low unit costs, the emphasis is on quantitative processing of job placement. This is in line with a relatively low skill level among employment office staff.

– Sweden on the other hand, proves to be the prototype of flexible, specialised, customised service production. With high resource input, high unit costs and a low workload, the strategy adopted is one of decentralised quality production with relatively good effectiveness and efficiency ratings. The employee skill structure is relatively high.

– The strategic location of Finland (and, more or less, that of Norway) is very much in accordance with the "stuck in the middle" hypothesis. Finland occupies the middle ground between the production regimes of efficient mass production à la Denmark and flexible and specialised service production à la Sweden. With a heavy workload and low unit costs, a relatively highly skilled workforce provides services which exhibit characteristics of both mass production and limited customer-orientation, attaining a relatively high efficiency and medium effectiveness level.

– The strategic location of Norway resembles to some degree that of Finland, with the important difference of having a low workload and being somewhat more traditionally organized and less on the way towards decentralization, flexible specialization and customer orientation. Norway has touched upon the same themes as the other Nordic countries, but to a lesser degree. Norway is not "yet" stuck in between, but one scenario would predict it is incrementally heading towards it. Norway is neither an efficient decentralized nor an efficient centralized mass producer, but somewhere "in between", too, but more to the traditional direction and with lower performance than the other Nordic countries. The Norwegian LMA has addressed many of the key questions of modernization in terms of reforms in steering and quality work, but has proceeded, as Norway in general, a rather incremental and cautious path. It will be seen in the next chapter that the local level of the Norwegian LMA would like to see more decentralization and both leeway and support for local initiative. This was also, as it was earlier pointed out, the general picture derived from the study by the Norwegians themselves on the Norwegian LMA. So, to a great extent, the same general picture as from the national macro level emerges.

A note on competition and complementarity between public and private services

Based on development trends at local government level, an earlier study by Naschold[11] put forward a hypothesis of the complementarity of public and private service production, provided the public sector retains a strategic "own competence" in this area and the complementary relationship is clearly regulated. This view is confirmed by the analysis of central government policies, illustrated in the following with respect to labour market policy.

Table 9.4 Market share for Public Employment services[12]

	Market Share
Monopoly Countries	
Austria (1992)	12%
Belgium (1992)	17%
W-Germany (1992)	24%
Spain (1990)	15%
Finland (1992)	20%
France(1992)	12%
Norway (1990)	17%
Sweden (1992)	25%
Japan (1990)	12%
Co-existence Countries	
Australia (1992)	17%
Bulgaria (1992)	-
Switzerland (1992)	3%
Cyprus (1990)	16%
Denmark (1991)	18%
G-Brit. (1992)	24%
Ireland (1992)	10%
Holland (1991)	12%
Portugal (1992)	-
USA (1991)	5%

Walwei, 1994, with Finland (1992) added

The market share of private agencies varies greatly (for example Switzerland 86% Netherlands 41%, Great Britain 17% and Denmark

11 Naschold 1996 using Walwei, 1994.

12 In co-existence countries, commercial placement services are not restricted geographically or occupationally. Sweden and Finland were still monopoly countries in 1992 (private services enabled 1993/1994). The appointment figures are national institution estimates in part.

11%). In Switzerland and USA the large share of private services is partly due to the "voluntary withdrawal" of public employment services to specific "difficult" labour market segments, e.g. the long-term unemployed and school-leavers (cf. Bishop 1992).

In principle though, private job placement complements the public service in all those countries in which the two coexist. Private job placement is primarily "job-oriented", concentrating on filling vacancies with higher-level and specialist requirements with the appropriate, usually already employed, applicants. The public placement service, on the other hand, is largely jobseeker-oriented. Not least due to their statutory commission, their clientele consists largely of the unemployed and other persons with placement difficulties. To this extent the public placement service tends to be used more frequently for jobs with lower skill requirements.

Further evidence for complementarity comes from the comparison of the relative market shares of public job placement services in "monopoly" and "coexistence" countries. Such a comparison shows that a monopoly – the prohibition of private job placement for profit – does not by itself endure a high market share for the public service, while conversely, the existence of private placement agencies does not necessarily imply a low market share for the public placement service (OECD, 1992; Walwei, 1994).

The example of Denmark, a country in which the two forms have coexisted for several years (since 1990), is a case in point. The aim of the Danish liberalisation policy was to raise the quantity and quality of

Figure 9.6

	Gt-Britain	Sweden	Finland	Denmark	Norway	Austria
MACRO-MODEL						
Generosity/control	low	medium	medium	high	medium	low
Centralization/decentr.	high	low	medium	high	high	high
Intern/ext	low	high	low	high	high	low
PERFOR-MANCE						
Work load	high	medium/low	high	high/medium	low	high
Effectiveness	high	medium/high	medium/high	high	medium/low	low
Efficiency	high	medium	high	high	medium	medium
Market share	high	high	medium	medium	medium	low

the jobs offered. In particular, employed jobseekers and firms facing difficulties in filling vacancies were to benefit from the new services offered by private agencies. The Danish Institute of Social Research has published a research report into the effects of the liberalisation (on the following cf. Csonka, 1993). According to the study, even by 1992 the market share of private job placement agencies was still very small. It clearly required a considerable length of time to establish a network of private agencies (supply side) and for enterprises and job-seekers to incorporate private agencies into their search efforts (demand side). Also in some business areas the absence of licensing in fact had a negative effect on the reputation of private services. Although the liberalisation did not actually initiate reforms within the public job placement service, it did serve to substantially accelerate on-going reforms and to better the reputation of public services. It lead to the creation of new job-oriented placement units and the option of charging for special services (like personnel selection). Similar developments have occurred in Sweden and Finland since 1993/94. Thus the aim of the Danish liberalisation, namely to improve the supply of placement services in both quantitative and qualitative terms seems to have been realised, although less (than had been expected) via the new offers and services provided by private agencies than by the improvement of the public job placement service. Thus the complex dialectic of the complementarity between public and private services, and not the simplistic dichotomy between private/market and public/state regulatory mechanisms, would appear to be an important motor behind the modernization process.

Summary

Referring to the macro-model combined with the Walwei performance comparison, the following overall picture emerges of the labour-market and employment policy constellations:

Great Britain emerges as a highly centralized, high performer, with a strict control approach in a high workload and low generosity environment. High performance on the sectorial level has to be proven on the local level. As it turns out, anticipating our findings in the next chapter, the "downside" of Britain's stringent approach is a high degree of front end turbulence and turndoor effect – and thus also a degree of ostensible performance. At the other end is conservative Austria, showing low performance with centralized steering in a high workload and low generosity environment.

The Nordic countries exhibit by no means a uniform picture.

Generosity is rather uniformly medium to high, with Denmark in the lead. Denmark and Norway come out as most centralized. Sweden – in the lead – and Denmark plus Norway have a high level of internalization of unemployment, whereas Finland, with an extremely high rate of unemployment, has here partly taken another path. In terms of performance Denmark leads with a high workload, followed by Sweden and Finland. Norway emerges as a medium performer in a low workload environment.

4. Effectiveness and efficiency of the local employment offices – a comparative perspective on micro-organizational processes

Introduction: More attention to the primary market?

In this chapter we benchmark qualitatively and quantitatively the local level of the Labour Market Authorities by comparing local employment offices. The material was compiled via intensive case studies executed by the authors in joint interviews and using other material.

But first we want to address two questions: is there a need for a change of focus in the employment offices and does it really make a difference in terms of welfare gains?

Especially in the Nordic countries there has been a long tradition of comprehensive employment services ranging from placements and information services to labour market training, labour market schemes, rehabilitation and unemployment benefits. Labour market policy, unemployment benefits and the service apparatus of the labour administrations were geared to deal with rather short-term cyclical changes and relatively low rates of unemployment.

In face of the current depression with huge public deficits, prolonged high unemployment and tremendously rising costs for both active labour market programmes (ALMPs) and benefits in the Nordic countries there are rising doubts about the sustainability and effectiveness of the general model, focus of employment office activities and the ALMPs. As we have seen, benefit policy – with some differences in the levels – has been generous in the Nordic countries. In a prolonged high unemployment situation this has proved extremely costly and also a disincentive to receive especially lower-to middle-range jobs. There is mounting evidence that would suggest that the ALMPs – so successful in the past decades especially in Sweden – in fact might slow down the recruitment process to primary market employment. A high level of ALMPs also can have negative effects on the functioning of the labour market.[13] There is growing doubt and evidence that local administration and monitoring of the various ALMPs and benefit-related tasks are very time-consuming and tend to bog down the service processes. All this is further aggravated by constant changes in legislation and rules about the ALMPs and benefits.[14]

It is against this severe European background that we are particularly interested in the arrangements and functioning of the core function of the employment office: the matching process of supply and demand and especially the placement function. The current issue is whether there is need for an "overhaul" of employment policies[15] and enough emphasis on the basic process of working with the primary market and placement process vs. concentrating more and more effort to the ALMPs – i.e. various schemes, labour market training and subsidised employment. Also the fundamental changes in the labour markets – in supply and demand pose challenges to the arrangement of service processes.

So our viewpoint on the employment office placement process and the benchmarking departs from the current debate on whether more attention should be directed to the primary market placement process in the public employment services. At any rate the placement process and connections to the primary market are at the core of the activities of public labour market services. Following this question we evaluate what setup of services at the local level of labour administration supports best result oriented practice of placements in local employment offices. We also assess the meaningfullness of the variance in service setup and performance i.e. does good practice really make a difference. If it does, this in turn has major implications for possible welfare gains or losses.

The changing framework: The variability of the placement process – does it make a difference?

Does variation in service setup and particularly the placement process really make a difference? Is the variation in performance really signifi-

---

13 A "rule of thumb" of over 5-6% on the average of the labour force covered by measures – a level already reached in Sweden and close in Finland). Calmfors, L. Will High Unemployment in Sweden be Persistent? Swedish Economic Policy Review. Vol. 2. 1995 pp. 5-12.

14 Ackum Agell, S. Swedish Labour Market Programs: Efficiency and Timing. Swedish Economic Policy Review. Vol. 2. 1995 pp. 101-129, Forslund, A. and Kruger, A.B. : An Evaluation of the Swedish Active Labour Market Policy. Occasional Paper/SNS No. 65 January 1995

15 White Paper of EU, 1993.

cant? If the variation is significant, it points to major possibilities in performance enhancement and conversely, bad performance points to significant direct and indirect welfare losses in terms of prolonged unemployment and inability to meet demand.

Despite the difficulties to assess this in precise terms, a comprehensive Finnish study[16] comparing the performance of Finnish employment offices gives us a possibility to roughly assess the possible magnitude.

The comparison was made 1994 of all Finnish employment offices (163) on several input and output variables. The comparison was made of the productivity of employment offices measuring mainly the number of placements (weight 61%) and training course starters (weight 25%). The average output would be indexed as 100. Thus an index of 200 would indicate that with the same input (number of personnel) an employment office would have a double output (mainly in placements) to the national average.

The variance of performance was considerable. There were offices clearly under the average, being able to produce less than half with the same staff and offices able to show productivity rates more than twice the national average. One can estimate that on the average the performance (output) differences in placements is about 50%. The differences can be largely attributed to differences in service setup, process priorities and office work culture factors. The magnitude points to strategic possibilities in performance enhancement.

Labour market exchanges and the public placement process

Traditional placement process

As on the macro level, also the modernization and reform process on the micro level has a critically viewed historical reference model as a point of departure. The 'traditional model' of the state and public government, characterized by centralization, strong and clear hierarchies and func-

16 For the methods and database see Talonen and Tuomaala, 1994. In the comparison it is possible to hold some important contextual and intervening variables constant. First, because this is an internal one-country comparison the variance due to differences in labour market policy is eliminated. Secondly because the comparison includes all the employment offices in the different regions of Finland, one can look at the variance within the different regional labour markets and eliminate the effect of environment. Thirdly, because the study shows that size is in negative correlation to output, variance due to size can be held constant. Fourth, in Finland, qualification levels of personnel are even throughout the country.

tional division of labour is duplicated on the local level of the labour market authority as an employment office with a compartmentalized structure and rigid division of labour. The employment office in the traditional administration is an unautonomous 'remote controlled' unit, strongly steered by the intermediate and central levels, with very little room for local initiative or customized solutions. It is against this model that we look at the modern challenges.

At the heart of the employment office is the matching process, mediating supply and demand of the labour markets. From this process, placements hold the key position. As long as the labour markets displayed a limited rate of change and complexity, the matching process could be arranged largely according to a "linear logic" of matching a supply A (a clearly defined need) through a specialized service A' (a department or responsibility in the employment office) with a demand A'' (likewise clearly defined and specialized, as still largely in industry in the 1970s) (see Figure 9.7).

Figure 9.7 The traditional matching and placement process

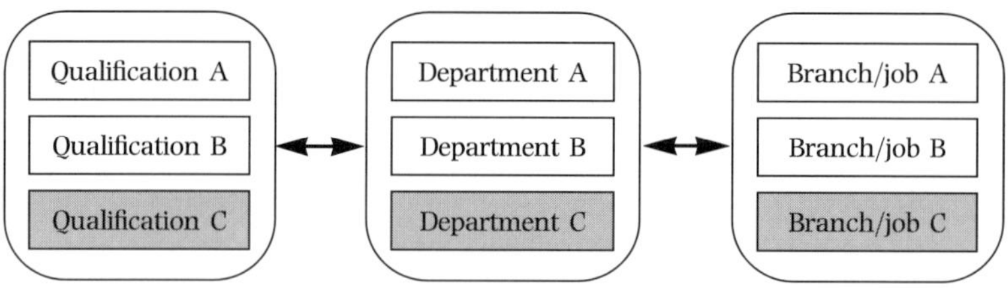

Supply
- lifelong careers
- one profession
- large groups with uniform skills
- clear "borders" of skills
- not consumer-conscious customers ("one down")

Matching and placement
- clear, compartmentalized division of labour
- working alone
- slow changes
- limited knowledge of demand (firms) and supply (job seekers)
- limited qualifications
- unequivocal matching

Demand
- slow changes
- specialized demand
- clear "borders" of demand

Naschold/Arnkil, 1997

On this basis the general organizational setup of the public employment services reflected the mass production model and division of labour in especially industry. Each main branch of industry or business activity had their own "isomorphic" representative – compartment or responsibility – in the organizational structure of the employment offices. There was very little "traffic" between the different departments in the employment office as there was indeed between the different walks of economic and working life. Also the qualifications of the employment offices reflected this general setup (mostly medium to low end of jobs).

The modern challenges

Both supply and demand in the labour market have considerably changed in the last decades and thus the nature and challenges of the matching process – and at the core of it placements – have considerably changed. The process includes an increasing degree of non-linearity. We can speak of the modern challenges of the employment office matching and placement process.

The (neo)modern matching and placement process has become more complex and demanding. Labour demand has become both more differentiated and "fuzzy" at the same time. Also time-tables have changed. There are more temporary jobs and changes are rapid both in supply and demand. On the one hand the ever increasing complexity of working life increases demand for very specialized and higher qualifications. On the other hand these demands have become more fuzzy in the sense that now you are looking for a unique combination of skills and qualifications, i.e. multi-tasking combined with personal qualifications. The demand now more and more takes a certain educational level as a self evident base-rate for recruitment and looks for more personal qualifications, i.e. psycho-social fitness for the job, special experience, ambitions and motivation, etc. [17]

Labour supply has changed, too. There is less stability in careers and typically people train themselves in a variety of skills.[18] On the one hand the customers of the public services have become more customer-conscious and qualified, on the other – with prolonged unemployment –

---

17 Growth, competitiveness, employment. White paper of EC. 1993. In a Finnish study on recruitment involving a questionnaire for 6000 employers, the most frequently encountered recruitment problems were 1) Special requirements of the job (35%) 2) Personal qualifications (16%), 3) Temporary nature of the job (16%) 4) Inadequate training (15%).

18 Hage, J. and Powers, C.H. *Post-Industrial Lives,* 1992. and Peavy, R.V. *Envisioning the Future, 1993*

customers are experiencing difficulties in motivation and initiative and are under the threat and process of marginalization. These put new pressures on the qualifications and skills of the employment officers.

In a recent paper[19], the Swedish labour market board, for instance, clearly recognizes the rising difficulty of the marching process and the increasing importance attached to the individuals personality and intangible qualifications and emphasizes the need to establish a large pool of job-seekers and vacancies and to act as an efficient broker between them.

In order to grasp the more complex and rapidly changing situation in the firms, the employment office needs a more comprehensive knowledge and contact to the demand side of the labour market. Likewise, in order to be able to assess the individual situations of the job-seekers the officers need a good contact to the customers and new and higher skills to do this. To support the activities of the customers also comprehensive self-service and general "transparency" is needed.

Accordingly the work process in the employment office must develop teamwork, combining skills and knowledge, flexible interaction and rapid exchange of knowledge. The modern challenges also emphasize the strategic importance of the "moment of truth" in services, i.e. the first encounters between the placement officer and the job seeker or employer. This "first encounter" should be as qualified as possible in order to get a good and quick assessment. (see Figure 9.8).

The priorities in the service process and its inversion[20]

The official policy of the labour administrations in all countries stress the importance and the priority of open market placements in employment services.[22] This is what is desired, but it appears that this is not quite so clear in terms of result definitions and priorities and especially the actual practice in the employment offices.

---

19 Labour Market Policy in Sweden, International Secretariat, AMS 1995

20 In general terms, the importance of priorities in service processes is emphasized in all TQM litterature on quality chains (cf. Oakland, 1993) , the importance of front office effort in literature on the service process and the "moment of truth" (Grönroos, 1990) as is the importance of the whole service setup and "value constellation" (Normann and Ramirez, 1994).

21 The Swedish labour market authority sets clear priority for placements. The number one key goal , with highest priority (Swedish Labour Market Board, 1995/1996) is filling vacancies. The second priority is stopping long term unemployment by active measures and third concerns immigrants and handicapped. In Finland the "marching order" is expressed in the Law of Employment and in the key result indicators (vacancies filled within required time, etc.).

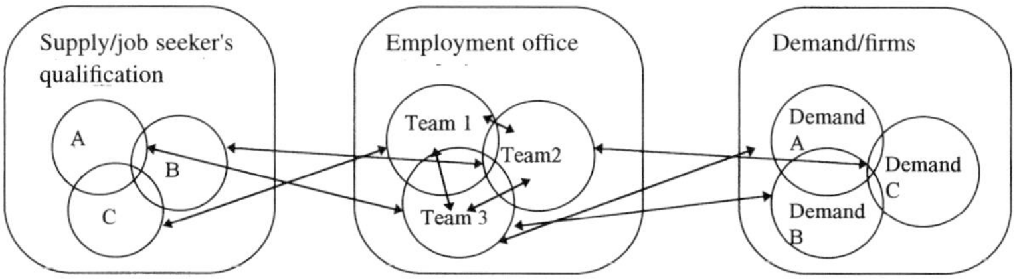

Changes in Supply	*Challenge for matching and placement*	*Changes in demand*
- less stability	- flexible division of labour	- less stability, rapid changes
- more individuality and locality	- teamwork and networking	- more emphasis on personal qualifications
- multi-skilling and qualifications	- rapid changes	- unique combinations
- many changes in career and workplace	- comprehensive knowledge of demand (firms) and supply (persons)	- more locality
- lifelong training	- qualified front office	- more "fuzziness": less clear "borders"
- consumer-conscious customers ("one-up")	- pressure on rising qualifications of personnel	
- more "fuzziness: less clear "borders"		

Naschold/Arnkil, 1997

Figure 9.8 The (neo)modern matching and placement process

In order to emphasize focus on activation and the primary market, the employment offices should have the following priority in the process chain of services:

1. Placements to open markets	2. Activating measures -training, re-training -work practice -individual schemes	3. Subsidies -enhancing placements for long-term unemployed	4. Benefits

Naschold-Arnkil, 1997

Figure 9.9 The Priorities of the Process Chain in Employment Office Services

The placement to open markets is a crucial function of the public employment service. A failure of the placement process in qualitative and/or quantitative terms has adverse effects on the reputation, contacts and market share of the employment office. This in turn reduces considerably the role of the employment office in the market, "drains the pool" and leaves very little leeway in terms of contacts and possibilities both at the "good" end of the labour market (i.e. qualified and active customer groups) and the "bad" end of the labour market (i.e. long term unemployment, handicapped, etc.). The better the contacts to the primary market, the more possibilities the office has to negotiate employment also to the less resourceful clients. In the opposite case, the office is left with only one way of helping people and that is working with the secondary market, subsidies and benefits. Working with the primary market is also a constant learning experience for the employment office having both direct (like attracting more vacancies and resourceful clients) and indirect advantages (like learning new methods and ideas from working life). In this sense, placements is not just a "function among functions", as it especially during hard times of unemployment apparently tends to be. In practice, there are several factors producing an inverse marching order (figure 9.10).

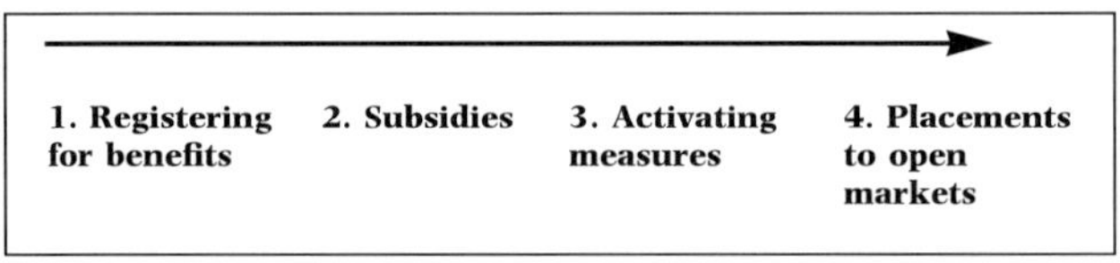

Figure 9.10 The inverse marching order Naschold-Arnkil, 1997

This can de due to many factors, some of which are summarized here:
1) *Rising complexity of demand and supply*: The qualitative change in the labour market generally increases the workload in the employment offices. Unless this is dealt with successfully it will generally slow down the work and lead to bad results. This leads to many adverse chain effects: loss of reputation, less vacancies, qualified labour not showing up, monitoring mistakes, etc. All this decreases the resources available. It effects most those functions which are less "tangible" in terms of legislation, pressing time-tables, clear and measurable results (like "networking").
2) *Rising customer flows*: The general rise in customer quantities rises the pressure on registering and benefits. Since these are very "tangible" jobs the less tangibles suffer.
3) *Long-term unemployment*: The tougher the unemployment scene gets, the more you have very tangible tasks related to it (ALMP:s, benefits) – and the more there is a danger of the primary market becoming a second order question.
4) *Working models of the employment offices*: If the priorities (goals, key results) and responsibilities in the employment office are unclear, if there

is diffuse "ownership" of priorities and results the work will tend to gravitate towards the "tangibles". Many experiences point to a need of establishing a "client–contractor" split (demand-supply) in this responsibility in the employment offices, i.e. having an own team for contacts with enterprises and another for job-seekers and establishing a good interface between them. Also experience strongly points to a need of good front office effort, because a failure here has many adverse chain effects.
5) *Policy-issues*: There are different ways of trying to establish a 'marching order' emphasizing the primary market. Great Britain is attempting a forceful turnaround by using placements, front-office effort and stringency in benefits largely in a control manner. This can have adverse chain effects. It can deteriorate the reputation of the employment services both in the eyes of the employers and job-seekers. This in turn is a starting point for a vicious circle of losing market share and cooperation. It also can lead to lots of front-end turbulence, i.e. people failing to reach sustainable placements only to return back to the office after some time. It also increases the share of useless monitoring leading to no results (but producing perhaps misleadingly good performance figures in terms of placement numbers, etc.). In all countries studied, the employment offices had rather limited knowledge about the real magnitude of this kind of turbulence.

The Nordic countries have a different kind of problem. With a generous benefit system and so little pressure on the customers topped with unclear priorities and responsibilities in the employment offices concerning particularly the primary market, you end up with an inverse marching order. With a generous benefit policy you have a strong disincentive to move away from the "cavalcade of ALMPs". This matter has been of major concern especially in Sweden, Denmark and Finland because of the public deficit.

In both regimes you can end up with a "circle of pretence": The employment officer pretends to give a genuine offer (when in fact it is for controlling purposes or an artificial job), the job-seeker, not wanting to lose his/ her eligibility, pretends to take it and goes to the employer pretending to be interested in the job (but, in fact, giving subtle hints of not wanting it). The employer, in turn, pretends to be assessing the suitability (when in fact rejecting at first hand) and pretends to send a genuine message to the employment office of not reaching a contract and the office pretends to take the message in earnest and the job-seeker manages to retain his/her eligibility. Lots of useless work, all eating away time from genuine primary-market, or front-office effort. (See Figure 9.11)

Factors producing an inverse order	Chain effects of unsuccessful coping
1) Rising complexity of demand and supply	Increase in workload > slowing down of work processes, bad results, less time generally > "less tangibles", like primary market contacts suffer
2) Rising customer flows	More and more claims for benefits > more registering > less time for else > "less tangibles" suffer
3) Rising long-term unemployment	More monitoring > less time for else >primary market contacts suffer
4) Working-models of employment office	Unclear coping > work gravitates towards tasks with pressing time-tables, clear definitions, strong laws and clear measurements > i.e. benefits, subsidies, schemes > primary market contacts suffer
5) Policy-issues	Britain: Forceful "turnaround" > superficial placement > lots of front end turbulence > 'circle of pretence' > lots of useless monitoring > loss of reputation with employers and job-seekers > vicious circle (and lots of ostensible "performance") Nordic countries: Unclear priorities > lots of effort on secondary market > primary market contacts suffer Generosity > circle of pretence > lots of ostensible "performance"

Naschold-Arnkil, 1997

Figure 9.11 Summary of some factors producing an inverse process

The qualitative and quantitative evaluation dimensions

In the following we benchmark the qualitative and quantitative performance of local employment offices particularly in the placement process, but also making an overall evaluation in terms of management and steering, organization, quality work and use of electronic data processing. Combining the general dimensions of the New Public Management criteria and the more contextual and specific process-criteria developed in the previous chapters we use a set of dimensions to qualitatively evaluate local employment offices (see figure 9.12):

Quantitatively the employment offices are compared in terms of workload (unemployed and vacancies per employee), efficiency (placements per employee) and effectiveness (placement ratio to vacancies). Also

Dimensions of evaluation for employment office model	Best practice criteria
I Organizational setting and development in employment offices	
1. Management reform: Steering and decentralization	Result and performance assessment and measurement - clearly set priorities and key results - special goals and measurements for: placements, contacts, teamwork, sustainable results (for employers, for job-seekers, little front end turbulence) Decentralization, autonomous and self-directive position in organization, local initiatives beyond "required"
2. Competition, comparison and transparency	Both private competition, general transparency and comparison within the public sector
3. Work organization	
- internal organization	Flexible interaction in office, quick communication (teamworking), conscious team model and effort, "ownership" of responsibilities, supply-demand split
- external work/ networking	Flexible interaction outside office (comprehensive networking)
4. Process development/ quality work	- comprehensiveness: external and internal customer, feedback, process development
5. Qualifications of personnel	Qualified personnel
II Placement process and organization	
6. Front office effort	Comprehensiveness of initial assessment, conscious effort & setup in office
7. Demand supply split and their interface: contact with firms and job-seekers	Clear and unambiguous split responsibility and priority for contact with firms (own team) job-seekers (own team) and connecting these (well established cooperation)
8. Information and self service	Well established and comprehensive information, easily accessible and well established self-service with good interface
9. Follow-up of placement and assessment of sustainable results	Follow-up and feedback on results & satisfaction of firms and job-seekers with placements. Evidence of sustainable results with little front-end turbulence or "turn-door" effect
10. EDP support for modern non-linear (fuzzy) matching	Well established EDP system with new innovations to tackle non-linear (fuzzy) matching, customized search and local initiatives

Naschold-Arnkil, 1997

Figure 9.12: Summary of Benchmark Criteria of Employment Offices

market share (placements ratio to appointments) is used, when available.[22]

The practical solutions were studied in the local employment offices via joint in-depth interviews by the authors. The study was executed in the following employment offices:

- Sweden: Stockholm City
- Norway: Drammen and Moss
- Denmark: Roskilde
- Finland: Rauma
- Great Britain: Braintree
- New Zealand: Christchurch

Benchmarking employment offices

Sweden: Stockholm City Employment office

Stockholm City employment office works in the centre of Stockholm with a staff of 40. It is one of 32 full service offices in Stockholm. There are additionally 6 occupationally specialized offices (building and transport, culture and media, staff and administration, technical and computers, tourism and maritime) and 10 special offices (university, youth under 25, temporary work, handicapped, foreign job-seekers).[23] It is evident already from this setup that a largely decentralized approach is applied in the Swedish employment services. In Norway, Denmark and Finland the office spread out is much more concentrated and less specialized than in Sweden.

The unemployment rate of the City office area is 6,1% with just over 4200 jobseekers of which 2400 unemployed (April -96) The labour market situation in Stockholm area is favourable and there are a lot of companies and vacancies. A total of 3% of all the vacancies in the country fall into the City office lot. This puts pressure on the office to be effective in placements.

The Stockholm City employment office has gone through a period of several changes in the organization. The last reorganization was planned

---

22 In the quantitative assessment workload, efficiency (placements/ employee) and effectiveness (placements to vacancies) can be reliabily counted. Assesment of market share (placements/ all appointments either locally or nationally) is more difficult because the figures are based on samples or varying degree of size. Sometimes the figures are not nationally or locally available at all or are impossible to discern.

23 This is by far the most decentralized setup in the capital cities of the Nordic countries.

in the spring of 1995 by having a couple of planning days, where the staff discussed – once again – what to do with the organization. The new organization was put into effect in August 1995. In general there was an air of change, an element of unpredictability, rapid re-adjustment and spontaneity about the office. There is also evidence of major results. After the change in organization the number of placements after referral went up from 40 in August to 130 in October, exceeding clearly the target level set at 80, so in the initial phase there is a performance rise of as much as 200%. The placement increase clearly exceeds the average in the whole Stockholm county which was only 17%. The number of all placements rose also from a level of 280 in July to 550 in October, a rise of 100%, county average being a rise of 40%. Here also other measures, like self-service has an impact. These results point to considerable possibilities in enhancing performance by work-model rearrangements along the lines we described in the best practice criteria.

In quantitative terms Stockholm City office emerges as a medium performer (see figure 16 in the summary of the micro-level analysis). The workload of Stockholm City office is medium in terms of unemployed jobseekers per employee but high in vacancies. The City office is a special case because it works in the capital city of Sweden and the "boundaries" of its environment are less clear than with the other cases. Effectiveness in terms of placements to vacancies is medium. Market share cannot be estimated in exact terms. There is clear evidence of higher performance than average, as pointed out above.

Organizational setting and development

The AMS has defined the key goals which also are the key goals for counties and local offices:

1) Filling vacancies and contacts to enterprises must be given top priority
2) Stop long term unemployment – create ways to activity and work
3) More emigrants and handicapped to work and active measures

The counties are responsible for taking care that the local employment offices make their own goals of these three in their own environment. Earlier the AMS and LAN (county-level) gave quite detailed guidelines, like stating how many percent of people should be in active measures, etc. Now the office itself sets the targets. The steering model is not explicitly identified in the employment office as "Management by Results" or the like. The office clearly works on its own initiative and does a lot of work to adjust to the labour market challenges. When asked about the role or value added by the county-level the answer is rather hesitant and the role is seen as limited as defining office hours and monitoring figures. The office now follows very closely the number of filled vacancies where they have made individual effort (placements after referral) and also the filled vacancies altogether. A target level is set for each month (over half a year ahead).

Private competition has been allowed in Sweden since July 1993. The role of private competition has remained quite marginal outside big urban areas and to some specific areas like job-hiring to office work and special head-hunting. The effect of private services is expected to grow as the market catches up.

The work organization in the office is a flat team-organization. The recent work reorganization is based on a split responsibility into a company-team (demand) and job-seeker team (supply) plus people responsible for administration. There is enthusiasm and commitment to this new setup. At the same time the team concept and its specific methods appear rather spontaneous. The influences for the reorganization are said to come from outside the administration. The Stockholm office has a modern appearance, rooms for both group-work and individual discussions. The office has an extensive front-office and ten self-service computers. The first thing a customer meets is the self-service and just behind it the front office in cubicles. Beyond that there are corridors with both group-work facilities and individual offices. One peculiarity about the office is that it works next to the Stockholm post office in the same building and uses the same entrance and entrance-hall. This gives a possibility of keeping the self-service spots open in a more extensive way. There is also more traffic than otherwise.

Also in terms of process development the office is clearly in a dynamic phase, but in a more spontaneous sense. The quality-work of the Swedish AMS was not known in the office other than in general terms and there was no systematic effort in customer feedback or monitoring quality as such. The qualification level of personnel is high, the highest in our case studies: all have a university degree and there is rather extensive in-house training, initially one year and after that at least 3 days a year.

Placement process and organization

The office has distinct upstream and front office effort. Placements have priority, qualified personnel is used in initial contacts and the10 self-service points (computers) for customers are used a lot. The procedure with a new customer is the following: on the first visit the customer is registered and then given a time within a week to a group information dis-

what confined, facility. The first thing the customer meets is a "cross-roads" with one way leading to initial registering at a desk in an open space and an adjacent (open) space for discussions. The other way leads to a hall/ corridor of information on vacancies and education. The information is on paper on the walls, quite well presented. There are no self-service computers for jobs (there used to be, but they were disbanded). There is one computer providing rather non-intuitive information on education. There is an officer to help with the matters. Beyond that there is an open office for the combined placement and enterprise-team. In the rest of the building, partly upstairs are rooms for counselling and administration. There are not many spaces for group work.

The general setup of the employment office services can be described as standard: a full repertoire of services – placements, information, counselling, training are provided in a standard way. The office does not appear to be in the midst of a turbulent change-phase either in priorities or work-arrangements. There was a general wish for further decentralization in the Danish labour administration. The regional/ local level was somewhat complaining that they are serving too much the AMS Arbetsmarknadsstyrelsen) "upwards" with too little time left to serve the local offices or concentrate on the local council. One gets a picture of various "AMS assignments" and changes coming top-down, with the regional and local levels left to execute them, whether locally relevant or not.

In quantitative terms, Roskilde emerges as a high performer under high workload, which is in line with the macro picture of the Danish LMA. The workload of Roskilde is high both in terms of unemployed job-seekers and vacancies per employee. Effectiveness in terms of placements to vacancies and efficiency as placements per employee is also high. Market share is 22% of placements/appointments which is rather low in this case comparison (see Table 9.5).

Organizational setting and development

The region has had the same goals for several years. The overall goals for the region are:

- offering suitable, well qualified labour to the enterprises
- predict and prevent bottle-necks of supply and demand
- prevent and defeat long-term unemployment

The position of local employment offices is less independent than in Sweden and Finland. On the other hand the region plays a rather central role and also the regional council plays a uniquely important role compared with the other Nordic countries.

Competition has been allowed in Denmark since 1989. It was the first

Nordic country to do so. At the time there was a lot of talk about it, and also concern about the consequences. So far this has had rather little impact and private competition was not mentioned as an important factor in the discussions with the local office. Neither was there evidence of special competition or comparison between different offices or regions. A developing trend has been the role of the local council and the local discussions and there is a wish to be able to devote more time and effort to this.

There are two main service groups, the IHP (individual action plan) -team and the Placement and Enterprise -team plus administration (provided by the county office) . The IHP (individual action plan) -team is responsible for initial registering, individual action plans for customers (essentially counselling) and also projects and outside contacts. The Placement and Enterprise -team is responsible for visits and information to the enterprises, placements and dealing with “bottlenecks” of supply and demand. There are 10 people on this team and they are responsible for both contacts to firms and job-seekers. They are expected to devote 50% of their time to each. Other people work in information service, counselling and projects. On top of this is the regional administration consisting of a secretariat and administration team. The different groups in the office are referred to as teams, but there is no specific adherence to a special team-concept.

There is a central administration initiative in quality work directed towards correct procedures. The guidelines are given by the administration and the regions make their own implementation on this basis. The quality work concentrates on defining the right procedures for registering the customer and the placement process. 15 – 20% of personnel are academically trained, which is a medium level. One typical background is a teacher from public schools.

Placement process and organization

A new entrant is registered in a routine way at a reception desk and given an appointment to individual discussions after a month. In this discussion the wishes and needs of the job-seeker are assessed. The rationale for giving a time for discussions as far as a month is that within that time many people find employment on their own initiative and thus the office avoids unnecessary work on registration. After that it depends whether the job-seeker is expected to be in a “risk-group” how frequently he/she will be called in for discussions and proving they are at the disposal of the labour market. If there is a risk for long-term unemployment, the customer will be called in six months.

There is no clear ownership along the lines of working either with enterprises or job-seekers. There is no special emphasis on the placement process, although it is one of the key functions to take care of. The team-members work with the whole repertoire of jobs and job-seekers without specialization. The team monitors their time themselves. There are no team goals or specific performance or result goals for the team. There was no indication that contact with firms was a special top priority in the office. The interface between supply and demand was established within the team, or more precisely, mostly within the work of the individual placement officer. The argument behind this is that this is how you secure knowing both the jobs and the job-seekers to find a good match. This is the traditional way of arranging the responsibilities of the employment officers and it certainly has its points. The critical argument is that unless there are special measures (and measurements) to secure working "out-house" with the enterprises there is a tendency of getting "bogged down" in the office.

Information about jobs and training was well – but in Nordic terms in a standard fashion – presented in paper form and there was assistance available. Two years ago there was also a self-service computer for jobs-seekers, but it was abandoned because it didn't work in a satisfactory way. There were no specific mentions about post-placement follow-ups or post-placement support or assessment of the sustainability of placement results. This is probably done "in-process". The EDP is of normal Nordic standard. The basic elements of the matching process are the job-codes and education. There were no indications of specific innovations to overcome the non-linear challenges.[26]

Norway: Drammen employment office

Drammen is a middle-size local employment office with about 50 employees. The qualification level of the office is medium in the case-comparison: 26% of the personnel have an academic background. Drammen is regarded as a good example of a Norwegian local employment office. It is located 50 km South-West of Oslo. Proximity to Oslo

26 Some additional remarks on brief observations of the Copenhagen City Employment office and an information service in Copenhagen :The office is large, over 100 employees and arranged in a traditional division of labour. In the entrance hall there is a traditional setup. No self-service. No evidence of special group-work or team facilities. Compared with Stockholm, the Danish setup in Copenhagen was more traditional and centralized. Information spot in Copenhagen: Written information was available in an open office. No self-service computers. If you had a special request, you consulted an officer. Thus the information service was more restricted than in especially Sweden and Finland.

has an effect on the general labour market situation. Drammen serves a population of 75.000, with 1800 employed customers and 2300 people receiving unemployment benefits and 1900 people in ALMPs.

Earlier Drammen has experienced a period of structural changes with closures of paper mills and other industry, which still has an effect as employment problems for the aged industrial workers. Otherwise presently there are no particularly difficult employment problem clusters and the economical and labour market situation is favourable.

The office has accomplished a reorganization in 1993. The whole office processed the need and solutions to change and the discussion is still going. The main emphasis has been on establishing more flexibility in ways of operating, introducing teamwork and a better contact with the enterprises and also getting more front-office effort. Mainly this has been done by forming a special team that devotes most of its effort to contacts with enterprises. The renewal was brought by both an emphasis by LMA for better results and a new manager initiating changes in the employment office.

In quantitative, international comparative terms, Drammen emerges as a low performer under medium workload (see figure 16 in the summary on the micro-level). The workload is twofold, however: it is low in supply (unemployed) and high in demand (vacancies). In an environment of high demand it is, as it was in the case of Stockholm City office, of course more difficult to reach high performance levels in the comparison of filling rates in vacancies.

Nevertheless, the situation in Drammen would suggest that even more attention should be devoted to the demand side in the primary market in recent times. There is clear evidence of improved performance due to some modernization changes in the office in terms of more emphasis and teamwork on the demand side as we shall see in the qualitative assessment.

Orgganizational setting and development

The office uses quite a comprehensive set of follow up figures on performance but we got the impression that the concept of management by results or objectives is not used as such in the office. The office doesn't seem to experience that there has been a major change in steering other than that there is more paperwork. There are no definite result goals the office was pursuing as a whole in the same sense that there is focused effort for instance in the Swedish or Finnish case. The general follow-up statistics of the central government were used (i.e. vacancies, placements, unemployment, etc.). On the other hand the renewal of the office into teams has produced self monitored goal-setting on team level.

The organization is divided into four main departments: 1) information-department, 12 persons, including reception, information ("job-club"), vocational counselling, administration 2) placement-department, 14 persons, including enterprise-group, labour market training and labour-market schemes 3) rehabilitation-department, 11 persons and benefits-department, 9 persons. Some people work across responsibilities, so the allocation here is a rough figure. The departments refer to themselves as teams, but no particular team concept or conscious methods were mentioned. The team concept can be seen as dynamic, but spontaneous.

The Drammen office is clearly in a dynamic phase and there is local initiative in the work with enterprises. The employment office would want to move even further into an initiative role, setting its own goals and priorities. The general impression is that Drammen would have more potential and wish to be locally active than the administration is on the average.

The interviewees were rather hesitant about the role and value added by the county-level (fylke). We got the impression that the local level feels that the county level doesn't really know the needs and problems of the local level well enough.

The quality campaign of the Norwegian labour administration, which emphasizes process control, didn't seem to raise much enthusiasm in Drammen. The written descriptions of correct procedures were felt to be more a restraint than a tool for higher quality. It was felt that in practice work is done in a faster and more flexible way than in the procedures and that in an office like Drammen, being in a dynamic and innovative phase, didn't really gain anything from these. Rather there was more unnecessary paperwork. The impression here was that the quality campaign served purposes of staff training and standardization with less focus on continuous development or outside customer orientation.

Placement process and organization

There are two people devoted to the reception, one at desk, the other further "inside". There is one self-service computer in the front-office and another in the information-point (job-club), which has 4 people. The procedure for a newcomer is the following: On the first meeting the persons is registered and asked to come within two weeks for individual discussions on benefit-matters only. Within three months the person is called in for a group-discussion on job-matters.

Concerning the placement-functions there is a fairly clear amount of ownership. The placement/ enterprise team of 5 people devote 70% of their time to contacts with firms and the rest, 30% goes to labour market training and schemes. One person in the group devotes 100% to working with firms. The group sets group- and personal targets on getting new vacancies. Before this arrangement the office got about 20 – 30 new vacancies a month, now 120 a month. So the new arrangement has produced a remarkable rise in the inflow of vacancies as it was also in the case of Stockholm. This can clearly be attributed to the more clear "ownership" on demand. The Drammen office has not here gone "all the way", i.e. established a clear-cut demand-supply split like Stockholm City office. Rather the arrangement in Drammen is quite close to Roskilde. Both arrangements have their strong and weak points. At any rate, the Drammen experience would in our mind suggest a need to move even further in the direction started. In a favourable labour market situation this is even more grounded.

There are two self-service computers and an information point, "job-club", with information on vacancies and training. A new development in Norway is a centrally provided information service for both employers ("blue line") and job-seekers ("green line"). You can get basic information about the numbers of job-seekers or vacancies available in different parts of the country. More detailed information is then provided by the counties or local offices. There was no special mention or special measures of post-placement assessment on the local level.

The EDP-system is of ordinary 'Nordic standard', with a rather limited number of extra search words, 8-10 altogether, approved by the central government.[27]

Finland: Rauma employment office

The city of Rauma is located on the west-coast of Finland and is renowned for its shipyards and export port and a long tradition of hand-

27 Additional remarks on the case study of Moss employment office corrobarate our picture: Moss office, a mid-size office with 28 employees South of Oslo has a traditional work arrangement: 1) Marketing and placements (9), 2) Benefits (8) and 3) Rehabilitation (11). The office arrangement was normal standard with a reception, one self-service spot and reception rooms. The picture of Moss corroborates our earlier findings on the Norwegian LMA and Drammen office; rather incremental changes, an expressed need by the local people to get more leeway and support for local initiative, quality work was considered as a routine standardization process, not innovation. Quantitatively, in international comparative terms, Moss emerges as a low performer (see table 16). It must be pointed out, though, that Moss has been shifting more to primary market orientation from ALMP-orientation, stressed the need for good front office effort and has been working in the local networks to get better results.

icrafts. With the slump in shipping industries Rauma has suffered a period of extremely difficult unemployment, with the rate rising to an all time high of 27,5 in 1993 after three years of continuous rise in unemployment. After that, with the recovery of export industries and some major industrial investments there has been a turnaround of development. Unemployment has dropped from the record high 27,5 % and 6600 unemployed to 20,4 and 4700 in just two years and the prospects are good. There have been two major industrial investment to the area – a new pulp-factory – the largest in the world and a new paper-factory – also one of the largest in the world and at the present time the largest construction site in Finland. The direct and indirect effect of these investments is thousands of new jobs for the larger area.

The Rauma employment office has 35 officials (23 permanent) and it has experienced a complete renewal of its organization within a year and a half. The office has been very closely involved with the above mentioned major industrial investments. The office was assigned to take care of the entire recruitment process of the new pulp-factory including the white-collar higher positions. There were 7000 applications submitted. In order to cope with this challenge, the office formed a special taskforce in collaboration with the regional office getting extra and special personnel (psychologists) to deal with the recruitment.

In the face of new challenges the office renewed its organization from a traditional functional and compartmentalized setup to a team-organization and is presently developing the team-concept further. It has become one of the forerunners of teamwork in the Finnish LMA. Similar development is occurring in many other offices in Finland.

In quantitative terms, Rauma emerges as a medium performer under high workload, which is in line with the macro picture of the Finnish LMA. The workload of Rauma is the reverse of Drammen: high on unemployed and relatively low in vacancies. Effectiveness in terms of placements to vacancies is high and efficiency as placements per employees medium. Market share is 42% of placements/ appointments, which is high.

Organizational setting and development

The Finnish labour administration has gradually moved from a strongly top-down steered management by results to a more decentralized approach emphasising the strategic role of the central administration and giving the counties and local offices more leeway in pursuing local initiatives.

The Rauma office defines its own goals and monitors its own achievement. It uses the strategic goals of the administration as a starting point, but defines its own goals and priorities each year. In 1995 the key goals were:

1) Developing teamwork
2) Enhancing employer/ business contacts
3) Enhancing job-seeker capabilities
4) Targeting special groups (youth, self-employment, etc.)

Each key goal is further defined in results, key performance and the follow-up figures used. A particular feature of the office is a thorough "developmental discussion" by the office manager individually to each employee and team. It is a personal appraisal of goal achievement, setting new goals, commenting on teamwork and other matters of the office.

Competition is allowed in Finland since 1994, but it has had no significant impact outside the capital city area, where it is confined to the hired-labour and the head-hunting markets.

The office was completely reorganized in 1995 on a team-basis. The office is devided into seven teams: 1) Front-office ("rapid services"), 2) Enterprise/ employer-team 3) Job-seeker -team 4) Training-team (vocational guidance and training-information) 5) Labour market schemes 6) Rehabilitation and 7) Administration. The team-concept has been worked out on several occasions with the staff and backed up by a team-network training program provided by the leading state training institution specialized in teamwork. The program runs 1995-96 with the whole staff participating for 5-6 days plus intermediate workshops and follow-up discussions.

Quality work in the Finnish labour administration has consisted of building a comprehensive customer feedback system to all employment offices in Finland. The employment offices gather a quality feedback from both job-seekers and employers and this information is compiled from all offices into a database that can be used on local, regional and national levels. The important part here is that it can be used on the local level and that the local level plays an active part in both getting the feedback and interpreting it. 20% of the personnel in Rauma are academically trained, which is a medium level.

Placement process and organization

Placement and front-office effort has been supported by a) forming a special team responsible for enterprise contacts (and also using major projects to this effect) b) developing a conscious model of a front-office team ("quick-service", 2 experienced officers) responsible for the initial discussions c) using information and 4 self-service computers

The office has implemented an effective "client – contractor" -split by having a special team for contacts with enterprises and a special team for job-seekers. There are 4 self-service computers in the front-office at the disposal of clients. The interface is reasonably good, but has the same shortcomings as the general matching in the face of modern challenges (i.e. fuzzy matching). Written information and officer support is easily available .There is no special effort in follow-up or post-placement support.

The Finnish EDP-system in the labour administration is under renewal. The present system affords some support for non-linear matching (30 search-words). There is also one innovation not present in any of the other countries: The job-seeker can write in free form a description ("advertisement") of her/himself in the system and can specify how it can be used – given to employers in written form or only read on the phone.

Great Britain: Braintree

The City of Braintree and Braintree employment office are located about 70 km North of London. The economic recession in the beginning of the 1980s had more effect in the Northern parts of England, but the recent one of the 1990s has had a bad effect in the South and the Braintree area. The present prospects are not particularly good, most of the jobs available in the office (60-65%), are part-time, unqualified jobs. Unemployment rate is 8%, National average 9% Braintree employment office has 40 staff. Workforce of 45.000. 300-500 enterprises, 2700 job-seekers, mostly unemployed. In May 1996 there were 173 vacancies.

In quantitative terms, Braintree emerges as a high performer under medium/ high workload, which is in line with the macro picture of the British LMA. The workload of Braintree is high/medium both in terms of unemployed job-seekers and vacancies per employee. Effectiveness in terms of placements to vacancies and efficiency as placements per employee are high. There is not an estimate on market share.

Organizational setting and development

The process of administration runs quite top-down in Great-Britain. The CEO agrees on the targets and budgets with regional management. "There is not much bargaining". The districts are then given their share. The regions hand down the objectives to district managers and the district managers are responsible for "steering the capacity" in the district according to objective indicators (number of unemployed, number of new clients). "It is called an agreement". If there is something particular in the district, it is taken into accord. Local initiative and leeway is scarce. The district manager has discussions with local staff once a month bringing knowledge of good practices elsewhere. There is a personal appraisal of the local manager every 3 months.

A comprehensive set of performance targets and indicators are given to the local office from above. They include Key indicators of placements, placements for long term unemployed and disabled, number of job interviews and work trial placings. Additionally there are indicators for various schemes and benefit payment accuracy and speed.

Private competition is allowed in Great Britain. There was no mention that it played a major role in the Braintree area.

The organization of employment services in Great-Britain used to be separated in benefits payment and employment offices (job centres). In 1988 they were joined into job centres. In Braintree the two functions were still in separate buildings but due to move into the same office in 1996. The organization is devided into three major sections: 1) Reception and advice 2) Placement, marketing and schemes and 3) Benefit payments. The job-centre part of the office was an open office, with rather little privacy either for clients or officials. There was limited room for group-work or teams, too. The benefits-part of the office had a shabby appearance of an open office. No mention of specific quality program was given.

There is no initial general level of education. The training is done on-the job, with emphasis on communicative skills, team ability and following instructions. Training is largely based on computer-based modules emphasizing correct procedures.

Placement process and organization

The new changes in employment benefits were expected to increase "forced" front office effort. The unemployment benefits will be changed into a "job-seekers allowance". The job seeker must frequently prove he/she has been active in finding employment. There is no split responsibility for employer vs. job-seeker contacts. Most of the effort is directed to the job-seekers, various job-interviews and schemes. Information and self-service was limited. The entrance-hall had information on walls about jobs with restricted information. If a job interested a client, the detailed information was behind the officer. There was no evidence of special follow-up. The EDP-support appears rather limited, clearly behind Nordic standard. In the Spring 1996 a new system was due, which would probably close the gap to some degree.

Dimensions of evaluation for employment office model	Sweden Stockholm City	Denmark Roskilde	Norway Drammen	Norway Moss	Finland Rauma	Great Britain Braintree	New Zealand Christchurch
I Organizational setting and development in employment offices							
1. Steering and result definitions	medium	low	low	low	high	medium	medium
2. Organizational position and local initiative	high	medium	medium	medium	high	low	medium
3. Work organization							
- internal organization	high	medium	medium	low	medium	low	high
- external work/ networking	high	medium	medium	medium	medium	low	high
4. Process development/ quality work	medium	medium	medium	low	high	low	low
5. Qualifications of personnel	high	medium	medium	medium	medium	low	low
II Placement process and organization							
6. Front office effort	high	low	medium	medium	medium	medium	medium
7. Responsibility and contact with employers and job-seekers and their interface	high	medium	medium	medium	high	low	high
8. Information and self-service	high	low	medium	low	medium	low	medium
9. Follow-up and assessment of sustainable results	medium	low	low	low	low	low	high
10. EDP support for modern non-linear ("fuzzy") matching	high	medium	medium	medium	medium	low	low

Figure 9.13 The qualitative summary of the employment offices

New Zealand: Christchurch Central employment office

The labour administration was established in 1988 in New Zealand. There are 4 regions, with a regional manager and 77 employment offices in NZ. Christchurch has 4 offices, the City office being the largest, with 34 staff. Unemployment rate in Christchurch is 5,8%, relatively low in national terms (average 6,6%). There are lots of jobs available – tourism and its spin-offs, hotels, retail, supermarkets and also manufacturing, electronics. footwear, clothing, forestry. Problem groups are the ethnic minority, maoris (20% unemployment), youth unemployment, women close-to retiring-age and middle management. The office has about 30% market share of vacancies (estimate). The office places a lot of emphasis on connections with employers and enjoys good relations with them.

Quantitatively Christchurch Central employment office is characterized by a high workload and medium performance.

Organizational setting and development

The office has a comprehensive number (14) key targets given by the central government) and it submits its own budget. The key targets cover roughly same kinds of subjects as those of Braintree, i.e. referrals to jobs and special job-seeker groups, various schemes, interviews and workshops, etc.

Private competition is allowed in New Zealand, but it doesn't play a major role in the field.

The personnel of the employment offices have typically "risen from the ranks" i.e. from working life with middle range education.

Placement process and organization

Earlier the office emphasized quick placements, but now more effort is devoted to make more qualified placements and have follow up on sustainable results and get feedback form the customers,

There is a basic split division of labour is into a "business focus team" and a "centre-based team", roughly in half. The office has devoted extra effort to "pre-placement" (finding jobs that suit the supply) and "post-placement" (follow-up and feedback from customers). The office has been an active player in the Christchurch initiative on youth employment. No mention of a specific quality programme was given. The job of the business focus team is especially to find the kinds of jobs suitable for the kinds of job-seekers. Written information was well available, but self-service computers weren't used.

The office made extra effort in post-placement-support for job-seekers and assessment of results from both job-seekers and employers. The Christchurch office was the only one in this study to demonstrate a conscious effort in this respect. There was no evidence of special innovation in the EDP field.

Summary of the local level benchmarking

Quantitative performance

Quantitative performance is assessed through the rate of placements per vacancies and placements per employees (Table 9.5). In quantitative performance, Roskilde from Denmark rates best, with Rauma from Finland and Braintree, Great Britain next. Stockholm, Sweden, Drammen and Moss from Norway rank lowest.

Table 9.5: The quantitative performance of the employment offices

	Work load Ue/ empl. 1995	Work load Vac/ empl. 1995	Effectiveness Pl/ vacancies 1995 (%)	Efficiency Pl/ employee 1995	Market share placements/ appointments
Stockholm[28]	59	100	32	37	-
Roskilde	138	88	93	84	22
Drammen[29]	38	90	26	30,6	-
Moss	44	60	26	16	-
Rauma	139	52	77	39,6	42
Braintree	67	92	63	58,6	30
ChCh	161	88	50	44	30

Qualitative performance

In the qualitative assessment (figure 9.13) of modernization, Stockholm City office rates best, with Rauma and Christchurch next. Qualitatively, Braintree from Great Britain ranks lowest.

We can see, that on the qualitative dimensions, the Swedish case-example presents an evenly high profile. In the Stockholm City office, which is working in a rather favourable environment, there was consid-

28 The Stockholm figures are assessed indirectly from Stockholm county figures. The rate of filling vacancies was 20% higher than the county average in September-November 1995. Due to being one of over 30 offices in the capital city, it is impossible to give an estimate of market share.

29 An estimate of market share could not be provided.

erable front-office effort and a conscious policy – backed up by the central administration priorities – to get more vacancies and fill them successfully. Since the renewal of the office on a "split team" model – a team devoting all its effort to enterprises and another to job-seekers there has been a sharp rise in vacancies and also successful placements. As a performer in quantitative terms, Stockholm is at the moment an average to low performer, however. There has been a considerable increase in performance in less than a year clearly attributable to the new service arrangement.

In Drammen, Norway, where a similar, but not as far going change was made, the number of vacancies attained in the office rose from 20-30 a month to 120 a month. One can argue that with the favourable labour market situation Norway has considerable untapped potential here. With more quantitative (personnel, time, contacts) and qualitative effort (team- & networking) productivity – and thus welfare gains – could be attained with very little restructuration costs. If the magnitude of variance due to mainly working model variables is correct, these gains are noteworthy.

A conscious effort to work on a special project with the primary market gave very good results also in the case of Rauma, where the huge challenge of a major recruitment process in fact spurred the renewal of the whole office. It is noteworthy that the close collaboration with the firm which was implementing a new team concept was a learning experience for the employment office.

So, in sum, the general picture of the Norwegian labour market authority on the local level is essentially the same as in the sectorial comparison and also the macro picture of the Norwegian public sector: in terms of productive capability moderate to low performance and the same in evolutionary capability.

An earlier study on the performance of employment offices (Naschold, 1996, ECON 1993) corroborates these findings:

According to the ECON, study Finland has the heaviest workload, followed by Denmark and then Norway and Sweden. The distribution of costs per job-seeker was precisely the reverse of this. In other words, in relative terms (i.e. per jobseeker) the Finnish employment offices devote the least amount of resources, those in Sweden the most. As far as the quality of placement procedures is concerned, a variable which is extremely difficult to determine, the study does at least provide two guidelines.

According to the ECON study, the Swedish employment offices spend the longest amount of working time on each job-seeker, followed by those in Norway, with Finland and Denmark spending the least number of working hours.

An additional dimension of quality is shown by the way in which computers are used in the placement process. The study clearly shows how the Swedish employment offices make intensive use of data processing technology for customised job-search process outside of routine procedures, whereas the Danish offices only do so in marginal cases, i.e. if explicitly requested to do so; the Finnish and Norwegian employment offices are situated between these two extremes.

Further, the skill structure of staff in the Swedish employment offices and in the Finnish offices is considerably higher than in Denmark and Norway. It should be noted, though, that it is not possible to determine exactly on the basis of the study to what extent these differences are offset or reinforced by internal training programmes and differences in the requirements set by national education systems. The interviews conducted by the authors would suggest that Sweden would pay most attention to staff training (also management training) with otherwise little differences between the other Nordic countries.

5. Modernization of the Labour Administration of Norway in Perspective

In this article we have compared the development and position of the Norwegian public sector particularly concerning the labour market and the labour market authority against an international perspective. We have been interested in two fundamental issues: 1) the productive capability (effectiveness and efficiency) and the evolutionary capability (ability to learn) of the Norwegian case compared with others. We have studied Norway on three levels: the macro-level, using selected OECD countries in the comparison, the sectorial level, using labour market authorities as case-examples and the micro level, studying local employment offices.

Our findings at all three levels converge, with small tolerances, on a robust result: Public sector reform in Norway has been incremental in nature and the Norwegian labour market authority is up to now characterized by structural conservatism and a moderate efficiency level both in terms of empirical comparison with other countries and against a theoretical reference model of an enlightened New Public Management vis-a-vis a Traditional Public Management Model. So Norway portrays a moderate to low productive capability and rather low evolutionary capability. This is a converging result with other studies portraying Norway as a "reluctant reformer" (Olsen, 1996) and placing the modernization of Norwegian municipalities clearly behind in an international comparison (Baldersheim and Ögård, 1996).

So in essence the evidence largely refutes the second scenario, Norway being an efficient welfare state, but is consistent with the fourth scenario hypothesis of Norway being welfare state conservative, with moderate productive and evolutionary capabilities. But let us also look at the other two possibilities – the issue being irrelevant to Norway or that Norway has been inefficient, but is catching up, like the wise tortoise.

Is modernization irrelevant for Norway?

We found that the Finnish study on the efficiency and effectiveness of employment offices (Talonen and Tuomaala, 1994) in placements points to considerable variance that can be attributed the service setups and culture. If one could get a large number of employment offices to rise their performance to best practice level we can extrapolate that we are looking at considerable direct welfare gains in terms of an increase in primary market placements. With an average output variance of the rate of 50% in placements, as was found on the Finnish national level, a rise in productivity in the Finnish environment, with around 60.000 placements per year this could be very significant indeed.

There are also many indirect benefits attached to better placements – building a virtuous circle of good reputation and contact with the primary market and also gaining more room to manoeuvre at the more troubled end of the labour market. Indirect benefits tend to be underestimated because of their complex and often intangible nature.

In Norway, with a lot of vacancies and favourable economic prospects, these issues carry a lot of weight. In addition, Baldersheim and Ögård's study (1996) and Naschold's research (1996) would suggest that there are probably similar untapped potentials also in the Norwegian municipalities and in central state organizations.

As we also pointed out in our findings on the public sector reform trends in the OECD-countries, there is no evidence of a linear homogenous trend in public sector development. Rather there is a limited plurality of developmental paths and also performance. So there are untapped possibilities also in learning. Let us finally look at these issues by exploring the third scenario – is Norway catching up?

Is the slow tortoise winning?

Olsen (1996) points out that in many ways the pattern observed in Norway was an antithesis to the international conventional "New Public Management-wisdom" of the 1980s. This antithesis is a rebuttal of the neo-liberal-Anglo Saxon model seen as a threat to the Nordic welfare state.

The international claim with regard to public sector reform has been that "major surgery" was needed. The welfare state had not lived up to its promises. The public sector was considered incompetent. It was unable to learn and adjust intelligently and rapidly to changes in society. The suggested remedy was to change its culture and structure along the lines of New Public Management. It was seen that to a large extent the Anglo-Saxon models and neo-liberal ideas challenged the core concepts of the welfare state and the public sector, as they have been institutionalized in Norway.

With the absence of a clear performance crisis and only modest ideological confrontation over the public sector coupled with oil money providing a buffer against public deficit and a lack of a strong central institutional basis for reform the sails of radical reform never caught much wind. So Norway has, along the years, made rather slight, incremental changes in an atmosphere of compromise.

So Olsen portrays Norway as a reluctant reformer. His first scenario is the "triumph of the tortoise". In sum, this scenario portrays the Norwegian public adminstration as plodding along, like Aesop's tortoise, learning slowly but steadily. Being a reluctant reformer, it has by and large avoided the misspecified medicine suggested by the international reform program in the 1980s. Slowness comes out as wisdom, since the largely Anglo-Saxon, neoliberal market-management medicines weren't a panacea for solving problems in the society. Rather, imitating the private sector has turned out to be a blind alley (Olsen, 1996). In contrast, in Norway, a capability for reforming and learning has slowly been built up. A process has started – as can also be seen in the case of the sectorial development of the Norwegian LMA. In this scenario the tortoise is winning.

His second scenario is that the tortoise is too slow. Western democracies are at a historical junction and the beginning of a new era. A rapidly changing world demands qualitative reorganizations of cognitive, normative, behavioral and organizational structures, as well as a reallocation of resources. Incrementalism will not be enough. Norway would need comprehensive reform. As a reluctant reformer, the Norwegian public adminstration gets too little empirical variation to explore, the number and types of trials are inadequate.

In line with Olsen´s second scenario our findings would suggest that the tortoise is not winning. First, as we pointed out in refuting the "Manna Scenario", there are already considerable direct and indirect welfare losses. What is more, we get the impression that there would be considerably more potential in modernization, as exemplified by the Norwegian labour market authority, than yet realised. The renewals could probably be accomplished with very little restructuration costs, since performance enhancement could be achieved with new work arrangements, focus and allocation of manpower. For instance our findings in the placement process suggest that even moderate changes in Drammen by focusing more attention and effort on the demand side produced remarkable gains, not to speak of Stockholm and Rauma.

Secondly we want to stress the importance of enhancing evolutionary capabilities in a turbulent environment of growing global competition. Crisis is not a good time to build up learning capabilities. Organizational conservatism is a particularly risky strategy in the case of external shocks or major transformation processes in the external environment. It has been suggested by Freeman (see chapter 2) that particularly the market reforms (capital controls and exchange rate policies) have reduced the number of policy instruments available, which suggests that the state may be less able to affect outcomes in the future than the past.

Further, one cannot identify modernization with the neo-liberal or the Anglo-Saxon version of New Public Management only, nor can one attribute efficiency to one specific regime. Nor is there an unambiguous or monolithic regime of a welfare state (defending itself against the evils of private market models), but rather various degrees of penetration, learning and innovations from different kinds of applications of modernization into the welfare state countries. We don't have an either or situation, but rather a challenge of assimilating in an innovative way the plurality and experience of the different regimes and countries.

So we see considerable untapped potential in Norway both in terms of qualitative and quantitative performance. We suggest a bolder approach in pursuit of best practice and an open mind to look at the rich experience and variability accumulated by the different countries in modernization. In stead of suggesting for the tortoise to just plod along, we would rather urge it to speed up the steps of modernization.

References

Alexander, J. (1994): "Modernisation theory after 'The' transition". In: *Zeitschrift für Soziologie* 23, 3, pp. 165 ff.

Arnkil, Robert (1995) *Restructuring Labour Administration – Investigating the Finnish Experience from a Regional-Local Perspective.* Ministry of Labour. Publications Nr. 90:1995

Aucoin, P. (1992): Administrative reform in public management: Principles, paradigms, paradoxes and pendulums. In: *Governance. An international journal of Policy and Administration,* Vol. 3, Nr. 2, April 1990, pp. 115-37.

Baldersheim, H. and Øgård, M. (1996): *Evaluering i kommunal organisasjonsutvikling.* Institutt for statsvitenskap. Universitetet i Oslo.

Bishop, J. (1992): *Improving job-worker matching in the U.S. labour market.* Center for Advanced Human Resource Studies, Working Paper 92-40.

Bishop, J., H. Key (1991): "*The Impact of Privatisation on the Performance of the U.K. Public Sector*", Vortrag für die CEPR/IMPG-Konferenz. Mailand.

Blöndahl, S. and Pearson, M. (1995) Unemployment and Other Non-employment Benefits. *Oxford Review of Economic Policy*. Vol. 11 No 1. Spring 1995.

BMAS (Österreichisches Bundesministerium für Arbeit und Soziales) (1992): *Die Effizienz der Arbeitsmarktverwaltung. Organisationsanalyse.* Forschungsberichte aus Sozial- und Arbeitsmarktpolitik, Nr. 45. Wien 1992.

Boyer, R. H. (1994): *Markets as a coordination mechanism. History, Theory, and Policy.* Paris: manuscript.

Brunsson, N., J. Olson (1994): *The Reforming Organization.* London: Routledge.

Bryntse, K. (1994): *The management of relationships in purchasing of services in local government.* Paper presented at the symposium "Externalisation and Internalization of Business Services", 29th and 30th of May, 1994, Roskilde University, Denmark.

Caiden, G. E. (1991): *Administrative reform comes of age.* Berlin/New York: de Gruyter

Carl Bertelsmann Prize 1993. *Democracy and Efficiency in Local Government.* Bertelsmann Foundation Publishers. Gütersloh.

Csonka, A. (1993): *Liberalisation of job-center services.* The Danish national insitute of Social Research. Copenhagen.

Davenport, Th. T. (1993): *Process Innovation.* Boston: MIT Press.

Downs, G., P. Larky (1986): *The Search for Government Efficiency. From Hubris to Helplessness.* Philadelphia: Temple University Press.

ECON (1993): *Samfunnsøkonomisk effektive arbeidskontorer i Norden* (1993) ECON Senter for Okonomisk Analyse. (Socio-economically Effective Employment Offices in Norden. ECON Center of Economical Analyses).

Forslund, A. and Kruger, A.B. : An Evaluation of the Swedish Active Labour Market Policy. *Occasional Paper/SNS* No. 65 January 1995

Fujimoto, T. (1996) *An Evolutionary Process of Toyota's Final Assembly Process.* University of Tokyo. Discussion Paper Series. January 1996.

Furabo, J. E. (1994): Learning from Evaluation: The Swedish Experience. In: F. L. Leeuw et al. (eds.): *Can Governments learn? Comparative Perspectives on Evaluation & Organizational Learning.* New Brunswick: Transaction Publishers.

Fölster, St. et al. (1993): *Sveriges systemskifte i fara? Erfahrenheter av privatisering, avreglering och decentralisering*/Ist der Systemwechsel in Schweden in Gefahr? Erfahrungen mit der Privatisierung, Deregulierung und Dezentralisierung, Stockholm: Industriens Utredningsinstitut. (Übersetzung C. Riegler.)

Grönroos, C. (1990): *Nyt Kilpaillaan Palveluilla,* Jyväskylä. (Service Management and Marketing. Managing the Moments of Truth in Service Competition)

Hage, J., Powers, Charles H. (1992): Post-Industrial Lives. Roles and relationships in the 21st Century. Newbury Park/London/New Delhi: Sage.

Häggroth, S. et al. (1993): *Swedish Local Government. Traditions and Reforms.* Stockholm: The Swedish Institute.

Häggroth, S. (1993): *From Corporation to Political Enterprise. Trends in Swedish Local Government.* Ds 1993:6. Civil departementet (Ministry of Public Administration), Stockholm.

Hammer, M., J. Champy (1993): *Reengineering the Corporation.* London.

Henning, R., D. Ramström (1989): *Förvaltningsförnyelse – Arbetsmarknadsverket inför 90-talet*/Verwaltungserneuerung – die Arbeitsmarktverwaltung von den neunziger Jahren. Stockholm: Carlssons. (Übersetzung C. Riegler.)

Leeuw, F. L., R. C. Rist, R. C. Sonnichsen (eds.) (1994): *Can governments learn? Comparative perspectives on evaluation and organisation leadership.* New Brunswick, London.

Locke, E. A., G. P. Latham (1990): *A Theory of Goal Setting and Task Performance.* Prentice Hall, New Jersey.

Lokaldemokratie-Kommittees (SOU) (1993): *Lokal demokrati i utveckling*/Lokale Demokratie in der Entwicklung (=Offizieller Abschlußbericht des parlamentarisch eingesetzten sog. Lokaldemokratie-Kommittees). Stockholm: Civildepartementet.

Luhmann, N., F. W. Scharpf (1989): "Politische Steuerung. Ein Streitgespräch." In: *Politische Vierteljahresschrift* 30 (1989), S. 4 – 21.

Mäki-Lohiluoma, K.-P., A. Niemi-Iilahti (1990): *Muuttaako vapaakuntakokeilu kuntien hallintoa? Vapaakuntakokleilu hallinnon uudistajana Suomessa ja Ruotsissa*/Does the free commune experiment change the municipal administration? Suomen Kaupunkiliitto (Finnish Association of Local Authorities). Helsinki. (Übersetzung M. Lahtonen.)

Mäki-Lohiluoma, K.-P. et al. (1994): *Vapauden aika? Tutkimus 11 vapaakuman kehityksestä vuosina 1988-93. Suomen Kuntaliitto, Vapaakuntaprojekti*/Time of Freedom? Study of developments in 11 municipalities of FCE in 1988 to 1993. Finnish Association of Local Authorities. Helsinki. (Übersetzung M. Lahtonen.)

Marcou, G. 1993: "New tendencies of local government development in Europe". In: Bennett, R. (1993): *Local Government in the New Europe.* London: Belhaven Press

Ministry of Finance Finland (1993): *The World's Best Public Sector?* International Public Management Comparison Project. Helsinki.

Montin, S. (1993): *Swedish Local Government in Transition. A Matter of Rationality and Legitimacy.* Örebro Studies 8, University of Örebro.

Naschold, F. (1996) *New Frontiers in Public Sector Management. Trens and Issues in State and Local Government in Europe.* Walter de Gruyter. Berlin. New York.

Nachhold. F. et al. (1996) *Leistungstiefe im Öffentlichen Sector. Erfarungen, Konzepte, Methoden.* Edition Sigma. Sonderband 4.

Naschold, F. (1993): *Modernisierung des Staates. Zur Ordnungs- und Innovationspolitik des öffentlichen Sektors.* Berlin: edition sigma.

Naschold, F. (1992): *Den Wandel organisieren. Erfahrungen des schwedischen Entwicklungsprogramms "Leitung, Organisation, Mitbestimmung" (LOM) im internationalen Wettbewerb.* Berlin: edition sigma.

Naschold, F., B. de Vroom (eds.) (1994): *Regulating Employment and Welfare. Company and national Policies of Labour Force Participation at the End of Worklife in industrial Countries. Berlin,* New York: de Gruyter.

Naschold, F., R. Cole, B. Gustavssen, H. v. Beinum (1993): *Constructing the new industrial society.* Assen/Maastricht: van Gorcum.

Niklasson, H. and D. Ramström (1989) *Att målstyra arbetsmarknadspolitik.* NAUT-projekt. Copenhagen: Nordisk Ministerråd.

Normann, R., Ramírez, R. (1994): *Designing Interactive Strategy. From Value Chain to Value Constellation.* Chichester: John Wiley & Sons.

Oakland, John S. (1993): *Total Quality Management.* Oxford: Butterworth-Heinemann

Olsen, Johan P. (1996), "Norway: Slow learner – or another triumph of the tortoise?", in Johan P. Olsen and B. Guy Peters, *Lessons from Experience. Experential Learning in Administrative Reforms in Eight Democracies,* Scandinavian University Press, Oslo

Nurmi, T. (1994): *Unitising of Rauma Employment Office.* Helsinki: manuscript.

OECD 1993: *Public Management Developments.* Survey. Paris.

OECD 1992: "The public employment service in Japan, Norway, Spain and The United Kingdom". In: *Employment Outlook,* p. 117 – 142.

OECD 1990: Public *Managment Developments.* Survey. Paris.

OECD (1994): *Economic Outlook.* June 1994. Paris.

OECD (1994): *Employment Outlook.* July 1994. Paris.

OECD *Economic surveys 1992-1993.* Finland. OECD, Paris.

OECD *Public management developments.* Survey 1993. OECD, Paris.

Osborne, D., T. Gabler (1992): *Reinventing Government.* Reeding.

Otter, C. v. (1992): *Personnel management in the public service: Sweden.* Stockholm: manuscript.

Peavy, R.V. (1993) Envisioning the Future Worklife and Counselling. *Canadian Journal of Counselling,* 27: 123-129

Pfeffer, N., A. Coote (1991): *Is Quality Good for You? A Critical Review of Quality assurance in Welfare Services.* Institute of Public Policy Research. London.

Pihlgren, G., A. Svensson (1989): *Målstyring – 90-talets ledningform för offentlig verksamhet*/Zielsteuerung – die Führungsform der 90er Jahre für öffentliche Tätigkeiten. Stockholm: Liber. (Übersetzung C. Riegler.)

Posner, B. (1994): "Sowing the Seeds of Change at the Department of Labor". In: *Harvard Business Review* May/June 1994.

Reichard, Chr., A. Wegener (1994): *Management by Objectives und Management by Results als Managementkonzepte.* Berlin: manuscript.

Rombach, B. (1991): *Why Decisions about Management by Objectives do not lead to Control with Objectives – the Stockholm Example.* Vienna: manuscript.

Rombach, B. (1992): *MbO in the Swedish Public Sector – Predicting a Failure.* Manchester: manuscript.

Senge, P. (1990): *The Fifth discipline.* New York: Doubleday Currency.

Swedish National Labour Market Board. Riktlinjer 1995/1990.

Talonen, M., Tuomaala, M. (1994): *Työvoimatoimistojen tuloksellisuus.* Helsinki. (Comparison of Results of Employment Offices in Finland). Ministry of Labour. Publications Nr. 79:1994.

Walwei, U. (1994): Reform der Arbeitsvermittlung in OECD-Ländern. Modernisierung öffentlicher Dienste und Zulassung privater Anbieter. In: *Mitteilungen aus der Arbeitsmarkt- und Berufsforschung.* Stuttgart u. a.: Kohlhammer, S. 94 ff.

Chapter 10

Making Solidarity Work? Summary and concluding remarks

Jon Erik Dølvik

1. Overview – same but different?

Over recent years the view has become widely held that internationalisation and political integration have drastically reduced the scope for national economic-political governance and undermined the viability of full employment welfare-state policies. It was in this context the Research Council of Norway asked Fafo to organise an international research project to analyse new challenges posed to the Norwegian labour market model by changing international circumstances. In this final chapter we highlight some main insights and questions which can be derived from the project. Section (1) reviews main features of recent labour market developments in Norway; (2) résumés factors that can account for the results and pin-points some critical factors for the future; (3) focus the need for societal commitment to resolve employment problems; (4) sketches co-ordinates for a way forward, while (5) asks whether a more encompassing solidarity pact is called for to restore full employment.

The international contributors to this project acknowledge that global change has posed new restrictions on nation-state policies, but nuance the picture by emphasising the scope for social choice and learning. Societal developments are not fully determined by convergent global economic imperatives. Politics and institutions still matter and have important impact on social outcomes. Mass unemployment is not an inevitable result of structural and technological change, but can be contained and fought against if political committment, imagination and endurance are there.

In line with international trends the Norwegian regime of economic-political governance has undergone substantial transformations. Capital movements and credit policies have been liberalised; exchange rate and monetary policies have been adjusted in conformity with the prevailing anti-inflationary international policy regime; and market reform has been pursued in accordance with the rules of the European single market.

In contrast to most West European and Nordic countries, however, the trend towards ever-increasing employment problems has in Norway been reversed over recent years. Contrary to the bedevilled choice between rising inequality and unemployment suggested by the US example, this turn around has been achieved in parallel with persistense of solidaristic income and welfare policies. Deregulation of labour markets and decentralisation of collective bargaining, as recommended by international agencies like OECD, have not been applied and facilitated by soaring oil revenues pursuit of expansionary Keynesian policy in one country has proved fairly efficient.

Despite this seemingly inconsistent hybrid of social-democratic traditionalism and market-oriented modernism, the Norwegian economy has over recent years fared better than most OECD-countries in terms of growth, employment, inflation and public finances. Unemployment has been brought down, the labour force has grown significantly and social marginalisation has been limited. After a severe crisis 1987–93 traditional exports have risen, competitiveness improved and private sector growth has created jobs at a fairly high pace. Female employment participation has grown and some social reform have been undertaken, contributing to the evolution of a "gender order" conducive to reduce inequality between the sexes in terms of involvement in work and family life.

Compared to the pervasive picture of massive employment crisis, rising inequality, social exclusion and failure of labour market policies prevailing throughout the OECD area, this is no minor achievement. Still, at 4-5 percent, unemployment is unacceptably high by Norwegian standards.

From the perspective of the abandonment of welfare-state corporatism by international economic orthodoxy and the dismissal of market reforms by labour orthodoxy, the achievements of the hybrid Norwegian policies may appear puzzling. The contributors to this book do not conceive that Norway has found a distinct new formula of restoring full employment or entered onto a third path between market liberalism and social-democratic traditionalism. Instead they tend to perceive that the performance of Norwegian labour markets over recent years reflects a virtuous combination of unusually favourable economic circumstances associated with soaring oil revenues and the development of a workable policy-mix by "muddling through", enabled by an institutional legacy of pragmatic cooperation between organised actors, better termed "reluctant reformers" (Olsen, 1996) than visionary innovators (Naschold and Arnkil chapter 9).

Norway as a slow learner of contemporary fashion appears to have prevented hasty failures and pursued retrenchment policies and rationalisation with less urgency. This has enabled Norway to reap the benefits of the institutionalised solidaristic legacy, while experiencing economic restructuring at a pace that has allowed scope for social adjustment to change (Keller, chapter 8). As suggested by Rødseth (chapter 5) the coincidal timing of change and events, perhaps more than political and institutional distinctions, seems to be an important factor why Norway has not been hit by such a drastic growth of unemployment as Denmark in the 1970s and Sweden in the early 1990s. In line with the image of a slow reformer the welfare state expansion in Norway took place a decade or so later than in Sweden and Denmark, serving as an important absorber of especially female labour throughout the 1980s and early 1990s. Indeed, as suggested by the "Golden Mean" hypothesis of Freeman (see chapter 2), the Norwegian welfare state has never reached the elaborated level of the Swedish, thereby avoiding the harsh consequences of having to roll it back later. The oil-crisis in 1986, perceived by some as a sign from God, forced consolidation and further helped rescue Norway from the Swedish malaise of delayed adjustment. Still, the Norwegian public sector seems to be an international laggard in terms of effectiveness and modernisation, accordning to Naschold/Arnkil (chapter.9).

A main conclusion that emerges from the analysis in this book is that the persistense of solidaristic welfare policies, gender equality and corporatist labour policies *per se* are not incompatible with the modern global economy. As stated by Freeman, "the world economy does not dictate any given wage structure/social spending policy. The problem of adjusting to a more open world economy lies with internal conditions relating to wage-setting institutions, not with trade per se" (chapter 2 p. 35). This might appear as a trivial insight, but contemporary trends make it worth acknowledging, even though some essential conditions are required, hereby qualifying and nuancing the thesis. While abolition of corporatist arrangements, marketisation and decentralisation of industrial relations have been considered essential to combat inflation and restore growth in most western countries, the contributors to this book seem to agree that the pursuit of centralised concertation and solidaristic incomes policies since the late 1980s have been important in containing inflation and ensuring credibility, acceptance and coherence of the adopted employment policies.

Thus, it seems reasonable to maintain that the officially embraced Norwegian "Solidarity alternative" has so far delivered. The various contributions, however, reflect uncertainty and in some cases doubts about the capacity of innovation, sustainability and viability of recent practices over the years ahead. The prerequisites and outcome of the "solidarity alternative" were facilitated by a unique constellation of political and economic circumstances which may not easily be replicated through the current boom. And as emphasised by Naschold/Arnkil in particular (chapter 9), the defensive adjustment of reluctant reformers may prove insufficient as strategy to match the challenges of the future.

2. Explanation – pragmatic combination of traditional means

What can account for the fairly positive developments of Norwegian labour markets over recent years? A reading of the various contributions in this book suggests that macro-economic and macro-political features have been central explanatory factors, while the institutional frameworks of Norwegian labour markets have played an important facilitating role.

(1) Soaring oil revenues, as analysed by Rødseth (chapter 5), have protected Norway from the constraining effects of current account and public debt problems, allowing scope to use macro-economic means for stabilising purposes, to defend the welfare-state and to use the public sector to bridge domestic slump in labour demand. Solid public finances have also eased the disciplining pressures of international financial markets, implying that expansionary fiscal policies could be pursued without a detrimental spill-over to monetary policy. Still noteworthy is that Keynesian policies have proved efficient in stimulating domestic employment in parallel with bringing down domestic inflation. So, provided solid public finances and institutional prerequisites are in place to contain cost-driving dynamics, it seems that the widely declared death of Keynesianism in one country has been somewhat precipitated.

(2) Despite the helpful "Mannah from heaven", frequently warned to cause a vicious circle of cost-inflation and crowding out of private industries (the so-called "Dutch disease"), Freeman (chapter 2) suggests Norway might have approached a "Golden Mean" of public and private means, preventing the negative effects on private growth and incentives claimed to undermine the Swedish welfare state. The oil-revenues evidently have cushioned public policies and, contrary to a common view, Eika (1996) has suggested that the oil-economy has provided positive spill-overs to mainland industries. Exports minus imports of non-oil goods was about 10% before 1973 and about 10 % in 1993, hardly indicating a "Dutch disease" problem. The robust surpluses of Norwegian budgets provide a safety-net securing room for manoeuvre to counteract

future slumps, but may also represent a continuous temptation to suspend long-term caution for short-term extravagance.

(3) It is worth noting in a world where fear of inflation seems to override most other policy goals that Norway, despite relatively tight labour markets and favourable macro-economic conditions over recent years has succeded in avoiding wage-cost spirals. This has been ensured by amongst other factors a vigorous reinforcement of centralised incomes policies, suggesting corporatism has served as a functional equivalent to market deregulation and economic retrenchment policy. Though, Norway has also benefited from reduced inflationary impulses from abroad and the competition policies of the European single market. In a situation where exchange rate policy and monetary policy have become more restricted by international finance markets, the system of industrial relations and labour markets are bound to carry a larger burden of adjustment to external economic fluctuations. Even though wage moderation has also been achieved in countries with market-based pay-setting, the solidaristic wage policies in Norway have effectively contained leap-frogging and pressures towards rising pay inequality, thereby providing credibility and social support for the overall policy approach (Dølvik et al, chapter 3).

(4) Solidaristic wage restraint has also contributed positively to the employment-effects of public spending (Keller, chapter 8) and allowed scope for substantial improvement of relative wages among the lowest paid, not least benefitting female labour (Ellingsæter and Rubery, chapter 4). A concern shared by most contributors, however, is to which degree this particular imposition of solidarity 'from above', freezing wage differentials, has caused underlying tensions which might unleash intensified distributive struggle in the years ahead. Under the current boom the social underpinning and legitimacy of the "solidarity approach" may thus be subject to erosion.

(5) Contrary to the current credo of labour market deregulation, the comprehensive regulatory frameworks of Norwegian labour markets, often assumed to inhibit employment generation, have seemingly not had detrimental effects on labour market performance in general. Contrary to the thesis of job-less growth, job creation has been high, also in low-skilled private labour market segments, while mobility rates and labour turn-over are similar to average figures within the OECD area, suggesting Norwegian labour markets are fairly flexible (Bosch, chapter 7). Most contributors, on the other hand, find it difficult to trace any significant solidaristic efficiency effects, as suggested by the argument that regulatory systems with high employment protection and cooperative labour relations is more conducive to functional, internal flexibility,

learning and innovative capacity at the workplace. As discussed particularly by Bosch (chapter 7) and Ellingsæter/Rubery (chapter 4) it seems that the innovative potentials of the egalitarian Norwegian system of pay, gender relations, work organisation and trust-based workplace cooperation have been realized to a very limited degree. Norwegian working life exhibits rather few examples of advanced, high-skilled production concepts, despite the relatively low costs of high-skilled labour, and is marked by conservatism e.g as to organisation of working time and pay systems. This may partly reflect the macro-oriented, distributive thrust of industrial relations, partly a kind of consensual easy-goingness at firm level (Bosch, chapter 7). According to Bosch, Norwegian management seems marked by weak decision-making capacity, a tendency to avoid conflicts and lack of training among supervisors, which all together limit the scope for learning and innovation at work. An excessively complex structure of representation and trade unions, also contributes to slow down change at firm level. In line with the image of a reluctant reformer, however, the institutionalised system of workplace cooperation seemingly engender ability to accomodate relatively conflict-free change by enhancing employee voice and acceptance.

(6) The comparatively slow pace of restructuring may, however, have provided some long-term benefits by halting drastic job-losses and hysteresis, allowing a more smooth absorption of excessive labour than in most other European countries. Moene et al. (chapter 6) argues that a distinction between fixed and flexible employment regimes may contribute to explaining why mass unemployment occurred later and might have become less entrenched in Norway than elsewhere. They suggest, however, that there has been a change towards more flexible employer manpower policies accompanying the rise of unemployment since the late 1980s, suggesting that a return to full employment may prove hard to achieve. Thus "Peer Gynt was wrong when claiming that the way forth and back was of equal length".

(7) The evolution of the public welfare sector has served multiple functions in Norwegian labour markets: as an employer absorbing increasing numbers of employees during the recession, especially among women, enabling the double income family; as a provider of benefits and incentives influencing individual choices of labour market adaption; and as a supplier of educational expansion and reform; all contributing to enhance the scope for social choice between work and other activities.

As emphasised by Ellingsæter and Rubery (chapter 4) the welfare state has given important impetus to a "gender order" of increased relative equality, also engendering new conflicts between men and women as to participation in work, family life and parenthood. The corollary to the new family life-styles has been a tacit mode of "job sharing" through female part-time work and rising flows in and out of work due to parental leave. Still labour markets are highly segregated and there are rare signs that women are entering the core masculine areas of the private sector or becoming the primary family breadwinner. Even though the new pattern of family-work relations contains promising potentials e.g. as to flexible adjustment of working time over the life-cycle, work-sharing and maintenance of wage moderation, the international contributors have also become concerned with new lines of social tension that may emerge. If public sector growth flattens out, women may in the future become more vulnerable to employment problems, distributional struggle may intensify between female high-skilled and low-skilled public employees, and womens' acceptance of part-time work and their status as secondary family wage-earners may prove questionable the years ahead. Such tensions might spill over to the system of pay determination and trade unions where changing gender, occupational and sectoral composition is likely to pose new debates about priorities and demands. Nevertheless, it should be recogniced that in international comparative terms Norway have made great progress towards a new gender order based on dual labour market participation without the increased household income inequality which can result from these changes in the distribution of employment.

(8) As to the complex effects of welfare state schemes on incentives to work and education, patchy empirical evidence has not provided the basis for the international contributors to arrive at clear-cut conclusions. Indeed Norway has comparatively generous benefits for certain groups enabling temporary absence from work, but labour participation rates have increased and the share of population outside the work-force has decreased in the 1990s, suggesting distortion of incentives to work does not represent a general problem. Compulsory participation in labour market schemes as eligibility criteria for an increasing number of benefits (the "working line"), may also serve as availability test, preventing labour market exit and increased dependence on social welfare.

The fact that enrollment in secondary and higher education has accelerated over recent years indicates that wage compression and decreasing returns to human capital have not eroded the overall motivation to acquire qualifications. On the contrary it seems that the growing propensity to enter higher education may outpace the rising skill requirements of vacant jobs, possibly generating a problem of over-qualification and mismatch in certain labour market segments and weakening the bargaining capital of many well-educated groups. If so the threshold into work may raise beyond the needs of actual jobs, threatening to cause frustration and tension between generations of labour market entrants and elder employees, presumably leaving the least skilled in a vulnerable position. Such prospects may suggest that positional struggle over job opportunities, demarcations and rewards among the working population might gain increased prominence, possibly to the detriment of newcomers and those outside work.

(9) Active labour market policy (ALMP), aimed at upgrading social and occupational skills of job-seekers and providing temporary employment and job-training for core groups of long-term unemployed, has been attributed central importance in Norway. The international researchers, however, tend to consider the gains of ALMPs are oversold in international discourse (Naschold and Arnkil chapter 9), suggesting "ALMPs are not a big gun in the fight against unemployment" (Freeman, chapter 2). Still they seem inclined to share the view that Norwegian labour market authorities have managed more succesfully than many countries (e.g. Sweden) to design and perform ALMP in a way that has contributed positively to accomodate labour market problems. Training schemes have plausibly improved job opportunities and rotation among the job-seekers and prevented marginalisation of the long-term unemployed during the slump. It has also been suggested that modestly paid and compulsory ALMPs may have an harassment effect, inducing people to find jobs or education on their own. It is however worth recalling that an important precondition for the effects of ALMP in Norway has been the stimulus of labour demand through macro-economic means. As labour markets are becoming tighter and employment problems increasingly structural, correctly targeted and designed schemes and selection of entrants become even more crucial to complement placement services. As pointed out by Naschold and Arnkil (chapter 9) excessive concentration on ALMPs might substitute for the core function of public labour market administration, placement services, which becomes even more crucial in periods of labour market recovery. The study of Naschold and Arnkil suggests that Norwegian placement services in comparative perspective have been marked by weak performance, modest efficiency and lack of innovation. Better quality of placement services might thus represent an untapped potential for improving the functioning of labour markets with positive welfare gains the years ahead.

(10) A common concern of the international contributors is whether the innovative capacity of the macro-oriented Norwegian labour market model will prove sufficient to cope with future competitive challenges. A critical factor thus will be to strengthen the linkages between macro and micro processes and between public and private actors, especially in the field of training, skill formation and R&D (Bosch chapter 7). If the disci-

plining effects of market pressures and unemployment are eased, the management-labour cooperation faces a particular challenge to develop more proactive adjustment of production. Ellingsæter and Rubery (chapter 4) suggest that more needs to be done to exploit Norway's potential comparative advantage in high skill industries resulting from a labour force with high educational levels but low premium for high skill and education. The quest for innovation applies not only to private actors exposed to international competition. Referring international, comparative studies, suggesting weak performance and adjustment capacity of the Norwegian public sector, Naschold/Arnkil argue that substantial welfare gains could be reaped by better organisation, more efficient utilisation of resources, improved quality and customer service in the public sector. In their words, "the tortoise" (Olsen, 1996) will have to change gear to remain competitive and maintain the credibility and popular support of public welfare provisions.

In conclusion, there is no "miracle-cure" that can account for the fairly positive labour market developments in Norway recent years. Even though favourable macro-economic conditions and policies stimulating labour demand have indeed been important, it rather appears to be the pragmatic combination of a number of traditional means, enhancing complementarity and coherence of applied policies which has been the "proof of the pudding". The egalitarian ethos of the centralised system of labour relations has by the international researchers been perceived as an indispensable societal foundation of the macro-political regime. The perception of a common responsibility for the unemployment problem was triggered by a sense of societal crisis in the late 1980s, enabling commitment of the main social partners to a tripartite social compromise from above, which proved capable of mustering social support and credibility from below. Despite popular criticism and impatience about results, the authors tend to conceive that the relative equality of Norwegian working life engender potentially important advantages which are not yet fully realised, but it might also engender new challenges.

If sustainable, egalitarian policies may provide increasing comparative advantage in terms of cheap skilled labour, social cohesion and utilisation of human resources, especially among women. In principle it might also reduce barriers to mobility and ease cooperative change at the workplace. On the other hand the difficult reconciliation of equality, efficiency and perceptions of just labour rewards might cause increased strains on the system of pay determination. Consequently consistency of the system of interest intermediation and collective bargaining will remain a critical, but presumably a vulnerable prerequisite for the capacity of

Norwegian society to cope with change and roll back unemployment. The contributors are hence concerned that interplay between economic affluence, more diverzified patterns of occupational interests and labour organisations, and increased tension over work renumeration (between employees in public and private sector; industries of traded and non-traded goods; high-and low-skilled; men and women, and different age groups) might undermine support of solidaristic pay and welfare policies. In that regard the relative success of recent policies may ironically turn out to become the main threat to its continuation.

3. Societal commitment to full employment?

The achieved progress and bright outlooks of the Norwegian economy engender a danger of delusion, potentially eroding political commitment. Norway is therefore approaching a cross-roads where the capacity of collective learning and choice will prove decisive for whether unemployment can be combated and employment rates increased. On the one hand Norway now has a golden opportunity to return to a full employment regime, on the other hand the affluence of the majority will make this an uphill battle. There are signs that commitment to continue the "solidarity approach" may be crumbling and employer voices have suggested the fight against unemployment is now accomplished.

A test of solidarity will thus be whether powerful organisations on the employer and union side are prepared to maintain the priority given to the needs of vulnerable groups in the labour market or revert to pursuit of narrower interests to secure a greater share of the cake for themselves. As unemployment ceases to be a visible threat of the majority there is an inherent risk that establishment in society tacitly accepts the view that a "natural unemployment" of some 4-5 percent is necessary to inhibit the danger of inflation.

However, if an open unemployment of 4-5 percent (in addition to sizeable groups with weak relations to the labour market) becomes politically accepted in the midst of peaking oil-revenues and the strongest economic up-turn since WW-II, there is ample reason to ask whether the concept of full employment will ever regain a meaningful content. If so it is likely that society adjusts to a development where every recession inevitably causes a rise in social exclusion until massive job-lessness has become "natural" also in Norway. Moreover, in a society with an ever rising level of education, screening of applicants and rationing of jobs become more efficient. It is therefore likely that groups excluded from employment will increasingly be regarded as victims of inferior individual abilities, socially legitimising their marginalised position. Therefore, if efficient policies are not conducted to help the hard-to-employ overcome the barriers surrounding working life and secure opportunities to acquire real training and job experience, a substantial minority of society may run the risk of being shut out from the community of social, economic and political rights associated with earning a wage in our society of work-protestantism.

In the longer term such a scenario may be a liability also from an economic perspective. In a society where things are valued by their price, unemployment represents a waste of human resources and a loss of society's capacity to solve common tasks. The ageing of society and demographic change imply that the labour force may shrink, unless the participation rate increases, while the need for manpower is likely to grow. One important lesson from the 1980s-early 1990s is that large welfare states cannot sustain high unemployment for very long (Freeman chapter 2). The possibility that oil revenues will decline, further strengthens the economic argument that contrary to accepting growing job-lessness, society should strengthen the efforts to promote a distribution of burdens and benefits that provides everybody a right to participate in productive activity.

4. The way forward – an uphill battle

A common thrust of the contributions in this book is that there is no magic formula to combat employment problems in (post) industrial societies. Design of appropriate strategies requires an adequate understanding of the increasingly complex, segmented and structural nature of prevailing labour market problems. Unemployment is not a static and homogenous stock feature, as often assumed in popular images, but a residual phenomenon pending from immense flows of labour exchange, complex matching processes between demand and supply of employees with different qualifications, and movements in and out of working life.

Commitment to increase labour participation and combat unemployment therefore will imply troublesome, patient struggle on several fronts where coherence and complementarity of policy instruments will be of crucial importance. Neither economic growth, expansion of public services, deregulation, more restrictive welfare state policies, social engineering of incentives, or job-sharing and working time reduction, can alone represent a viable response to the challenge. They may however all be parts of a possible answer, provided appropriate targeting and consistency is ensured. As there is never only one pathway to achieve societal goals, we will maintain that each society, if possible, should try to find a way which builds on and makes the most of acquired experiences, advantages and distinctions. Hence Norway ought to strike a careful balance between preservation of what is achieved and innovation of past practices, recalling that small changes might sometimes cause large differences.

As the nature of current Norwegian employment problems are not conjunctural, the potentials of further macro-economic demand-side stimulus are limited. Likewise onesided uniform measures to achieve job-sharing by reducing normal working time appear likely to overshoot, possibly aggravating bottlenecks and raising labour costs, whereas tax reform to raise the competitiveness of labour vis-a-vis other productive sources may give a positive impetus to employment demand.

Enhancement of flexible and differentiated reorganisation of working time; educational and parental absence of leave; reduced overtime; options for voluntary shortening of working time for specific categories of employees; and more flexible retirement schemes, reflecting the varying social needs and capacities over the life-cycle, might contribute to provide easier access to and rotation of jobs (see Ellingsæter and Rubery, chapter 4, Bosch, chapter 7 and Keller, chapter 8). Such initiatives might also enhance sharing of jobs and better distribution of burdens and rewards between groups of employees. A striking paradox of modern working life is that sizeable groups suffer from unhealthy, excessive work-hours, whereas other groups are suffering from a lack of meaningful activities. Resolution of this dilemma is primarily a question of organisational imagination and commitment, posing important challenges to the central and local organisations of working life in particular. In this regard Ellingsæter and Rubery call for greater awareness of the advantages that could accrue to Norway from having already made the transition to a dual breadwinner system, providing an asset rather than a constraint on future development.

To reduce the structural and frictional component of unemployment, policies to improve matching of skills by means of education, training and re-training combined with more efficient placement services are indeed pivotal. Segmentation of labour markets due to occupational and professional job protection is an inherent feature of a modern labour market. Policies to enhance a more flexible deployment of tasks between different categories of employees are indeed a desirable, though contentious undertaking, but much could presumably be achieved by a better monitoring and scaling of professional education and labour supply. In a situation with excessive supply of candidates with university grades and scarcity of manpower and educational places in several professional labour markets, a shift of emphasis towards the latter might be helpful. This might, possibly in combination with better financial support of education, also ease tendencies of professional wage drift.

One of the most promising intiatives in Norwegian working life recent years has, according to Bosch (chapter 7) been the reform of vocational training, supposed to raise skill-levels and improve transition from school to work.Whether the practical outcome will match the expectations, hinges on the ability to provide sufficient apprenticeship places. So far the Norwegian model seems to suffer from a lack of means to induce employers to take on this collective responsibility in a satisfactory way. Improved vocational training among labour market entrants is likely to influence job-rationing processes and cause pressures for more training among supervisors and less skilled elder workers. An interesting, but controversial, initiative thus is the proposal of the main trade union confederation (picked up by Government) to prioritise individual rights to vocational retraining over the life-cycle, rather than the increase of real wages. Such a reform would indeed raise a range of complicated questions to be solved by the concerned social partners (e.g. the issue of labour costs and flexibility), but a fundamental precondition seems to be a profoundly improved supply of adequate training facilities. As emphasised by Bosch, the scattered nature of Norwegian society, with few regional centres and industrial clusters large enough to provide a fully-fledged supply of competent training facilities, implies that public agencies will have to play a key role in developing an adequate nation-wide supply of vocational education in cooperation with private actors.

To increase labour market participation of outsiders and help the long-term unemployed back into work, the main approach will, as suggested, have to rely on positive means, comprising the (long-term) upgrading of skills and social qualifications, the development of targeted ALM-schemes to provide job-experience, the combating of discriminatory screening practices and the enhancement of recruitment. While neither the precarious, low-paid US service-job option, nor the general expansion of public sector to absorb the unemployment, are considered serious policy alternatives, it might yet be considered whether specific public schemes could be designed to provide appropriate job opportunities for those not having acquired a job after all ordinary schemes have been tried. To reduce marginal labour costs and bolster demand of un-skilled labour, particularly in the service sector, differentiated easing of levies on employees might be helpful.

In the longer term, especially if oil revenues decline, the growth and job-creating capacity of the Norwegian economy outside the public sector will be decisive for the combating of employment problems. To bolster competitiveness, make the most of productive resources, and ensure the credibility of public services in a climate of tougher international competition, the international authors view it as essential to foster the capacity of innovation and renewal of working life. (While this book has concentrated on macro-economics and labour market institutions, enhancement of product innovation by means of R&D, socio-technical infrastructure and industrial policy are indeed important in that regard.) Even though the cooperative system of industrial relations may be conducive to defensive change, simplified structures of representation and trade unions seem recommendable to improve the ability of proactive change at a decentralised level. The persistence of the centralised system of corporatism appears more viable if stronger emphasis is given to develop support, expertise and advice to actors at lower levels, more attentive to issues of production. A challenge to the social partners, and perhaps trade unions in particular, would thus be to strengthen the micro-foundation of the cooperative Norwegian model in a way that provides more offensive flexibility and tangible results also from an employer point of view.

5. Case for a more encompassing solidarity pact?

A constraint on all countries trying to roll back unemployment is the monetarist bias of the international political economy towards fighting the spectre of inflation, inhibiting international initiatives to promote growth and employment. In the medium term each country will therefore mainly have to rely on national strategies to combat the crisis of employment. In such an undertaking each country will have to build on their own experience and distinctions. This implies that the conclusions we have drawn as to evolution of a Norwegian approach is not easily applicable to other countries with different traditions. That does not exclude the possibility that the Norwegian experiences can provide useful insights and inspiration for actors from other nations.

Restoration of full employment in Norway will amount to a demanding balancing act between preservation and innovation, requiring prudence and courage. As emphasised, a key prerequisite will be that all central actors maintain commitment to prioritise the goal of employment above special interests.

In a situation with economic boom, an increasingly strong currency and falling interest rates, the Norwegian model of concertation is thus heading for a strong robustness test. Whereas economic bonanzas ended with devaluations and wage laws in the late 1970s and 1980s, exchange rate adjustment and use of monetary policies for stabilising purposes have now been abandoned (Rødseth chapter 5). This implies that fiscal restraint and moderate incomes policies will have to resolve the task of preventing overheating of the Norwegian economy, indeed no easy task in a situation with soaring budget surpluses and a minority government.

As discussed in several of the contributions the main challenge to the Norwegian labour market model does not stem from outside, but from within. Currently there are signs that the legitimacy and support of solidaristic policies are crumbling, suggesting a renewed and more comprehensive social compromise is called for. The imposition of solidaristic incomes policies from above has caused a feeling among certain groups that wage structures have been frozen in an unfair way, implying that important organisations lack identification and feel alienated from the previous compromise, despite its leverage. This has been fuelled by the economic boom, causing growing expectations and feeling of relative deprivation among less advantaged groups. The fact that profits have soared and employer representatives and management have allowed themselves conspiquous increases of salary, option deals etc., while simultaniously preaching moderation to wage-earners, represents a symbolic demonstration of ignorance which might seriously add to erosion of the solidaristic legacy. The fairly generous 1996 pay round indeed implied an easing of tension over relative wages, but signalled also that employees may prove less willing to comply with the quest for moderation in the years ahead. If a dynamic of rising inequality and wage competition is gaining ground, a new consensus may prove hard to achieve, easily triggering tendencies towards leapfrogging and fragmentation of the system of interest intermediation. The losers in such a race are likely to be the unemployed and social groups threatened by marginalisation.

The overall challenge to the actors of the Norwegian labour market model therefore seems to be the construction of a more encompassing social compromise that combines the virtues of distributive justice with responsiveness to the increasingly differentiated demands of production and employee expectations. A particular challenge will be to provide full-time employment opportunities among women, decreasingly inclined to accept part-time jobs. To succeed in such an undertaking it seems desireable to include a wider range of issues and involve a broader set of actors than the current solidarity alternative, in practice focussing mainly on macro-policies and wage moderation. Acknowledging the legitimacy of securing profitability and predictability for business, long-term reciprocity requires employer commitment to ensure that company surpluses are not wasted on unfounded "out-flagging" and "casino-capitalism", but invested in production of real value and jobs beneficial to all parties of the domestic economy. In this section we have suggested some issues which might feed into negotiations over such a compromise, but a crucial task apparently will be to define envisaged sacrifices and benefits in a more tangible way, enabling greater social involvement, consent and monitoring from below. This may amount to a strainful pedagogical and political task, but considering the alternative of entrenched unemployment such a pathway may be worth the price of trying.

Reference

Eika, T. (1996) "Petroleumsvirksomheten og norsk økonomi". *Økonomiske analyser*, 15: pp. 26-33

Olsen, Johan P. (1996), "Norway: Slow learner – or another triumph of the tortoise?", in Johan P. Olsen and B. Guy Peters, *Lessons from Experience. Experential Learning in Administrative Reforms in Eight Democracies*, Scandinavian University Press, Oslo.

Participants of the research team

Prof. Dr. **Gerhard Bosch**, born 1947, sociologist from University of Cologne. Researcher at several research institutes and universities in Germany and for the German Trade Union Federation. Since 1993, Professor in Sociology at the Gerhard Mercator University of Duisburg and Vice President of the Institute for Work and Technology, Science Center of Northreine-Westphalia. Member of the High Level Expert Group on the Social and Societal Aspects of the Information Society, 1995. Recent publications in English: *Retraining not Redundancy* (ILO Geneva, 1992); with P. Dawkins, F. Michon (eds) *Times are Changing. Working Time in 14 Industrialized Countries* (Geneva, 1993); with D. Anxo et al. (eds) *Working Patterns and Capital Utilisation. An International Comparative Study* (Deventer, 1995); *OECD Flexible Working Time, Collective Bargaining and Government Intervention* (Synthesis Report) (Paris, 1995); and *Building the European Information Society for Us All.* Interim Report (European Commission, 1996).

Dr. **Anne Lise Ellingsæter**, born 1950, sociologist from University of Oslo and Research Director at the Institute for Social Research in Oslo. Her current research interests are gender relations in the labour market, the temporal organization of work and family, comparative research on the relationship between institutional–political factors and gendered labour market relations, and the gender–class issue. Among her main works may be mentioned *Gender, Work and Social Change. Beyond Dualistic Thinking* (Institute for Social Research, 1995).

Prof. Dr. **Richard B. Freeman,** Ph.D. in Economics at Harvard 1969. His current positions are Professor of Economics at Harvard University, Program Director for Labour Studies at the National Bureau of Economic Research and Executive Director, Programme in Discontinuous Economics, London School of Economics, Centre for Economic

Performance. Professor Freeman has served on several official panels and commissions in different countries. He recently completed his role as member of the United States Secretary of Labor and Commerce's "On the Future of Worker–Management Relations". Professor Freeman was Project Director for the joint NBER-SNS project on "Reforming the Welfare State: the Swedish Model in Transition". He has published over 250 articles and written and edited 16 books on such topics as youth labour market problems, higher education, trade unionism, traditional economics, social mobility, income distribution and equity in the marketplace. Some of his recent books include: *What do Unions Do?* (1984), *Small Differences that Matter: Labor Markets and Income Maintenance in Canada and in the United States* (1993), *Working Under Different Rules* (1994), *Differences and Changes in Wage Structures* (1995), *The Welfare State in Transition* (forthcoming 1997).

Prof. Dr. **Berndt K. Keller**, born in 1946, sociologist from University of Bochum. Professor at the Department of Public Policy at the University of Konstanz since 1987. Guest professor at the University of Berkeley 1992–1993 and at the University of Warwick 1994. Most important books are *Arbeitsbeziehungen im öffentlichen Dienst. Tarifpolitik der Gewerkschaften und Interessenpolitik der Beamtenverbände* (Frankfurt/New York, 1983); *Arbeitspolitik des öffentlichen Sektors* (Baden-Baden, 1993) and *Arbeitsbeziehungen und Arbeitsmarkt in sozialwissenschaftlicher Perspektive* (Munchen/Wien, 1996).

Per Kleppe, born 1923, Cand. Oecon. Minister of Trade 1971–1972, Minister of Finance 1973–1979, Minister of Planning 1979–1981, Secretary General of EFTA from 1981, and leader of the Norwegian Employment Commission in 1992.

Prof. Dr. **Karl Ove Moene,** Department of Economics, University of Oslo.

Prof. Dr. **Frieder Naschold**, born 1940, Professor for Administration Sciences at the University of Constance, Special Professor for Organizational Sciences at the Free University of Berlin, Visiting Professor at Harvard, Berkeley, Oxford, Oslo, Stockholm and Vienna. Managing Director of the Research Unit Technology–Work–Enviroment at the Science Center Berlin (WZB) and Special Advisor to the European Commission. His recent publications in English are: *The Modernisation of the Public Sector in Europe: A Comparative Perspective on the Scandinavian Experience* (Ministry of Labour, Helsinki, 1995); *New Frontiers in Public Sector Management: Trends and Issues in State and Local Goverment in*

Europe (Berlin: Walter de Gruyter, 1996); and *Public Sector Transformation; Rethinking Markets and Hierarchies in Government* (Amsterdam/Philadelphia: John Benjamins Publishing Company, 1996) (co-written with Carsten von Otter).

Prof. Dr. **Jill Rubery**, Economist from University of Cambridge. Professor of Comparative Employment Systems at the Manchester School of Management. Coordinator of the EUC network of experts on the situation of women in the labour market. She has written five reports for the EUC on occupational segregation, wage determination sex segregation, changes in work and working time, women and the European employment rate and trends and prospects for women's employment. Recent publications include: *Employment Strategy and the Labour Market* (Oxford: Oxford University Press, 1996); "The British production regime. A societal specific system?" *Economy and Society*, 1996; "Performance-related pay and the prospects for gender pay equity", *Jounal of Management Studies*, 1996; and "Gender segregation in societal context", *Work, Employment and Society* 1996.

Prof. Dr. **Asbjørn Rødseth,** born in 1951. Rødseth teaches macroeconomics and is professor at the University of Oslo. His main research areas have been open macroeconomics and wage formation, but he has also published articles in other branches of applied economics. He is a member of the Banking, Insurance and Securities Commission of Norway and has served as an advisor to the Norwegian Central Bank and the Ministry of Finance on economic modelling and research. Selected articles: "Macroecononomic policy in a small open economy" *Scandinavian Journal of Economics* 1979; "Wage formation in Norway", in Calmfors (ed.): *Wage Formation and Macroeconomic Policy in the Nordic Countries*, 1991; "Efficiency wages and local versus central bargaining", *Oxford Economic Papers* 1993; "Exchange rate versus price level targets and output stability", *Scandinavian Journal of Economics* 1996.

Researcher, Mag.art. **Jon Erik Dølvik,** born in 1955, sociologist from the University of Oslo, previous work in the Norwegian Ministry of Labour, research director at FAFO, guest researcher at the European Trade Union Institute, attached to ARENA – Advanced Research on Europeanization of the Nation-State, University of Oslo. His main fields of research are labour relations and labour market policies, and he is currently writing a doctoral thesis on the Europeanization of trade unions. Recent international publications: "Norwegian model in transition" (with D. Stokland) in A. Ferner and R.Hyman (eds) (1992);

"Europäisierung oder Re-Nationalisierung? Zur Zukunft skandinavischer Gewerkschaftsstrategien", in W. Lecher and H.W. Platzer (eds) (1994); "Nordic Trade Unions, the EU and European Works Councils", Transfer No.1 (1995); "Trade unions, the citizens and the European Union – the democratic challenge", ETUI (1996).

Managing Director **Arild H. Steen** at the opinion polling institute OPINION in Norway. Born in 1957, sociologist from the University of Oslo. Previously researcher at the Institute of Transport Economics in Oslo and until 1996 managing director of the Centre for Labour Relations and Industrial Policy at FAFO. Steen has been a member of the official expert panel on Youth, Salaries and Unemployment (1993). He has headed several research projects on labour relations, employment and industrial policy and has written or a number of reports on these topics.

Research Assistants

Mona Bråten, born in 1970, research assistant at FAFO and student in sociology at the University of Oslo.
Frode Longva, born in 1971, research assistant at FAFO and student in sociology at the University of Oslo.

Appendix

ANNEX - Comparative Labour Market Statistics

Table A1 **Growth of real GDP in selected OECD countries**[a]
Annual percentage change

	Average 1983-1993	1994	1995
Canada	2.7	4.6	2.2
Denmark	1.9	4.4	2.6
Finland	1.1	4.4	4.2
France	2.0	2.8	2.2
Germany	2.8	2.9	1.9
Norway	2.7	5.7	3.7
Sweden	1.2	2.6	3.0
U.K.	2.2	3.8	2.4
U.S.	2.9	3.5	2.0
OECD Europe	**2.4**	**2.5**	**2.7**
Total OECD	**2.8**	**2.7**	**1.9**

[a)] Aggregates are computed on the basis of 1991 GDP weights expressed in 1991 purchasing power parities.
Source: OECD, Employment Outlook, July 1996, table 1.1

Table A.2 **Unemployment[a] and incidence of long-term unemployment[b] in selected OECD countries, 1995**

	Total unemployment, percentage of labour force	Unemployed 6 months and over, as a per cent of total unemployment	Unemployed 12 months and over, as a per cent of total unemployment
Canada	9.5	27.1	13.8
Denmark	10.0	46.6	27.9
Finland	17.2	47.4	32.3
France	11.6	68.9	45.6
Germany	9.4	65.4	48.3
Norway	4.9	43.3	26.5
Sweden	7.7	35.2	15.7
U.K.	8.2	60.7	43.5
U.S.	5.6	17.3	9.7
OECD Europe	**10.3**	.....	......
Total OECD	**7.6**		

a) According to commonly used definitions.
b) These figures are based on data from labour force surveys.
Sources: OECD, Employment Outlook, July 1996, table 1.3; OECD, Employment Outlook, July 1996, table Q.

Table A.3 **Employment/population ratios[a] by sex, 1983 and 1995**
Percentages

	Men		Women		Total	
	1983	1995	1983	1995	1983	1995
Canada	77.8	73.9	55.0	61.4	66.4	67.7
Denmark	78.3	.....	65.0	.....	71.7	73.4
Finland	77.4	64.1	69.0	58.5	73.2	61.3
France	73.4	67.7	48.3	51.6	60.8	59.5
Germany	76.6	74.6	47.8	55.3	62.2	65.1
Norway	84.4	78.7	63.0	69.1	73.9	74.0
Sweden	83.0	72.4	73.9	69.8	78.5	71.1
U.K.	75.9	73.0	52.6	62.6	64.3	67.8
U.S.	76.5	80.3	56.2	66.7	66.3	73.5
OECD Europe[b]	**75.2**	**71.3***	**44.4**	**48.2***	**59.7**	**60.1**
Total OECD[b]	**77.6**	**77.5***	**50.3**	**54.4***	**63.7**	**66.2**

* 1994.
a) Defined as total unemployment divided by the working age population (15-64).
b) Above countries only.
Source: OECD, Employment Outlook, July 1996, table A.

Table A.4 **Employment and labour force growth in selected OECD countries**
Percentage changes from previous period

	1986	1987	1988	1989	1990	1991	1992	1993	1994	1995
Canada										
Employment	3.0	2.7	3.2	2.1	0.6	-1.9	-0.6	1.4	2.1	1.6
Labour force	1.9	1.9	2.0	1.8	1.3	0.6	0.5	1.3	1.1	0.7
Denmark										
Employment	2.6	0.9	-0.6	-0.6	-1.0	-1.5	-0.6	-1.0	-0.6	1.8
Labour force	1.3	0.8	0.2	-0.7	-0.5	0.2	0.2	-0.7	-0.6	-0.6
Finland										
Employment	-0.3	-0.3	0.3	1.6	-0.1	-5.2	-7.1	-6.1	-0.8	2.2
Labour force	0.1	-0.6	-0.3	0.5	-0.1	-0.9	-1.2	-0.7	-0.2	0.7
France										
Employment	0.5	0.4	1.0	1.4	1.0	0	-0.6	-1.4	0.3	1.1
Labour force	0.6	0.5	0.5	0.7	0.5	0.6	0.4	0.2	0.9	0.3
Germany										
Employment	1.4	0.7	0.8	1.5	3.0	2.5	-1.8	-1.8	-0.7	-0.2
Labour force	1.0	0.7	0.8	0.7	2.2	1.7	-0.7	-0.5	0.1	-0.4
Norway										
Employment	3.5	1.9	-0.6	-3.0	-0.9	-1.0	-0.3	0	1.5	2.0
Labour force	2.9	2.0	0.6	-1.3	-0.6	-0.7	0.2	0	0.9	1.5
Sweden										
Employment	0.8	1.0	1.4	1.5	1.0	-1.9	-4.3	-5.8	-0.9	1.6
Labour force	0.4	0.6	1.0	1.2	1.1	-0.6	-1.9	-2.7	-1.2	1.3
U.K.										
Employment	0.3	2.4	3.5	2.7	0.4	-3.1	-2.4	-0.8	0.7	0.6
Labour force	0.3	1.0	1.2	0.9	0.1	-0.6	-0.6	-0.4	-0.4	-0.5
U.S.[a]										
Employment	2.3	2.6	2.3	2.0	1.3	-0.9	0.7	1.5	2.3	1.6
Labour force	2.1	1.7	1.5	1.8	1.6	0.4	1.4	0.8	1.4	1.0
Total OECD[b]										
Employment	1.5	1.7	2.0	1.9	1.5	0.1	0.1	0.1	0.9	1.0
Labour force	1.5	1.3	1.4	1.4	1.4	0.8	0.8	0.6	0.9	0.7

a) Break in series as of January 1994.
b) Totals exclude Mexico prior to 1988.

Sources: OECD, Economic Outlook, June 1996, annex table 20; OECD, Economic Outlook, June 1996, annex table 18.

Table A.5 **Labour force participation rates[a] by sex**
Percentages

	Men			Women			Total		
	1983	1993	1995[b]	1983	1993	1995[b]	1983	1993	1995[b]
Canada	88.5	82.4	81.8	62.2	67.7	67.6	75.3	75.1	74.8
Denmark	87.6	86.9	......	74.2	78.3	......	80.9	82.6	78.7
Finland	82.0	77.6	77.5	72.7	70.0	70.2	77.4	73.9	73.9
France	78.4	74.5	74.8	54.3	59.0	60.0	66.4	66.7	67.3
Germany	82.6*	81.2	80.3	52.5*	61.8	61.3	67.5*	71.7	71.0
Norway	87.2	82.0	83.0	65.5	70.8	72.4	76.5	76.5	77.8
Sweden	85.9*	79.4	79.0	76.6*	75.8	74.9	81.3*	77.6	77.0
U.K.	87.5	84.0	82.1	57.2	65.3	65.4	72.4	74.7	73.8
U.S.	84.7	84.7*	85.0	61.9	69.0*	70.7	73.2	76.8*	77.8
Total OECD[c]	**84.4**	**83.2**	**83.5[d]**	**55.2**	**58.6**	**59.2[d]**	**69.5**	**70.9**	**71.4**

a) Defined as the total labour force divided by the working-age population (15-64).
b) Secretariat estimates based on OECD, Economic Outlook, No. 59, June 1996.
c) Above countries only.
10 1994.
*) Break in series.

Sources: OECD, Employment Outlook, July 1996, Table J; OECD, Employment Outlook, July 1996, Table K.

Table A.6 **Civilian employment by sector**
As a per cent of total employment

	Agriculture		Industry		Services	
	1983	1995	1983	1995	1983	1995
Canada	5	4	26	23	69	73
Denmark	7	5[a]	28	27[a]	64	68[a]
Finland	13	8	33	28	54	64
France	8	5	34	27	58	69
Germany	5*	3	41*	38	54*	59
Norway	8	5	27	23	65	71
Sweden	5	3	30	26	65	71
U.K.	3	2	33	26	64	72
U.S.	4	3	28	24	68	73
OECD Europe[b]	**13**	**10[a]**	**33**	**29[a]**	**53**	**61[a]**
Total OECD[b]	**9**	**8[a]**	**32**	**28[a]**	**59**	**64[a]**

a) 1994.
10) Above countries only.
* Break in series.
Source: OECD, Employment Outlook, July 1996, table D.

Table A.7 **Average annual hours actually worked per person in employment in selected OECD countries[a]**

	1975	1983	1995
Canada	1839	1731	1737
Finland	.....	1809	1775
France	1865	1711	1631
Germany	1801	1733	1559
Norway	1671	1487	1424
Sweden	1516	1453	1544
U.K.	1886	1719	1735
U.S.	1890*	1882*	1952

* Break in series.
a) The concept used is the total number of hours worked over the year divided by the average numbers of people in employment. The data are intended for comparisons of trends over time. They are unsuitable for comparisons of the level of average annual hours of work for a given year, because of differences in their sources. Part time workers are covered as well as full-time.
Source: OECD, Employment Outlook, July 1996, table C.

Table A.8 **Incidence and composition of part-time employment (percentages)**

	Part-time employment as a proportion of total employment				Women's share of part-time employment			
	1983	1993	1994	1995	1983	1993	1994	1995
Canada	16.8	19.1	18.8	18.6	69.8	68.3	68.8	68.8
Denmark	23.8	23.3	21.2	21.6	84.7	74.9	74.4	73.3
Finland	8.3	8.6	8.5	8.4	71.7	63.1	63.6	64.7
Germany	12.6	15.1	15.8	16.3	91.9	88.6	88.1	87.4
Netherlands[a]	21.2	35.0	36.4	37.4	78.4	73.7	73.8	73.6
Norway[b]	29.6	27.1	26.5	26.5	77.3	80.6	80.6	80.8
Sweden[c]	24.8	24.9	24.9	24.3	86.6	81.3	80.1	80.1
U.K.	19.4	23.4	23.8	24.1	89.8	84.5	83.6	82.3
U.S.[10]	18.4	17.6	18.9	18.6	66.8	66.0	67.3	68.0

[a] Break in series after 1985.
[b] Break in series after 1987.
[c] Break in series after 1986 and after 1992.
[d] Break in series after 1993.

Source: OECD, Employment Outlook, July 1996, table E.

Table A.9 **Evolution of trade union density rates in selected OECD countries, 1970-90**
Trade union membership as a per cent of wage- and salary-earners

	1970	1980	1990
Canada[a]	31.0	36.1	35.8
Denmark	60.0	76.0	71.4
Finland	51.4	69.8	72.0
France	22.3	17.5	9.8
Germany	33.0	35.6	32.9
Norway	51.4[b]	56.9	56.0
Sweden	67.7	79.7	82.5
U.K.	44.8	50.4	39.1
U.S.	23.2[c]	22.3	15.6

[a)] Data from Canada is based on recorded membership, not corrected for possible retired, unemployed and self-employed members. Data from all the other countries is based on employed members only.
[b)] 1972.
[c)] 1977.

Source: OECD, Employment Outlook, 1994, table 5.7

Table A.10 **Trends in earnings dispersion**[a]

		D5 / D1			D9 / D5		
		1980	1987	1991	1980	1987	1991
Canada[b]		2.24	2.43	2.23	1.79	1.83	1.88
Denmark		1.41	1.41	1.38[c]	1.52	1.56	1.57[c]
Finland		1.49	1.48	1.44	1.65	1.70	1.68
France		1.69	1.62	1.44	1.65	1.70	1.68
Germany		.....	1.55	1.53	.....	1.64	1.64
Norway		1.41	1.45	1.32	1.46	1.49	1.50
Sweden		1.30	1.33	1.36	1.57	1.57	1.55
U.K.		1.67	1.77	1.77	1.67	1.81	1.85
U.S.[d]	Males	1.85	2.06	2.01	1.76	1.91	1.95
	Females	1.66	1.87	1.89	1.76	1.87	1.94
	Total	.....	.....	2.05[d]	....	.....	2.03[d]

a) D1 and D9 refer to the upper earnings limits of, respectively, the first and ninth deciles of employees ranked in order of earnings from lowest to highest, i.e. 10 per cent of employees earn less than the D1 earnings limit and 90 per cent earn less than the D9 earnings limit. D5 are defined similarly and, thus, corresponds to median earnings.

b) The figures are from 1981, 1986 and 1991.

c) 1990.

d) OECD (1996) does not provide total figures for the U.S. between 1979-92. The only total figure available refers to 1993.

Source: OECD, Employment Outlook, July 1996, table 3.1

Table A.11 **Business sector labour costs in selected OECD countries**[a]
Percentage changes from previous period

	Compensation per employee			Unit labour costs		
	Average 1983-93	1994	1995	Average 1983-93	1994	1995
Canada	4.6	1.8	1.1	3.3	-0.8	0.8
Denmark	4.8	3.3	3.7	2.7	-1.8	3.1
Finland	7.8	5.3	3.8	4.0	-1.5	1.5
France	4.8	1.6	1.8	2.4	-1.5	0.5
Germany	4.3	3.5	3.4	2.0	-0.5	1.0
Norway	6.0	2.9	2.5	4.4	-0.8	1.6
Sweden	7.9	5.6	4.7	5.6	1.6	3.8
U.K.	7.1	2.5	2.4	5.4	0.4	1.1
U.S.	4.2	2.5	2.8	3.2	2.0	2.8
OECD Europe	**6.2**	**3.4**	**3.4**	**4.0**	**0.1**	**1.4**
Total OECD	**6.1**	**2.8**	**3.4**	**4.4**	**1.1**	**2.7**

a) Aggregates are computed on the basis of 1991 GDP weights expressed in 1991 purchasing power parities.

Source: OECD, Employment Outlook, July 1996, table 1.4

Table A.12 **Job gains and job loss**[a]
Average annual rates as a per cent of total employment

	Canada 1983-1991	Denmark 1983-1989	Finland 1986-1991	France 1984-1991	Germany 1983-1990	Norway (manu-factoring) 1985-1992	Sweden 1985-1992	U.K. 1985-1991	U.S (manu-facturing) 1984-1988
Gross job gains	**14.5**	**16.0**	**10.4**	**12.7**	**9.0**	**8.1**	**14.5**	**8.7**	**8.2**
Openings	3.2	6.1	3.9	6.1	2.5	2.1	6.5	2.7	1.4
Expansions	11.2	9.9	6.5	6.6	6.5	6.0	8.0	6.0	6.7
Gross job losses	**11.9**	**13.8**	**12.0**	**11.8**	**7.5**	**10.6**	**14.6**	**6.6**	**10.4**
Closures	3.1	5.0	3.4	5.5	1.9	3.1	5.0	3.9	2.7
Contractions	8.8	8.8	8.7	6.3	5.6	7.5	9.6	2.7	7.7
Net employment change	**2.6**	**2.2**	**-1.6**	**0.9**	**1.5**	**-2.5**	**-0.1**	**2.1**	**-2.2**
Job turnover	**26.3**	**29.8**	**22.4**	**24.4**	**16.5**	**18.7**	**29.1**	**15.3**	**18.6**
Continuing establishments only	20.0	18.7	15.2	12.9	12.1	13.5	17.6	8.7	14.4

a) Sampling months/periods vary across countries.
Source: OECD, Employment Outlook, July 1996, table 5.1

Table A.13 **Active Labour Market Policies as share of GDP and of Unemployment, 1993.**[a]

	Active schemes	Passive schemes	Total	Public exp. for labour market policy as % of GDP relative to unemployment
Denmark	1.88	4.89	6.77	0.56
Finland	1.77	5.12	6.89	0.38
France*	0.98	2.01	2.99	0.24
Germany	1.58	2.60	4.18	0.61
Japan	0.09	0.26	0.35	0.12
Norway	1.30	1.60	2.90	0.56
Sweden	2.56	3.13	5.69	0.66
U.K.	0.52	1.23	1.75	0.18
U.S.	0.24	0.45	0.69	0.12

* The figures are from 1992.

[a] Active schemes consist among other things of qualification and training schemes, whereas passive schemes consist of expenditure for unemployment benefits, early retirement schemes etc.

Source: The Norwegian Directorate of Labour, Annual Report, 1994, table 22.

Table A.14 **Overview of Active Labour Market Schemes in Norway**

* Temporary employment in the public sector involving special projects or other extraordinary work to prevent displacement and substitution. Participation is for 1 to 10 months, combining training and work experience, ordinary payment for hours worked, especially targeted at long term unemployed.

* Temporary employment in the private sector: a wage subsidy is granted to the employer, equivalent to 25 to 75 per cent of ordinary wages for a maximum of 6 to 12 months, aiming at permanent employment. Target groups include youth, women, seniors, immigrants and the disabled.

* Training courses, mainly classroom training, 4 to 40 weeks, various vocational and general subjects. Most prominent are the so-called AMO-courses whose aim is to qualify job seekers for ordinary work by providing skills which are in demand from employers.

* Youth training programmes, combining work experience and training, both class-room and on-the job-training of 1 to 10 months duration.

* Substitution schemes granting employees in the private and public sectors leave for further education provided the attendant work is substituted by an unemployed.

* Special rehabilitation programmes based on within-the-plant training, special training centers combined with temporary work in public enterprises.

* Diverse special schemes including job clubs, mobility grants, apprentice positions in the public sector, subsidies for firm-internal training.

Source: Torp, H. 1995 Norway Baseline Study. Oslo: Mimeo, ISF

Table A.15 **Overview of Norwegian pay rounds in the LO/NHO area**

Year	Type of settlement	Level of bargaining	Centrally agreed wage increase	Locally bargained wage drift	State intervention	Government
1974	Main settlement	Industry by industry	16.6	7.9	No interv.	Labour party
1975	Intermediary	Tripartite	8.9	4.3	No interv.	Labour party
1976	Main settlement	Tripartite	9.4	5.8	No interv.	Labour party
1977	Intermediary	Tripartite	2.9	7.1	No interv.	Labour party
1978	Main settlement	Centrally coordinated	2.1	3.9	Compulsory arbitration	Labour party
1979	No regular bargaining	Wage stop	0.3	2.4	Wage and price freeze	Labour party
1980	Main settlement	Industry by industry	5.0	8.2	No interv.	Labour party
1981	Intermediary	Centrally coordinated	1.7	6.8	Compulsory arbitration	Labour party

Table A.15 **Continued**

Year	Type of settlement	Level of bargaining	Centrally agreed wage increase	Locally bargained wage drift	State intervention	Government
1982	Main settlement	Industry by industry	5.4	6.0	Compulsory arbitration	Conservative minority governm.
1983	Intermediary	Centrally coordinated	0.9	5.7	No interv.	Nonsocialist coalition from May
1984	Main settlement	Industry by industry	3.0	5.9	No interv.	Nonsocialist coalition
1985	Intermediary	Centrally coordinated	0.5	6.9	No interv.	Nonsocialist coalition
1986	Main settlement	Industry by industry	11.4	6.9	No interv.	Labour party from May
1987	«Exception year»	Centrally coordinated	0.2	8.3	No interv.	Labour party

Table A.15 **Continued**

Year	Type of settlement	Level of bargaining	Centrally agreed wage increase	Locally bargained wage drift	State intervention	Government
1988	"Exception year"	Centrally coordinated	1.7	0.7	Wage law	Labour party
1989	"Exception year"	Centrally coordinated	4.1	-0.2	Wage law	Conservative minority governm.
1990	Main settlement	Centr.coord/ industry	3.3	3.0	No interv.	Labour party
1991	Intermediary	Central.coord.	1.6	2.5	No interv.	Labour party
1992	Main settle-ment	Centr-coord./ industry	0.5	2.4	No interv.	Labour party
1993	Intermediary	central.coord.	0.8	1.8	Contribution to early retirement scheme	Labour party
1994	Main settle-ment	Industry by industry	1.3	1.1	Contribution to early retirement	Labour party

Table A.15 **Continued**

Year	Type of settlement	Level of bargaining	Centrally agreed wage increase	Locally bargained wage drift	State intervention	Government
1995	Intermediary	Central. coord.	1.1	2.7	No intervent.	Labour party
1996	Main settlement	Industry by industry	2.5		No intervent.	Labour party

Sources: Sivesind et al (1995:302), Høgsnes (1995:12), NOU 1996:4, Stortingsmelding 2 (1995-96).